Borderless Education

GLOBAL TEACHER EDUCATION

SERIES EDITORS

Mary Curran, PhD, The State University of New Jersey

Nilufer Guler, PhD, Rockhurst University

This series provides broad and multiple perspectives on the emerging and crucial field of global education, and acts as an agenda-setting catalyst for the urgent call for teachers who can prepare students with the knowledge, skills, and dispositions for ethical action in today's global society. This series addresses the needs of multiple, overlapping global audiences, including:

- Academic researchers;
- Faculty who design and teach courses in teacher preparation, educational leadership and administration, and evaluation;
- P-16 practitioners and P-16 system leaders;
- Community and education partners;
- Social innovators; and
- Policy makers.

Titles in Series

At School in the World: Developing Globally Engaged Teachers, edited by Carine E. Ullom and Nilufer Guler

The Human Rights Imperative in Teacher Education: Developing Compassion, Understanding, and Advocacy, edited by Gloria T. Alter and William R. Fernekes

Borderless Education: A Pedagogical Framework for Cultural Responsiveness and Global Competence, edited by Christina Wright Fields, Novea McIntosh, and Rochonda Nenonene

Borderless Education

A Pedagogical Framework for Cultural Responsiveness and Global Competence

Christina Wright Fields, Novea McIntosh, and Rochonda Nenonene

BLOOMSBURY ACADEMIC
NEW YORK • LONDON • OXFORD • NEW DELHI • SYDNEY

BLOOMSBURY ACADEMIC
Bloomsbury Publishing Inc, 1359 Broadway, New York, NY 10018, USA
Bloomsbury Publishing Plc, 50 Bedford Square, London, WC1B 3DP, UK
Bloomsbury Publishing Ireland, 29 Earlsfort Terrace, Dublin 2, D02 AY28, Ireland

BLOOMSBURY, BLOOMSBURY ACADEMIC and the Diana logo are trademarks
of Bloomsbury Publishing Plc

First published in the United States of America 2026

Bloomsbury Publishing Inc does not have any control over, or responsibility for, any
third-party websites referred to or in this book. All internet addresses given in this
book were correct at the time of going to press. The author and publisher regret
any inconvenience caused if addresses have changed or sites have ceased
to exist, but can accept no responsibility for any such changes.

A catalog record for this book is available from the Library of Congress.

ISBN: HB: 978-1-5381-9391-4
         PB: 978-1-5381-9392-1
         ePDF: 979-8-8818-5466-9
         eBook: 978-1-5381-9393-8

Series: Global Teacher Education

Typeset by Integra Software Services Pvt. Ltd.
Printed and bound in the United States of America

For product safety related questions contact productsafety@bloomsbury.com.

To find out more about our authors and books visit www.bloomsbury.com
and sign up for our newsletters.

To my mom and father-in-law, I remember both of you asking me when I was going to finish that first book, and now here I am wrapping up a second one— your prayers have truly kept me on this path, guiding every step of the way. To my partner, José: Your unconditional love and support mean the world to me. I couldn't imagine having anyone else by my side in this journey of life. To my son, Tré: Thank you for your patience as I worked on my writing, and for being such a big help with your little sister. To my daughter, Javae: Thank you for being my little administrative assistant, keeping me on task, forwarding calls to voicemail, and making sure I took breaks. And to my sista scholars, Rochonda and Novea: It's been such a joy to share those sista circles with you, talking about life in the academy, family, and, of course, writing. To future scholars from humble beginnings: never underestimate the power of your voice and your story— through liberatory writing, you have the ability to spark transformative change and pave the way for the next generation. Sawubona (I see you!)
~ Christina Wright Fields, PhD

To my husband and soulmate, Mario, your abounding love and support have been the stabilizing force in my journey. We are a team, two immigrants, collectively honoring our Afro-Caribbean roots, feeding our souls together as we navigate spaces. Thank you for encouraging me to engage others interculturally to broaden my own worldview. To my amazing son, Zade, you have inspired me so much with your gifts. As I watch you joyfully thrive in your endeavors, a strong young man of faith, I am thankful for you. Your humility encourages me to be a better human being every day. And to the "village" of prayer warriors, family members, educators, and friends on the beautiful island of Jamaica and across the globe, whose daily WhatsApp prayers, phone calls, messages, and island vibe stories ground me in my culture, "One love." To my scholar sistas! Rochonda and Christina, thank you for embracing me. Our collaboration is symbolic of our rich intersecting ancestral history of collectivism, activism, and emancipation. All praise be to God who has given us the strength to do His will in furnishing a tool to energize and mobilize future educators, scholars, and disruptors to advocate for our children—His heritage.
~ Novea McIntosh, EdD

To my husband, Kwasi, who inspires me and I love beyond bounds. Thank you for being steadfast in your support, and encouraging me to think and dream beyond the present. Always you, Always me, Always us. To my children, Mawusi, Delali, Mawuena, and Enyonam, who amaze me with their talents, and whose happiness brings joy to my soul. I pray you all continue to pursue your passions, do good wherever you can, and live life without limits. Always choose to fly. To my two sister colleagues, Novea and Christina, thank you both for inviting me into this project. We have demonstrated the power of collectivism and the audacity to say the "dangerous things" that need to be said. We made a great team. Much love and solidarity! To those in education who have committed themselves to being advocates for equity and justice, stay strong. Your voice and work are necessary and important—don't stop. And finally, to my younger self, I will keep all my promises to you, A Luta Continua (the struggle continues).
~ Rochonda L. Nenonene, PhD

Contents

12 Designing a Unit Plan Utilizing the Integrative Global CRSP Framework *Christina Wright Fields, Rochonda Nenonene, Novea McIntosh, and Jennifer Wu-Pope* 195

13 The Quilted Classroom Poem: Harnessing Poetry to Cultivate Global and Cultural Awareness *Novea McIntosh, Christina Wright Fields, Rochonda Nenonene, and Isabella Lundgren* 203

14 Examining Organization's Culturally Sustaining Global Education Strategies through an Audit of Integrative Global CRSP Framework *Christina Wright Fields, Rochonda Nenonene, and Novea McIntosh* 207

Foreword

When Christina Wright Fields, Novea McIntosh, and Rochonda Nenonene expressed their vision and passion for cultivating *Borderless Education: A Pedagogical Framework for Cultural Responsiveness and Global Competence*, we were thrilled to include it as part of the Rowman & Littlefield Global Teacher Education Book Series, as we urgently need to articulate the intersections between global teacher education and equity, and asset-based pedagogies. The authors in this edited volume have done just that: they have called for opening a dialogue around the powerful intersections between these two deeply interconnected and mutually informative fields, which in many ways have developed in parallel, without acknowledging and articulating the power gained when joining, reimagining, and expanding these frameworks.

We live and learn in our local contexts, but those local contexts are informed and impacted by global issues. At the same time, our actions in our local contexts have ripple effects in global contexts. To become aware of this interplay (which is erroneously dichotomized as local/global as if there are clear demarcations between the two), requires, as the authors state, "a fundamental shift in our understandings of the importance of the interconnectedness of local and global issues and the importance of addressing both within education contexts" (see Introduction). But how do we go about making this shift? Where do we begin?

Reading and reflecting on the ideas, programs, and questions shared in this book is one way to embark on the professional development educators need to see, understand, and then act upon the intersections between culturally responsive and sustaining pedagogy and global teacher education. The authors demonstrate how this intersection must inform educators' knowledge, skills, and dispositions so they can move away from normative pedagogical practices and expectations and reimagine a new educational landscape without borders, which recognizes and learns from global intellectual traditions, perspectives, and the many ways of being in this world. Actively engaging with this text supports us to question and expand existing frameworks and approaches to articulate the global culturally responsive and sustaining principles and practice that can guide our work. This new framework impacts many things, for example, how we design teacher education programs, courses, and projects; choose curriculum context; and select and implement pedagogical tools and practices. It calls for a critique of our US-centric, hegemonic beliefs and practices, which are evident in existing accreditation standards, K-12 and community partnership practices, protocols for teacher observations, etc.

This integrative global approach grounded in equity and asset-based pedagogy is demanding as it requires that we operate at a point of tension that both centers and sustains our students' multiple identities, while also engaging in education that locates our students, their education, and ourselves within the shifting dynamics and power at play in our shared world. Thank you, Christina, Rochonda, and Novea for providing teacher educators with this enticing map (that includes spaces where we can reflect, question, and learn from examples from around the world) as we enter this new territory and are called to action.

Mary Curran, PhD
New Brunswick, New Jersey, USA

Preface

Women {of African descent} have experiences that provide them specific angles of vision on their experience. Their point of view, if uncensored, provides fresh, albeit potentially dangerous, ideas ... (Hill Collins, 2013: 22).

We believe in the idea of happenstance—that everything happens for a reason. But, sometimes, it is more than the right place and time. It's about being with the right people. This book was initially ignited by our work with the Longview Foundation Global Teacher Education Fellows Program and the American Association of Colleges of Teacher Educators' (AACTE) Programmatic Committee for Global Diversity; both constituents provided valuable connections, offering opportunities to engage with, be mentored by, and co-create alongside leading global scholars in the field. When Novea and Christina attended a global education reception at the 2023 AACTE's Annual Meeting, they did not know that night would lead to collaboration in a book series with a theme of globalizing teacher education. Through conversations, the series editor, Dr. Mary Curran, noticed our passion, commitment, and expertise to provide an intersectional global and culturally responsive teaching approach that offers futuristic possibilities of reimagining learning without borders.

We discussed the need for dismantling the traditional silos of global education and Culturally Relevant Sustaining Pedagogy (CRSP), and rather advocating for a call to action that illuminates the synergistic possibilities of a globalized CRSP framework to holistically support students' cultural competence development. With the intention of highlighting the evolving needs of education in an interconnected world, the idea of creating a unified framework that incorporates global competencies grounded in CRSP principles that could address systemic inequities and promote belonging and inclusion started to take shape. We wondered what research, praxis, and practice would look like between two fundamentally important pedagogical frameworks (CRSP and global education), recognizing that each of the frameworks has a long-standing legacy and impact in teacher education. In light of our educational ecosystem, now is a time for the convergence of these frameworks.

This fourth book in the series aims to offer a practical and conceptual model, one that has been thoughtfully developed by scholars of color. We are among the 2 percent of tenured Black women in academia (Williams and O'Leary, 2021). We recognize and embrace that this is our moment to help shift the conversation. We offer our voices here to represent those, ourselves included, who have been marginalized and silenced, while simultaneously as women scholars being expected to bear the burden of excessive workloads, "mothering" of our students, and producing the next generation of educators for America's diverse classrooms. The context for needed change, accountability, and action is clear. For us, the words of Lorde ring true, "the master's tools will never dismantle the master's house" (1984: 110). New ideas, new frameworks, and new ways of thinking and seeing are needed. This is the impetus for our work.

We align our work with the theoretical framework of Black feminist scholar Hill Collins (2013), as she reminds us that liberation and resistance to oppressive structures that lead to social change rest in the work of engaged scholarship. Indeed, we are building on the foundation of many Black scholars such as Crenshaw (2005), hooks (1994), Jordan (2002), Lorde (1984), and Wynters (2015) who have identified, problematized, and offered solutions. We join their calls of understanding to action to centering, advancing, and validating Black women's funds of knowledge. Specifically, we situate our work within the field of educator preparation. A field that remains entrenched in the Eurocentric educational tapestry that centers whiteness in the teaching learning process. Indeed, there is an "epistemic violence" (Dominguez, 2019) in schools intentionally designed to oppress minoritized people, cultures, and ways of thinking. Ultimately, this schooling process builds both visible and imperceptible walls and borders that dehumanizes students, limits academic potential, and reinforces societal disparities.

Currently, 82 percent of the teaching workforce is White, while teachers of color make up just 18 percent. Additionally, only 25 percent of students in teacher education programs nationwide are future educators of color (US Department of Education, 2016). Under these circumstances, we believe it is vital that the preparation of teacher candidates has a foundation in culturally responsive, sustaining, and global understandings. The teaching population may not reflect the diversity that exists in the classrooms, but their understandings and actions should respond as such. In order to provide a high-quality education that is relevant, engaging, and meaningful, the intent of the classroom environment, curriculum design/instruction, and student experiences should be infused with local and global cultural contexts.

We share our positionalities to underscore how our unique experiences as Black women educators and scholars influence our perspectives and approach to this work. When these viewpoints are expressed authentically, we bring forth fresh insights that challenge the status quo, by illuminating counternarratives that are often overlooked or suppressed. This is who we are. We—Christina, a daughter of an immigrant from Jamaica, Novea, an Afro-Caribbean immigrant, and Rochonda, an African American woman and wife of an immigrant from Ghana, are teacher educator faculty in higher education spaces where preparing teachers to meet the needs of students is our passion. Initially, our commonality was our shared immigrant experiences, but we recognize and appreciate that each of us brings our own complex and multifaceted identities to the table. Thus, we must share with you our why. Why have we chosen this work? Why do we prioritize global perspectives in education? Why do we want you to join us in this work?

Christina—Nia, the fifth principle of Kwanzaa, is all about purpose. Rooted in the rich traditions of Africa, it encourages us to focus on our goals and contribute to the greater good of our community. It's a reminder to live with intention, to make our actions meaningful, and to work toward a collective future. My journey in education began with a purpose. My nia is greatly influenced by my identity. I am a womxn, a first-generation college graduate, daughter of a single parent. I come from humble beginnings (low socioeconomic status). I am a mother of two Black school age children. I am unapologetically Black. My intersectionalities shape my worldview and substantially impact my understanding of self and others.

I view education as an instrument to promote and engage individuals in social transformation, by bridging the gap between people from different backgrounds and identities. Globalization impacts students on local, national, and international levels, and our teacher education programs must prepare students for these new realities. Global education promotes communication skills, critical thinking, and reflective techniques all of which are crucial to a student's development. As a teacher educator, I help my students recognize the interconnectedness of our increasingly global world. In my teaching, I break down the what, the why, and the how—but most importantly, I always ask, "For whom am I doing this?" I think about the future generation of scholars, including my own children, and the teachers I am helping mold. I want to inspire them to think how they can engage in transformative and meaningful change that affirms and sustains cultural identity, both here at home and on a global scale.

Novea—"Wi likkle but wi tallawah" an affirmation in Jamaican patois of one's strength, power, resilience, and refusal to be constrained by any boundaries, is at the heart of my Jamaican upbringing and upstanding, cultural heritage. My why starts with my Afro-Caribbean formation, my beginning and becoming, an identity, shaped by the village of collective emancipated and liberated educators who taught me to embrace my native cultural assets. Growing up in my country, my educational journey was steeped in a Eurocentric system, but my Blackness and Black history were centered, giving me voice and agency to interrogate and dismantle the colonizer's systems. Now as an immigrant, my belonging is fraught with complexities. I am living outside the margins, minoritized by White America and secondarily marginalized within my Black race. I am an immigrant with an accent that does not fit into the normalized racialized culture. So, I center my Blackness, undergirded with my strong African ancestral legacy, giving me an arsenal of decolonial practices and an activist academic voice to decenter whiteness in spaces of learning.

I view education as an equalizer providing opportunities for everyone to honor and exchange ideas, cultural practices, and knowledge to celebrate each other's human dignity and self-worth. How can our schools value the cultural capital present in our classrooms? How can we unearth the joy of learning in all our students whether native or immigrant? I strongly believe we bear the responsibility to advance authentic culturally sustaining global education to all students. As an Afro-Caribbean immigrant, I intentionally maintain a cultural and racial bond with my ancestral heritage throughout the diaspora, feeding my soul. As a mother passing on traditions to my Black son born to foreign-born immigrants, as so many other Black, Indigenous, and children of color in America's classrooms, I transmit and sustain multiplicities of cultures, sustaining their heritage. As a teacher educator, I teach with a global attitude, perspective, and knowledge base, embedding Black consciousness and minoritized intellectual traditions in my classroom thus disrupting the traditional canon, and broadening my students' worldview. And as a scholar, I take a closer view now with reflexivity at the heart of my research using my platform to amplify Blackness and global voices. Ultimately, I seek to mold and shape future teachers who respect, appreciate, empathize with, and collectively engage in learning environments where students thrive as they joyfully celebrate their identities, cultures, and lives across the globe. This book is an example of living within the margins, a framework of belonging. I embraced the village with my sister scholars, Christina and Rochonda, as we collectively unearth the assets of educators who are globally engaged. "Wi tallawah"!

Rochonda—My why starts with my entry into schooling through a Head Start program in Cleveland, Ohio, in the 1970s. I was immersed in a nurturing space, surrounded by teachers of color who recognized my eagerness to learn. I clearly remember feeling that I belonged. I was encouraged and the work we did was place based (not even sure that was a consideration of the profession at that time), relevant, and provided multisensory opportunities to learn and share understandings. This beginning experience was wonderful and my elementary school years as a student in Cleveland Public Schools mirrored what I experienced in Head Start. However, as my family sought to move to a better neighborhood and what my parents perceived to be a better quality education, we moved to the suburbs. There, I was one of a few Black students and no teachers of color. I quickly came to realize that in this space, I was not welcome. As I matriculated through middle school and high school, my experiences were detrimental to my development as a learner. Teachers openly questioned my intelligence, made assumptions with respect to my potential, and offered little guidance and support. Eventually, after prodding my mother we moved back to the city, and I again was immersed in spaces where my identity and culture were reflected, appreciated, and celebrated.

I share this snippet of my educational journey because I experienced first hand how the presence or absence of culturally responsive educators can impact the trajectory of a student. Indeed, this is what drew me to the teaching profession, and eventually educator preparation. I come to this work with the knowledge that all students need to experience a sense of belonging and acceptance in educational environments. At the core of this experience for students is the action of the teacher. As we move forward in a rapidly growing global society with classrooms reflecting the anticipated demographic shifts, these same ideals apply to our wonderful multi-lingual, immigrant, and first-generation students. Without hesitation, I was delighted when my colleagues, Novea and Christina, invited me to envision and create a framework that would help educators understand and create spaces of support and inclusion for students.

We recognize that we are not alone in this work; there are many others around the world engaged in the global education trenches lending their voice and ideas fighting to be seen, heard, and accepted. Everyone wants a seat at the table, but sometimes you may have to build your own table. The framework we offer and the chapters in this book offer a blueprint for building a global table. A table where the "others" will now have seats, and will help plan the menu. Bringing with them, their own identities, culture, funds of knowledge, and joy as the primary ingredients for educational success. We are fortunate to be a part of the process and honor those who have chosen to build with us and sit besides us.

We are no longer guests at someone's else's table; rather, we are now the hosts of our own. This book features a diverse group of global authors actively engaged in meaningful work in various regions of the world including Brazil, Costa Rica, Ghana, Italy, Jamaica, Kenya, Malawi, Northern Ireland, South Korea, Turkey, Togo, Ukraine, and the United States. We extend our sincere appreciation and walk in solidarity with them all. Additionally, we extend our gratitude to our colleagues in the AACTE Programmatic Committee for Global Diversity, Longview Foundation Global Teacher Education Fellowship, and our respective institutions (Marist University and University of Dayton) whose mission and strategic plans advance our work within our local communities.

We have committed ourselves to this work because our experiences have shown us the necessity of it. Showcasing the nexus of intersectionalities evident in our professional work informed by our own lived experiences and cultural identities, providing a comprehensive model that is not only relevant but actionable for those seeking to foster change and promote culturally rich and contextually relevant learning environments. We fully recognize that the work ahead for educator preparation is daunting as we expand our curricula, learn from our diverse students and communities, stand in solidarity with those who have been marginalized, and advocate for justice. But, in today's political climate of division and exceptionalism, our work is more relevant and needed. Schools have always functioned as democratic spaces (Collins et al., 2019; Dewey, 1916), our conceptions of who we are and the work we do, must continue to live up to this expectation. As you read the text, we ask you to consider your role in promoting equity and inclusion, and take up our call to action. Your classroom can be and should be a welcoming place for every student.

Throughout our education and career journey, this has always been our why. We harness the power of operationalizing a global CRSP framework that fosters borderless, futuristic, and limitless possibilities within education. We hope after reading this book, it becomes yours too. We invite you to join us in this work toward radical hospitality, where all are welcome. Where we cross borders, embrace the collective, dismantle normative educational structures, and create and cultivate transformative spaces.

Acknowledgments

Haramabee—a Kiswahili word meaning "let's pull together"—beautifully captures the essence of unity and the power of shared purpose. It's a call to embrace the strength found in reinforcing core cultural values while celebrating the richness of global diversity. This book stands as a testament to that idea, illuminating the transformative potential of blending culturally relevant sustaining pedagogy with a global perspective. In this journey, we stand on the shoulders of our ancestors, Black Indigenous People of Color, by honoring the wisdom of those who came before us, recognizing that the work we do today is not just ours but a collective legacy we carry forward together.

We express immense gratitude to our series editor, Mary Curran, who invited us to not only take a seat at the table but also encouraged us to make this table our own by sharing our unique cultural recipes, globally engaged guests, and leaving the table full of worldly wisdom and joy. It was at this table that we were able to center our identities, cultures, and lived experiences as minoritized individuals and marginalized scholars, adding a secret ingredient, infusing the intellectual cannon with bold flavors and fresh ideas that not only enrich but also strengthen the global education series. A big thank you to the series editors, Mary Curran and Nilufer Guler for selecting our book.

We are thankful for the support from the editorial team from Bloomsbury for your guidance throughout the process.

Many of the scholars cited in this work have been radical and transformative voices in the field of scholar-activism, Black feminism, culturally relevant and sustaining pedagogy, social justice, decolonizing, and global education. Their groundbreaking contributions have shaped the way we approach education, challenging norms, and paving the way for more inclusive and empowering pedagogical practices.

We deeply appreciate our institutions (Marist University and University of Dayton) for recognizing the importance of our work, encouraging our transformative thinking, and supporting our passion for culturally sustaining global pedagogy. We would like to express our appreciation for our contributing chapter authors for not only providing rich chapters but also serving as peer reviewers for each other's work. Also, we acknowledge that we were unable to include everyone who submitted a proposal, but we recognize the value of their work in advancing efforts to create globally and culturally inclusive environments. A special thanks to our graduate and undergraduate students, Casey Bogues, Isabella Lundgren, and Stephanie Merino.

It was through this collective work and responsibility, or *ujima*, that we were able to bring this book to life. Each page, each idea allowed us to harness the power of the collective to offer a text grounded in efforts to disrupt and dismantle systems that we know are harmful. By coming together, we blended our efforts, knowledge, and spirit to center humanity, reimagine schools and communities as borderless inclusive spaces, and empower educators to take action.

Asante sana (Thank you very much)

Introduction: The Case of a Globalized Pedagogical Framework in Teacher Education

In today's increasingly interconnected world, the ability to understand others, transcend boundaries, and recognize the interwoven fabric of our pluralistic society is needed now more than ever. This book continues the evolution of culturally relevant teaching and culturally sustaining pedagogy, expanding its scope to embrace a global perspective. By incorporating global understanding, narratives, and viewpoints, this book provides educators with the tools to foster a more inclusive and empathetic learning environment. It highlights the importance of recognizing and celebrating diverse cultural backgrounds, preparing students to navigate and contribute to a globalized society with greater awareness and sensitivity.

This book builds on the work of scholars who have called for culturally relevant, responsive, and sustaining teaching and pedagogies in education. The goal of this text is to provide an intersectional, global, and culturally responsive teaching approach that offers futuristic possibilities of reimagining learning without borders. Opening the conversation for readers to consider dialogue, collaboration, and research between two fundamentally important pedagogical frameworks, that each have a long-standing legacy and impact in teacher education. In light of our educational ecosystem, now is a time for the convergence of these frameworks to fully incorporate the principles and practices of culturally relevant sustaining pedagogy (CRSP) with the multifaceted elements of global competencies. The authors share a new globalized pedagogical framework to empower teacher educators to reimagine, strengthen, and develop new literacies that seamlessly and intentionally recognize the nexus of CRSP and global competencies. This is a pivotal moment in education to create and foster more inclusive and collectivist globally engaged classrooms, where students thrive, educators are empowered, and communities are connected. Gone are the days of silo approaches and ethnocentric strategies that default to hegemonic pedagogical practices in schools. What new possibilities emerge with a borderless education, where all constituents are connected, honored, and sustained?

Currently, CRSP and global education tend to operate independently or within isolated frameworks rather than being integrated or connected. We propose a dismantling of these two silos to instead foster interdisciplinary collaboration and recognizing and validating the intersectionality of CRSP and global education. A globalized pedagogical framework needs to address both cultural responsiveness and global competencies interconnectedness seamlessly, if educators and teacher educators desire to provide borderless teaching and learning opportunities for students. It involves recognizing that CRSP is fundamental for understanding and respecting diverse perspectives within a local context, while global education necessitates understanding and engaging with perspectives and ways of knowing from around the world. By bridging these silos, educators can create and support a more inclusive and comprehensive pluralistic education ecosystem that meets the needs of not just the traditional United States students, but also foreign-born, culturally and linguistically diverse, Indigenous, and refugees.

Historical Context of CRSP

The concept of culturally responsive education can find its roots in the aftermath of the Landmark 1954 Brown Decision which called for the integration of American classrooms with, "all deliberate speed" (*Brown v. Board of Education of Topeka,* 1955: 301), thus schools were given the mandate of creating equal and equitable classrooms while the nation continued to be embattled in battle for civil rights. This decision, while groundbreaking in its efforts, did not resolve the long-standing discrimination faced by Black students and teachers during this era. In fact, one of the direct results of the court's order was the decimation of the Black teacher population, which to this date has never significantly recovered in terms of numbers of teaching professionals (Milner, 2020). Desegregations' move toward equality inadvertently or unintentionally led to the fracturing of the Black school ethos, which while underfunded and resourced, by all accounts was successful in terms of serving the needs of students, requiring and producing academic success, and operating as a vital institution in the community. Prior to Brown, collectivism and cultural appreciation were evident in the fabric and identity of Black schools. Yet, after Brown, what schools needed was a new interpretation of collectivism that would be reflective of integrated classrooms and schools that petitioners imagined and the courts demanded. Reflective of this sentiment is Baldwin's (1963) candid "*Talk to Teachers*" which charged educators to situate revolutionary practices in their classrooms, to empower and engage Black students by embracing their historical and cultural identities in the classroom to thrive in a broken system. This influenced minoritized and underrepresented scholars' work to center diverse cultures, histories, and narratives in education, thereby influencing subsequent research and pedagogical practices in classrooms.

During the twentieth century, scholars such as James Banks and Geneva Gay offered new perspectives by advocating for educational practices that addressed diverse cultural backgrounds, emphasizing equal representation and inclusion. Bank's work, influenced by the liberatory praxis of Freire (1970), called for revolutionary ideas to transform the American classrooms. He explained that one of the goals of multicultural education is "to help students acquire the knowledge and commitment needed to think, decide and take personal, social and civic action" (Brandt, 1994: 31). Building on the work of Banks, Gay coined the term culturally responsive teaching to describe pedagogy that uses students' cultures (i.e., customs, characteristics, experiences, and perspectives) as essential tools to improve classroom instruction (Gay, 2002). In 1995, Gloria Ladson-Billings' seminal work, "*Towards a Theory of Culturally Relevant Pedagogy,*" introduced the concept of culturally relevant pedagogy (CRP), as a way of teaching that fosters student achievement by centering students' cultural references in all aspects of learning (Ladson-Billings, 1995). Similarly, Lisa Delpit's book *Other People's Children* (1995) noted the importance of acknowledging students' cultural backgrounds and being aware of the power dynamics at play in classrooms.

A few years later, Ladson-Billings (1998) explored the significance and impact of Critical Race Theory (CRT) in education emphasizing its role in examining systemic inequalities and the lived experiences of marginalized communities. Her work demonstrated how CRT can be employed to understand and challenge the pervasive nature of racism within educational systems.

In the mid-2010s, Django Paris and H. Samy Alim expanded on Ladson-Billings's CRP with the concept of culturally sustaining pedagogy (CSP), by extending the ideas of CRP to also encompass sustaining and revitalizing cultural practices within education contexts. They urged educators to go beyond simply acknowledging diverse perspectives and experiences in the classroom, advocating instead "to *sustain*–linguistic literate, and cultural pluralism as part of the democratic project of schooling and as a needed response to demographic and social change" (Paris and Alim, 2014: 88). Additionally around this same time, inclusive pedagogy emerged to include not only cultural diversity but also encompassing different learning needs and identities, within promoting equity and social justice education. Kendi's (2019) anti-racist work challenges educators to reexamine systemic racism within schools, by providing a historical and contextual understanding to create more inclusive and equitable learning environments. Love's (2019) call for abolitionist teaching advocates for a decolonized curriculum and classroom where the learner's history is centered and nurtured. Muhammad's (2023) culturally and historically responsive education (CHRE) framework empowers teachers to design curricula that center students' identities, histories, and literacies, by critically engaging with, celebrating, and sustaining the funds of knowledge students bring to the classroom, fostering a sense of joy.

Culturally responsive-sustaining pedagogy (CRSP) (Figure I.1) in the United States underscores the growing recognition of the critical and essential role evolving cultural relevance and responsiveness play in education. Evolving from the early days of multicultural education to the current emphasis on culturally sustaining practices, CRSP continues to shape the way educators approach teaching and learning in diverse classrooms. Integrating global competencies into CRSP practices can provide a more holistic approach, ensuring that educators not only address local diversity issues but also prepare individuals to thrive in a global context.

The section provided an overview and genealogy of culturally responsive-sustaining pedagogy in education in the United States. Through a historical and critical examination highlighting the necessity for the inclusion of the global lens to the existing framework, readers will have the foundation needed to understand the evolution of global competence in teacher preparation, while also considering practical P-16 implications, with the hope of developing a critical mass of globally and culturally competent educators. The book will

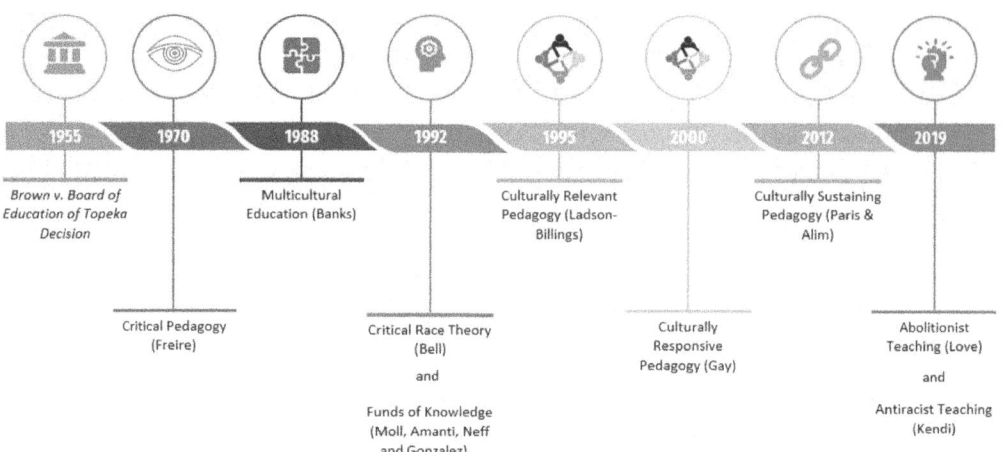

Figure I.1 Evolution of culturally responsive/sustaining pedagogy. *Created by the authors.*

draw on the narratives of educators and practitioners from domestic and global spaces, sharing lived experiences engaging diverse students.

Historical Context of Global Education

The roots of global education can be traced back to the post–World War II period, when there was a strong emphasis on promoting international understanding and cooperation. Global leaders acknowledged the need to foster peace and prevent future conflicts by encouraging and supporting cultural understanding among nations. This development led to the creation of numerous international organizations such as the United Nations Educational, Scientific and Cultural Organization (UNESCO) in 1945, which focused on international cooperation in education pivotal at the end of World War II, as an impetus to rebuild and promote peace in the world to prevent future conflicts and promote sustainable development.

In 1948, the United Nations Declaration of Human Rights created a context not only for advancing respect among each other but to advance global education to bridge cultural gaps across the world. Interestingly, Martin Luther King Jr.'s last message of an interconnected world united irrespective of cultural differences influenced the UN's thrust to embrace global understandings. In the 1960s and 1970s, global awareness increased significantly as international exchange programs, such as study abroad, became more prevalent and global issues began to be included in school curricula. During this time, there was the creation of world studies, an interdisciplinary approach of combining geography, history, and social studies to foster a global perspective. The next two decades (1980s and 1990s) focused on expanding global competencies by raising awareness of global development issues, such as poverty and illiteracy and numeracy of basic skills, in hopes of promoting a more equitable world (United Nations Educational, Scientific, and Cultural Organization 1990). Interestingly, at this time, the United States of America was looking inward at its own failing education system, documented in the "Nation at Risk," detailing schools' inadequate preparation of students to compete in the global marketplace. Initiatives such as "No Child Left Behind" and "Race to the Top" as antidotes to the glaring educational crisis especially to support students from diverse populations who were instructional casualties of schools. Globally, education emerged a priority during the 2000s. UNESCO has led this effort prioritizing education and promoting Education for Sustainable Development (ESD) now at the forefront of the UN's agenda (SDGs) with SDG 4 focused on education as a basic human right from primary through tertiary institutions (2024). Organizations such as OECD/PISA produced comparable data impacting education systems and standards globally. Key frameworks such as UNESCO's global citizenship education (GCE) emerged, underscoring the importance of developing cognitive, socioemotional, and behavior dimensions of learning thereby creating more inclusive classrooms producing students who are global citizens of the world, (Global Citizenship Foundation, 2022). Many organizations, programs, and curricula arose across the globe such as ESD, Oxfam's Global Citizenship Curriculum, Asia Society's Global Competence Framework, and OECD's Global Competence Framework. The global organizations centered the work of many scholars and theorists whose research and pedagogical frameworks questioned and disrupted the traditional Eurocentric Western intellectual traditions such as decoloniality theory (Quijano., Peruvian sociologist 1991).

The emergence of scholarship from minoritized scholars in higher education in the United States has underscored the significance of global education in relation to multicultural education, decentering whiteness. Works such as Friere's *Pedagogy of the Oppressed* (1970), Mill's concept of the racial contract (1997), and Wynter's exploration of human emancipation (2015), highlight the intersections between these fields. Despite the progress made in addressing the multifaceted global diversity, there remained a critical gap in the consideration of students' cultural backgrounds. Although significant strides were made in the development of TESOL and ESOL programs in the 1960s, aimed at supporting culturally and linguistically diverse students, these initiatives primarily focused on language development and acquisition and often overlooked the importance of understanding students' culture and recognizing their funds of knowledge. Scholars, including Deardoff (2006), have emphasized the importance of intercultural competence with cultural awareness as essential elements of cross-cultural knowledge. This research supports programs in higher education such as study abroad, service, and mission-driven experiential learning initiatives, which aim to enhance students' global awareness and intercultural understanding. Building on and critiquing traditional models of service learning, recent scholars Collopy et. al. (2020) have advocated for reciprocal service learning, which promotes a more mutually beneficial approach to experiential learning for both local and international students. Unlike conventional service learning, which can perpetuate unequal power dynamics by positioning students as "helpers" or "voyeurs," and communities as passive recipients.

Andreotti's (2015) work on global citizenship intersects with decoloniality theory advancing building relationships with others addressing differences and inequalities as we appreciate the histories, positionalities, and narratives in the world. In consideration of factors such as increased migration, world crisis, wars, and shifting demographic trends, Mansilla and Jackson (2012) emphasized a need for fostering global competence through transdisciplinary, design-based research. They advocated for an approach that draws upon students' cultural capital and funds of knowledge, allowing educators to better meet the needs of foreign-born, immigrants, and refugee students in domestic classrooms. The Tichnor-Wagner et. al (2019) book *Becoming a globally competent teacher* also seeks to advance the global dimensions of teaching as educators need to be equipped to foster cross-cultural interactions in their classrooms. Educators must be intentionally engaged in humanizing education by actively acknowledging and addressing the profound impact of students' lived experiences, cultural background, global issues, and personal dignity within the learning process. Moving beyond the one-size-fits-all approach and embracing empathy, curiosity, cognitive complexity, varying perspectives, and cultural humility that emerge from having a global mindset. The Bajaj et al. (2022) book *Humanizing education for immigrant and refugee youth: 20 Strategies for the classroom and beyond* recognizes the possibilities that can exist in schools where students feel seen, valued, and respected, ensuring a sense of belonging fostered through deeper connections and enhanced learning outcomes.

More recently, the digitalization of global education became paramount. Mansilla and Jackson's (2023) *Educating for global competence,* published digitally first after the COVID -19 pandemic, captured the attention of educators who were all forced to teach and engage with students on a digital platform. Contemporary trends arose through the integration of digital technology and global competencies, which expanded global learning being offered on online platforms to advance global learning, enabling cross-cultural exchanges and collaborative learning. For example, the emergence of Collaborative Online International Learning (COIL), global literacy learning and its impact on curricular practices in schools across the globe, programs such as global literacy day.

Evolution of CRSP with Global Competencies

Educators have been engaging in CRSP and global education independently; however, we propose a reframing or an expansion of the understanding and the context in which global competence situates itself in American classrooms and beyond our borders. This perspective aims to recognize, enrich, and affirm the identities and lived experiences of all students in the classroom. Such a perspective requires a fundamental shift in our understanding of the importance of the interconnectedness of local and global issues and the importance of addressing both within educational contexts. Furthermore, the evolution of CRSP with global competencies emphasizes the need for intercultural competence, cross-cultural interactions through immersive experiences, which will impact curriculum development and revision, as well as educator's philosophical, epistemological, and pedagogical practices.

In today's rapidly changing world, developing a unified CRSP and global competency approach is more crucial than ever. While the student demographics are changing rapidly, the teacher demographics are not, thus the urgency of developing culturally responsive and globally competent teachers is crucial as students' identities are not reflected in the teacher demographics. Striving toward the goal of ensuring that every instructional leader in the classroom, regardless of their racial or cultural identity, embodies both cultural responsiveness and global competency. The relevance of equipping educators with this valuable knowledge becomes increasingly important for fostering inclusive and equitable learning environments.

Appreciating the work of Kelly and Fields (2020), joining the concepts of CRSP and Universal Design Learning (UDL) we extend their efforts to broaden the traditionally isolated approaches to an asset-based framework. By doing so, teacher educators can create a more inclusive preparation experience for all candidates. This Integrative Global-CRSP Framework encourages educators and practitioners to implement an intersectional, globally, and culturally responsive teaching approach. This approach not only acknowledges but nurtures and sustains students' cultural identities to enhance their academic achievement, increase their sense of belonging and inclusion in a pluralistic society, while raising their sociopolitical consciousness and commitment to activism as a citizen of the world.

In the image below, we visualize this framework as a combination of a series of pedagogies, or the way in which teacher educators and teachers can enact globalized culturally responsive and sustaining curriculum. This proposed framework opens the conversation for educators to engage in dialogue, collaboration, and research between two fundamentally important pedagogical frameworks, Culturally Responsive-Sustaining Pedagogy–CRSP (Ladson-Billing, 1995; Paris Alim, 2014; Gay, 2002) and global competency (PISA). Each of these frameworks has a long-standing legacy and impact in teacher education. Given the current state of our educational ecosystem, now is a time for the convergence of these frameworks to fully incorporate the principles and practices of CRSP with the multifaceted elements of global competencies (Table I.1).

Global Competence +CRSP→Academic Success

The internationalization of the American classroom is here, making it crucial to integrate this framework into candidate preparation from introductory courses to student teaching. America's pluralistic society already exists, with diverse, diasporic cultural spaces in our local communities. It is important to recognize that local global competency is distinct from domestic cultural competency. We critique America's Educator Preparation Programs (EPPs) for their limited approach to global education because of the reductionist and ethnocentric perspective embedded within the educational tapestry. Instead, teacher candidates should be compassionate and empathetic allies who understand and value a holistic global approach. There is a necessity for a comprehensive and integrative approach that includes global competencies that support teacher candidates' development of an appreciation for diversity and sensitivity of all individuals within our local spaces as part of a larger cross-cultural environment. A new globalized pedagogical framework that incorporates CRSP theoretical and conceptual approaches, with consideration of how these frameworks can be applied in both local and international contexts to enhance teaching and learning experiences.

What if the aim of education extended beyond fostering students' awareness and deepening their cultural understandings, to actively shaping students into citizens of the world? Confronted with the realities of immigration debate and reform; legislation that seeks to eliminate the teaching of diverse histories; and growing international conflicts that seek to dehumanize and oppress groups, teachers will have to learn outside of the traditional canon in educator praxis. Educator preparation must shift to recognize the relevance and importance of preparing candidates to have a global frame of reference. Integrating these competencies should become a new benchmark for transformative and culturally responsive teacher preparation. This imperative shift is essential if education aspires to reach its fullest potential in fostering the holistic, inclusive, and equitable development of all learners.

Table I.1 Global Competence Dimensions, Culturally Responsive-Sustaining Pedagogy, and Integrative Global-CRSP Frameworks

Global Competence Dimensions	Culturally Responsive/ Sustaining Pedagogy (CRSP)	Integrative Global CRSP Framework
1. Examine local, global, and intercultural issues (OECD PISA, 2022) to magnify and illuminate the interconnectedness of humanity across the globe (Mansilla and Jackson, 2012) in curricular practices (Kerkhoff, 2022).	Develop sociopolitical consciousness, identify root causes of injustice, increase self-awareness and intersectionalities (Crenshaw, 1989), and incorporate these issues in instruction from an informed stance so that students are able to understand and critique systems and society (Ladson-Billings, 1995; 2021).	Examine local, global, and intercultural issues while developing socio political consciousness for understanding and critique of educational systems and policies. 1. Analyze how integrative global education can be applied both within and beyond traditional classroom spaces to cultivate sociopolitical consciousness. 2. Demystifying the local and global dichotomized educational landscape to foster sociopolitical consciousness and transnational understandings. 3. Support complex multifaceted identity development and self-awareness from different nations to foster intercultural competence across differences.

Global Competence Dimensions	Culturally Responsive/ Sustaining Pedagogy (CRSP)	Integrative Global CRSP Framework
2. Understand and appreciate the perspectives and world views of others (Deardoff, 2006) through self-reflection using inner development goals both individually and collectively to create a sustainable educational ecosystem (Inner Development Goals, 2021).	Focus on cultural competence and equip students to navigate systems not designed to enable their success. (Ladson-Billings, 1995; Matias and Liou, 2014). Explicitly engage students in critical thinking, reflection, and action to spur emancipation and liberation for the community through the students. (Gay 2002, 2018; Villegas and Lucas, 2007). Funds of Knowledge (Moll et al., 1992) and HILL Model (Muhammad, 2023). The cross-pollination of CSP with Universal Design for Learning and queer frameworks explicitly attends to dis/ability and sexual and gender identity as essential components in the construction of fluid cultural identities (Kelly and Fields, 2020). Curriculum changes from CRP to Anti-Racist Activism (Kendi, 2019), which seeks to reimagine, reclaim, agitate, and inspire through content that is culturally relevant, racially affirming, and socially meaningful. (McIntosh and Nenonene, 2022).	Commit to an inclusive pedagogical framework that values social perspective taking, cultural appreciation, and decolonizing education. 1. Engage in practices to actively dismantle hegemonic systemic practices that have historically and currently marginalized immigrants, first generation, linguistically diverse, and racial minoritized groups. 2. Reimagine the world as a curriculum that fosters critical thinking, reflection, and action, while embracing multiple intellectual traditions and ways of knowing; and acknowledging the cultural wealth of both students and teachers. 3. Utilize approaches such as Universal Design for Learning to develop, restructure, and reimagine the world as a curriculum centering Sustainable Development Goals (SDGs) while scaffolding content, identifying key conceptual benchmarks, and fostering a more nuanced understanding of intersectionalities in educational settings across the globe.

Global Competence Dimensions	Culturally Responsive/ Sustaining Pedagogy (CRSP)	Integrative Global CRSP Framework
3. Engage in meaningful, humanistic, and intercultural dialogic interactions to develop and foster reciprocity, empathy, and engagement (OECD, 2022). Deardoff's (2006) model of intercultural competence highlights the importance for teachers' understanding of diverse perspectives through active engagement and reflection on working with students and parents, in their local communities.	Seek to "perpetuate and foster—to sustain—linguistic, literate, and cultural pluralism as part of the democratic project of schooling" (Paris, 2012: 93). Enhance the learning of all students, not only international, but multilingual, marginalized communities with complex intersectionalities (Dimitrov and Haque, 2016).	Understands the multifaceted dynamics of cross-cultural interactions grounded in responsive and sustaining equitable educational practices. 1. Create global-centric environments that nurture criticality, encouraging individuals to explore diverse perspectives to cultivate mutual understanding and promote personal and collective growth. 2. Engage in critical, reciprocal, and mutually beneficial partnerships that promote global awareness that is purposeful, sustainable, and productive for all to thrive through education.
4. Taking action toward collective well-being through emancipatory and liberatory practices that advocate for shared responsibility, systemic change, and justice-centered education (Wynter, 2015; Mansilla and Jackson, 2012).	Love (2019) advances the use of abolitionist teaching as a means of advocating for student voice and social cohesion. Hammond (2015) emphasizes the power of community collaboration, where educators and learners partner together to drive collective action toward educational equity. Promoting the development of critical consciousness in relation to civic engagement that leads to social justice (Hill Collins, 2013). Seek to sustain "heritage and community" language, literacy, and cultural ways of knowing and being and offer "access to dominant cultural competence" (Paris, 2012: 95) while embracing the fluidity of culture and community.	Harnesses the power of collectivism through which community cultural assets foster belonging, well-being, and overall 1. Decenter traditional Eurocentric ways of knowing to establish a new inclusive and globally centered frame of reference. 2. Provide space for community engagement and agency to promote transformative globalized learning and action in educational spaces that transcends borders. 3. Empower students, as cultural translators and bridge-builders, facilitate understanding and connection between globally diverse cultures.

Global Competence Dimensions	Culturally Responsive/ Sustaining Pedagogy (CRSP)	Integrative Global CRSP Framework
5. Embedding and assessing practices that support intercultural competence and global citizenship education (Andreotti, 2015) through dialogic approaches fostering reciprocal engagement among diverse global populations. Using tools such as Deardoff (2020) "Story circles" and Boix Mansilla's "Global thinking routines" to go beyond theoretical learning into lived experiences in a globalized society. Utilizing UN Sustainable goals alongside traditional academic standards (United Nations Department of Economic and Social Affairs, 2024).	Emphasize preparing students for life-long learning through interactions that lead to individual and collective academic achievement and empowerment (Ladson-Billings, 1995), HILL Model (Muhammad, 2023) and the Black Gaze Framework (Bertrand and Porcher, 2023). Transform schools and societies through student-centered approaches to curriculum, instruction, and assessment (Gay 2002, 2010; Villegas and Lucas, 2002). Foster reciprocal service learning engagements disrupting power dynamics and creating opportunities for intercultural learning (Collopy et al., 2020).	Design academic outcomes are directly correlated to the implementation of relevant cultural and global instructional and assessment practices. 1. Center student academic success and well-being as the primary focus of education facilitated through the use of global thinking routines that offer a variety of relevant, culturally rich materials, modalities, activities, and experiences. 2. Reconceptualize assessment practices to draw on the globally diverse assets students bring to the classroom to promote academic achievement.

Indeed, our book responds to this imperative by highlighting the need for an integrative global diversity approach that recognizes, critiques, and expands the complexity of bridging the local, national, and global education landscape. Capturing the interconnectedness of culturally relevant pedagogy to global consciousness, delineating how "teaching affects competence and practice whereas pedagogy affects attitude and disposition" (Aronson, Amatullah, and Laughter, 2016: 167). Our aforementioned framework encompasses not only the necessity of cultural awareness but also brings attention to the multifaceted elements of global competency, where understanding that those traditional areas: knowledge, skills, and dispositions, highlighted by our education profession, are enhanced and informed by this globalized pedagogical perspective. Additionally, we propose reflective questions to help educators and students delve deeper into the importance of utilizing a global diversity approach to develop and support students' cultural awareness and responsiveness in their teaching and learning.

Knowledge

Educators must not only be aware of themselves, but they must be aware of "The Other" (Delpit, 1995). Specifically, knowledge of group ancestry, identities, histories, cultural traditions, rituals, observances, mannerisms, and individual and collective orientations. It's not just navigating other cultures, it's being intentional in offering enriching experiences so students will be equipped to function in an ever changing world. Shifting education's focus to not only encompassing student-centered education, but simultaneously centering the "world" in education (Andreotti, 2021b). What would world-centric education encompass? An embracing of the vast and diverse intellectual traditions within the diaspora, moving beyond the focus on centering whiteness.

Reflective Questions for Teacher Educators/In-service Teachers/Pre-service Teachers

1 In what ways do my personal experiences and background influence my interaction with others from different cultural backgrounds?
2 What steps am I taking to learn about the ancestors, identities, and cultural traditions of my students and colleagues?
3 Can I identify specific ways my teaching practices (e.g., planning, instruction, and assessment) to honor and respect the cultural identities of others?
4 What intentional actions do I implement to provide and support enriching experiences that prepare students for a globally diverse world?
5 What strategies do I utilize to foster an environment where all students feel seen and valued?

Reflective Questions for K-12 Students

1 How am I learning about the world?
2 Am I aware of what's happening outside my national setting?
3 Do I understand how it influences my local context?
4 Do I understand the impact of my local context on people and societies in the world outside my context?
5 How can I intentionally begin to engage in this learning?

Skills

A clear appreciation and inclusion of domestic and international cultures and identities.

Educators should develop students' awareness and understanding, when coupled together, educators begin to implement a more holistic approach fostering students' success. Aligned with the recommendation of Paris (2012), educators should embrace a value system that seeks to sustain "heritage and community" language, literacy, and cultural ways of knowing and being and offer "access to dominant cultural competence" (p. 95) while embracing the fluidity of culture and community.

Equally important in terms of skills is the development of sociopolitical consciousness as an asset-based pedagogical necessity for student engagement and learning (Ladson-Billings, 1995). Educators must commit to identifying root causes of injustice, increase self-awareness on matters related to privilege, advocacy, and allyship; and incorporate these issues into curriculum and pedagogy from an informed stance so that students are able to understand and critique systems and society (Howard, 2021; Ladson-Billings, 1995).

What skills should an educator demonstrate that reflect cultural competence in a global context while simultaneously supporting and valuing equity, inclusion, and social justice? Our hope is that these skills reflect the aspirational intentions many felt after the 1954 Brown decision, which hoped, "to produce an active and diverse citizenry committed to advancing democratic principles, our students must be able to learn with and from peers of different races, ethnicities, languages, faiths, and economic status" (James, 2024).

Reflective Questions for Teacher Educators/In-service Teachers/Pre-service Teachers

1 How do I actively incorporate both domestic and international cultural perspectives into my curriculum and pedagogical practices?
2 How do I support and sustain students' heritage and community languages, literacies, and cultural ways of knowing in my classroom?
3 Is the development of a sociopolitical consciousness evident in my pedagogical practices, selection of learning materials, and experiential learning opportunities?

Reflective Questions for K-12 Students

1 How does domestic and global diversity impact my lived experiences?
2 How do I engage with students who are different from me (e.g., immigrants, refugees, Black Indigenous People of Color [BIPOC], linguistically diverse, etc.)?
3 How do I demonstrate, validate, and sustain my own cultural identity?
4 How do I honor and respect my classmates' heritage and community languages, literacies, and cultural ways of knowing?

Dispositions

Dispositions are the possession and consistent demonstration of values, behaviors, commitments, and ethics that exemplify cultural competence in a global context that supports issues of equity, inclusion, and social justice. This translates to tangible, intentional pedagogical practices that foster, support, enhance, and develop students' cultural awareness and understanding. Thus, fostering "cultural pluralism as part of the democratic project of schooling" (Paris, 2012: 93).

To promote a learning environment of respect and educational reciprocity, in which students recognize that learning comes from sitting with one another in community and mutually benefiting from the interactions. Ultimately, the goal is to move students from being passive outsiders or spectators in the educational process and emerging into actively empathetic participants who engage in inquiry, truth seeking, and genuine understanding of the other. Aligning with Biesta's (2013) differentiation between "learn from," in which there is a preconceived notion and anticipation of what the learning experience will entail and "be taught by," which requires a challenge and critique of established oppressive notions of "others" and a reorientation that allows for new way of thinking and application, encompassing unexpected and unpredictable influences. Thereby, manifesting a fresh lens through which to view the interconnectedness of self, other, and the world. By learning about the global realities of others, educators can develop an appreciation of both domestic and global diversity. As such, we propose educators engaging in cultural fluidity that blurs the lines between local and global, essentially fostering borderless learning.

Reflective Questions

1 How do I envision or adapt my teaching methods to reflect the fluid and dynamic nature of culture and community in my students' lives?
2 In what ways do I create a learning environment that emphasizes respect and educational reciprocity, encouraging students to learn from and with one another in a community setting?
3 How do I challenge and critique established oppressive notions of "others" in my teaching, encouraging students to rethink and reorient their perspectives?
4 What strategies do I utilize to facilitate a learning experience where students are receptive to being taught by the unexpected and unpredictable influences of diverse cultures and perspectives?

Reflective Questions for K-12 Students

1 Do I understand how my culture and community influence my perceptions of myself and peers?
2 What insights have I gained from my classmates' cultural identities that I can appreciate and incorporate into my own life?
3 How have I shown empathy for classmate's diverse lived experiences?
4 How might I use these diverse perspectives to become a global citizen?

We pose these reflective questions as a way to encourage both educators and students to engage in meaningful, human-centered dialogue, with the intention of inspiring actions that promote and support collective well-being. Unearthing both the knowledge and power within educators and students to engage in emancipatory and liberatory practices that cultivate shared responsibility, systemic change, and justice-centered education.

The purpose and organization of *Borderless Education: A Pedagogical Framework for Cultural Responsiveness and Global Competence* is to address global education through the lens of pre-service teacher training, PK-12 setting, and community-engaged partnerships. It offers recommendations on how to extend the nexus between culturally responsive educational practices and global education. The chapters offer relevant and replicable examples of how educator preparation can reimagine program curriculum, enhance experiential learning, and foster community partnerships that lead to a more inclusive interpretation and recognition of culturally and linguistically diverse student populations. Gay (2002) suggests that diverse students are more responsive to teaching when their "cultural characteristics, experiences, and perspectives" are authentically embedded in the curriculum (p. 106). Strengthening the global competency of educators is crucial, especially as today's classrooms mirror the growing demographic changes in the United States. Despite numerous teacher pipeline initiatives aimed at increasing the number of people of color in the profession, the majority of classroom teachers remain predominantly White and female (Diamond, Posey-Maddox, and Velázquez, 2021).

Considering the new landscape of education where global diversity is a necessity, not a choice, teacher educators should consider integrating global competencies into every aspect of teacher preparation. By intentionally challenging conventional understandings of research and knowledge, while advocating for social justice and equity in education, they can develop epistemologies grounded in global intellectual traditions. This approach ensures that teacher candidates are prepared to meet the needs of a diverse student population with compassion, empathy, and a deep appreciation for the cultural wealth that students bring to the classroom.

The book serves as a conduit between global and domestic diversity by bridging the gap between global and cultural competence. Practitioners, researchers, scholars, and activists will share their expert knowledge, pedagogical skills, and strategies of how they intentionally infused global understandings to meet the needs of students. Readers will interrogate their identities and positionalities as they explore domestic and global issues in the classroom, thus gaining a voice of agency as they reflect and re-envision teaching and learning through a global intersectional approach. When students proactively engage in social issues, they build self-esteem, compassion, and advocacy and hopefully become empowered to become active citizens or change agents for the next generation of students.

The three parts of this book seek to contribute to the ongoing conceptualization, implementation, facilitation, and application of global education with respect to educator preparation. Each section is rich in contextualizing history, examining and challenging long-held institutional policies and practices, offering relevant and informative frameworks and experiences as exemplars of teaching, practice, and application. The work presented here represents the efforts of a diverse group of undergraduate and graduate students; PK-teachers and school leaders; community organizers; and teacher educators. All focused on demonstrating the importance and power of inclusive global practices that engage students, enrich the learning process, and contribute to academic success.

We encourage you to read this book and take action. Read to expand your knowledge and deepen your contextual understanding. Read to be inspired by the work of others. Read to reflect on what you can do. Then, take action. Act for yourself, nurturing your growth and well-being, thus becoming not only an advocate but a catalyst. Act for the immigrant, multilingual, and diverse students who need recognition, affirmation, and support. Act to create meaningful, impactful, and sustainable change.

Part I—Operationalizing the Global Pedagogical Framework in Curriculum and Content

Chapters in Part One focus on the lived experiences of children of immigrants, the recent migration of families in the United States, and our international educational colleagues' experiences in their local contexts. The chapters will vary in context, author roles (e.g., researchers, scholars, community partners, K-12 teachers, etc.), and positionalities, validating the findings and lessons learned from each narrative. Contributors share examples of reimagining within a global context by challenging normative pedagogical practices and expectations associated with traditional subjects such as Math and Art as well as offer recommendations for educator preparation programs to consider for embedding global frameworks and understandings into the preparation of future teachers with respect to curriculum, dispositions, and experiences.

In Chapter 1, Gajasinghe et al. detail considerations for curriculum revision by the inclusion of intellectual traditions and other ways of knowing through an "Anti-Conquest" curriculum. Employing currere and confabulation methods of inquiry to demonstrate how two educators created space for their students to imagine the world otherwise by attuning to diverse places and ways of knowing, being, and feeling that resist US hegemony and anthropocentrism.

Chapter 2, using the narrative inquiry process, explores the experiences of international and immigrant students at a predominantly White institution. Through this qualitative approach, Kavimandan et al. seek to offer understandings and recommendations for institutions of higher education (IHE) and educator preparation programs with regard to being responsive to the needs of diverse students. Their work highlights the urgency and crucial need for a global pedagogical framework rooted in the principles and practices of intercultural responsiveness, multicultural/lingual competencies, and an individual's positionality.

Highlighting a unique, place-based program in the Global South known as Mathkind, Chapter 3 is the work of Powell et al. Mathkind exemplifies how traditional subjects like mathematics can be grounded in culturally responsive practices without instituting missionary practices, such as uncritically transplanting programs from the North and behaving parasitically or paternalistically. This chapter underscores the potential of mathematics education to be both locally rooted and globally informed, fostering mathematics leaders who not only honor and respect their own cultural contexts but also strategically adapt relevant global ideas to meet their educational goals.

In Chapter 4, Falk et al. offer a reflective analysis of their experience as faculty leaders on a study abroad program in Northern Ireland, guiding undergraduate pre-service teachers. The chapter explores the historical and ongoing nature of conflict in Northern Ireland, drawing parallels to the escalating social and political tensions in the United States. Through this comparative lens, the authors highlight key lessons on peacebuilding, emphasizing the transformative role of education in fostering reconciliation and understanding in divided societies.

Part II—Blurring the Lines between Local and Global: Fostering Borderlessness

Global diversity is borderless, confronted with the realities of immigration, legislation, and growing diversity of domestic populations, educators must expand their practice beyond the traditional canon. Bridging the local, national, and global education landscape presents a complex challenge, yet underscores the necessity for an integrative approach to global diversity. Schools are core institutions in communities and serve as the place and space for cross-cultural interactions that are paramount to the development and sustainability of the inclusive communities that we all seek.

To bring theory to life, these chapters will feature narratives from educators and practitioners both in the United States and abroad. Offering firsthand accounts of the challenges and successes encountered while implementing a globalized CRSP framework in diverse educational settings. In Chapter 5, Wilkins presents the nexus of Art and culturally sustaining pedagogy through the framework of Critical Visual Literacy. Exemplifying the importance of incorporating culturally responsive practices, educators can ensure that the curriculum fosters a sense of belonging and respect for diversity through critical consciousness. Through the medium of visual arts, students can learn empathy, understand how to navigate cultural differences, and develop a better understanding of the world.

In the next chapter, Hwang examines an innovative online conversation partners program (Turkish Students Conversation Partners) that facilitated borderless intercultural engagement between college students in the US and Turkey. The chapter illustrates how digital technology broadened the scope of cross-cultural encounters, providing students with global cultural learning opportunities. Through these virtual exchanges, students enhanced their religious literacy, developed a deeper, more authentic understanding of culturally responsive and sustaining teaching, and gained critical awareness of how social and environmental factors impact oppressed groups—all without leaving their home countries.

In Chapter 7, Jeon explores how civil society organizations (CSOs) in South Korea are implementing global citizenship education (GCED) in K-12 schools. This author critically examines the dynamic interplay between the South Korean context—marked by strong social cohesion rooted in shared history and culture—and the principles of GCED. This chapter provides insights into how unique contextual factors and preservation of heritage can influence the practice of global citizenship education and understanding of diversity, shaping both its challenges and its potential impact on students' development as global citizens.

Landa, in Chapter 8, delves into the impact of school organizational structures on immigrant students with disabilities and their access to inclusive, least restrictive environments. The author's findings highlight how inadequate support for coordination between staff and between staff and parents contributes to delayed disability identification, overly restrictive segregated placements, and denial of appropriate language services for immigrant children. The chapter concludes with practical recommendations for redesigning elementary school organizational structures to better support school staff in effectively including all students in the learning process.

In the final chapter of Part Two, Koubek and Rojas utilize duoethnography to examine the collaborative journey of a US teacher educator and a Costa Rican bilingual school principal as they facilitate a study abroad program for US pre-service teachers in Costa Rica. Their findings illuminate the transformative impact of cross-cultural interactions, emphasizing the mutual benefits for both the pre-service teachers and the host communities. This chapter provides critical insights into the power of immersive educational experiences in fostering intercultural understanding and professional growth.

Part III—Conclusion, Recommendations, and Resources

In the end, it's the "So what? Now what?" questions that Ladson-Billings always prompts us to consider that you should keep in mind. You can make a measurable difference in your local community using global considerations. Educator preparation must shift to recognize the relevance and importance of preparing candidates to have a global frame of reference. These competencies include (1) examining local, global, and intercultural issues, (2) understanding and appreciating the perspectives and worldviews of others, (3) taking action for collective well-being and sustainable development, and (4) engaging in open, appropriate, and effective interactions across cultures (OECD/Asia Society, 2018). Including such competencies becomes a new standard for transformative and culturally responsive teacher preparation.

We conclude the book with Part III, as it explores global futurism in the context of teacher education, recognizing the anticipation and preparation for the evolving challenges and opportunities that educators will face in a rapidly changing world. Noting the importance of implementing interdisciplinary approaches that blend insights from various fields such as arts, technology, and science. This prepares educators to approach complex global issues holistically.

Part III's recommendations and resources should be considered by readers as a means to construct a new landscape of education where global diversity is a necessity, not a choice. We hope you utilize these tools as a means to seek an end to epistemic violence, develop a voice of advocacy, and enhance your global pedagogical activism. By disrupting the traditional canon in teacher education through questioning existing pedagogical methodologies, educators can offer and sustain much richer, fuller, and inclusive praxis for the times. Now is the time to advocate for teaching practices that foster and support sustainability and social responsibility, while preparing students to become active, informed global citizens who contribute positively to their communities and the world.

References

Andreotti, V. de O. (2015). Global citizenship education otherwise: Pedagogical and theoretical insights. In Ali Abdi, Lynette Shultz, and Tashika Pillay (Eds.), *Decolonizing Global Citizenship Education*, pp. 221–30. Sense Publishers.

Andreotti, V. de O. (2021). Depth education and the possibility of GCE otherwise. *Globalisation, Societies and Education*, *19*(4), 496–509. https://doi.org/10.1080/14767724.2021.1904214.

Bajaj, M., Walsh, D., Bartlett, L., and Martinez, G. (2022). *Humanizing Education for Immigrant and Refugee Youth*. Teachers College Press.

Baldwin, J. (1963). *A Talk to Teachers*. ESED 5234 Master List. https://www.zinnedproject.org/materials/baldwin-talk-to-teachers (accessed November 11, 2025).

Bertrand, S., and Porcher, K. (2023). Shifting the gaze to Blackness in ELA: Using the Blackgaze framework in literacy teacher education courses. *Language Arts*, *101*(1), 27–39. https://doi.org/10.58680/la202332598.

Biesta, G. (2013). Receiving the gift of teaching: From "learning from" to "being taught by." *Studies in Philosophy and Education*, *32*(5), 449–61.

Brandt, R. (1994). On education for diversity: A conversation with James A. Banks. *Educational Leadership*, *51*, 28–32.

Brown v. *Board of Education of Topeka*, 349 U.S. *301* (1955). https://www.archives.gov/milestone-documents/brown-v-board-of-education (accessed October 24, 2025).

Collopy, R., Tjaden-Glass, S., and McIntosh, N. (2020). Attending to conditions that facilitate intercultural competence: A reciprocal service-learning approach. *Michigan Journal of Community Service Learning*, *26*(1), 19–38.

Crenshaw, K. (1989). Demarginalizing the intersection of race and sex: A Black feminist critique of antidiscrimination doctrine. University of Chicago Legal Forum, 139–68.

Deardorff, D. K. (2006). Identification and assessment of intercultural competence as a student outcome of internationalization. *Journal of Studies in International Education*, *10*(3), 241–66.

Deardorff, D. K. (2020). *Manual for Developing Intercultural Competencies*. *Story Circles*. Routledge.

Delpit, L. (1995). *Other People's Children: Cultural Conflict in the Classroom*. New Press.

Diamond, J. B., Posey-Maddox, L., and Velázquez, M. D. (2021). Reframing suburbs: Race, place, and opportunity in suburban educational spaces. *Educational Researcher*, *50*(4), 249–55. https://doi.org/10.3102/0013189X20972676.

Dimitrov, N., and Haque, A. (2016). Intercultural teaching competence: A multi-disciplinary model for instructor reflection. *Intercultural Education*, *27*(5), 437–56.

Freire, P. (1970). *Pedagogy of the Oppressed*. Seabury.

Gay, G. (2002). Preparing for culturally responsive teaching. *Journal of Teacher Education*, *53*(2), 106–16.

Gay, G. (2018). *Culturally Responsive Teaching: Theory, Research, and Practice* (3rd edn.). Teachers College Press.

Global Citizenship Foundation. (2022). Global Citizenship Schools. https://www.globalcitizenshipfoundation.org/project/globalcitizenshipschools-2022 (accessed November 11, 2025).

Hammond, Z. (2015). *Culturally Responsive Teaching and the Brain: Promoting Authentic Engagement and Rigor Among Culturally and Linguistically Diverse Students*. Corwin.

Hill Collins, P. (2013). *On Intellectual Activism*. Temple University Press.

Howard, T. C. (2021). Culturally responsive pedagogy. In J. A. Banks (Ed.), *Transforming Multicultural Education Policy and Practice: Expanding Educational Opportunity*, pp. 137–63. Teachers College Press.

Inner Development Goals. (2021). Inner Development Goals: Background, method and the IDG framework. https://innerdevelopmentgoals.org (accessed November 11, 2025).

James, W. (2024). *In Pursuit of Justice: Fulfilling the Promise of Brown v. Board of Education.* Center for American Progress. https://www.americanprogress.org/article/in-pursuit-of-justice-fulfilling-the-promise-of-brown-v-board-of-education (accessed November 11, 2025).

Kelly, M., and Wright Fields, C. (2020). Unlocking the doors: Opening spaces for inclusive pedagogy and practice in teacher education. In C. K. Clausen and S. R. Logan (Eds.), *Integrating Social Justice Education in Teacher Preparation Programs*, pp. 1–28. IGI Global.

Kendi, I. (2019). *How to Be an Anti-racist.* Random House.

Kerkhoff, S. N. (2022). A pedagogical framework for critical cosmopolitan literacies. *Changing English, 29*(3), 262–84 https://doi.org/10.1080/1358684X.2022.2042673.

Ladson-Billings, G. (1995). Toward a theory of culturally relevant pedagogy. *American Educational Research Journal, 32*(3), 465–91.

Ladson-Billings, G. (1998). Just what is critical race theory and what's it doing in a nice field like education? *International Journal of Qualitative Studies in Education, 11*(1), 7–24. https://doi.org/10.1080/095183998236863.

Ladson-Billings, G. (2021). Three decades of culturally relevant, responsive, & sustaining pedagogy: What lies ahead? *Educational Forum, 85*(4), 351–54. https://doi.org/10.1080/00131725.2021.1957632.

Love, B. (2019). *We Want to Do More than Survive: Abolitionist Teaching and the Pursuit of Educational Freedom.* Beacon Press.

Mansilla, V. B., and Jackson, A. (2012). *Educating for Global Competence: Preparing our Students to Engage the World.* ACSD.

Mansilla, V. B., and Jackson, A. W. (2023). *Educating for Global Competence: Preparing our Students to Engage the World* (2nd edn.). ASCD.

Matias, C. E., and Liou, D. (2014). Tending to the heart of communities of color towards critical race teacher activism. *Urban Education, 50*(5), 601–25.

McIntosh, N., and Nenonene, R. (2022). Developing culturally responsive antiracist activists. In S. Browne and G. Jean-Marie (Eds.), *Reconceptualizing Social Justice in Teacher Education: Moving to Anti-racist Pedagogy*, pp. 215–230. Palgrave Macmillan.

Mills, C. W. (1997). *The Racial Contract.* Cornell University Press.

Milner, H. R. (2020). Disrupting punitive practices and policies: Rac(e)ing back to teaching, teacher preparation, and Brown. *Educational Researcher, 49*(3), 147–60. http://doi.org/10.3102/0013189X20907396.

Moll, L., Amanti, C., Neff, D., and Gonzalez, N. (1992). Funds of knowledge for teaching: Using a qualitative approach to connect homes to classrooms. *Theory into Practice, 31*(2), 132–41.

Muhammad, G. (2023). *Unearthing Joy: A Guide to Culturally and Historically Responsive Teaching and Learning.* Scholastic.

Organization for Economic Cooperation and Development. (2022). *Education at a Glance 2022: OECD Indicators, OECD Publishing.* Paris. https://doi.org/10.1787/3197152b-en.

Organization for Economic Cooperation and Development/Asia Society. (2018). *Teaching for Global Competence in a Rapidly Changing World.* https://www.oecd.org/content/dam/oecd/en/publications/reports/2018/01/teaching-for-global-competence-in-a-rapidly-changing-world_g1g8938c/9789264289024-en.pdf (accessed November 11, 2025).

Paris, D. (2012). Culturally sustaining pedagogy: A needed change in stance, terminology, and practice. *Educational Researcher*, *41*(3), 93–7. https://doi.org/10.3102/0013189X12441244.

Paris, D., and Alim, S. H. (2014). What are we seeking to sustain through culturally sustaining pedagogy? A loving critique forward. *Harvard Educational Review*, *84*(1), 85–100.

Tichnor-Wagner, A., Parkhouse, H., Glazier, J., and Cain, J. (2019). *Becoming a Globally Competent Teacher*. ASCD

United Nations Department of Economic and Social Affairs. (2024). https://sdgs.un.org/goals (accessed October 24, 2025).

United Nations Educational, Scientific, and Cultural Organization. (1990). *Education for All: Status and Trends*. https://unesdoc.unesco.org/ark:/48223/pf0000096125 (accessed November 11, 2025).

Villegas, A. M., and Lucas, T. (2007). The culturally responsive teacher. *Educational Leadership*, *64*(6), 28–33.

Wynter, S. (2015). *On Being Human as Praxis*. Duke University Press.

Part I

Operationalizing the Global Pedagogical Framework in Curriculum and Content

1

Storytelling for an Anti-conquest Curriculum: Nurturing Epistemological Diversity in the Global Education Ecology

Kasun Gajasinghe, Alyssa Morley, and Yetunde Alabede

Abstract

Scholars within and beyond the field of education call for reimagining curriculum to confront the logics of conquest that endanger multispecies survival. Global education (GE) is a space for not only learning to inhabit an ecologically collapsing world of multiply entangled uncertainties but also to "compost" violent systems and "cultivate the soil in which genuinely different and wiser futures might grow" (Stein et al., 2023: 999). In this chapter, we invite the reader to reflect on what it means to enact an "anti-conquest" curriculum for GE, building from ecological and expansive notions of curriculum (e.g., Aoki, 2005) and employing currere (Pinar and Grumet, 1976) and confabulation (Barros et al., 2022) as methods of inquiry. The paper offers stories that emerged through our work with pre-service teachers at a Midwestern university in the United States. The first story narrates a teacher candidate's study abroad experiences and sets the stage for the next two stories, which demonstrate how two educators created space for their students to imagine the world otherwise by attuning to diverse places and ways of knowing, being, and feeling that resist US hegemony and anthropocentrism. The confabulations unfold as invitations (both evocative and analytical as they appear) for the reader to think about GE beyond Global North-centered and human-centered worlds.

Key Terms: *global education, anti-conquest, curriculum, storytelling*

Multispecies survival faces at least four intertwined threats: anthropogenic climate change, undermining of democracy, nuclear (weapons) production, and militarism (Chomsky, 2020; McCormack and Gilbert, 2022). These threats cannot be separated from the heteronormative patriarchal global racial capitalist system, and this imbrication necessitates ways of being, knowing, and feeling that challenge this reproductive system of violence. While much has been written in the humanities and social sciences on suffering and misery produced by these threats,[1] we follow calls to recenter hope and for "a moratorium on damage-centered research" (Tuck, 2009: 422). This moratorium opens space for scholars to focus on the possibilities for inhabiting an ecologically collapsing world of multiply entangled uncertainties (Haraway, 2016; Loveless, 2019; Tsing, 2015). These possibilities often converse with ways of knowing, being, and feeling from people who have consistently tended and cared for more-than-human worlds, resisting multiple colonizing forces (Huaman and Swentzell, 2021; Kimmerer, 2013; Voyles, 2015).

Scholars within and beyond the field of education call for reimagining curriculum to confront the logics of conquest that endanger multispecies survival. For instance, Stein et al. (2023) offer an invitation to climate education "otherwise" that upends the modern/colonial[2] systems of violence and helps "people to identify, interrupt, and 'compost' the harmful and unsustainable system that lives within all of us so that we can cultivate the soil in which genuinely different and wiser futures might grow" (p. 999, see Haraway, 2019 on compost writing). We agree and encourage educators of/for the world (who think beyond the militarized ethnonationalist neoliberal patriarchal nation-state and human exceptionalism) to engage their students not only with the myriad tragedies but also the possibilities of reimagining livability for all beings. We contend that GE is a space for this reimagining, and this chapter presents an inquiry into these possibilities.

We approach our work—a pan to the "global"—with caution, given the ways that global has been narrowly and instrumentally understood. Building from the critical work of Andreotti (2014) and other scholars (e.g., Estellés and Fischman, 2021; Stein et al., 2023; Stein at al., 2024), we contend that the pervasive model of GE reflects "soft" global citizenship that responds superficially to complex problems while leaving untouched the structuring inequalities that maintain these problems. We join scholars committed to reimagining GE "otherwise" and invite educators to think beyond "soft" and "critical" global (citizenship) education (Andreotti, 2014). Our attempt in this chapter is to seek possibilities to (re) imagine the GE curriculum along this invitation through storytelling. Such an education includes fostering epistemological diversity through an anti-conquest curriculum. The stories we share present sparks of such an orientation in our teaching and research, while stopping short of prescribing toolkits, goals, or standards for curriculum design.

Global Education

The landscape of GE began developing in the mid-twentieth century. In part, this landscape was a reactionary development, as educators and scholars across the globe assessed the damage of two world wars, centuries of colonial violence, and unevenly distributed extreme poverty.

World Wars I and II had also given rise to new international bodies—such as the United Nations (UN) and its agencies, the International Monetary Fund (IMF), and the North Atlantic Treaty Organization (NATO)—that were important to understand for their roles in both sustaining and remediating global inequalities. New fields of study under the broad umbrella of GE emerged, seeking to prepare students for global understanding and international engagement. International organizations, like the United Nations Educational, Scientific and Cultural Organization (UNESCO), aimed to promote peace and development and played a central role in promoting education for international understanding (Nygren, 2016).

To understand GE's implications for teachers and teacher educators, the American Association of Colleges for Teacher Education (AACTE) commissioned a study of the GE field in the 1980s. The study came at a time when the term "globalization" was emerging from the business sector and would soon animate media and political discourse. Further, visible political interventions were being enacted on global stages—from the Cold War to the imposition of structural adjustment policies in (post)colonial states, and the rise of conditional bilateral aid flows and US hegemony (Tabulawa, 2003). In the AACTE report that emerged from the study, the authors argued that GE was important for teachers since "world affairs now significantly touch all domains of human activity" (Alger and Harf, 1985: 3). Alger and Harf defined the then-emerging field of GE as "education that enables people to make decisions while taking into account the ways in which they are affected by a diversity of economic, social, political, military, and natural phenomena that link together peoples of the world" (1985: 3). They argued that GE is a diverse and decentralized field of study that responds to issues such as resource scarcity, environmental catastrophes, human rights issues, population growth, terrorism, and colonization.

The decentralization of GE is quite apparent as one traverses this discipline that spans historically and ideologically diverse fields such as International Education (e.g., Cambridge and Thompson, 2004), Comparative Education (e.g., Mundy et al., 2008), and Global Citizenship Education (e.g., Andreotti, 2014). These fields overlap in their recognition of the necessity of education about the world and world affairs, the urgent need for better education for all humans, and the interdependence of nation-states and/or world actors, including individuals (Alger and Harf, 1985). Consequently, in this chapter, we use the term GE as a project that requires educators and students to think beyond national boundaries. However, we maintain that a GE committed only to thinking beyond national boundaries is incomplete, as it can uphold human exceptionalism and other logics of conquest. Therefore, decentering the human within curriculum imaginaries is crucial. Given that human beings have brought the world to the sixth mass extinction, scholars have pointed out the importance of challenging human exceptionalism (e.g., Haraway's *The Camille Stories*, 2016: 134) to reflect on possibilities to reimagine the world where all beings are indispensable for the liveliness of this mortal planet. In this paper, by decentering the human, we mean that—through our stories—we place the human on the same plane of existence (instead of placing the human at the top of a hierarchy) with other beings and objects. In other words, we argue that humans are not superior to other(ed) beings and objects. We also hold that even within the human species, the hierarchies are formed because of the desire to conquer the other and make the other "human" (e.g., The White Man's Burden) or exploit for profit. Consequently, "being human" is not merely biological, but discursive.

Toward an Anti-conquest Curriculum in Global Education

Before presenting how we envision an anti-conquest curriculum through stories, some clarification of how we conceptualize **curriculum** might be helpful. Gershon and Helfenbein (2023) broadly describe curriculum as "ecologies where educational understandings reside" (p. 251). Recognizing curriculum as ecologies of knowledge highlights how this space is animated by politics, desires, aspirations, struggles for control, and resistance (Kelly, 2009). This ecological perspective challenges an inert understanding of curriculum (as a "paper" or a "plan"). It foregrounds the liveliness and tensions in what is known (and knowable), how it is known, and why. As an onto-epistemological space where values, lifeworlds, and relations are negotiated and enacted, the curriculum is both an elastic orientation to the world and a reflection of changing consciousness. In conceptualizing curriculum in this expansive and ecological manner, we join other critical scholars who disturb the "traditional landscape, with its single privileged curriculum-as-plan awaiting implementation" (Aoki, 2005: 204).

Drawing on Cicero's work, Egan notes that curriculum, in certain instances, refers to "the temporal space in which we live; to the confines within which things may happen; to the container, as opposed to the contents" and to the contents or the materials one studies as well (Egan, 1978: 66). In this sense, curriculum is always more than itself, spilling out and refusing to be contained. He concludes that "curriculum is the study of any and all educational phenomena" and is not restricted to or by any methodology (Egan, 1978: 71). While, on the one hand, a non-instrumentalist definition of curriculum might be disorienting, on the other, this capaciousness enables scholars to explore various topics such as instructional methods, learning experiences, implicit and apparent objectives, and assessment (Egan, 1978; see also, Kelly, 2009). This approach also promotes inquiry into the moral, cultural, and political dimensions of curriculum, given that, at its core, "curriculum is about producing children who are productive, moral, and ethical citizens" (Popkewitz, 2014: 17). In our GE work, we contend that looking at curriculum, in its broadest possible sense, is essential to allow for new ways of knowing, being, and imagining.

In the attempt to approach a curriculum that attends to embodied and planetary issues as we desire cohabitation in a more-than-human world, we have crafted the concept of an **anti-conquest curriculum.** According to Andreotti, (2021), "conquest is the driving force of modernity/coloniality: the colonial desires to 'discover,' to conquer, occupy, own, rule, and control … " (p. 30). In other words, conquest is tightly bound not only with any urge to civilize/develop/subjugate the cultural/economic/political *other* or nature but also with everyday human interactions that enable and cover over the banality of such violence. For us, the anti-conquest curriculum has two crucial orientations. First, it embraces Andreotti's (2021) invitation to hospice modernity by imagining education otherwise as educators and students identify how, both in (post)colonial and settler colonial contexts, education plays a key role in genocides, ecocides, and epistemicide (de Sousa Santos, 2015) in this era of development-through-nuclear-power. In this regard, culturally relevant pedagogy (Ladson-Billings, 1995), culturally sustaining pedagogy (Paris, 2012), and culturally responsive pedagogy (Howard, 2021) are helpful theoretical approaches to disrupt dominant conceptions of knowledge and self and the other. However, we observe that these approaches are centered in humanism and conceptualize knowledge and being within the nature–culture divide. Therefore, those who aspire to imagine education otherwise for the survival and sustenance of all species could explore ways of knowing and being that consistently decenter "the human" from the matrix. Second, anti-conquest curriculum imaginaries, as we present in our confabulations in this chapter, could attempt to disrupt the nature–culture divide, enabling responses to questions such as: "Can we and our students easily answer questions regarding our sources of water, food, material for our clothes, homes, daily use items, and what sacrifices have been made by whom in order for these to be present?" (Huaman and Swentzell, 2021: 24).

In addition to imagining otherwise, an anti-conquest curriculum deconstructs claims of self-righteous activism in the name of the planet that ignores diverse forms of complicity with genocides, ecocides, and epistemicide around the world. This orientation responds to the acknowledgment that the "anti-conquest" discourse is co-opted as a part of "strategies of representation whereby European bourgeois subjects seek to secure their innocence in the same moment as they assert European hegemony" (Pratt, 2008: 9). For instance, the sensitivity to how tourism and travel writing hides coloniality and colonial infrastructure in place while assigning a sense of innocence to (European) bourgeois travelers, distinguishing them from (European) colonizers (Pratt, 2008) is crucial in GE.

We emphasize that central to an anti-conquest curriculum in GE are the deep queries which it enables to problematize the often taken-for-granted desires for conquest enacted not only on humans in the forms of genocide and epistemicide, but ecocide as well (see Eichler, 2020). Within this anti-conquest curriculum is abundant space to both acknowledge the multiple forms of conquest and to imagine an education delinked from conquest imperatives. Importantly, an anti-conquest curriculum imaginary needs to move beyond attempts to standardize education (e.g., PISA) and coercively creating a norm-abiding community (see Fendler, 2006, on community and its discontents) while supporting and sustaining epistemological diversity. Rather than inculcating competencies to fix global problems, the anti-conquest curriculum is an orientation through which one can begin to self-critically identify and unpack individual and systemic desires that drive multiplicities of conquests.

Currere as Collaborative Storytelling Toward an Anti-conquest Curriculum

The Latin root of curriculum, currere, refers to the following: "a running," "a race," "a course," "a race-course," "a career" (Egan, 1978). It also establishes a direction for currere as a method of inquiry, which aims to make visible the ideologies, movements, interactions, and introspections—to run with one's curriculum as memory work (Barros et al., 2022). **Currere,** according to Pinar and Grumet (1976), is "a uniquely educational method of inquiry, one that will allow us to give truthful, public and usable form to our inner observations" (p. 5) or rather, it is an invitation to sit with one's curriculum in conversation with others, meditating on curriculum moves that bear witness to its orientation(s) and how the course and interruptions reflect the changing consciousness of the students and teachers. According to Pinar (1994), this reflection manifests in three steps entailing (1) a stream of consciousness memories of one's past experiences regarding education and teaching; (2) projecting oneself into the future and recording "memories" of things that are likely to happen based on one's past experiences of education and teaching, and (3) connecting the past and conjectured future to find common themes that are worthwhile for the present. The currere steps suggested by Pinar are enacted in the process of confabulation as "method, process, and outcome" (Barros et al., 2022: 21). **Confabulation**[3] has three meanings associated with it: to talk, to discuss, and to fill in gaps in memory by fabrication. Confabulation is an attempt to resist "being conditioned to live in an endless and uncertain present, reduced to being citizens in a state of forgetfulness" (Berger, 2016: 139–40). Consequently, confabulation as method, process, and outcome brings together memory work, dialogue, and storytelling (see Barros et al., 2022). As they complement each other, currere (as inner observation) and confabulation (as method, process, and outcome) help us collaboratively theorize how our educational, teaching, and research experiences and intellectual commitments intersect toward imagining possibilities for an anti-conquest global education.

The confabulations shared in the next section—generated through journal entries, memories, photographic narratives, and interview data—not only demonstrate sparks of an anti-conquest orientation to the world and a reflection of our own (and sometimes students') changing consciousness but also they are products of our "attunement to the role that confabulation plays in shaping collaborative autoethnographic research through the sharing and analysis of life-writing activities" (Barros et al., 2022: 21). Our confabulations in the following section are examples of what Aoki (2005) calls daily stories; daily stories disrupt master stories that privilege modernism.

"What Stories Make Worlds; What Worlds Make Stories"

What follows are three confabulations that emerged through our work with pre-service teachers at a Midwestern university in the US. We invite you to read these stories with Haraway's (2016) words in mind: "It matters what matters we use to think other matters with; it matters what stories we tell to tell other stories with … It matters what stories make worlds; what worlds make stories" (p. 12). The first story, titled, *Coming to know*, which narrates a teacher candidate's study abroad experiences, sets the stage for the next two stories. The second story, titled, *Memory of their past* and the third, titled, *Specter of violence* demonstrate how two educators created space for their students to imagine the world otherwise by attuning to diverse places and ways of knowing and being that resist US hegemony and anthropocentrism. Therefore, for us, the confabulations unfold as invitations (both evocative and analytical) for the readers to think about GE beyond Global North-centered and human-centered worlds.

Coming to Know

Kayla sat with the PI for the post-interview in a qualitative study on study abroad experiences.[4] She had just returned from eight weeks in France, where she took French language classes that were peppered with culture and history. Before deciding to go to France, she had sieved through the many study abroad options in Germany, Portugal, Lithuania, Australia, Japan, Ireland, Colombia, Taiwan, Denmark, Indonesia, South Korea, Belgium, Tanzania, and others. Brochures were posted around her Midwestern university—in the halls, near the elevators, even in bathroom stalls. One read: "Consider spending May in Tanzania. You will teach in local schools, go on a 4-day safari, climb to 9,000 ft on Mt. Kilimanjaro, learn Swahili and local culture, tour a coffee plantation, volunteer in a local orphanage and much more."

But she had always dreamed of living in France for a longer period, and it made sense to her to learn French from native speakers, at least for a summer. Her minor was French, and she was seriously considering taking a teaching position in France after graduation.

The study abroad program was split into two parts, with a week-long break in the middle. During the first three weeks, she had classes from 9:00 a.m. to noon and had the afternoons for herself. Being immersed in French was a big confidence boost for her. She spent a lot of time outside in parks, meeting people, and hanging out with her host family. The weather was great for so much of the trip. The classes met three days a week. The food truck that was parked close to the school sold delicious crepes. In classes, she found herself among other international students, mostly North American, and it was a pleasant coincidence to meet one of her peers from her Midwestern university.

Three weeks into the program, during the short break, Kayla's boyfriend visited her, and they met in Paris. The second half of the program kicked off with a little bit more intensity in class schedules. They had six-hour classes, which were pretty unstructured. One French teacher made Kayla feel insecure about her competency in French. The teacher constantly corrected her on her accent, and that was really frustrating for Kayla, who minored in TESOL and had learned that accent shouldn't be the focus. Outside of her classes, Kayla and her friends explored their surroundings. Fairly early in the trip, she and a few friends rented a car and drove down to the South of France. They went on many excursions; the trip to Mont-Saint-Michel was a highlight for her. Some excursions were canceled or moved around, which was frustrating because the students were not going to be refunded. "You pay a lot of money for a trip like this, and you expect to get a certain amount of support," she explained.

When asked about courses or readings that Kayla thought about while studying abroad, Kayla said, "I think I thought a little bit about concepts from one of the classes. I don't know exactly what it is … I can't think of the actual term, but the cultural comparisons we make and how to become more of a culturally sensitive, culturally—not relevant—I wish I had the name of it … " The interviewer said, "Is it cultural competence?" Kayla said, "Yes, I think it's that." And added "I really appreciate the food culture that they have where a meal is a significant thing."

The trip had made Kayla think a lot about the United States' position in the world and how privileged she was to have grown up in the United States. "If I needed to" she said, "I could have spoken English to anyone, and most people would've been able to help me out, or at least understand me." She was getting right off the Metro in Paris when she received the Apple News notification on the overturning of *Roe v. Wade*. It was just such a shock. "I hadn't really been following anything in the lead up to that," she recalled. That night, her host mom had said, "If it can happen in the US, it can happen here too, and that makes me afraid." Kayla reflected in the interview,

> It was interesting to hear her perspective on how it was something in a completely different country that's so far removed, but that it has ripple effects there too … I think it is an indication of how connected we all are. Especially the US has so much more cultural and even just literal power than I had not previously really understood.

But toward the end, she wanted to be home and spent much time talking to her parents and boyfriend. She had never thought she would miss her family so much. It was strange for Kayla to be on the outside of everything that was happening that summer and be so far removed from what was happening in the United States.

The Fourth of July shooting around Chicago was very close to her hometown. "That was something that I didn't necessarily expect, but something that I think I'm gonna probably continue to—it's not good to be desensitized to those things, but at the same time, it's also a survival mechanism. Just being taken out of my culture helped me realize that I do have a culture." Being far away helped her see familiar elements of her life and culture in new ways, but it also made her miss the familiar.

"France was good for a short trip," she concluded. The researcher wanted to know more about how Kayla had come to this realization since she had imagined living in France for a longer period of time before the trip. Kayla thoughtfully said that the program was disorganized and mismanaged, particularly on the part of her university. The host family exceeded her expectations. They were so wonderful. They cared for her like she was their own family when she got COVID during the last part of the trip. But ultimately, Kayla felt too uncomfortable in France:

> I think, basically, I came to the realization that there are so many little things that are different from what I'm used to at home, that after a certain point, they really started to add up. Really little things, like the fact that there was no AC for the summer, and then there was a huge heat wave in Europe for like two weeks, and it was just brutal. [The city where I lived in France] was definitely a larger city than I'm used to, and so, using public transportation every day was something that I was not—it worked out and the system was really good, but I just so much prefer being able to rely on myself and my car, than using public transportation.

She was very happy to have the life she has here in the United States, but at the same time she was quite frustrated with a lot of the larger political and governmental issues. "Oh, my gosh, everything is so much easier. Not only because I can speak English, but also because I understand how the system works," she said.

Memory of Their Past

She was not the first Nigerian to teach undergraduates in a US university. And it was not the first class she had taught in her life. Yet, she was surprised that her professors had (en)trusted her with twenty-five students by the third semester of her PhD journey. The course focused on examining the dynamics of social inequalities and the interconnectedness between educational systems and broader societal structures, analyzing the reciprocal relationship where schooling both influences and is influenced by these disparities and structures. Since she signed the contract, every time she thought about teaching single-handedly, a surge of excitement mixed with trepidation overwhelmed her. The course was predominantly focused on the educational inequalities in the US. Though she immersed herself in the course content and rehearsed, over and over again in her mind, how to start the first class or what to say if she didn't know the answer to a question, a distant echo of her English-as-a-Second-Language-learner-self was making her wonder if she was good enough to meet the expectations of her professors and the students. She couldn't just delete the fifteen years of schooling in Nigeria; the formal education inherited from the British colonizers was carried forward by the Nigerian National Policy on Education that had etched in the students' minds that they were never good enough without English. Colonization, racism, globalization, capitalism, civil wars, famines, and her own sojourn as a doctoral student in the US were tightly tethered with (the) English. She recalled how she had failed some of her high school students in Nigeria, emulating her own teachers, for not being able to write in correct spelling and grammar. "It was too drastic," she regretted later, but remorse always comes too late.

***

On the day of the first class, as she embraced her toddler tightly at the daycare and caught a glimpse of her own reflection mirrored in her daughter's teary eyes before saying goodbye, she recalled a history of education lesson from her undergraduate days in Nigeria. She told her daughter, born in the US, that Babatunde Fafunwa had said, "History is to a people what memory is to an individual, a people with no memory of their past suffer from collective amnesia groping blindly into the future without guideposts of precedence to shape their cause" and kissed her on her cheeks. Her daughter giggled as if she had understood her mom had found her confidence. As she drove to the university to teach that first class, questions about history and inequalities flooded her mind. What past was Babatunde Fafunwa referring to? Where were the guideposts of precedence to shape her cause? How would she construct a past for her daughter born in a country where Black people—stolen from Africa—were enslaved and continue to be marginalized? Black students in a nearby city recently sued the state for denying them their fundamental right to learn to read and write.[5] So many public schools had failed Black children, a fact that added to her mix of emotions as she prepared to lead a class of future teachers at a predominantly White institution. How could she prepare future teachers to embrace the intelligence, joy, and complexity of students like her daughter? She realized that accepting consistent disorientation (and reorientation) was an important part of engaging with her students, her daughter, and her history as she sought out guideposts.

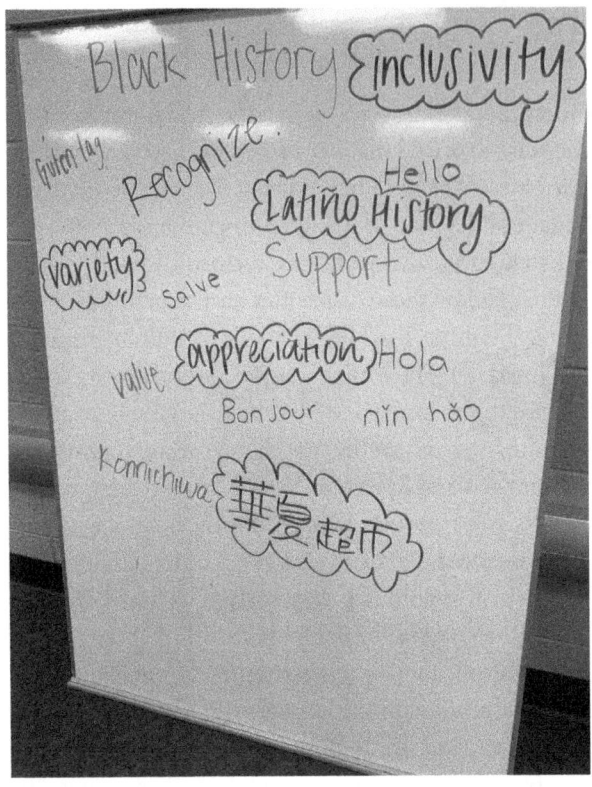

Figure 1.1 Imagining a perfect school. *Author made.*

She started the class by telling her students that she was feeling a bit anxious. Then she felt a bit better. They discussed the syllabus and segued into a discussion around schools and schooling in the US. Students expressed their surprise that many critical issues and topics included in the course syllabus were not a part of their K-12 school curriculum. In response, she invited her students to imagine what a perfect school would look like for them. The students, in small groups, wrote their thoughts on whiteboards that surround the classroom.

They imagined an inclusive and diverse school where all cultures and languages were sustained (Figure 1.1). "The school would foster inclusion by teaching Black history, Latino history, foreign languages and cultures, and expand our horizons," one student explained. "The school will also teach the history of various countries," another student added. She was impressed by what the students had shared and posed a question for further reflection, "How will you achieve this if the school district does not approve such content in the curriculum and this is not what the students are assessed on?" The classroom became silent as a grave until a student finally said, "I don't think we are better prepared to think globally because we are confined to seeing ourselves as better than others." "That's an insightful response to my question" she said, and invited the students to write a brief reflection on what it means to think globally when they have been taught to think nationally for much of their life.

Specter of Violence

The provost had said that reopening the university for in-person classes just a week after the on-campus mass shooting should not be considered "resumption of normal operations." That gloomy Wednesday, neither the teacher nor the students wanted to be in class, but they were all huddled together on Zoom. The students chatted among themselves in breakout rooms: some expressed their anger against the university, others shared retriggered trauma from school shootings, some said they were with their family, some were with their friends, and a few were alone in their dorm rooms. Despite how far away they went from the campus, there was no escaping the sounds of choppers, sirens, dings of news alerts, and ringing phones.

Since the university had communicated that the classes were to recommence in-person, the teacher had been wondering, worrying, planning, and panicking about how to start the class, let alone what to teach that day. The dreaded moment had arrived. Something had to be taught. There was something on the syllabus, but no one wanted to go there. Then he told his students, "Given the nature of our course, I cannot ignore how shootings in the US relate to most of the topics that are on our syllabus." He explained how, through a necessary tangent:

"As international people, my partner and I have always been terrified by gun violence being a daily occurrence in the US and how different mechanisms normalize it." He sighed.

"We live on campus. When my father called me that night, we were sitting in the dark in our bedroom. Our building number had just been mentioned on the live police audio stream. The darkness made me feel less distressed because I only heard my partner cry; I didn't have to see her tears. I suggested we sleep, knowing well that there was no sleep for many nights to come. When my phone vibrated, I automatically answered. It was my dad wanting to tell me about his visit to the doctor. I said, 'I can't talk right now; there is a shooter in our building.' 'There is a what?' he said. 'A man with a gun,' I whispered into the phone. 'A terrorist attack?' he asked me. 'No! I don't know! Will call you later.' I ended the call."

"While sitting in the dark, hugging my partner, I wondered how to respond to my dad's question. Was it a terrorist attack? Part of me wanted to scream 'YES!' and part of me said 'NO!' because, for him, a terrorist is someone who fights for a separate nation-state, ethnically minoritized: an image of a Tamil or a Muslim. Images of people who formed the boundary between the outside and inside. What meaning would he make of this story, that a Black man killed students who were in a class? That would add to the racialized narratives of violence. He would want to know the motive. Something like fighting for a separate nation-state, religious fanaticism, or at least poverty. I would say 'mental illness.' Then he will have more questions: 'Do mentally ill people in other countries go around shooting people? How did the sick man get a gun? Doesn't the mental health narrative cover over the actual problems like nationalism, capitalism, racism, (settler)colonialism, insecurities of an empire?' I wouldn't know how to respond. But I would try to explain to him how the mental health narrative helps unsettle the racialization of violence."

"The following day, when I called, my dad asked me 'How did that man get that gun? Did he get it from the underworld?' Everyone had seen the tragedy on campus on live TV in Sri Lanka. 'NO! He is a citizen who can legally purchase as many guns and bullets as he wants. That's a constitutional right. That is why I didn't know what to say when you asked me whether he was a terrorist.' He said, 'Why don't they change the laws?' I said, 'It's complicated.' He said, 'What is not!' and gave the phone to my mum. 'What an unsafe country. What kind of madness is that?' she said. I didn't like that she spoke self-righteously about Sri Lanka, at least implying that. I said:

How many times have we elected presidents in Sri Lanka, including a woman president, to change the executive presidency that keeps our presidents above the law? But no one has changed it. The constitution is not just a law it is a part of the culture of ethnonationalism. People are proud of it. Some people benefit from it. Here also, it is the same. Guns are sold in shopping malls. Walmart says: 'Shop Sports Shooting and Supplies at Walmart and find all your shooting needs in one place, all at a price that helps you save money and live better.' This 'American multinational retail corporation that operates a chain of hypermarkets, discount department stores, and grocery stores in the United States' promotes guns in their back-to-school advertisements. It's all in the game. Every subject, human or animal, of the state is game. Like in the colonial times. Here, when people are killed by shooters a lot of flowers get sold, T-shirts, candles; therapists get more work, and more antidepressants get sold. We don't have the money to do all that in Sri Lanka.

"My mom listens silently. 'I'm sorry, *amma*, I shouted at you. I know you get what I'm thinking.' I apologized."

Absorbed in his thoughts, he continued talking to his students.

"The empires, desires, weapons, tax, violence, mass killings, numbers, terrorists, stateless people, immigrants, more numbers, migrants, hurricanes, droughts, wildfires, wars, warming seas, more and more numbers, refugees, more guns. Animals disappear into thin air, no numbers. Spectacle after spectacle, I'm reminded of our 'internationalness,' and the precarity that gives rise to international studies, Muslim studies, area studies, South Asian studies, African Studies, African American Studies as well as the complete erasure of other studies that empires are determined to eliminate from the archives of memory itself. Names of people, names of communities I'm forced to be silent of in fear of losing my job! And that's a facet of global education for us to meditate on."

***

Despite the looming specter of violence haunting the campus, the students came to class. Somedays, death seemed unsettlingly near. On another Wednesday during class, a police notice popped up on their computer screens saying, "A person with a knife was seen on campus." The classroom did not have any blinds, shades, or curtains, and the door couldn't be locked from inside. To barricade the door with no lockable lock, the teacher and a few students pushed their tables and chairs around the door. Then, while most of them stayed staring at their phones, some of them kept watching out through the large glass window that opened the classroom to a large courtyard.

***

On the last day of class, one student knocked on her table during student presentations to get everyone's attention. They had just finished a discussion on the environment and "otherwise" futures. She gets her classmates' full attention. She doesn't seem angry; she is concerned and curious. She poses a question to the class: "What would it take to make people in the US understand that even when a nuclear weapon is fired, a retaliation with nuclear weapons is not justifiable?" The silence following the question is the longest silence that the teacher had ever experienced in a class. Why were they so quiet, he would never know. The question interrupted the curricular assumptions of the planned international education curriculum on what knowledge matters and what knowledge doesn't in a world of competing empires and multifaceted conquests. After a long period of silence, he said, "during the summer try to find some time to read Chomsky's *Internationalism or Extinction*; might help us all start processing that question."

Postscript

The confabulations we shared are not isolated episodes. Together they present how students and teachers struggle to make sense of the present world that normalizes "appropriation, exploitation, extractivism, and extinctionism" (Haraway, 2018: 67), which threaten multispecies survival. In this context, we invite educators to consider imagining an anti-conquest curriculum through storytelling that entails deeply critiquing logics of conquest and to nurture epistemological diversity in the global education ecology. An anti-conquest curriculum draws attention not only to acts of forceful colonization by using weapons of mass destruction or blatantly unequal trade agreements among nation-states but also to seemingly innocent ways in which conquest is justified and promoted. Such a curriculum would consider the precarity of the world that human exceptionalism and its myriad consequences have created for all beings. It would supersede the rush for quick results with a meditative or slow curriculum (Kauper and Jacobs, 2019) that makes one comfortable with, to borrow from Haraway (2018), "no guarantees and no pre-set directions" (p. 68). Another consideration in such a curriculum is to trouble the normalization of the centrality of the West in reimagining education. An anti-conquest curriculum is just one way to (re)orient ourselves and our students to the dystopian present. This chapter is not didactic in terms of representing what should be considered or accomplished as sensible teaching in GE in teacher education, rather we are interested in how our curricula moves open up possibilities to imagine GE "otherwise." Rather than closing the conversation with a list of "must haves" in an anti-conquest curriculum, we open the conversation with more questions to create space to imagine an anti-conquest curriculum from diverse onto-epistemological orientations.

In the process of creating this chapter, particularly the confabulations—asking each other reflective questions and helping one another recall and acknowledge often painful memories of everyday violence with global significance—we often came across the following three questions from each other as well as colleagues who closely read the chapter:

1 How is an anti-conquest curriculum similar to or/and different from other radical and subversive invitations to (re)think curriculum (e.g., antiracist curriculum, anti-supremacist curriculum, critical curriculum)?
2 To what extent does one need to make peace with stepping out of comfort zones and accepting consistent disorientation (and reorientation) as a part of engaging oneself in an anti-conquest curriculum?
3 What would anti-conquest curriculum orientations look like across various subjects such as social studies, biology, music, and mathematics?

To keep the conversation moving around imagining an anti-conquest curriculum in as many directions as possible, we invite the reader to sit with us as we grapple with these questions. Moreover, in the process of creating the stories in conversation with our ongoing research and memories, we realized that "Self and Other become expansive concepts" and that "we may limit how we imagine the world through them, or we may stretch our imagination to think about the world and its problems with these concepts" (Barros et al., 2022). As we reflect on these concepts (e.g., anti-conquest (curriculum), epistemological diversity, self/other) borrowing from Paul McCartney and John Lennon (1966), we ask: Who are they for? Where do they all come from? and Where do they all belong? In response to these questions and the spirit of "compost writing" or "compost narration" (Haraway, 2019) and decentering the human, let us offer one more story, because "stories nest like Russian dolls inside ever more stories and ramify like fungal webs throwing out ever more sticky threads" (Haraway, 2019: 565).

In the flamboyant city of Omelas, there is a child imprisoned in a dark basement closet whose unfathomable suffering gives the city its peaceful luster and prosperity (Le Guin, 1993). Residents know that the city's peace depends on the tortured child's pain. Those who choose to walk away from Omelas never return to tell the stories of what they witnessed in faraway lands. We can only speculate, like Le Guin and Haraway invite us to, and tell stories for "otherwise" futures. But let's sit with the present for a bit more. We are in Omelas, here and now, wherever we are. From chimney sweepers that industrialism produced (that William Blake wrote about in 1789) to mica mining children produced by the global electronic and makeup industries of the late industrialism, and from millions of child soldiers to Devika Balakrishnan—a Dalit girl from India who killed herself for being deprived of access to online classes (Al Jazeera, 2020)—we hear a loud and clear cry about the violence of modern|colonial|development. There is no walking away or repairing this Omelas, knowing that when the child in the basement closet dies modern|colonial|development replaces it with another. We need to construct a new residence altogether, one where we can weave our stories into a new tapestry of being and knowing.

Notes

1 We are reminded of various (humanitarian) disasters such as Hiroshima and Nagasaki, Chernobyl, Fukushima, Bhopal, Auschwitz, and the gradual obliteration of Palestine with such catastrophes still increasing.

2 In this chapter, we use the forward slash (/) sometimes to indicate options as in "of/for" or "and/or" and sometimes to show the interconnection between concepts or phenomena, as in "modern/colonial" or "civilize/develop/subjugate." In the postscript, we use the vertical bar (|) to invite readers to consider "modernity," "coloniality," and "development" as one and the same instead of conceptualizing them as different phenomena, discourses, or concepts that enable people to understand phenomena. Similarly, we want to emphasize

the significance of creating a language that goes beyond our traditional uses of punctuation marks (given that language is limited and limiting what is imagined and imaginable) that allows educators to communicate and understand the complexity of the issues we are engaging with within global education.

3 Confabulation as "filling in memory by fabrication" refuses to make "the human disappear under abstract concepts" and gives credence to lapses and gaps as an unavoidable aspect of inquiry (see, Barros et al., 2022). Since we are not endeavoring to establish factual accuracy, we are untroubled by the claims of "falsehood" often implied in the term confabulation. In fact, we use this term counter intuitively resisting the reverence for truth and factual accuracy in academia.

4 In a separate manuscript, we analyze the interviews with multiple pre-service teachers for this broader study (Morley et al., 2025). This study received IRB approval, and names and identifying details are changed to conceal participant identities.

5 Here, we are reminded of the 2016 lawsuit alleging that the state of Michigan denied Detroit's schoolchildren a basic education by failing to teach them to read (see Bakuli, 2023, July 7). Detroit's $94 million "right to read" lawsuit settlement is finally coming through for DPSCD. *Chalkbeat.* https://www.chalkbeat.org/detroit/2023/7/7/23787399/detroit-public-schools-right-to-read-settlement-whitmer-emergency-management (accessed October 24, 2025).

References

Al Jazeera. (2020, June 3). India: Unable to access online classes, Dalit girl kills herself. *Al Jazeera.* https://www.aljazeera.com/news/2020/6/3/india-unable-to-access-online-classes-dalit-girl-kills-herself (accessed October 24, 2025).

Alger, C. F., and Harf, J. E. (1985). *Global Education: Why? For Whom? About What?* Working Paper for the "Guidelines for International Teacher Education" Project of AACTE, pp. 1–30.

Andreotti, V. D. O. (2014). Soft versus critical global citizenship education. In S. McCloskey (Ed.), *Development Education in Policy and Practice*, pp. 21–31. Springer.

Andreotti, V. D. O. (2021). *Hospicing Modernity: Facing Humanity's Wrongs and the Implications for Social Activism.* North Atlantic Books.

Aoki, T. T. (2005). Curriculum implementation as instrumental action and as situational praxis. In W. F. Pinar and R. L. Irwin (Eds.), *Curriculum in a New Key: The Collected Works of Ted T. Aoki*, pp. 111–23. Routledge.

Bakuli, E. (2023, July 7). Detroit's $94 million "right to read" lawsuit settlement is finally coming through for DPSCD. *Chalkbeat.* https://www.chalkbeat.org/detroit/2023/7/7/23787399/detroit-public-schools-right-to-read-settlement-whitmer-emergency-management (accessed October 24, 2025).

Barros, S. R., Hadeer, R., and Gajasinghe, K. (2022). Confabulating research: Performing memory-work as inquiry. *International Review of Qualitative Research*, *15*(1), 21–41.

Benjamin, W. (2019). The storyteller. In H. Arendt (Ed.) and H. Zohn (Trans.), *Illuminations: Essays and reflections*, pp. 26–55. Mariner Books, Houghton Mifflin Harcourt.

Berger, J. (2016). *Confabulations.* Penguin Books.

Cambridge, J., and Thompson, J. (2004). Internationalism and globalization as contexts for international education. *Compare: A Journal of Comparative and International Education*, *34*(2), 161–75.

Chomsky, N. (2020). *Internationalism or extinction* (C. Derber, S. Moodliar, & P. Shannon, Eds.). Routledge, Taylor & Francis.

de Sousa Santos, B. (2015). *Epistemologies of the South: Justice Against Epistemicide*. Routledge.

Egan, K. (1978). What is curriculum? *Curriculum Inquiry*, *8*(1), 65–72.

Eichler, L. J. (2020). Ecocide is genocide: Decolonizing the definition of genocide. *Genocide Studies and Prevention: An International Journal*, *14*(2), 9–26. https://doi.org/10.5038/1911-9933.14.2.1747.

Estellés, M., and Fischman, G. (2021). Who needs global citizenship education? A review of the literature on teacher education. *Journal of Teacher Education*, *72*(2), 223–36. https://doi.org/10.1177/0022487120920254.

Fendler, L. (2006). Others and the problem of community. *Curriculum Inquiry*, *36*(3), 303–26.

Gershon, W. S., and Helfenbein, R. J. (2023). Curriculum matters: Educational tools for troubled times. *Journal of Curriculum Studies*, *55*(3), 1–19.

Haraway, D. (2016). *Staying with the Trouble: Making Kin in the Chthulucene*. Duke University Press.

Haraway, D. (2018). Making kin in the Chthulunene: Reproducing multispecies justice. In A. E. Clarke and D. J. Haraway (Eds.), *Making Kin Not Population*, pp. 67–100. Prickly Paradigm Press.

Haraway, D. (2019). It matters what stories tell stories; it matters whose stories tell stories. *A/b: Auto/Biography Studies*, *34*(3), 565–75. https://doi.org/10.1080/08989575.2019.1664163.

Howard, T. C. (2021). Culturally responsive pedagogy. In J. A. Banks (Ed.), *Transforming Multicultural Education Policy and Practice: Expanding Educational Opportunity*, pp. 137–63. Teachers College Press.

Huaman, E. S., and Swentzell, P. (2021). Indigenous education and sustainable development: rethinking environment through Indigenous knowledges and generative environmental pedagogies. *Journal of American Indian Education*, *60*(1–2), 7–28. https://doi.org/10.1353/jaie.2021.a840601.

Kauper, K., and Jacobs, M. (2019). The case for slow curriculum: Creative subversion and the curriculum mind. In C. A. Mullen (Ed.), *Creativity Under Duress in Education? Resistive Theories, Practices and Actions*, pp. 339–60. Springer. https://doi.org/10.1007/978-3-319-90272-2.

Kelly, A. V. (2009). *The Curriculum: Theory and Practice*. Sage.

Kimmerer, R. W. (2013). *Braiding Sweetgrass: Indigenous Wisdom, Scientific Knowledge and the Teachings of Plants* (First paperback edition). Milkweed Editions.

Ladson-Billings, G. (1995). Toward a theory of culturally relevant pedagogy. *American Educational Research Journal*, *32*(3), 465–91.

Le Guin, U. K. (1993). *The Ones Who Walk Away from Omelas*. Creative Education.

Loveless, N. (2019). *How to Make Art at the End of the World: A Manifesto for Research-Creation*. Duke University Press.

McCormack, K., and Gilbert, E. (2022). The geopolitics of militarism and humanitarianism. *Progress in Human Geography*, *46*(1), 179–97. https://doi.org/10.1177/03091325211032267.

Morley, A., Gajasinghe, K., Alabede, Y., Bizhanova, A., and Selezneva, E. (2025). Committing to "stay with the trouble": Theorizing global commitments through future teachers' study abroad reflections. *Frontiers: The Interdisciplinary Journal of Study Abroad*, *37*(3), 250–78. https://doi.org/10.36366/frontiers.v37i3.1015.

Mundy, K., Bickmore, K., Hayhoe, R., Madden, M., and Madjidi, K. (Eds.). (2008). *Comparative and International Education: Issues for Teachers*. Economic Policy Institute and Teachers College.

Nygren, T. (2016). UNESCO teaches history: Implementing international understanding in Sweden. In P. Duedahl (Ed.), *A History of UNESCO: Global Actions and Impacts*, pp. 201–30. Palgrave Macmillan.

Paris, D. (2012). Culturally sustaining pedagogy: A needed change in stance, terminology, and practice. *Educational Researcher*, *41*(3), 93–7. https://doi.org/10.3102/0013189X12441244.

Pinar, W. F. (1994). The method of "Currere" (1975). *Counterpoints*, *2*, 19–27.

Pinar, W. F., and Grumet, M. R. (1976). *Toward a Poor Curriculum* (3rd edn.). Educator's International Press, Inc.

Popkewitz, T. S. (2014). *The Reason of Schooling: Historicizing Curriculum Studies, Pedagogy, and Teacher Education*. Routledge.

Pratt, M. L. (2008). *Imperial Eyes: Travel Writing and Transculturation*. Routledge.

Stein, S., Andreotti, V., Ahenakew, C., Suša, R., Taylor, L., Valley, W., Siwek, D., Cardoso, C., Duque, C., Calhoun, B., Sluys, S., Pigeau, D., and D'Emilia, D. (2024). Education beyond green growth: Regenerative inquiry for intergenerational responsibility. *Nordic Journal of Comparative and International Education (NJCIE)*, *8*(2), 1–25.

Stein, S., Andreotti, V., Ahenakew, C., Suša, R., Valley, W., Huni Kui, N., Tremembé, M., Taylor, L., Siwek, D., Cardoso, C., Duque, C. "Azul," Oliveira Da Silva Huni Kui, S., Calhoun, B., Van Sluys, S., Amsler, S., D'Emilia, D., Pigeau, D., Andreotti, B., Bowness, E., and McIntyre, A. (2023). Beyond colonial futurities in climate education. *Teaching in Higher Education*, *28*(5), 987–1004. https://doi.org/10.1080/13562517.2023.2193667.

Tabulawa, R. (2003). International aid agencies, learner-centred pedagogy and political democratisation: A critique. *Comparative Education*, *39*(1), 7–26. https://doi.org/10.1080/03050060302559.

Tsing, A. L. (2015). *The Mushroom at the End of the World: On the Possibility of Life in Capitalist Ruins*. Princeton University Press.

Tuck, E. (2009). Suspending damage: A letter to communities. *Harvard Educational Review*, *79*(3), 409–28.

Voyles, T. B. (2015). *Wastelanding: Legacies of Uranium Mining in Navajo Country*. University of Minnesota Press.

2

Borderless Curriculum: Shaping Instruction through Re-imagined Pedagogies and Practices for a Global Community

Shabina Kavimandan, Amanda Lickteig, Éder Intriago-Palacios, and Mona Menking

Abstract

This chapter, while problematizing the current perspectives on cultural responsiveness and globalized pedagogies and practices within our Institutions of Higher Education (IHE), highlights the urgency and a need for a global pedagogical framework rooted in the principles and practices of intercultural responsiveness, multicultural/lingual competencies, and an individual's positionality. Through a narrative inquiry process, it examines the intersectionality of international students' cultural/ linguistic competencies, the role their positionalities play, and an IHE's responsiveness in preparing them by examining the experiences of ten international students at a predominantly White institution. It also aims to share implications for university faculty as they prepare pre-service educators for the diverse spaces in which they will ultimately teach. The two overarching questions for this study are:

1 To what extent does an IHE consider its students' intercultural competencies while planning curricular and pedagogical approaches?
2 What can we learn about the pedagogical preparedness of future educators around issues of diversity, equity, and globalization?

Key Terms: *global competencies, international students, positionality, narrative inquiry, institutional responsiveness*

Introduction

Khalil Gibran, in his 1926 address to young Americans of Syrian origin, said, "I believe that you can say to the founders of this great nation, Here I am, a youth, a young tree whose roots were plucked from the hills of Lebanon, yet I am deeply rooted here, and I would be fruitful." Almost a hundred years later, this quote continues to highlight a significant challenge where immigrants and newly arrived individuals are still grappling with their place within the United States. Even though immigrant students help strengthen America's higher education community, driving an increase in overall enrollment in IHEs while contributing to the success of the US economy (Higher Ed Immigration Portal, 2025) yet, we see gaps and a lack of overall understanding regarding the creation of equitably diverse spaces for our students.

Similarly, within PK-12 settings, the literature establishes what it is that students ought to know about global competencies, yet we remain unsure of how teachers instill these mindsets and skillsets in students, what responsibility policymakers and teacher educators have in moving teachers toward these directions (Tichnor-Wagner et al., 2016). Hence, this study aimed to examine the experiences of ten international students at a predominantly White institution, thereby focusing on on the intersectionality of students' cultural/linguistic competencies and their individualized positionalities and views regarding the levels of responsiveness an institution exhibits in preparing its diverse students. It also aims to share implications for university faculty as they prepare pre-service educators for the diverse spaces in which they will ultimately teach.

Our educational ecosystems are a diverse network of varied ethnic and linguistic repertoires. As Ramos et al. (2020) share, today's youth live, work, and interact in an interconnected world that aims to create a just and sustainable world and for this, teacher educators must integrate teaching for global competence. This argument becomes critical due to what Sandell and Tipsy (2015) argue, as cited in Yeh and Wan (2018), the roles educators play are crucial because their knowledge (i.e., global literacy skills and intercultural competence), attitudes, and practices in culturally diverse classrooms impact how students interact and communicate with peers from diverse backgrounds. They further emphasize that it is important that educators understand social and intercultural contexts to develop mutual understanding and healthy relationships with their students and families. Something that this research aims to highlight through its academic and social experiences at the institution.

On the importance of culturally competent educators, Ateh and Ryan (2023) argue that it is critical to develop teachers who are respectful of diverse student identities and develop a philosophical and ideological framework for their practice that is committed to elevated expectations, social justice, and equity in education (Ladson-Billings, 1995, 2009). Hence, we hope that the narratives shared through this chapter highlight ways to create spaces for advancing global competence among students (Chandir and Blackmore, 2024).

Research Questions

- To what extent does an IHE consider its students' intercultural competencies while planning curricular and pedagogical approaches?
- What can we learn about the pedagogical preparedness of future educators around issues of diversity, equity, and globalization?

Literature Review

Intercultural Competencies and Classroom Environment

Intercultural competency (IC) at the university level is usually left up to individual faculty and diversity-specific programs. Typically, students take one or two diversity courses as part of their coursework. However, this is not enough. Schwarzenthal et al. (2019), as cited in Guillén Yparrea and Montoya (2023), state, IC is not limited to intergroup attitudes but also involves awareness and knowledge of different world views and the capacity for behavioral flexibility to face them. In their extensive study on intercultural competencies, Romijn et al. (2021) concluded that they encompass interrelated and reciprocal knowledge, values, attitudes, skills, and action. Knowledge within these parameters refers to knowledge of the self, of language and communication, and of the world in a broad sense—which cannot be understood just by taking a "diversity class." Values and beliefs comprise a wide variety of topics, such as diversity, inclusion, human rights, and justice, and are considered to be knowledge-based but also imply a certain judgment or evaluation in contrast to knowledge which is neutral in nature (e.g., Flores and Smith, 2009; Nespor, 1987).

At the same time, Pastori et al. (2018) share that positive intercultural attitudes express openness to cultural otherness and other beliefs, world views, and practices, which goes back to the research questions for this study, especially regarding institutional preparedness. One of the reasons why intercultural competence was considered a variable in this study is what Van and Ferreira (2023) shared—as the workplace becomes more globalized, intercultural competence becomes important in the professional field and employers require employees to cooperate with people from other cultural backgrounds (Spitzberg and Changnon, 2009). This is important for our pre-service candidates as our schools and classrooms continue to become more diverse.

Scholars generally agree that intercultural competency is a multi-layered construct that enables individuals to function contentedly and successfully across cultures (Zhang and Zhou, 2023). Therefore, within the context of intercultural competency, the authors framed interview questions that prompted participants to reflect upon ideals of cultural responsiveness (Gay, 2018) and multicultural education (Banks, 2004) and whether these frameworks were being at all utilized by their professors.

Responsiveness

Merolla et al. (2024) bring forth the argument that responsiveness originally proposed as an "organizing construct" encompasses various theoretical perspectives focusing on the interlinkages between social interaction and well-being indicators (Reis et al., 2004). At the same time, an individual's ability to be responsive has been linked to various positive outcomes, such as perceived psychological safety, interpersonal trust, positive emotion, and openness to others (Reis et al., 2022). Therefore, this inquiry aimed to also focus on the examples of responsive interactions at the institutional level that provided students a feeling that there were people around them who "get them" and will care for them even in moments of vulnerability (Kang and Fay, 2023; Biesta, 2013).

With more and more US colleges enrolling international students (Mahalingappa, Polat, and Kayi-Aydar, 2021) and seeing a high number of US-born culturally and linguistically diverse students, it becomes imperative for IHEs to be culturally and linguistically responsive through pedagogical actions and frameworks. We felt this is an important construct of the global education debate, especially since, through international teaching experiences, participants can build global competencies and intercultural awareness, have more responsiveness to the individuals who may enter their classrooms from increasingly diverse backgrounds (Byker and Putman, 2019).

Positionality

The third prong of this argument, positionality construct, suggests that we are not simply actors of predetermined scripts, but also agents and authors in our social participation (Acevedo et al., 2015). This narrative inquiry aimed to capture the role students' positionalities, identities, and experiences played as they engaged with professors and fellow students (Acevado et al., 2015). Secules et al. (2021) argue that positionality captures the dynamic ways an individual is defined by socially significant identity dimensions. At the same time, focusing on what Hult (2013) as cited in Torres-Olave and Lee (2020) share, positionality inevitably "involves the negotiation of multiple identities in relation to different people and social settings." Since this is a narrative inquiry, we interrogated students' positions while focusing on how their realities and social worlds informed their relation to themselves and one another (Spangler, 2023). At the same time in their story line, individuals take different positions reflecting their understanding of the institutions that they navigate, their agency, their decision-making, transformation, and their own interpretations of their actions (Patino-Santos and Poveda, 2022), which is important to share with the faculty members at the institution.

Theoretical Lens

Teaching for Global Readiness: A Model for Locally Situated and Globally Connected Literacy Instruction (Kerkhoff, 2018) was utilized as a theoretical lens. Kerkhoff's (2017) GTM (Global Teaching Model) is based on K-12 settings and works under the assumption that global teaching is contextualized within a nation (Fujikane, 2003). The GTM comprises four factors: situated, integrated, critical, and transactional. GTM's first factor is **situated practice**, meaning teaching is culturally relevant to both students in the class and sociopolitical issues at the local level. Situated practice includes the dispositions of valuing diversity and students' voices. Situated practice is culturally relevant (Ladson-Billings, 2004) and acknowledges local and global connections. Teachers also reflect on their own cultures, assumptions, and biases (Hull and Stornaiuolo, 2014). During the interviews the discussions moved back and forth between the preparation of faculty members and the way diverse perspectives were being situationally utilized in the classrooms.

The next factor, **integrated**, closely aligns with this study through its focus on educators building a repertoire of resources related to global issues in the disciplines they teach. It prompts educators to focus on the interconnectedness of the world and analyze global challenges and inequities through a disciplinary lens. By doing this, teachers show students how their lives and their studies are globally interconnected. This was an important discussion throughout the interview process with the students.

Interview questions focused on global teaching through a **critical** frame based on what Delpit (2006) and Kerhoff (2017) consider as issues of power, privilege, and oppression, often creating hierarchies found in the world. Part of critical framing is reflexivity, or what O'Connor and Zeichner (2011) referred to as "sociocultural consciousness," where teachers acknowledge they are cultural and political beings and examine their biases.

Transactional experiences involve international partnerships, through which students engage in intercultural dialogue and construct knowledge about the world (Kerkhoff, 2018). Transactional experiences mean learning with other people through active listening and critical thinking. It also means problem-solving with others in solidarity, rather than solving others' problems in ways that reinforce colonial power relationships. All four factors were critical in the development of interview questions and data analysis.

Research Design

Narrative inquiry—which is "the study of experience interpreted by and through stories of practice"—is a methodology that examines lived experiences and reflects "knowledge accumulated, and experience gained over time" (Clarke, 2023: 238). Due to the sensitive nature of this research (most participants are on a student visa and/or belong to countries that are currently facing economic and social turmoil), this approach seemed the most appropriate due to what Riessman (2008) argues—that storytellers use narratives to help excavate memories, persuade skeptical audiences, and mobilize others into action for progressive change by engaging listeners in the storyteller's perspectives.

Authors' Positionality and the Interpretive Process

The framing of this research, and the subsequent analysis of data, was heavily influenced by the researchers' own experiences of:

- being international students themselves,
- teaching first generation, underserved populations, and international students, and
- being study abroad advisers.

While natural and unavoidable, the authors' unique ability to relate to participants supports a narrative methodology. Narrative inquirers come alongside participants and begin to engage in narrative inquiry through participants' stories. This process of coming alongside participants and inquiring into the stories is called retelling stories. Because both participants and researchers are changed in this process of coming alongside each other, they may begin to relive their stories (Johnson and Christensen, 2017: 426).

Participant Recruitment and Selection

Potential participants were identified through mixed purposeful sampling (Patton, 1987). A funneling of purposive, convenience, and opportunistic sampling was used to identify ten participants. As the interviews were conducted during our winter intersession, we needed individuals who were available and willing to participate during the busy time of year (convenience), who further met our specific characteristics as international students and who had spent time living and studying in the United States (purposive), and had participated in some of our distinct opportunities that could yield the potential for rich narrative (opportunistic). The sampling size of ten allowed us to craft a detailed story of their experiences through a narrative inquiry (Clandinin and Connelly, 2000). Table 2.1 represents some general demographics and profiles of the participants, with participant-generated pseudonyms and self-identified ethnicities.

Data Collection

We collected a variety of data to achieve understanding and adhere to the three dimensions of narrative research: the temporal, social, and spatial (Clandinin and Connelly, 2000). Participant profiles, which consisted of questions about their positionality, their professional and academic background, and an overall profile as a learner, provided mostly temporal and social data. Additionally, surveys that examined participants' academic, linguistic, and cultural experiences were collected using Qualtrics. The items in the survey ranged from fully anchored Likert scales to open-ended responses, and the emphasis

Table 2.1 Participant Information

Participant Pseudonym	Ethnic Origin	Sex	Age Range	Length of Experience and Visa Type	Highest Level of Education
Spark	Hispanic, Latino, Spanish	Male	36–45 years	Short-term Scholar	Master's Degree
Gaviota	Hispanic, Latino	Female	56–65 years	Short-term Scholar	Doctorate Degree
Ahmar	Asian (but prefers to be identified as Middle Eastern)	Female	25–35 years	Long-term International Student	Master's Degree
Butterfly	African (from Africa)	Female	35–45	Long-term International Student	Master's Degree
Stonecat	Hispanic but also indigenous/ Native American	Male	36–45 years	Short-term Scholar	Doctorate Degree
Roshni	Asian	Female	45–55 years	Long-term International Student	Master's Degree
Aurora	White (but not American White)	Female	26–35 Years	Long-term International Student	Master's Degree
Maria	Hispanic/Latino	Female	56–65 years	Short-term Scholar	Doctorate Degree
Tilda	Hispanic/Latino	Female	36–45 years	Short-erm Scholar	Doctorate Degree
Britney	Jamaican	Female	26–35	Long-term International Student	Bachelor's Degree

was more about the spatial dimension—the contexts that shaped their experiences. The primary form of data collection was the semi-structured interviews, which emphasized the temporal dimension by focusing on participants' narrated reflections. These interviews were conducted in English over Zoom and lasted between 45–75 minutes each.

Data Analysis

The data analysis was conducted through four interconnected stages: Restorying, Narrative Analysis, Summarizing, and Horizontal Analysis (Foxall et al., 2021). Semi-structured interviews provided individual and collective insights regarding the experiences of these individuals. Interviews were individually transcribed and later analyzed for isolation of words, thought patterns regarding experiences, and positionalities which set the stage for subsequent themes to emerge (Moustakas, 1994).

Field notes were kept during the interview process for the data analysis process (Foxall et al., 2021). The analysis of the transcription and the field notes led to the preliminary restorying (Foxall et al., 2021), which was achieved by noticing the patterns and themes of participant experiences. Every effort was made to keep the meaning and the emotional context of the participants' words. The narratives emerging from the restorying were interpreted from an emic perspective—starting with the ideas leading to descriptive labels, themes, and observed behaviors that emerged from the data. Summary of the analysis included each individual narrative being analyzed to highlight commonalities/ uniquenesses with other participants. Finally, stage four focused on the themes emerging across the entire data set (Reid et al., 2014).

Themes/Findings

Throughout this investigative process, the researchers remained aware, monitored, and accounted for their own values, beliefs, knowledge, and biases that might impact the data generation, relationships with research participants, and data analysis (Berger, 2015)—thus also engaging in the critical factor of the Global Teaching Model. Member checks were conducted, and the findings of the inquiry were analyzed through the lens of three prongs of intercultural competency, responsiveness, and positionality and the theoretical lens. These dimensions were utilized to report the final findings and help shape the strategies to be shared with the faculty members.

Participants' Sense of Self: Lessons for the University Faculty

The participants repeatedly talked about strengths gained from traveling across borders to study, getting to know the world, and keeping a strong self of identity. Therefore, this theme is reflective of both the situated and critical factors of the Global Teaching Model. As Butterfly shared, "I felt like when I first started, I was penalized for having a different point of view and writing papers from my country's perspective, but now I make sure I let the professors know about my different perspective and I am mindful of sharing my positionality early on." This sentiment shows Butterfly's realization that her perspectives are different because she is from a different culture. At the same time, her comment holds significant impact for the faculty working with pre-service educators. We must prepare our pre-service educators to honor and accept the divergent views that their students might exhibit in their future classrooms. Yet at the same time, our faculty members working with ISCs must realize that students' journeys and positionalities are a source of empowerment and a focus on these two factors can help us develop pedagogical supports rooted within the principles of humanizing pedagogy (Freire, 1970; Salazar, 2013), that can ultimately help us create learning spaces where students' sociocultural resources are valued and extended. Further Tilda said,

> I have received a lot of scholarships; I have traveled a lot. I felt like I have a very competitive profile with a postdoc. I have always taken advantage of the opportunities to travel and learn. Coming to the US to learn was just that—I wanted to keep myself updated. It had been ten years since I left my country, and I wanted that experience of being in another place to gain that perspective again.

This quote is a great testament to students' view of self and the sense of empowerment about their own identity and positionality in the world. Also, it poses an important question for the institutions regarding their own preparedness and responsiveness toward diverse students. How are the faculty being prepared to create learning spaces where engaging students means focusing on their sociocultural resources and students are motivated through a responsive and positive teacher-student relationship?

Unique Positionalities/Belief Systems: Lessons for the Classrooms

United in their positionalities as international students—yet vastly different due to their experiences, outlooks, and trajectories—participants shared stories that highlighted the uniquenesses and similarities of their identities. The most striking of them was what Ahmar said,

> The language I speak is one that is derived from a widely used language. It has borrowed words from other languages like Hindi, Persian, and Turkish, with its own unique phonological system. It is part of my identity and I want others to understand that the English language borrows many words. I had a student teacher who suggested to take out the words such as Zafran (Saffron), and Gazal (Gazelle) from a passage and I had to explain that these are the words that have been borrowed from another language and incorporated into the English language so you will need to keep these when you are working with students who speak that language because these are part of their linguistic competencies.

This quote holds so much power for the faculty as well as K-12 educators especially with the shifting narrative regarding reading and literacy development. While revealing a superior sense of student's metalinguistic awareness, it highlights that languages are fluid and students' previous linguistic knowledge can directly impact their use of second language across contexts, an important consideration for K-12 settings.

Participants discussed the role positionality played in their emerging mindsets. As Stonecat shared,

> I have always felt different. Even in my home country, there are certain things that are difficult to avoid. Living in Europe also gave me a different perspective and bring [sic] my positionality out further. I try not to judge but there is always something there that will inform your perspective differently. I have a career that is typically different than most.

When people find out about my career and what I do, people are interested in it and want to ask questions. But we can't just have one perspective. I don't want to have a superficial discussion; I want to have deeper conversations.

This quote from Stonecat speaks to the power of an individual's positionality, something that has been stressed throughout this chapter. By attending to our students' journeys and positionalities, we might be able to increase their self of belonging while also attempting to provide more meaningful opportunities for interaction where students have a chance to discuss, unpack, and extend their intellectual and social abilities. In this theme, we see that transactional experiences of the GTM are emphasized in the quotes of Ahmar and Stonecat.

It is important to consider that these are the individuals whose children might be integrated into our schools. Our pre-service candidates must be exposed to this diversity of perspectives that many immigrants to this country hold. When the question of unique viewpoints came up, Britney overwhelmingly expressed that she was different, "I feel that I am in a totally different mindset, and I have different goals. I feel that I am always planning and always worried about the next thing. I must always be on my toes." Both the quotes speak to the power of unique mindsets and students' funds of knowledge that must be brought into our coursework discussions. It is critical that the faculty share these insights with their pre-service candidates and at the same time integrate a diverse and multifaceted lens in their own coursework. In this regard, the integrated factor of the Global Teaching Model is emphasized.

Move to a Foreign Country: Lessons for Our Institutions

Based on the stories these participants shared, their reasons for coming to a new country varied, whether it be to learn new ways, new strategies, or to dispel any stereotypes about the United States. Students were fully aware of the fact that their linguistic competencies varied because of their accents and differences in vocabulary and yet they wanted to be heard and express themselves to their fullest potential because they were here to learn and be acknowledged—another resounding reality for our K-12 settings. So many of our young scholars want to express themselves to their fullest potential and yet hold themselves back due to their linguistic competencies, which ties back to the idea of classroom environment and how a focus on students' intercultural competencies might help us in creating spaces that are responsive and yield meaningful outcomes for students regardless of their linguistic repertoires.

As Maria also shared,

I felt very appreciated as a Latino person here, but I felt like it was my language that was limiting. Idioms are different and words are different sometimes here. It was a humbling experience (which is also a phrase I learned here in the US). Being in the US and being in these uncomfortable situations made me think about my students that I teach statistics [to] back home in my country. I need to simplify things for them. Do they feel about the subject how I felt sometimes when I was there? I want to use my own example, so I can simplify things for students in my stats class just like I needed things in the US.

This anecdote is an ultimate testament to the power of being a global student. Not only did she learn new things, but she also took a lifetime of lessons with herself. Yet at the same time, if a well-traveled graduate student with social capital feels uncomfortable in a new linguistic environment, then we must think about how our young students relocating to a new country and a new environment might feel. And whether this sense of vulnerability might lead to alienation and a feeling of isolation in a foreign classroom. Implications for educators are plenty through these examples. Maria's quotes demonstrate both critical and transactional factors from the Global Teaching Model.

Another meaningful connection was shared by Spark. As he mentioned,

When you have another culture, your behavior is related to that culture. Of course you have cultural differences. But everyone was kind to me. You can feel it. But you also must understand that you may have an idea and someone else has another idea in their mind and everyone wants to share. In that case it was the patience of the professors that helped me. We need that patience.

These reflections have such relevant implications for the universities serving ISCs. This quote speaks to the power of intercultural dialogue (or, transactional experiences in the GTM) and collaborative discussions at the classroom level and the need to accommodate for linguistic differences to help students share to their highest potential.

Experiential learning was important for these students. As Gaviota shared,

I have represented my country everywhere—Argentina, Cuba, Budapest, Taiwan, and many other places. So, I came to the US to improve my English to communicate in my traveling and to communicate with other citizens. I am a very philosophical person inside. I want to know about other persons [sic]. English is an international language, so I want to know more. So, I feel like, sometimes, I needed a longer time for English to calibrate in my brain to have discussions and reflections; it takes time. You need to figure out how to start your life in English here in the US before you learn and study something.

Multiple lessons for faculty members may be gleaned from what Gaviota shared. On one level, it is important to consider the cognitive dissonance and the impact on executive functioning that many bi/multilingual learners experience as they traverse between two languages at the same time; we must reflect upon the importance of providing an experiential learning environment where students can practice their linguistic skills and improve their learning outcomes and build linguistic competencies. This is something that must be shared with pre-service educators as well.

The Role That Students' Competencies Play

In response to the questions regarding their competencies, the responses ranged from, "I was reminded of the holes in my own linguistic abilities" to "I had no idea that even though I grew up in an English-speaking environment, I did not know how different this

English was going to be." There were responses such as, "I feel the proudest of my linguistic abilities and competencies when I am with people from my own country" to "because of my ability to speak my language, I can actually teach a class in modern languages." These students' linguistic competencies were not going to shake their conviction of studying in a predominantly English-speaking environment. They highlighted that they have bilingual or multilingual abilities but for most of them it is a label, an idea, often a sense of identity that neither deters nor diminishes their ability to function in English-speaking spaces. This aspect resonated with the authors as well who had to sift through their linguistic competencies as students in this country and have their own kids now studying in a US public institution.

As Maria shared,

> I think it is important for the professors to get some knowledge about our context. In a class with a professor, we talked about our journal, and I feel like they only know their context, but maybe some information about our context is good for them to understand as well. Especially about our academic work. In my case I have a long experience of publishing articles, books, and chapters and I know, and I apply in my daily work but if you don't know the level we are at, maybe it will become boring for us to be in your class. So, learn the context. I know it's difficult, if you need to check about one person but it is important to know about your students.

These students exhibit their academic intentionality through the experiences they have had and their own positionalities. They understand the deficits that exist within the university's preparedness and pedagogical actions. And they want to help inform the field through their own narratives and stories. This theme emphasizes the Global Teaching Model's situated practice.

Lesson from Traversing the Stereotypes and Physical Borders

The key players in this quest were students who traversed a physical border to come to a country so different from theirs, yet with an unconditional desire to learn. As Roshni so eloquently shared,

> The country I belong to, the official language there is English. When I was there, I wasn't thinking too much about the linguistic differences that I was about to encounter upon coming to the US; I wasn't aware of a lot of things because technology also wasn't there. But then I moved here, and I sensed a lot of challenges because of the language. When I met a few people, they told me that your language is different. Then I thought, 'Oh okay, this is not a little bit, it's a lot.' But I wasn't scared of that. My mom's encouragement and motivation were behind me. My mother's dedication brought me here and that's why I wasn't scared even though there were a lot of challenges.

Roshni's words reminded us of an important task IHEs have in front of them: to have modifications available for students to express themselves and to provide students with opportunities to elaborate on their experiences. A student's ability cannot be measured by the level of their linguistic competency, rather the linguistic competency they bring with them can be utilized as a conduit for exploratory discussions in the classrooms.

Families and the societies they had to leave behind were brought into the discussion several times. For some, it was a matter of "getting ready for the new culture and the new system needs time" and they had to do it all while also getting things ready for the families they were leaving behind. As Aurora said,

> The most helpful conversations I have ever had was the ones that I had with my adviser […] because when I got here, I was very confused and really overwhelmed by everything because everything was different. So, in the beginning, I didn't know how to rent a place. I didn't know how to open a bank account. I know I don't know anything. It was, like, different. Food was different, culture was different. And I think all of that made me overwhelmed for a period. And the only person I could refer to was my adviser, who did a great job letting me know, where I am, and gradually kind of like mentoring me, where I should be of the conversations that we have.

This theme, which is more comprehensive in what it touches, features elements of all four factors of the GTM: situated, integrated, critical, and transactional.

Discussion

Many parallels to K-12 systems were noted throughout the research process along with the focus on students' intercultural competencies, faculty responsiveness, and the power of their positionalities:

1 Students shared the importance of understanding their collective and individual intercultural competencies, linguistic abilities, and backgrounds, and the faculty's responsiveness to attend to the diverse perspectives they bring, aligning with the idea of situated practice in GTM.

2 Students' positionalities cannot be painted with a single narrow stroke. Just like these international students shared their divergent views and experiences, immigrant students coming into K-12 settings are diverse in their linguistic, cultural, and socioeconomic profiles. Not only is this imperative for our institutions of learning to focus on the wide range of competencies students bring but also to stress on the global connectedness and the rich tapestries we can weave in our classrooms through an interconnected transaction of learning between these diverse minds. Something that was brought up repeatedly by the study participants.

3 Participants expressed a desire for the institutions to understand that:

   a Their positionalities impacted their perspectives and could lead to a learning process that is situated in student voices and the diversity of thought they represent, sharing traces of GTM's situated practice.

    b Intercultural/linguistic competencies could become catalysts for deep critical thinking and student engagement to occur, leading to the transactional practice of GTM.

    c Faculty members must embrace that our world is shrinking due to increased geographic and digital mobility and as consumers of digital knowledge our students are at the frontlines of this global interconnectivity. Global issues are being discussed at a much deeper and faster rates among our younger population because social media has made it visible to them.

4 Students' experiential knowledge plays a critical role in their instructional trajectory. It is important for the faculty not to assume the knowledge level of their ISCs. Not every student is coming to a foreign country for the sole purpose of learning, rather they might be coming to advance their knowledge by learning a specific skill or fulfilling degree requirements, which is also important for the faculty to share with their pre-service teacher candidates.

5 Students shared traces of GTM's global teaching through a critical frame as they discussed the levels of institution's responsiveness. It is critical for educators to provide students with a space to utilize their experiences.

6 Collaborative discussions in classrooms help students extend their thought processes.

Future Implications and Connections to Classroom Practice

For many ISCs, often the road to completion is paved with confusion, uncertainty, and a longing for their native countries. However, the important thing is that they are here and want to make the best of their situations. Therefore, it becomes imperative for IHEs to consider that if students are choosing us as their institution of choice, then we must provide opportunities for them to utilize their intercultural competencies to the fullest and be prepared to learn more about their unique positionalities.

Keeping in line with the fact that to create equitable and inclusive learning environments that support learners in achieving their educational potential, teachers must be equipped with a range of competencies, knowledge, and attitudes (Cerna et al., 2021), we are proposing a global competency framework (see Figure 2.1) that could be utilized by institutions to avoid ambiguity and lack of preparedness within pedagogical and instructional frameworks. At the conclusion of these narratives and the perspectives that were shared, we believe that a Global Competency Framework comprising Intercultural Responsiveness, an Individual's Positionality, and Multicultural and Linguistic competencies is important for the universities to help strengthen their ecologies and to best prepare their pre-service candidates.

Such a framework that focuses on the core power of students' competencies and positionalities could engage an individual's identity and sociocultural competencies in such a way that their core knowledge, skills, attitudes, and values ultimately help them overcome

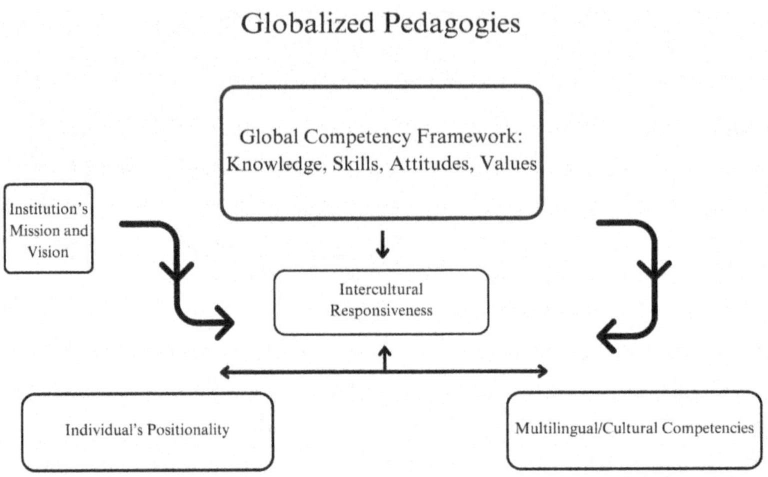

Globalized Pedagogies

Figure 2.1 Globalized Pedagogies Framework. *Created by the authors.*

the systemic barriers often posed through a lack of understanding of diversity in higher education (OECD, 2018). It is the authors' belief that a framework rooted within these three core principles along with an individual's knowledge, skills, attitudes, and values they bring with themselves can help build strong institutional ecologies and create more faculty responsiveness regarding students' multicultural/lingual competencies.

Ultimately, we would like to emphasize emphatically that internationalization is not a program. Although we provide recommendations for faculty and IHEs based on the narratives of our participants, there is not a single act or initiative or workshop or mandate that encompasses a culture of internationalization. Rather, we see internationalization as a curated anthology featuring the rich and colorful stories of individuals' lived experiences—a true compilation of multiple voices brought together to further a borderless curriculum.

Questions to Consider

1 One participant highlighted the importance of recognizing that languages often borrow words from one another. What other strategies can educators or researchers employ to incorporate this understanding into their classrooms or work environments?

2 Participants expressed the benefits of studying abroad to gain a broader perspective on themselves and the world. However, studying abroad isn't feasible for everyone. How can educators integrate cultural responsiveness or globalized pedagogical framework into teaching practice without the opportunity to study abroad? How do you create and implement a borderless study abroad experience, where students do not need to physically leave their IHE's? With this approach can IHE's still foster and sustain cultural competence?

3 Given that intercultural competency is a multi-layered construct essential for successful and harmonious functioning across cultures, how can teachers, pre-service teachers, and administrators meet the needs of linguistically and culturally diverse students (i.e., international students, immigrants, etc.)? How can they prepare students to meet the demands of an increasingly globalized workplace?

References

Acevedo, S. M., Aho, M., Çela, E., Chao, J., Garcia-Gonzales, I., Macleod, A., Moutray, C., and Olague, C. (2015). Positionality as knowledge: From pedagogy to praxis. *Integral Review*, *11*(1), 28–46.

Ateh, C., and Ryan, L. (2023). Preparing teacher candidates to be culturally responsive in classroom management. *Social Sciences & Humanities Open*, *7(1)*, 100455. https://doi.org/10.1016/j.ssaho.2023.100455.

Banks, J. A. (2004). Multicultural education: historical development, dimensions, and practice. In J. A. Banks and C. A. M. Banks (Eds.), *Handbook of Research on Multicultural Education* (2nd edn.), pp. 3–29. Jossey-Bass.

Berger, R. (2015). Now I see it, now I don't: Researcher's position and reflexivity in qualitative research. *Qualitative Research*, *15*(2), 219–34. https://doi.org/10.1177/1468794112468475.

Biesta, G. (2013). Responsive or responsible? Democratic education for the global networked society. *Policy Futures in Education*, *11*(6), 733–44. https://doi.org/10.2304/pfie.2013.11.6.733.

Byker, E. J., and Putman, S. M. (2019). Catalyzing cultural and global competencies: Engaging preservice teachers in study abroad to expand the agency of citizenship. *Journal of Studies in International Education*, *23*(1), 84–105. https://doi.org/10.1177/1028315318814559.

Cerna L., Mezzanotte C., and Rutigliano A. (2021). Promoting inclusive education for diverse societies: A conceptual framework. *OECD Education Working Papers, No. 260*, OECD Publishing. https://doi.org/10.1787/94ab68c6-en.

Chandir, H., and Blackmore, J. (2024). Situated enactments of global competence in three schools in Victoria. *Journal of Education Policy*, *39*(5), 1–21. https://doi.org/10.1080/02680939.2023.2299471.

Clandinin, D. J., and Connelly, F. M. (2000). *Narrative Inquiry: Experience and Story in Qualitative Research*. Jossey-Bass.

Clarke, A. (2023). Teacher inquiry: By any other name. In R. J. Tierney, F. Rizvi, and K. Ercikan (Eds.), *International Encyclopedia of Education* (4th edn.), pp. 232–42. Elsevier. https://doi.org/10.1016/B978-0-12-818630-5.04026-4.

Del Carmen Salazar, M. (2013). A humanizing pedagogy: Reinventing the principles and practice of education as a journey toward liberation. *Review of Research in Education*, *37*(1), 121–48. https://doi.org/10.3102/0091732X12464032.

Delpit L. (2006). *Other People's Children: Cultural Conflict in the Classroom*. New Press.

Flores, B. B., and Smith, H. L. (2009). Teachers' characteristics and attitudinal beliefs about linguistic and cultural diversity. *Bilingual Research Journal*, *31*(1–2), 323–58. https://doi.org/10.1080/15235880802640789.

Foxall, F., Sundin, D., Towell-Barnard, A., Ewens, B., Kemp, V., and Porock, D. (2021). Revealing meaning from story: The application of narrative inquiry to explore the factors that influence decision making in relation to the withdrawal of life-sustaining treatment in the intensive care unit. *International Journal of Qualitative Methods*, *20*, 160940692110283. https://doi.org/10.1177/16094069211028345.

Freire P. (1970). *Pedagogy of the Oppressed*. Continuum.

Fujikane H. (2003). Approaches to global education in the United States, United Kingdom and Japan. *International Review of Education, 49*, 133–52.

Gay, G. (2018). *Culturally Responsive Teaching: Theory, Research, and Practice* (33rd edn.). Teachers College Press.

Guillén-Yparrea, N., and Ramírez-Montoya, M. S. (2023). Intercultural competencies in higher education: A systematic review from 2016 to 2021. *Cogent Education, 10*(1), 1–14. https://doi.org/10.1080/2331186X.2023.2167360.

Higher Ed Immigration Portal. (2025). National Data on Immigrant and International Students in Higher Education. https://www.higheredimmigrationportal.org/national/national-data (accessed November 12, 2025).

Hull G. A., and Stornaiuolo A. (2014). Cosmopolitan literacies, social networks, and "proper distance": Striving to understand in a global world. *Curriculum Inquiry, 44*(1), 15–44.

Hult, F. M. (2013). Covert Bilingualism and symbolic competence: Analytical reflections on negotiating insider/outsider positionality in Swedish speech situations. *Applied Linguistics, 35*(1), 63–81.

Johnson, B., and Christensen, L. B. (2017). *Educational Research: Quantitative, Qualitative, and Mixed Approaches* (666th edn.). Sage.

Johnson, B., and Christensen, L. B. (2019). *Educational Research: Quantitative, Qualitative, and Mixed Approaches* (77th edn.). Sage.

Kang, H., and Fay, L. (2023). Teacher responsiveness as a core feature of justice- and equity-centered instruction. *The Science Teacher, 90*(5), 38–43. https://doi.org/10.1080/19434871.2023.12290282.

Kerkhoff, S. N. (2017). Designing global futures: A mixed methods study to develop and validate the teaching for global readiness scale. *Teaching and Teacher Education, 65*, 91–106.

Kerkhoff, S. (2018). Teaching for global readiness: A model for locally situated and globally connected literacy instruction. In E. Ortlieb and E. H. Cheek, Jr (Eds.), *Addressing Diversity in Literacy Instruction*, pp. 193–205. Emerald Publishing.

Khalil, G., and Khalil, J. (1926). *Beyond Borders*. Simon & Schuster.

Ladson-Billings, G. (1995). Toward a theory of culturally relevant pedagogy. *American Educational Research Journal, 32*(3), 465–91. https://doi.org/10.3102/00028312032003465.

Ladson-Billings G. (2004). Culture versus citizenship: The challenge of racialized citizenship in the United States. In J. A. Banks (Ed.), *Diversity and Citizenship Education: Global Perspectives*, pp. 96–126. Jossey-Bass

Ladson-Billings, G. (2009). *The Dreamkeepers: Successful Teachers of African American Children* (2nd edn.). Jossey-Bass.

Mahalingappa, L., Kayi-Aydar, H., and Polat, N. (2021). Institutional and faculty readiness for teaching linguistically diverse international students in educator preparation programs in U.S. universities. *TESOL Quarterly, 55*(4), 1247–77. https://doi.org/10.1002/tesq.3083.

Merolla, A. J., Neubauer, A. B., and Otmar, C. D. (2024). Responsiveness, social connection, hope, and life satisfaction in everyday social interaction: An experience sampling study. *Journal of Happiness Studies, 25*(1–2), 7. https://doi.org/10.1007/s10902-024-00710-5.

Moustakas, C. (1994). *Phenomenological Research Methods*. Sage. https://doi.org/10.4135/9781412995658.

Nespor, J. (1987). The role of beliefs in the practice of teaching. *Journal of Curriculum Studies, 19(4)*, 317–28. https://doi.org/10.1080/0022027870190403.

O'Connor, K., and Zeichner, K. (2011). Preparing US teachers for critical global education. In Vanessa De Oliveira Andreotti (Ed.), *The Political Economy of Global Citizenship Education*, pp. 208–23. Routledge.

OECD. 2018. Preparing Our Youth for an Inclusive and Sustainable World: The OECD PISA Global Competence Framework (accessed November 12, 2025).

Pastori, G., Mangiatordi, A., Ereky-Stevens, K., and Slot, P. L. (2018). ISOTIS Virtual Learning Environment. Development, progress and on-going work in WP3, 4 and 5. Reis et al., pp. 239–257. ISOTIS.

Patiño-Santos, A., and Poveda, D. (2022). Bilingual education: English and the life projects of youth in contemporary Spain. In E. Codó (Ed.), *Global CLIL*, pp. 149–73. Routledge.

Patton, M. Q. (1987). How to Use Qualitative Methods in Evaluation. Sage.

Ramos, K., Wolf, E. J., and Hauber-Özer, M. (2021). Teaching for global competence: A responsibility of teacher educators. *Journal of Research in Childhood Education*, 35(2) 311–30. https://doi.org/10.1080/02568543.2021.1880998.

Reid, A. D., Hart, P. E., and Peters, M. A. (2014). *A Companion to Research in Education*. Springer.

Reis, H. T., Clark, M. S., and Holmes, J. G. (2004). Perceived partner responsiveness as an organizing construct in the study of intimacy and closeness. In D. J. Mashek and A. P. Aron (Eds.), *Handbook of Closeness and Intimacy*, pp. 201–25. Erlbaum.

Reis, H. T., Itzchakov, G., Lee, K. Y., and Yan, R. (2022). Sociability matters: Downstream consequences of perceived partner responsiveness in social life. In J. P. Forgas, W. Crano, and K. Fiedler (Eds.), *The Psychology of Sociability: Understanding Human Attachment*, pp. 239–57. Routledge. https://doi.org/10.4324/9781003258582.

Riessman, C. K. (2008). *Narrative Methods for the Human Sciences*. Sage.

Rokeach, M. (1972). *Beliefs, Attitudes and Values: A Theory of Organization and Change*. Jossey-Bass.

Romijn, B., Slot, P., and Leseman, P. (2021). Increasing teachers' intercultural competences in teacher preparation programs and through professional development: A review. *Teaching and Teacher Education*, 98, 103236. http://doi.org/10.1016/j.tate.2020.103236.

Sandell, E. J., and Tupy, S. (2015). Where cultural competency begins: Changes in undergraduate students' intercultural competency. *The International Journal of Teaching and Learning in Higher Education*, 27, 364–81.

Schwarzenthal, M., Schachner, M. K., Juang, L. P., and van de Vijver, F. J. R. (2019). Reaping the benefits of cultural diversity: Classroom cultural diversity climate and students' intercultural competence. *European Journal of Social Psychology*, 50(2), 323–46. https://doi.org/10.1002/ejsp.2617.

Secules, S., McCall, C., Mejia, J. A., Beebe, C., Masters, A. S., L. Sánchez-Peña, M., and Svyantek, M. (2021). Positionality practices and dimensions of impact on equity research: A collaborative inquiry and call to the community. *Journal of Engineering Education*, 110(1), 19–43. https://doi.org/10.1002/jee.20377.

Spangler, V. (2023). On positionalities in research with international students. *Journal of International Students*, 13(4), 234–39. https://doi.org/10.32674/jis.v14i3.6090.

Spitzberg, B. H., and Changnon, G. (2009) Conceptualizing intercultural competence. In D. K. Deardorff (Ed.), *The SAGE Handbook of Intercultural Competence*, pp. 2–52. Sage.

Tichnor-Wagner, A., Parkhouse, H., Glazier, J., and Cain, J. M. (2016). Expanding approaches to teaching for diversity and social justice in K-12 education: Fostering global citizenship across the content areas. *Education Policy Analysis Archives*, 24(59), 1–31.

Torres-Olave, B., and Lee, J. J. (2020). Shifting positionalities across international locations: Embodied knowledge, time-geography, and the polyvalence of privilege. *Higher Education Quarterly*, 74(2), 136–48. https://doi.org/10.1111/hequ.12216.

Van M, J., and Ferreira, M. M. (2023). An essay about intercultural sensitivity and competence in higher education. *European Journal of Education and Pedagogy*, 4(2), 149–55. https://doi.org/10.24018/ejedu.2023.4.2.624.

Xiaotian Z., and Mingming, Z. (2023). Information and digital technology-assisted interventions to improve intercultural competence: A meta-analytical review. *Computers & Education*, *194*, 1–26. C. https://doi.org/10.1016/j.compedu.2022.104697.

Yeh, E., and Wan, G. (2018). Intercultural competence for teachers of young ELLs. In G. Onchwari and J. Keengwe (Eds.), *Handbook of Research on Pedagogies and Cultural Considerations for Young English Language Learners*, pp. 192–216. IGI Global. https://doi.org/10.4018/978-1-5225-3955-1.ch010.

Zhang, X., and Zhou, M. (2023). Chinese university students' intercultural competence: Reconceptualization and assessment. *Journal of International Students*, *14*(3), 5593. https://doi.org/10.32674/jis.v14i3.5593.

3

Collaborative Mathematical Endeavors as Pillars of Global Education

Arthur Powell, Hanna Haydar, and Chadd McGlone

Abstract

This chapter addresses the global interconnection of educational challenges, emphasizing the importance of equitable social and economic opportunities. It presents an example of a challenge to the conventional nationalist approach to international education, advocating instead for a commitment to global justice. The example is Mathkind, a US-based nongovernmental organization that collaborates with local partners in Global South countries to co-create culturally responsive mathematics education programs. Initially established to expose US teachers to diverse educational traditions, Mathkind has evolved into a year-round endeavor co-designing professional development initiatives with Global South educators, fostering leadership, and enhancing mathematics teaching practices. The chapter highlights Mathkind's use of Culturally Responsive and Sustaining Pedagogy (CRSP) to adapt global educational standards to local needs, illustrating the benefits of co-constructed, culturally aware educational strategies. Mathkind's partnerships, involving countries such as Ecuador, Guatemala, Nepal, and Zimbabwe, showcase the importance of collaboration and mutual learning in developing sustainable educational models. Through these efforts, Mathkind contributes to a global dialogue on the application of CRSP, advocating for educational practices that honor and incorporate Global South students' cultural and linguistic identities.

Key Terms: *Culturally Responsive-Sustaining Pedagogy, Mathkind, International Education, Global Education*

Introduction

Educational challenges are globally interconnected, with an emphasis on improving social and economic opportunities to ensure global well-being and justice. US agencies like the Departments of State and Education advocate for international education (The US Department of Education, 2022). However, it is crucial to move beyond nationalism and contribute to global justice. Governments and NGOs from the Global North should help develop educational programs in the Global South. The challenge is to do so without instituting missionary practices, such as uncritically transplanting programs from the North and behaving parasitically or paternalistically. In response to this challenge, a Global North nongovernmental organization called Mathkind is evolving to co-create mathematics education programs with partners in Global South countries. Mathkind's Culturally Responsive and Sustaining Pedagogy (CRSP) perspective shows how an organization can evolve while supporting Global South mathematics leaders who respect and value their culture, adapting beneficial global ideas to achieve their mathematics education goals.

Mathkind

In this chapter, we describe an educational project headquartered in the United States, a Global North[1] nation, focused on collaborative approaches to mathematics learning and teaching: Mathkind. Established in 2014, it began as a summer travel program with two objectives. First, it aimed to expose US teachers to the rich cultural and educational traditions of the students they teach from Central and South American countries. At the same time, in those countries, the second objective was for US teachers to support their professional peers' growth in their knowledge of US perspectives of mathematics and its pedagogy. Since its start, those initial objectives have been examined and continually modified. Mathkind, in its current and unfinished state, is currently a year-round endeavor partnering and collaborating with local Global South organizations, schools, and teachers to transform mathematics instruction through high-quality programs. It has grown from a small group of US-based mathematics educators into an international network of researchers and practitioners. While still primarily US-based, they now collaborate with mathematics leaders in Global South countries to co-construct educational programs in schools that are committed to high-quality instruction but face systemic barriers.

Mathkind's programs now emerge from co-constructive efforts to provide professional development programs to enhance Global South mathematics educators' and teachers' content knowledge and provide them with evidence-based pedagogical practices that address their identified challenges. Mathkind co-designs its programs with partners in the countries where it works to respond to their articulated needs. For instance, based on a model developed by an Ecuadorian mathematician in the Guayaquil area, MathMobile is a Mathkind program that travels to coach teachers in various Guatemalan communities, whereas Girls STEM Clubs is a Guatemalan-developed program where Guatemalan teachers support girls to engage and enjoy STEM disciplines. Each of Mathkind's co-designed programs aims to include three foundational components: instructional support, quality resources, and collaborative spaces.

Through Mathkind programs, country-based teachers enhance their content knowledge and pedagogical strategies, and later, country-based Mathkind staff members further support those teachers in applying their learning in their classrooms. Graduates of Mathkind programs have developed into leaders who, in turn, coach their colleagues. Mathkind conjectures that this combination strengthens teachers' specialized knowledge for teaching mathematics, consequently leading to positive outcomes for their students.

Currently, Mathkind is at different stages of development and implementation and has partnerships in several Global South countries, including Ecuador, Guatemala, Nepal, and Zimbabwe. Later in this chapter, to provide insight into how Mathkind, a nongovernmental organization of the Global North, co-constructs professional enhancement projects with partners in Global South countries, we will describe aspects of those partnerships to illustrate the evolving theory of Mathkind's work toward implementing CRSP. As a final example of Mathkind's implementation of CRSP, we will present an initiative that transcends specific national borders, called Global Math Stories.

Mathkind's Theoretical Framework

This section examines the theoretical foundations supporting CRSP and global education. This examination is crucial to understanding the development of Mathkind's CRSP framework, revealing the influences that guided its evolution within the domain of international initiatives.

Culturally Responsive and Sustaining Pedagogy

In contemplating three decades of culturally relevant, responsive, and sustaining pedagogies, Ladson-Billings (2021), a pioneering figure in culturally relevant pedagogy, emphasizes that teaching that prioritizes advancing student learning, cultivating cultural competence, and nurturing critical consciousness is the sole approach that authentically embodies the essence of Culturally Relevant Pedagogy. This definition has given rise to diverse initiatives, appellations, methodologies, and theories, all aimed at placing "culture" at the core of the education of students who have been historically marginalized.

Later, scholars such as Gay (2002) sought to reframe pedagogy and curriculum beyond mere relevance to students' lives, emphasizing the necessity of designing pedagogy and curriculum specifically for culturally marginalized students. They adopted the term "culturally responsive pedagogy" to describe this approach. Building on this work and recognizing its limitations, Paris (2012) initiated a discourse on a new paradigm, coining the term "culturally sustaining pedagogy." This conceptual evolution positioned Culturally Sustaining Pedagogy as the cornerstone for constructing an educational framework explicitly designed to resist the prevailing status quo. It motivates marginalized communities to advocate for recognizing and respecting their linguistic and cultural identities. To enable students to recognize and affirm their cultural identity, education should bridge the gap between students' school and home lives (Paris and Alim, 2014). Furthermore, teachers should acknowledge, affirm, and incorporate the "funds of knowledge" that students bring from their communities and homes, treating those funds as valuable forms of capital that schools should strive to activate (Rios-Aguilar et al., 2011).

We emphasize that acknowledging, validating, and incorporating cultural dimensions should not be understood as advocating for an invariable perspective of the world and students. Educators must avoid the tendency to "enforce assumptions that culture is a static set of rules of behavior in which all group members abide by, presuming coherence within groups which may not exist" (Kolovou, 2022). On the contrary, our perspective views CRSP as promoting a dynamic, varied, and contextualized understanding of culture and students. The following section uses this dynamic lens to consider CRSP in mathematics education.

Culturally Responsive and Sustaining Pedagogy in Mathematics

Although there have been some encouraging outcomes, adopting CRSP in mathematics education remains limited and inconsistent (Neri et al., 2019). Mathematics teachers often struggle to identify clear connections between their subject matter and the cultural and ethnic backgrounds of their students (Boutte, Kelly-Jackson and Johnson, 2010). Educators emphasize the need for increased efforts in supporting teachers to translate effectively culturally relevant theories into their practice, especially within mathematics education (Brown et al., 2019).

Several misconceptions are compounded when implementing CRSP in mathematics classrooms. These include the following: (1) the mistaken belief that the mathematics taught in schools is the exclusive form of mathematics worldwide (Bishop, 2002), (2) the perception that mathematics possesses universal applicability and is indifferent to color (Martin, 2009), (3) the pervasive Eurocentric dominance in school mathematics (Powell and Frankenstein, 1997), (4) the persistence of traditional instructional practices that prioritize basic skills over sense-making and conceptual understanding (Ellis and Berry, 2005), and (5) the standardized educational approach that severs students' cultural strengths and experiences from the teaching and learning of mathematics (Leonard, 2008).

Nevertheless, mathematics educators have succeeded recently in crafting ways to implement CRSP across grade levels. For instance, for elementary classrooms, educators such as Matthews, Jones, and Parker (2022) have developed a practical approach to the design, adoption, and implementation of research-based, learner-centered CRSP mathematical tasks that empower students to connect mathematics to themselves and their surroundings. Focusing on elementary and secondary school classrooms, other scholars have developed frameworks and specific lessons for teachers to engage their students in exploring how mathematics can be used to understand and analyze social injustices (Bartell et al., 2022; Berry et al., 2020; Childs and Staley, 2025).

Global and International Education

Essentially, global education calls for enabling students to achieve their career goals in an interconnected global economy (Asia Society and Center for Global Education, 2021). It also instills in them individual and collective responsibility as global citizens, contributing to creating more just and sustainable local communities, countries, and a world that benefits all of humanity (Banks, 2015)

Global and international education competence, a multifaceted concept outlined by various sources (OECD, 2018; UNESCO, 2015), encompasses learning's cognitive, social-emotional, and behavioral dimensions. The cognitive domain involves acquiring the knowledge and thinking skills necessary for a comprehensive understanding of the world and its complexities. Simultaneously, the social-emotional dimension focuses on cultivating values, attitudes, and social skills that foster respectful and peaceful coexistence. Finally, the behavioral domain pertains to conduct, performance, practical application, and engagement (UNESCO, 2015). Critically, global education competence should not be treated as a stand-alone content area but should be grounded in disciplinary and interdisciplinary knowledge across all subjects (Mansilla and Jackson, 2011). It should not be considered an "add-on" but seamlessly integrated into existing courses and curricula, ensuring exposure for all students throughout the school year (Tichnor-Wagner et al., 2019). This integrative approach extends to international mathematics education, where curriculum frameworks often embed global competencies. For example, Singapore's mathematics frameworks incorporate applications of mathematics relevant to today's world, promote pedagogies that encourage critical thinking, effective communication, and the use of digital technologies, and present problem contexts that raise students' awareness of both local and global issues (Ministry of Education, 2020).

Mathkind and Global Mathematics Education

Our perspective on global education is grounded in three fundamental stances. First, we recognize the nuanced nature of globalization, which, according to Henry and Taylor (2000), encompasses contradictory impulses of integration, fragmentation, and differentiation. It is imperative not to equate globalization with universalization. Nash and Willey (2010) argue that a global culture is inherently fragmented and pluralistic, promoting greater openness and responsibility toward cultural differences.

Second, our approach to global education involves scrutinizing partnerships between Global North organizations and Global South communities. Drawing from the insights provided by Newton and Early (2015), we advocate for a thorough examination of intentions and strategies when collaborating with Global South partners. The five critical principles proposed—respecting and valuing people, building trust through relationships, engaging in collaborative efforts, ensuring feedback and accountability, and evaluating each step of the process—guide our interactions to transform what may be good intentions into positive outcomes that are the joint result of Global North and South partnerships (Newton and Early, 2015). We consider these principles aspirational, recognizing that partnerships are inherently fraught with power imbalances (Lee, 2021).

Third, we emphasize the complementary relationship between CRSP and global education. Recognizing that CRSP teaching supports self-awareness about identity, culture, and sensitivity to differences, we view those dispositions as integral to global competence (González-Salamanca et al., 2020). Fostering those dispositions through CRSP teaching sends a powerful message that all students are valued, and that multiculturalism is an asset, aligning with global education. Mathkind's interconnected approach, as described in the examples section below, strives to create a holistic and inclusive educational framework that values diversity and fosters positive international engagement.

Mathkind's Evolution to CRSP in Its Global Work

In the diverse educational landscapes Mathkind navigates, from urban schools in Ecuador to rural classrooms in Nepal, CRSP serves as a guiding principle for its educators. By embedding students' cultural narratives and epistemologies into the fabric of mathematics education, Mathkind's embodiment of CRSP fosters a learning environment where mathematical concepts are understood and felt in a manner that is profoundly relevant and personal to each student. The diverse contextual and cultural implementations of this CRSP approach will be detailed in the examples section of this chapter. By investing in the growth and development of country-based educators, Mathkind is committed to nurturing a globally competent yet locally sensitive cadre of mathematics educators. This commitment is evident in the change observed in educational practices and the heightened sense of community involvement in the educational process. From those observed changes in country-based leadership, Mathkind envisions a future where educational reform resonates profoundly with each community's cultural and contextual realities, contributing significantly to the global discourse on educational equity and excellence. Further exploration and discussion of these aspects will be presented in the later sections.

Mathkind's approach to mathematics education is distinguished by its inherent adaptability, a fundamental quality in navigating the multifaceted landscape of global education. Rather than adhering to a static methodology, its pedagogical strategies continuously evolve to resonate with the varied cultural and educational ecosystems encountered.

In practice, this means that whether operating within the bustling urban schools of Kenya or the close-knit rural communities of Ecuador, Mathkind's methodologies are negotiated and crafted to address each locale's specific educational needs and challenges. This process involves a collaborative and dialogic engagement with local educators and stakeholders, ensuring that local educational philosophies and practices are respected and integrated into teaching approaches. This evolved and shaped how Mathkind uniquely operates in each community.

This tailored approach results in pedagogical strategies that are both culturally relevant and pedagogically robust, creating an educational environment where mathematical concepts become accessible, meaningful, and empowering for students. Mathkind's adaptive methodologies respect the uniqueness of each educational setting while simultaneously upholding the principles of inclusivity and academic excellence in mathematics education. The intended outcome is a dynamic, context-sensitive pedagogy that effectively bridges global education with the rich tapestry of local educational narratives.

To sum it up, Mathkind's CRSP approach has undergone refinement over time, and several vital principles now articulate it as shown in Figure 3.1. First, CRSP is the cornerstone, emphasizing cultural responsiveness and context sensitivity in educational practices. Second, Mathkind prioritizes adaptive methodologies in diverse educational ecosystems, recognizing the dynamic nature of learning environments and adapting its methodologies accordingly. Third, its approach centers on co-constructing partnerships

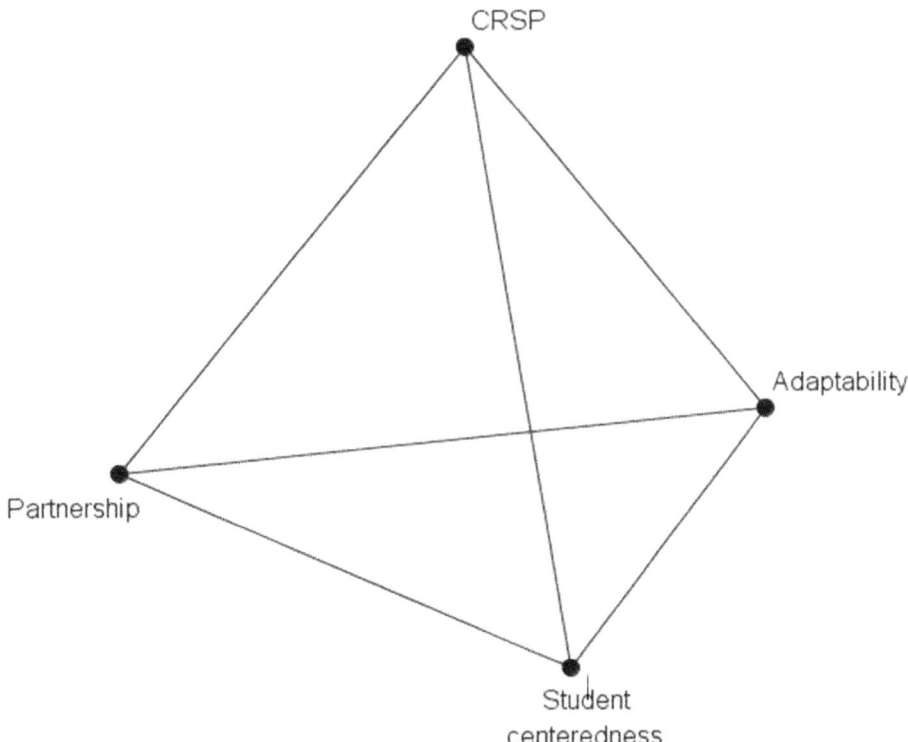

Figure 3.1 The Four Key Principles of Mathkind's CRSP Approach.

Note: In this figure, the label of the vertices summarizes each of the four principles: (1) Culturally Responsiveness and Sustaining Practice (CRSP), the cornerstone of educational practices; (2) Adaptability, diverse educational ecosystems shaping learning and teaching methodologies; (3) Partnership, collaborating with in-country educators with a focus on community engagement; and (4) Student-centeredness, prioritizing student engagement, sense-making, and attentiveness to student thinking and culture.

with in-country educators characterized by collaboration and active community engagement. Lastly, Mathkind is committed to sense-making, student engagement, and teacher attentiveness to student thinking and culture, ensuring that its educational endeavors create an environment attuned to local communities' unique needs and contexts. Through these four main principles, Mathkind's CRSP approach aims to create a comprehensive and inclusive educational framework responsive to the diversity of global and local educational landscapes. In the following section, we will illustrate examples of this framework being implemented in four countries and multiple initiatives.

Examples of Mathkind's Global CRSP Work

Methodological Actions

To report on the implementation examples of Mathkind's CRSP work, we draw from several data sources. These include textual data such as organizational policy documents, websites, annual reports, and teacher case studies collected at various moments over Mathkind's past decade. To discover themes from those data sources, we employed a methodological procedure for interpreting meaning from the content of textual data as described by qualitative methodologists such as Lune and Berg (2021) and Hsieh and Shannon (2005). According to Hsieh and Shannon (2005), contemporary content analysis applications reveal three distinct approaches: conventional, directed, and summative. We implemented conventional content analysis, allowing us to code categories and themes derived directly from our data. That approach aims to describe a specific phenomenon when an existing theory or research literature is limited. With conventional content analysis, researchers avoid using preconceived categories; instead, they inductively develop keywords, codes, categories, themes, and their names from the data by becoming immersed in the data and unbiasedly allowing insights to emerge.

For the presentation of this chapter, our phenomenon of interest is the reflection of CRSP in the work of Mathkind through its international interactions with mathematics educators and practitioners in Guatemala, Ecuador, Nepal, and Zimbabwe. What we describe in the following four subsections results from applying the procedures of conventional content analysis (Hsieh and Shannon, 2005).

Examples of Mathkind's International Educational Projects

Guatemala and Ecuador

In Guatemala and Ecuador, Mathkind is working with partners to transform mathematics education through a fusion of innovation, cultural sensitivity, and pedagogical excellence.

Mathkind's journey began with teacher service trips and evolved into extensive conferences, workshops, and training projects that have reshaped the educational dialogue and practices across the country. The organization's partnership and mutual learning laid the foundation for a sustainable educational transformation model, emphasizing local educators' development as agents of change.

Mathkind's partnerships in both countries have presented unique challenges and opportunities. Nevertheless, its adaptable and responsive approach has consistently fostered educational environments where, at the forefront are critical thinking, problem-solving, and cultural relevance.

Mathkind in Guatemala: Building Educational Expertise

In Guatemala, Mathkind's involvement illustrates the organization's commitment to building educational expertise through an evolving, responsive approach. Starting with teacher service trips that facilitated an exchange of cultural and mathematical content knowledge and pedagogical strategies, Mathkind's CRSP approach laid the groundwork for a deeper, more sustained engagement in the country's educational landscape. Those initial forays were crucial for learning to establish mutual respect and understanding so that, instead of displaying unilateral expertise, mathematics educators in the country in which Mathkind worked along with Mathkind's US-based mathematics educators set a collaborative tone of mutual learning.

As Mathkind's experience interacting with Guatemalans grew, so did its understanding of Guatemala's educational needs and cultural dynamics. Recognizing that annual workshops and US-teacher trips were insufficient to instigate more beneficial change in Guatemalan mathematics education, Mathkind shifted its focus to more scalable and sustainable initiatives, such as hiring Guatemalan education leaders to form partnerships with their teachers and administrators and Guatemalan teacher trainers to develop professional development programs for teachers. These actions led to the convening of annual mathematics education conferences, designed not just as events to disseminate specialized content knowledge but also to build peer relationships and provide platforms for experiential learning and professional enhancement for Guatemalan teachers by Guatemalan mathematics education leaders. The conferences rapidly grew in popularity and scale, reflecting the desire of Guatemalan teachers and mathematics educators to examine and share innovative teaching methods. Moving from a modest attendance of twenty-three teachers in the inaugural year to hosting 147 self-selected participants in 2023. The growth in attendance is an indication that teachers felt the need for such professional interactions and learning. Many teachers would take time off from second jobs to participate. The conferences have become a cornerstone of Mathkind's collaborative engagement in Guatemala.

An outgrowth of these conferences, which are now entirely Guatemalan led, is a clear articulation of Mathkind's evolved framework: Learn–Apply–Lead. This three-part approach guides all Mathkind's professional development initiatives for mathematics educators. The framework describes a transformative journey in which educators acquire new methodologies, apply them in their local contexts, and eventually assume leadership roles by training others. It establishes a continuous cycle of learning and professional development, building collaborative peer networks within countries. Mathkind's CRSP approach is weaved in all the stages of this framework and ensures that the new methodologies are not only effective but also culturally responsive and sustaining. This approach values and leverages the unique cultural assets of Guatemalan educators while they lead and innovate within their own contexts.

Our analysis of various case studies involving Guatemalan teachers who engaged in Mathkind's activities, shaped by the organization's evolving and dynamic CRSP model, reveals a notable trend of local teachers advancing through the Learn–Apply–Lead framework. As expressed by one Guatemalan teacher, "Mathkind helped me evolve from a traditional mathematics teacher to my current role [math coach], which involves not only guiding teachers in my school but also participating in virtual training workshops, extending the impact beyond local boundaries" (translated from Spanish to English).

Mathkind in Ecuador: Cultivating a Community of Educators

Mathkind's initial foray into Ecuador involved partnerships with larger, established organizations, laying the foundation for a broad and impactful reach. Building on its work in Guatemala, Mathkind began by focusing on collaborating with local mathematics educators. This focus necessitated the navigation of diverse settings, seeking a nuanced understanding of each one's unique educational needs. A notable aspect of Mathkind's endeavors in Ecuador is the desire of local educators to gain knowledge about research-based teaching methods. The growth in attendance of virtual conferences vividly captured this spirit. Offered in 2020 as a one-day event akin to the conferences in Guatemala but held online due to pandemic restrictions, the "Math Marathon" grew exponentially in scope and reach. The first iteration saw forty-six teachers engaged in a day of learning and collaboration. By 2021, participation soared to over 1300 participants. The conference's growth demonstrated the thirst for professional learning opportunities among Ecuadorian mathematics educators and underscored the success of Mathkind's approach in cultivating an educational community. This is exemplified by an Ecuadorian teacher's reflection: "My professional goal each school year is to help students learn through games, and I truly feel that this approach has been effective. This [Mathkind] workshop was very productive, as new ideas emerged, and when applied in class, the students were very enthusiastic' (translated from Spanish to English)."

Furthermore, in Ecuador, Mathkind's CRSP has been diverse, spanning from the bustling streets of the country's capital, Quito, to remote Afro-Ecuadorian communities along the Onzole River. Moreover, Mathkind engaged with the Galapagos Conservancy and the Ecuadorian Ministry of Education to provide a multi-year series of culturally relevant professional learning workshops for Ecuadorian mathematics teachers built around the environmental challenges of the Galapagos archipelagos.

Key Insights from the Implementation of Mathkind's CRSP Framework

The progression of Mathkind's initiatives in Guatemala and Ecuador illustrates how its flexibility and responsiveness have led to its CRSP framework over time. The examples presented in the preceding sections prove its positive educational potential and influence in two crucial dimensions: the professionalization of teaching through local expertise and the acknowledgment of linguistic diversity.

By supporting teachers in becoming creators of meaningful learning experiences, Mathkind has contributed to a fundamental shift in the perception and delivery of mathematics education. At the core of this professionalization process is identifying and cultivating local talent. In Guatemala and Ecuador, Mathkind has identified and nurtured educators with the potential to emerge as leaders in their educational communities. Through training programs, learning labs, and collaborative platforms, these educators have polished or gained evidence-backed pedagogical skills and the confidence to innovate and tailor their practices to distinct cultural and educational contexts. This journey has enabled them to assume control of the learning process, crafting an educational experience that is both globally informed and locally relevant.

In the pursuit of establishing an inclusive and equitable learning environment, Mathkind's CRSP honors linguistic diversity. Mathkind staff collaborated with country-based partners to assemble a team of translators and interpreters to ensure participants could access oral presentations and written materials in their native or second language, Spanish. This perspective on linguistic identity parallels the evolving country-based educational leadership. Initially, resources and professional development were mainly available in English, provided by Mathkind's US team with the assistance of interpreters and translators. Recently, however, professional coaching and conferences have been conducted entirely in Spanish by country-based educational leaders, reflecting a significant linguistic and leadership transition.

Mathkind's CRSP enriched the educational experience and outcomes for all participants and cultivated a transformative atmosphere that acknowledged cultural and linguistic diversity. Mathkind's approach aligns with global educational trends that underscore teacher agency, continuous professional learning, and sensitivity to cultural context and language (Asia Society, 2021).

The following examples explore how Mathkind implements and adjusts its CRSP framework in other international settings. We provide insights into initiatives undertaken in Nepal and Zimbabwe at different development stages.

Mathkind's Engagement in Nepal: Enhancing a Robust Educational Framework

Underscoring the importance of contextual adaptation, Mathkind has tailored its engagement in Nepal to the country's established mathematics education infrastructure.

Unlike the grassroots initiatives in Guatemala and Ecuador, Mathkind's entry into Nepal leveraged an existing, comprehensive network of mathematics education professionals.

Nepal's mathematics education system, overseen by its Council for Mathematics Education (CME), is distinguished by a well-established array of teacher training and professional development programs. The CME, influential in shaping the nation's mathematical curriculum and pedagogy, extends its influence through journal publications, university collaborations, and involvement with the nationwide Ministry of Education. Mathkind's role, therefore, was to strengthen this pre-existing structure through collaboration.

As Nepalese mathematics educators affirm, enhancing foundational mathematics skills during the early grades is pivotal in improving math achievement in Nepal's higher levels of basic education and beyond. However, Nepalese scholars also observe the persistence of traditional instructional methods, including mathematics teaching, which predominantly rely on rote memorization with insufficient emphasis on conceptual understanding (Mainali and Belbase, 2023). Recognizing this challenge, Mathkind directed its efforts in Nepal toward elucidating effective mathematics teaching and learning practices.

Mathkind's collaboration with the CME in Nepal facilitated a significant exchange of pedagogical expertise during their 2023 visit. This partnership culminated in a special journal issue, with contributions from the Mathkind team and Nepalese mathematics educators, focusing on strategies that promote conceptual understanding in mathematics and build on local context. This joint effort reflects a promising synergy that leveraged the CME's established infrastructure to advance further mathematics education in Nepal (AIEM, 2023).

Mathkind in Zimbabwe: Virtual Transformations and Community Empowerment

Mathkind's initiatives in Zimbabwe echo its early ventures in Guatemala, operating without the benefit of established local educational infrastructure. It revolved around online, virtual engagements necessitated by logistical constraints and the worldwide COVID-19 pandemic. Though challenging, the virtual format presented unique opportunities for innovation and adaptability of the Mathkind CRSP framework. The focus was on a small, dedicated group of mathematics educators introduced to a range of student-centered and inquiry-based teaching strategies, fundamentally different from the traditional teacher-focused approaches prevalent in Zimbabwean schools.

The adaptive nature of the engagement was vital. Each session was a collaborative exploration of materials and instructional techniques, with continual feedback from the country-based educators. This dialogical process allowed Mathkind to tailor its approach, ensuring that the pedagogical strategies discussed were applicable in the Zimbabwean context. Those virtual sessions marked the first step in the Learn–Apply–Lead framework. The Apply phase occurred in school-based STEM clubs, where Zimbabwean educators adapted and implemented student-centered strategies. As the educators experimented with new methods, virtual coaching with Mathkind staff provided ongoing support.

This flexible approach underscores Mathkind's dedication to creating effective and sustainable educational change. In Zimbabwe, the ability to engage virtually and learn alongside local mathematics educators showcases Mathkind's capacity to overcome barriers. Our analysis of teacher case studies is helping us understand the multidirectional influences between teachers' participation across the professional development and classroom settings (Kazemi and Hubbard, 2008).

Global Math Stories: Transcending Borders through Mirrors and Windows

Mathkind integrates its dedication to CRSP through Global Math Stories (GMS), a central component of its framework. GMS employs storytelling as a primary tool, immersing students in diverse cultural and mathematical scenarios to bridge the gap between abstract mathematical concepts and real-life applications, rendering math more tangible and relatable. This aligns with research indicating that incorporating stories in mathematics education benefits students in various ways, such as making mathematical connections, learning concepts and language, alleviating anxiety, improving problem-solving skills, increasing achievement, and correcting misconceptions (Durmaz and Miçooğulları, 2021). Additionally, integrating stories and mathematics can foster positive attitudes toward mathematics, enhance engagement and motivation, and create a more inclusive classroom environment by showcasing diverse cultures globally (Goral and Gnadinger, 2006).

From Amazonian biodiversity to Ohio festivals, GMS allows students to explore mathematics within varied cultural contexts and instills an appreciation for diverse cultures. In line with Sims Bishop's work (2011), GMS functions as a mirror, reflecting students' experiences and identities, and as a window, offering views into different parts of the world, enriching students' comprehension of their place in a globally interconnected world. This aligns with Mathkind's commitment to global education with local cultural relevance, as discussed in the theoretical framework section.

GMS is available in both English and Spanish, and plans exist for further AI language translation. This aligns with the explicit goals of CRSP to promote multilingual and multicultural education. This enhanced accessibility and inclusivity aligns with the discussion of how Mathkind's framework acknowledges and respects language diversity.

While formal research studies on the effectiveness of GMS are still pending, preliminary evidence and teacher feedback suggest a positive impact on students' understanding of mathematics. GMS facilitates authentic problem-solving experiences, enhancing both student engagement and comprehension. Teachers appreciate key features within GMS, including a focus on pedagogical strategies and supporting the implementation of student-centered lessons emphasizing critical thinking and active learning. Additionally, teachers find GMS beneficial for incorporating interdisciplinary connections into math lessons (Haydar et al., 2023), highlighting the versatility of mathematics as a subject that intersects with various disciplines. Furthermore, GMS has proven effective in fostering deep engagement among students, allowing them to actively participate in constructing mathematical concepts. This transformative approach shifts the classroom dynamic from passive learning to active exploration, echoing Singh's (2020) assertion that highlighting stories similar to those of the students helps them develop their mathematical identities and connections to mathematics and each other.

Concluding Thoughts

In this chapter, we examined how Mathkind's emphasis on CRSP parallels the foundational work of scholars such as Gloria Ladson-Billings (1995), who advocate for pedagogical approaches acknowledging diverse cultural perspectives within educational practices. Furthermore, prioritizing adaptive methodologies within diverse educational ecosystems aligns with broader CRSP literature recognizing the dynamic nature of learning environments. Scholars like Rios-Aguilar et al. (2011) underscore the importance of flexible teaching strategies to meet the diverse needs of learners in various educational contexts. Mathkind's focus on co-creating empowering conditions with local educators and communities resonates with CRSP literature's emphasis on community involvement. Researchers such as Paris and Alim (2014) argue for the significance of community collaboration in education, emphasizing that meaningful partnerships contribute to the success of CRSP. Additionally, Mathkind's commitment to balancing global mathematics education standards with local relevance aligns with CRSP principles, emphasizing the need to contextualize education while acknowledging the complementary relationship between CRSP and international education.

Upon comprehensive analysis of Mathkind's initiatives across diverse countries, recurring themes manifest at varying stages and depths contingent upon our partnership's distinctive local context and duration. A central theme revolves around cultivating beliefs and experiences associated with teaching mathematics. This process unfolds uniquely based on the specific characteristics of each locale and the duration of Mathkind's collaborative efforts. Furthermore, a fundamental aspect of these endeavors centers on fostering a paradigm shift in views and practices within mathematics education. Mathkind's goal is to guide this transformation toward innovative and student-centered pedagogies, recognizing that the pace and depth of this shift are intricately tied to the particularities of the local context and the duration of engagement. Additionally, Mathkind's work consistently places a spotlight on collaborative partnerships and the cultivation of leadership within mathematics education. This theme becomes particularly pronounced in the increasing leadership roles assumed by country-based staff and partners, and its impact varies across different stages and durations of partnerships.

In conclusion, Mathkind's collaboration with country-based educators, notably in diverse international contexts, illustrates an ongoing reciprocal learning model grounded in CRSP. Initially, Mathkind's team, comprised of mathematics education thought leaders and experienced educators, shared their expertise with an emphasis on receptiveness and co-construction, listening to and learning from country-based educators to comprehend unique cultural nuances and educational needs (Ladson-Billings, 1995; Paris, 2012). The role of country-based educators has evolved into leadership, marking a crucial shift toward sustainable educational development. This phase has involved innovation in CRSP strategies. In a transformative reversal, the role of Mathkind experts has transitioned from mentors to learners, gaining insights from country-based educators and contributing significantly to the global discourse on CRSP. This cyclical knowledge exchange underscores Mathkind's CRSP transformative potential and reality.

Questions to Consider

1 How can educational programs and policies be designed and implemented in a way that respects local contexts and avoids the pitfalls of uncritically transplanting practices from more privileged regions, such as the North? What strategies can be employed to ensure that these programs support authentic local needs and perspectives without adopting a parasitic or paternalistic approach?

2 How can educators better support teachers in effectively translating culturally relevant theories into their mathematics instruction (or other content areas), and what are the key challenges and strategies involved in making content-specific education more inclusive and responsive to diverse cultural contexts?

3 How can mathematics education curricula effectively integrate global competencies while maintaining the depth and rigor of mathematical content? What are the potential benefits and challenges of embedding these global competencies within mathematics frameworks, and how can educators balance the need for both local relevance and global perspective in their teaching practices?

Note

1 Since the late twentieth century, instead of using labels that suggest value judgments or hierarchies such as "First World," "Third World," and "developed and developing" countries, social scientists have used the terms Global North and Global South to categorize Earth's countries along socioeconomic and political lines. On the one hand, the Global South broadly comprises countries in Africa, Latin America and the Caribbean, Asia (excluding Israel, Japan, and South Korea), and Oceania (excluding Australia and New Zealand). On the other hand, the Global North consists of countries in Northern America and Europe, as well as Israel, Japan, South Korea, Australia, and New Zealand (https://en.wikipedia.org/wiki/Global_North_and_Global_South). Nevertheless, the terms are contested; Mignolo (2011) explains that from the perspective of capitalism and the expansion of Western, the "Global South" is the location to be developed economically and liberated from non-democratic regimes. From the perspective of the emerging political society, the "Global South" is where liberation from Western democratic to justify economic takeover and cultural management (p. 165).

References

AIEM. (2023). Mathematics Education Forum, *23*(41), Special Issue. https://doi.org/10.35763/aiem23.

Asia Society, Center for Global Education. (2021). *Five Reasons Why Global Competence Matters.* https://asiasociety.org/education/five-reasons-why-global-competence-matters (accessed October 26, 2025)

Banks, J. A. (2015). Multicultural education, school reform, and educational equality. In The Equity Project (Ed.), *Opening the Doors to Opportunity for All: Setting a Research Agenda for the Future,* pp. 54–63. American Institutes for Research.

Bartell, T., Yeh, C., Felton-Koestler, M. D., and Berry, R. Q. I. (2022). *Upper Elementary Mathematics Lessons to Explore, Understand, and Respond to Social Injustice.* Corwin Press.

Berry, R. Q. I., Conway, B. M. I., Lawler, B. R., and Staley, J. W. (2020). *High School Mathematics Lessons to Explore, Understand, and Respond to Social Injustice.* Corwin Press.

Bishop, A. (2002). Mathematical acculturation, cultural conflicts, and transition. In G. Abreu, A. Bishop, and N. Presmeg (Eds.), *Transitions Between Contexts of Mathematical Practices,* pp. 193–212. Kluwer.

Boutte, G., Kelly-Jackson, C., and Johnson, G. L. (2010). Culturally relevant teaching in science classrooms: Addressing academic achievement, cultural competence, and critical consciousness. *International Journal of Multicultural Education, 12*(2), 1–20.

Brown, B. A., Boda, P., Lemmi, C., and Monroe, X. (2019). Moving culturally relevant pedagogy from theory to practice: Exploring teachers' application of culturally relevant education in science and mathematics. *Urban Education, 54*(6), 775–803.

Childs, K. J., and Staley J. W. (2025). *Teaching Mathematics for Social Justice: A Guide for Moving from Mindset to Action.* Corwin Press.

Durmaz, B., and Miçoogullari, S. (2021). The effect of the integrated mathematics lessons with children's literature on the fifth grade students' place value understanding. *Acta Didactica Napocensia, 14*(2), 244–56. https://doi.org/10.24193/adn.14.2.18.

Ellis, M. W., and Berry, R. Q., III. (2005). The paradigm shift in mathematics education: Explanations and implications of reforming conceptions of teaching and learning. *The Mathematics Educator, 15*(1), 7–17.

Gay, G. (2002). Preparing for culturally responsive teaching. *Journal of Teacher Education, 53,* 106–16.

Global North and Global South. (2024, January 7). In *Wikipedia.* https://en.wikipedia.org/wiki/Global_North_and_Global_South (accessed October 26, 2025).

González-Salamanca, J. C., Agudelo, O. L., and Salinas, J. (2020). Key competences, education for sustainable development and strategies for the development of 21st century skills: A systematic literature review. *Sustainability, 12*(24), 10366. https://doi.org/10.3390/su122410366.

Goral, M., and Gnadinger, C. M. (2006). Using storytelling to teach mathematics concepts. *Australian Primary Mathematics Classroom, 11,* 4–8.

Haydar, H. N., Kaya, M., and Weaver, J. C. (2023). Promoting interdisciplinary connections and mathematics collaborations through literacy-centered lesson study. In S. Dotger, G. Matney, K. Chandler-Olcott, J. Heckathorn, and M. Fox (Eds.), *Lesson Study with Mathematics and Science Preservice Teachers Finding the Form,* pp. 170–81. Routledge. https://doi.org/10.4324/9781003326434-20

Hsieh, H.-F., and Shannon, S. F. (2005). Three approaches to qualitative content analysis. *Qualitative Health Research, 15*(9), 1277–88. https://doi.org/10.1177/1049732305276687.

Kazemi, E., and Hubbard, A. (2008). New directions for the design and study of professional development: Attending to the co-evolution of teachers' participation across contexts. *Journal of Teacher Education*, 59, 428–41.

Kolovou, M. (2022). Embracing culturally relevant education in mathematics and science: A literature review. *The Urban Review*, 55(1), 133–72. https://doi.org/10.1007/s11256-022-00643-4.

Ladson-Billings, G. (1995). Toward a theory of culturally relevant pedagogy. *American Educational Research Journal*, 32(3), 465–91. https://doi.org/10.2307/1163320.

Ladson-Billings, G. (2021). Three decades of culturally relevant, responsive, & sustaining pedagogy: What lies ahead? *Educational Forum*, 85(4), 351–4. https://doi.org/10.1080/0013172 5.2021.1957632.

Lee, Jenny J. (Ed.). (2021). *U.S. Power in International Higher Education*. Rutgers University Press.

Leonard, J. (2008). *Culturally Specific Pedagogy in the Mathematics Classroom: Strategies for Teachers and Students*. Routledge.

Lune, H., and Berg, B. L. (2021). An introduction to content analysis. In *Qualitative Research Methods for the Social Sciences* (9th edn.), pp. 349–85. Pearson.

Mainali, B. R., and Belbase, S. (2023). Job satisfaction, professional growth, and mathematics teachers' impressions about school environment. *Education Policy Analysis Archives*, 31(22), 1–24. https://doi.org/10.14507/epaa.31.7424.

Mansilla, V. B., and Jackson, A. W. (2011). *Educating for Global Competence: Preparing Our Youth to Engage the World*. Council of Chief State School Officers.

Martin, D. B. (2009). Researching race in mathematics education. *The Teachers College Record*, 111(2), 295–338.

Matthews, L. E., Jones, S. M., and Parker, Y. A. (2022). *Engaging in Culturally Relevant Math Tasks, 6–12: Fostering Hope in the Middle and High School Classroom*. Corwin Press.

Mignolo, W. D. (2011). The global south and world dis/order. *Journal of Anthropological Research*, 67(2), 165–88. http://www.jstor.org/stable/41303282.

Ministry of Education. (2020). *Mathematics: Teaching and Learning Syllabus Primary*. Curriculum Planning and Development Division.

Nash, K. (2010). *Contemporary Political Sociology Globalization, Politics, and Power*. Wiley.

Neri, R. C., Lozano, M., and Gomez, L. M. (2019). (Re)framing resistance to culturally relevant education as a multilevel learning problem. *Review of Research in Education*, 43(1), 197–226. https://doi.org/10.3102/0091732X18821120.

Newton, C., and Early, F. (2015). *Doing Good … Says Who? Stories from Volunteers, Nonprofits, Donors, and Those They Want to Help*. Two Harbors Press.

OECD. (2018). Preparing our youth for an inclusive and sustainable world. *The OECD PISA Global Competence Framework*. OECD.

Paris, D. (2012). Culturally sustaining pedagogy: A needed change in stance, terminology, and practice. *Educational Researcher*, 41(3), 93–7.

Paris, D., and Alim, H. S. (2014). What are we seeking to sustain through culturally sustaining pedagogy? A loving critique forward. *Harvard Educational Review*, 84(1), 85–100.

Powell, A. B., and Frankenstein, M. (Eds.). (1997). *Ethnomathematics: Challenging Eurocentrism in Mathematics Education*. State University of New York Press.

Rios-Aguilar, C., Kiyama, J. M., Gravitt, M., and Moll, L. (2011). Funds of knowledge for the poor and forms of capital for the rich? A capital approach to examining funds of knowledge. *Theory and Research in Education*, 9, 163–84. https://doi:10.1177/14778785114097761.

Sims Bishop, R. (2011). Windows, mirrors, and sliding glass doors. *Perspectives: Choosing and Using Books for the Classroom*, 6(3), ix–xi.

Singh, P. (2020). Mathematics and social justice: How stories can help us understand our roots and our connections. *Mathematics Teacher: Learning and Teaching PK-12, 113*(1), 16–22.

Taylor, S., and Henry, M. (2000). Globalisation and educational policymaking: A case study. *Educational Theory, 50*(4), 487–503.

Tichnor-Wagner, A., Parkhouse, H., Glazier, J., and Cain, J. M. (2019). *Becoming a Globally Competent Teacher*. ASCD.

UNESCO. (2015). *Global Citizenship Education: Topics and Learning Objectives*. UNESCO.

U.S. Department of Education. (2022). *Succeeding Globally Through International Education and Engagement.*

4

Conflict and Peacebuilding in Northern Ireland and the United States: A Comparative Educational Study

Thomas M. Falk, Colleen Gallagher, and

Lindsay A. Gold

Abstract

In this chapter, the authors reflect on a study abroad experience for which they were faculty leaders. Three teacher-educator faculty members spent four weeks in Northern Ireland with twenty-five undergraduate pre-service teachers. Through coursework and experiential learning opportunities, students and faculty immersed themselves in a society still recovering from the effects of twentieth-century sectarian unrest that left a legacy of trauma but also an example of peacebuilding and transformative healing. This chapter summarizes key events during the conflict in Northern Ireland, draws comparison with intensifying conflict in the United States, synthesizes prominent themes from the summer abroad curriculum, and concludes with possibilities for applying lessons on peacebuilding, with attention to the social and emotional dimensions of education, from Northern Ireland to the United States.

Key Terms: *Teacher education, study abroad, conflict, race, peacebuilding, Northern Ireland, United States*

Introduction

In the summer of 2023, the authors led a study abroad program for university students in Belfast, Northern Ireland. Prior to departure, we designed a curriculum comparing issues of segregation, diversity, and conflict in the schools and societies of Northern Ireland (NI) and the United States (US). In Belfast, the capital of NI, we found educational institutions enlisted to promote peace. Based upon their experiences, our students—all pre-service teachers at a private, Catholic and Marianist university—learned to see dynamics of segregation, diversity, and conflict with fresh eyes. In particular, the people of Belfast taught us that attention to the social and emotional dimensions of education is paramount in efforts to foster peace, justice, and equality in an erstwhile divided society.

Below, we review the background context of NI. Next, we describe the curriculum and pedagogy of our study abroad program. Subsequently, we illustrate curricula and pedagogies that Belfast educational institutions employ to manage conflict and promote peace. Within these curricula and pedagogies, the ethics of diversity and *empathetic engagement*, characterized by Halpern (2001: 130) as "an affective experience of connecting—wanting to relate to another person as another self, as a center of meaning and initiative," feature prominently. For ourselves and our students, first-hand exposure to Belfast society and the people working for peace revealed significant problems in American schools and society, along with potential solutions. Conspicuously, several of our hosts highlighted ways in which the British Empire wielded religious and ethno-nationalist identity—coded as race—as tools to divide and conquer the people of NI. They also articulated the indispensability of diverse perspectives and attention to the affective dimensions of conflict in countering these efforts. As American society has become increasingly polarized—in significant part along racial lines—we submit that the ethics of peacebuilding and empathetic engagement across differences deserve to feature more prominently in American education. Teacher candidates who participated in this program reflected that, by incorporating diverse perspectives and attending to the affective dimensions of conflict, their classrooms may serve as spaces in which to foster empathy and peace.

Background

First conquered by the Normans in 1169, Ireland has been shaped by centuries of British imperialism (Bardon, 2011). Since this time, writes Jane Ohlmeyer (2020), Ireland has "served as a laboratory both for imperial rule and for resistance to that rule." During the seventeenth century, the monarchy imported Scottish planters to dispossess, indenture, and enslave native inhabitants of the north of Ireland. Some Irish folk, as Ohlmeyer recounts, were enticed by "the king's shilling" to perpetrate similar crimes in India, Pakistan, and other conquered lands. Following an early-twentieth-century home rule movement and civil war, the island became partitioned into a Catholic-dominated Irish Republic and a Protestant-dominated territory of the United Kingdom (UK) (Lynch, 2019). In the North, a Protestant, Unionist, and Loyalist majority ruled over an Irish, Catholic, and Nationalist minority that lived as second-class citizens deprived of the ballot, housing, employment, and equal protection of law. Communities and schools remained segregated according to these ethno-nationalist divisions. In response to persistent violence in interface communities, municipalities erected more than sixty peace walls to separate neighborhoods. Some went so far as to construct subterranean barriers between Catholic and Protestant cemetery plots, exemplifying the adage, "As above, so below." For many generations, children of NI grew up surrounded only by those who shared their religious and ethno-nationalist identity.

During the 1960s, Irish Catholics inspired by the American Civil Rights Movement initiated their own Civil Rights Movement for access to housing, jobs, business ownership, and the ballot (Maney, 2012). However, many Protestant Loyalists, animated by their own grievances, perceived this as a threat. The British government and Ulster Volunteer Forces (UVF)—a Protestant-Unionist paramilitary organization—opposed the Irish Catholic Civil Rights Movement, which many Loyalist citizens viewed as a front for the Irish Republican Army (IRA), which the UK considered to be a terrorist organization. Over the next decade, NI conflagrated into what became known as *the Troubles*, a thirty-year period of conflict that killed at least 3,700 people, mostly civilians, from a total population of only 1.5 million (McKittrick et al., 1999). Brian McKee (personal communication, July 10, 2023), a teacher and peace activist who grew up at the epicenter of the deadliest years of *the Troubles*, attributes many deaths beyond this figure to the addiction, post-traumatic stress disorder, miscarriages, cancers, and other ailments that have resulted from the mass trauma of violent conflict. As late as 2010, ongoing segregation and ethno-nationalist violence earned Belfast the title of "race hate capital of Europe" (Knox, 2011: 387).

In 1998, aided by the international political and business class, parties to the conflict signed the Good Friday Agreement, which stated that "an essential aspect of the reconciliation process is the promotion of a culture of tolerance at every level of society, including initiatives to facilitate and encourage integrated education and mixed housing" (Borooah and Knox, 2015: 40). Rooted in the agreement, the British education ministry's *Shared Future* policy emphasized that "separate but equal is not an option. Parallel living and the provision of parallel services are unsustainable both morally and economically" (Borooah and Knox, 2015: 40). Despite adversity, Belfast has achieved notable success in quelling hostilities through educational efforts—including integrated schooling, shared education, and peacebuilding—to bring together children from across the divide.

Throughout our time in NI, we encountered individuals and institutions deeply committed to peacebuilding by working together on common projects across differences of identity and politics. Inspired by these examples, our students considered their application to teaching in the US. For example, one student reflected that "our experiences in Northern Ireland … serve as living examples of reconciliation, acceptance, and mutual respect. We can inspire our students to build bridges across differences and dismantle walls, physical and metaphorical, that divide" (personal communication, July 25, 2023).

Curriculum and Pedagogy

Our comparative study of education in NI and the US focused on issues of segregation, diversity, and conflict, with an eye toward peacebuilding. This theme emerged from several sources: (1) pre-departure research into issues of concern among professional educators and citizens in NI and the US; (2) speakers and experiential learning opportunities arranged by a non-profit education abroad company; and (3) the public curriculum of NI society. In terms of methodology, we assumed the role of students alongside our own students, attempting to learn from our hosts and surroundings. Our class meetings served as opportunities to share observations, draw connections to readings, and contemplate lessons relevant to teaching in American schools. The theme and thesis of this essay emerge out of these experiences and discussions. Based upon the perspectives and narratives of our hosts, as well as the public curriculum of NI, we draw connections to contemporary social and educational issues in the US.

Our curriculum offered experiences intended to heighten our teacher candidates' awareness of global issues relevant to the aims and ethics of their future profession. Formally, this included both experiential learning opportunities and coursework in philosophy of education, cultural and intellectual diversity, and language awareness. Along with our students, we spent time in youth centers that provide summer programs and activities for area youth. We listened to community members who lived through the conflict, fought as paramilitaries, and currently work as peace activists. In addition, we examined scholarly literature on educational efforts to help students see the conflict from multiple perspectives. Beyond this, we spoke with local and national politicians, professors, youth workers, tour guides, cab drivers, and pub goers who informed our perspective and influenced our feelings about the conflict. We also found ourselves immersed in public murals, museums, marches, and memorials that communicated the identities and historical narratives of Belfast residents.

Among the first observations that several students reported was the division of Belfast according to religious and ethno-nationalist identities. Seeing segregation expressed in this distinctive form appeared to heighten our students' awareness of the existence and effects of racial segregation in the US. In their final reflections, two students observed that:

> Separation of education [in NI] due to personal identity and religious background correlates with segregation between races in the United States. Both situations convey the message that one group is inferior to the other ... Even though many discriminatory policies of our past are no longer in place, our country still experiences its generational effects. As we have learned here in NI, segregation is not something you can always see. Segregation in education can reinforce social divisions, limit opportunities for children to interact with one another, and perpetuate stereotypes and prejudices between communities (personal communication, July 25, 2023).

Our students would go on to articulate ways in which they can apply these lessons in their future work as teachers.

The Irish Catholic community of NI credits the American Civil Rights Movement for inspiring its own Civil Rights Movement during the 1960s. Throughout NI, we encountered public imagery and iconography of figures such as Frederick Douglass, Sojourner Truth, Rosa Parks, Martin Luther King, Jr., Mohammad Ali, and Angela Davis. Phrases such as "Black Lives Matter" and "I Can't Breathe," in conjunction with images of Irish political prisoners and victims of police misconduct—namely a fourteen-year-old boy named Noah Donohoe—confronted us with regularity. These helped us forge connections between the unfamiliar and the familiar. Although more difficult to relate to, rarely far removed were the imagery and iconography of the Loyalist community, typically featuring Queen Elizabeth, King Charles, and Ulster Volunteers.

During our stay, veterans from both sides of *the Troubles,* who currently work in the fields of peace, reconciliation, and conflict resolution, instructed us to see the whole of NI society as a casualty of the empire. Liam Stone (personal communication, July 10, 2023), who fought with the IRA, and William Mitchell (personal communication, July 17, 2023), who fought with the UVF, argued that the British Empire, in its pursuit of wealth and power, maintained conditions intended to mire NI in sectarian warfare. Religion, language, and ethno-nationalist identity—which Belfasters code as race—served as lines of division and points of hostility that produced "acceptable levels of violence." While fighting amongst one another, the people of NI remained distracted from their common grievances against the British government.

For many in Belfast, the intergenerational trauma of violent conflict remains fresh. At a visceral, embodied level, folks carry this trauma and feel compelled to prevent it from conflagrating. Anne Marie McKee (personal communication, July 21, 2023), who came of age during the conflict, explained that warfare and military occupation robbed her of a genuine childhood. Born into a community in which silence and stoicism were survival adaptations, she struggled to form healthy emotional attachments with others, including her future spouse and children. Peace and reconciliation, in McKee's view, have granted rising generations authentic childhoods and emotional lives that many her age never enjoyed.

While visiting Action for Community Transformation, a Progressive Unionist museum and education center, we spoke with former UVF fighters who described finding community, purpose, and healing through dialogue with fellow combatants whom they had once sought to kill. Mitchell, who guided our tour, believes that everyone in NI, regardless of affiliation, has a story worth sharing. Through their narratives, folks can connect with one another in authentic ways and see that each has something valuable to contribute to the society they share. Veterans and survivors with whom we spoke described such conversations as integral to the work of healing from the traumas of war. Schools, youth clubs, and other educational institutions in Belfast utilize similar approaches to promote the social and emotional welfare of children and adolescents.

Prior to visiting seven different youth centers in Belfast that serve youths with after-school and summer activities, staff warned that we would encounter anger, hostility, and other antisocial behavior resulting from intergenerational trauma. Academically trained in developmental child psychology and trauma response, these professional youth workers explained that violence, alcoholism, poverty, unemployment, and other social ills reverberate from *the Troubles* to afflict individuals and communities. Relative to the US, we found that trauma-informed care and social and emotional competencies feature much more prominently in the preparation of NI educators. Before considering parallels and applications to the US, we explore below how NI's policies promoting integrated and shared education embed social and emotional dimensions of learning.

Integration, Shared Education, and Peacebuilding in Northern Ireland

Throughout our time in NI, our hosts conveyed the sense that peace is a delicate balance. Forms of structural violence—oppression and deprivation, segregation and inequity, etc.—easily give rise to direct violence. Peacebuilding aims to challenge each of these forms of violence (Brantmeier, 2011). Beginning in the 1980s, citizen peacebuilders established integrated schools, attended by students from both sides of the conflict, in efforts to short-circuit the internalization of prejudice that prevailed throughout the larger society. Officially, NI's *Cross-community Contact Scheme,* introduced in 1987, promoted recurrent inter-group activities among school communities, with the intention of breaking down myths and providing youths from different backgrounds opportunities to work together toward common goals. Subsequently, the *Education Reform Order* of 1989 established a common curriculum, including "education for mutual understanding and cultural heritage," which sought to teach students to respect others, recognize their social interdependence, and appreciate non-violent means of resolving conflict (Borooah and Knox, 2015: 22). Toward this end, the UK established a national, non-sectarian history curriculum in 1991 that elevated no single identitarian narrative and instead emphasized critical inquiry of multiple perspectives (Barton and McCully, 2010: 149).

Although most parents report supporting integration in theory, in practice, they prioritize education that aligns with their sectarian identity. Despite the noteworthy success of some integrated schools, 90 percent of NI students attend segregated schools. Many do not interact with members of the other ethno-nationalist community until university. As a result, stereotyping and prejudice persist (Hughes, 2011: 829). Undeterred, reformers developed an alternative policy known as *shared education*, in which students continue to attend separate Catholic and Protestant schools, but wherein these schools collaborate to offer professional development for teachers, networking opportunities for administrators, and shared classes and extracurricular activities for students (Borooah and Knox, 2015: 127–8). In this way, students receive instruction aligning with their sectarian identity, yet also develop relationships with children who are different from them.

According to Brian McKee (personal communication, July 10, 2023), shared education has proven to be a sustainable and culturally responsive means of promoting diversity and subduing sectarian hostility. While allowing schools to inculcate a particular religious and ethnic identity, shared education affords students chances to work with out-group peers on pressing issues—including drugs, alcohol, and social relationships—that transcend religion and ethno-nationalism. Shared education, observed a Belfast secondary school teacher, affords kids the chance to "lift the clouds of suspicion that may have existed. They now believe that it is okay to be different and that it is okay to be yourself. I am convinced that those involved in the programme will be more likely to challenge prejudice either in their homes or beyond" (Borooah and Knox, 2015: 130).

Studies comparing history education in NI and the US are instructive in this regard. US history textbooks notoriously propagate national myths and omit heterodox narratives (Loewen, 1995). Hence, many US students believe that their schooling aims to instill a common "story of us." Such is not the case for students in NI. "We cannot stress strongly enough how different the Northern Ireland curriculum is from that of most nations," write McCully and Barton (2019: 20–2):

> There is no attempt to present a single narrative of national development … the curriculum is grounded in inquiry, the interpretation of evidence, and consideration of multiple perspectives … At no point does the NI curriculum attempt to initiate students into a consensual narrative of national origins and development.

Any teacher doing otherwise, insist McCully and Barton, would be considered unprofessional.

However, Barton and McCully also find that most NI high school history curricula culminate in 1921. Students do not spend much time investigating the modern history of the conflict. Although teachers tend to play it safe by avoiding questions of how history bears upon the present, McCully and Barton find that many students appear genuinely interested in moving beyond the perspectives of their family and community, even though most ultimately remain committed to their sectarian identities and concomitant frameworks for making sense of the past. Nevertheless, some students attest that their studies of history have shattered and reconstituted their worldviews. Following a visit to Kilmainham Jail in Dublin, where the British executed Irish Nationalist leaders of the 1921 Easter Rising, one undergraduate teacher candidate from a Protestant and Loyalist community shared that:

> The visit to Kilmainham really challenged me. I have to admit I had some inbred feelings … I realized how much historical events like this get distorted as a result of the current political situation. My views of the Easter Rising were totally tainted by my opinions on the situation in Northern Ireland and, I guess, this was the lens I used to view the past. But Kilmainham really shattered that lens (as cited in McCully and Barton, 2019: 24).

This future teacher, believes McCully, will be in a stronger position to work with students from across the sectarian divide.

In perhaps their most intriguing discovery, some of Barton and McCully's respondents—who happened to attend integrated schools—reported aligning themselves with neither religious nor ethno-nationalist identities, but rather universal values such as peace, justice, and equality. In one case, high school students viewed history not through a lens of sectarianism, but rather a contest between rulers and those who have fought for social change, including Nelson Mandela and the leaders of the Easter Rising and Civil Rights Movements (Barton and McCully, 2012: 392–3). These students' perspectives appear compatible with NI's officially neutral and balanced approach to history instruction.

Parallel to conflicts over "the story of us" in US schools and society, Belfast teachers must sensitively navigate issues of identity and intergenerational trauma. Just as Americans have battled over the teaching and omission of racist elements of our national history, Belfasters have argued passionately over how to teach controversial aspects of their history. While Americans have fought over Confederate statues and iconography during recent years (Barakat, 2024), Belfasters have similarly clashed over statues and iconography featuring heroes and martyrs from both sides of the NI conflict (Borooah and Knox, 2015: 47).

At the heart of the politics of trauma, asserts Zembylas (2008), lie emotions. Key to navigating sectarian conflict, he argues, is attending to its emotional dimensions by listening to others' stories and building rapport. Similar to Zembylas, Halpern (1993) places *empathetic engagement* at the center of conflict resolution. Curiosity and emotional imagination, writes Halpern (2001: 130), are "grounded in an affective experience of connecting—wanting to relate to another person as another self, as a center of meaning and initiative … When one person actually listens to another person's story, emotional resonance and empathy often occur effortlessly." These sentiments resonate with those expressed by our teachers in Belfast. Storytelling, insisted Mitchell (personal communication, July 17, 2023), Stone (personal communication, July 10, 2023), McKee (personal communication, July 21, 2023), and Cross (personal communication, July 19, 2023), is an essential component of productive dialogue with "the Other." Some of our students connected these insights to their NI youth center experiences and future work as teachers. For example, one student reflected that, "I think my biggest takeaway is that we are all more similar than we think. While we all have our differences and separate identities, we all have some common ground" (personal communication, July 25, 2023).

According to Barbara McDade (personal communication, July 21, 2023), a professor of Education and Religious Studies at Stranmillis University College, controversial subject matter can and should be addressed in shared classrooms after students and teachers have built rapport. Once students have changed the channel from tribal and political consciousness to a frequency of empathy and mutual respect, they can begin to dialogue through their biases and prejudices. The primary job of the teacher in such conversations is to set rules, enforce boundaries, and foster a climate of trust in which students can see and hear one another. "I have found," remarked a veteran teacher from Belfast, "if you treat pupils like normal human beings rather than label them as being from different religious backgrounds, you can establish trust. Only then, and it can take a while to build trust, can you begin to tackle the controversial issues" (Borooah and Knox, 2015: 133). Acknowledging that social and political conflict will inevitably impact them as teachers, our students responded powerfully to this lesson. "Because we all come from different backgrounds, we need to be able to push our biases to the side in order to hear others' stories," reflected one of our students:

> We are taught that we should be sensitive to the struggles of our students, but this experience made me realize the wide variety of situations young people could be dealing with. We can never really know what a student is going through. Everyone comes from some kind of conflict, so it is important as a teacher to take that into consideration when getting to know my students … Every student should feel safe, cared for, and heard. They need to feel that the classroom is an open and safe place to share their feelings (personal communication, July 25, 2023).

The contemporary climate of fear and distrust surrounding controversial school subject matter in the US proves this student's insight essential.

Race, Conflict, and Collective Trauma in the United States

In both NI and the US, race has served as a fault line of division and conflict. Whereas race assumes ethno-nationalist dimensions in NI, it derives from the ideology of white supremacy in the US (Roediger, 2007). For more than 400 years, racial segregation in the US has allowed myths and prejudices about "the Other" to thrive. "Following Reconstruction," writes Rana, "white Southern politicians aimed to eliminate spaces where white and Black people could congregate and develop a sense of both community and solidarity. If poor white people had less contact with their Black neighbors, they would be far more likely to defer to white elites" (Rana, 2022, para. 3).

Understandings of the past inform attitudes about contemporary social issues. Regrettably, many US teachers may be unprepared to productively engage students with controversial history. As of 2011, the majority of US high school history teachers did not major in the subject. Of those who did, half had no coursework centered on the Civil Rights Movement (Southern Poverty Law Center, 2017: 9). In recent years, at least twenty-three state legislatures have introduced bills to censor Black History and restrict student access to ideas that explore, and information that challenges, hegemonies of race and class (FutureEd, 2024). Teachers have lost jobs and experienced revocation of teaching licenses for broaching these topics (Mystal, 2021). "What we are witnessing in Florida," contends LeRoy Pernell, a law professor at Florida A&M, "is an intellectual reign of terror. There is a tremendous sense of dread right now, not just among faculty; it's tangible among students and staff as well. People are intellectually and physically scared" (Stanley, 2024: 19). Jason Stanley (2024: 19), a professor of philosophy, warns that this undermines a core civic function of public education:

> Democracy is a system where we let ourselves be affected by our fellow citizens' perspectives. Cutting students off from exposure to the perspectives of their neighbors therefore preempts democracy. Such erasures are more conducive to an education for authoritarianism, where an autocratic leader can more easily set groups against one another, relying on mutual estrangement and mutual misunderstanding.

Amidst lingering segregation, attitudes about race remain inextricably implicated in contemporary cultural and political conflict. While the language and logic of antiracism—Black Lives Matter—has become prominent in American public discourse, a reactionary language and logic of *anti-antiracism* has risen to meet it. Coined by Wetts and Willer (2022), anti-antiracism refers to beliefs and attitudes hostile toward antiracism, including denial and revanchism. In their study of racial schemas related to political parties, Zhirkov and Valentino (2022) conclude that political parties "are increasingly seen as distinct racial and ethnic camps rather than institutions for delivering unique policy bundles, and this has major implications for understanding current political processes in the United States." We have become tribalized, observe Jilani and Smith (2019), "into groups that compete against each other in a zero-sum game where negotiation and compromise are perceived as betrayal." As of 2024, nearly a quarter of surveyed Americans agreed that political violence may be necessary to save the country (Lerer, 2024). Intensifying polarization and resort to violence, argues Cox (2023), can be understood as a collective trauma response.

In his account of the 1977 Buffalo Creek flood that killed 125 people and destroyed a mining town in Logan, West Virginia, Kai Erikson described *collective trauma* as "a blow to the basic tissues of social life that damages the bonds attaching people together and impairs the prevailing sense of communality" (Cox, 2023: 16). Despite tremendous social progress over recent generations, the traumatic shocks of the twenty-first century—including mass shootings, January 6, the opioid epidemic, and a global pandemic—have catalyzed violent and antisocial behavior throughout the nation (Cox, 2023). A primary lesson that we took from NI is that individuals, institutions, and societies can retard these behaviors through peacebuilding.

Conclusion

Studying the nexus of conflict and peacebuilding between NI and the US can meaningfully inform a global pedagogical framework for the twenty-first century. As teacher educators at a Catholic and Marianist institution, we seek to raise teacher candidates' awareness of structural violence in schools and the larger society—poverty, patriarchy, racism, segregation, accountability regimes, and the oppressive knowledge paradigms that these spawn—together with possibilities for transformative action toward peace, justice, and equality. This pedagogical framework also coheres with global values expressed in the United Nations Sustainable Development Goals (UN, n.d.), namely the goals of quality education, well-being, peace, justice, and strong institutions. In NI, we observed that these goals require people to change their frequency from territorial confrontation to mutual recognition, whereby they can see one another not as Red or Blue, Liberal or Conservative, Irish or British, Catholic or Protestant, but as fellow human beings who experience fear, anger, pain, and are possessed of will, conscience, and meaningful work to do in the world.

Schools throughout the US have laid important groundwork toward peace, justice, and equality with attention to the social and emotional dimensions of education. Like our hosts in Belfast, the US-based Center for Reaching and Teaching the Whole Child (CRTWC, 2022) supports teachers' skills in forming positive relationships across differences, building community, and fostering self-reflection. Additionally, the Collaborative for Academic, Social, and Emotional Learning (CASEL, n.d.) advocates for student identity development through self-awareness, self-management, social awareness, relationship skills, and responsible decision-making within an equitable context. Teachers must first build these capacities in themselves in order to foster them in students.

Study abroad programs may contribute to teachers becoming global citizens by engendering humility, self-knowledge, empathy, and cultural awareness. Anecdotally, over the course of a month, we witnessed our students acclimate to and appreciate cultural differences, while finding common touchstones of identity, values, and historical struggle. Specifically, they identified ways in which professional educators in NI assumed responsibilities for managing conflict and building peace. Considering worrisome conflicts in the US, our students articulated professional responsibilities to build relevant social and emotional capacities in their own students.

Some of the most powerful conclusions from this group of teacher candidates illustrated the personal connections that they formed in the NI youth centers. The bonds of affection formed with NI youths appeared to rank among our students' most significant experiences during the trip. We believe that such personal connections across cultures are foundational to global citizenship. Expressing the sentiment that we grow to become more understanding and compassionate through interaction with diverse others and appreciation for their perspectives, one student reflected:

> The only way to discover more about yourself is to be among people unlike you … Engaging with diverse cultures gives us the tools to be better educators. If young brains are allowed the chance at multiple perspectives, I think we would live in a much more empathetic society. It is when we are forced out of our comfort zone that we can truly learn about ourselves (personal communication, July 25, 2023).

Curiosity about the boys and girls at the youth centers appeared to transfer to our students' thinking about teaching in the US. Several reported greater confidence that they could successfully teach children from different cultural and linguistic backgrounds. One student emphasized the importance of learning each child's story:

> During our labs at the youth center, I was so interested in the lives of these kids because they are from another country and have completely different backgrounds than I do. I have realized that still goes for my classrooms in the future because I will have students that come from all different backgrounds, have different family situations, and might even be from another country and speak another language. It has made me curious, and I know I will use this curiosity in my classroom to really get to know each and every one of my students on an individual level (personal communication, July 25, 2023).

Finally, our students shared that cultivating a healthy classroom climate is essential to their vocational mission. One student captured this insight:

> We live in a very divided society, and it is important that we create an unbiased classroom that is welcoming to all. We can do this by creating an open, kind, nurturing environment … Learning how to combat my own biases and acknowledging my privileges is essential for my personal growth and development. As a teacher, I can use my experiences as a teaching moment for my students on the importance of actively working towards peace and understanding amidst conflict (personal communication, July 25, 2023).

In his Gettysburg Address, Abraham Lincoln (n.d.) reminded Americans that democracy is an experiment, the goal of which is to figure out how to go on living together. Considering that the US is one of the most conflicted and heavily armed societies in the world today, we believe that the wisdom of NI deserves a more central role in our educational mission.

Reflection Questions

1 How can NI's approaches to conflict resolution and peacebuilding through empathetic engagement be applied to the US? How might societal differences—including demographics and culture—limit the effectiveness of these approaches?

2 In what historical and contemporary ways do racial divisions serve the interests of empire in the UK and the US? How have these divisions and interests been reflected and imparted through schools?

3 What would it take for US teachers to practice peacebuilding in their classrooms? What social, emotional, and cultural understandings and competencies would they need? How could they develop these?

References

Barakat, M. (2024, May 10). In reversal, Virginia school board votes to restore Confederate names to 2 schools. *The Hill*. https://thehill.com/homenews/ap/ap-top-headlines/ap-an-education-board-in-virginia-votes-to-restore-confederate-names-to-2-schools (accessed October 26, 2025).

Bardon, J. (2011). *The Plantation of Ulster*. Gill & Macmillan.

Barton, K., and McCully, A. (2010). "You can form your own point of view": Internally persuasive discourse in Northern Ireland students' encounters with history. *Teachers College Record*, *112*(1), 142–81.

Barton, K., and McCully, A. (2012). Trying to "see things differently": Northern Ireland students' struggle to understand alternative historical perspectives. *Theory & Research in Social Education*, *40*(4), 371–408. https://doi.org/10.1080/00933104.2012.710928.

Borooah, V., and Knox, C. (2015). *The Economics of Schooling in a Divided Society: The Case for Shared Education*. Palgrave Macmillan.

Brantmeier, E. (2011). Toward mainstreaming critical peace education in U.S. teacher education. In Malott, C. S. and Porfilio, B. (Eds.), *Critical Pedagogy in the Twenty-first Century: A New Generation of Scholars*, pp. 349–75. Information Age Publishing.

Center for Reaching and Teaching the Whole Child. (2022). Anchor competencies framework. https://crtwc.org/framework (accessed October 26, 2025).

Collaborative for Academic, Social, and Emotional Learning. (n.d.). What is the CASEL framework? https://casel.org/fundamentals-of-sel/what-is-the-casel-framework (accessed October 26, 2025).

Cox, A. M. (2023, October). America the traumatized. *The New Republic*, 15–21. https://newrepublic.com/article/175311/america-polarized-traumatized-trump-violence (accessed October 26, 2025).

FutureEd. (2024). Analysis of legislation restricting the teaching of racism. https://www.quorum.us/spreadsheet/external/KBYQbCxNgAheAgQCtQZC (accessed October 26, 2025).

Halpern, J. (1993). Empathy using resonance emotions in the service of curiosity. In H. Spiro, M. G. M. Curren, E. Peschel, and St. D. James (Eds.), *Empathy and the Practice of Medicine*, pp. 160–73. Yale University Press.

Halpern, J. (2001). *From Detached Concern to Empathy: Humanizing Medical Practice*. Oxford University Press.

Hughes, J. (2011). Are separate schools divisive? A case study from Northern Ireland. *British Educational Research Journal*, *37*(5), 829–50.

Jilani, Z., and Smith, J. A. (2019, March 4). What is the true cost of polarization in America? *Greater Good Magazine*. https://greatergood.berkeley.edu/article/item/what_is_the_true_cost_of_polarization_in_america (accessed October 26, 2025).

Knox, C. (2011, April). Tackling racism in Northern Ireland: The race hate capital of Europe. *Journal of Social Policy*, *40*(2), 387–412. https://doi.org/10.1017/S0047279410000620.

Lerer, L. (2024, January 13). On the ballot in Iowa: Fear. Anxiety. Hopelessness. *New York Times*. https://www.nytimes.com/2024/01/13/us/politics/iowa-caucuses-anxiety-fear.html (accessed October 26, 2025).

Lincoln, A. (n.d.). Gettysburg Address. Library of Congress. https://www.loc.gov/resource/rbpe.24404500/?st=text (accessed October 26, 2025).

Loewen, J. (1995). *Lies My Teacher Told Me*. Touchstone.

Lynch, R. (2019). *The Partition of Ireland: 1918–1925*. Cambridge University Press.

Maney, G. (2012). The paradox of reform: The Civil Rights Movement in Northern Ireland. In S. Erickson Nepstad, and L. Kurtz (Eds.), *Nonviolent Conflict and Civil Resistance*, pp. 3–26. Emerald Group Publishing.

McCully, A., and Barton, K. (2019). Schools, students, and community history in Northern Ireland. In A. Clark and C. Peck (Eds.), *Contemplating Historical Consciousness: Notes From the Field*, pp. 19–31. Berghahn Books.

McKittrick, D., Kelters, S., Feeney, B., Thornton, C., and McVea, D. (1999). *Lost Lives: The Stories of Men, Women, and Children Who Died as a Result of the Northern Ireland Troubles*. Random House.

Mystal, E. (2021, June 3). The miseducation of white children. *The Nation*. https://www.thenation.com/article/society/critical-race-theory-white (accessed October 26, 2025).

Ohlmeyer, J. (2020, December 29). Ireland has yet to come to terms with its imperial past: Some celebrate and some excoriate connections with the British Empire. *The Irish Times*. https://www.irishtimes.com/opinion/ireland-has-yet-to-come-to-terms-with-its-imperial-past-1.4444146 (accessed October 26, 2025).

Rana, A. (2022, Fall). Our segregation problem. *Dissent*. https://www.dissentmagazine.org/article/our-segregation-problem (accessed October 26, 2025).

Roediger, D. (2007). *The Wages of Whiteness: Race and the Making of the American Working Class*. Verso Books.

Southern Poverty Law Center. (2017, October). *Teaching the Movement: The State of Civil Rights Education in the United States*. https://www.learningforjustice.org/sites/default/files/2017-10/Teaching-the-Movement-2011-v2-CoverRedesign-Oct2017.pdf (accessed October 26, 2025).

Stanley, J. (2024, June). Education: The end of civic compassion. *The New Republic*, 18–19. https://newrepublic.com/article/181274/end-civic-compassion (accessed October 26, 2025).

United Nations. (n.d.). *Sustainable Development Goals*. https://www.un.org/sustainabledevelopment/sustainable-development-goals. (accessed October 26, 2025)

Wetts, R., and Willer, R. (2022). Anti-racism and its discontents: The prevalence and political influence of opposition to antiracism among white Americans. *SocArXiv*. https://doi.org/10.31235/osf.io/xvcf2.

Zembylas, M. (2008). *The Politics of Trauma in Education*. Palgrave Macmillan.

Zhirkov, K., and Valentino, N. (2022). The origins and consequences of racialized schemas about U.S. parties. *Journal of Race, Ethnicity, and Politics*, 7(3), 484–504. https://doi.org/10.1017/rep.2022.4.

Part II

Blurring the Lines between Local and Global: Fostering Borderlessness

5

Developing Empathy through Activist Art: Young Adult Texts with Culturally Sustaining Practices

Elizabeth Wilkins

Abstract

Global literacy and culturally sustaining classroom practices are critical for fostering an inclusive educational environment. Art serves as a universal language that transcends linguistic and cultural barriers, providing a unique medium for students to explore and express diverse perspectives and reflect on their own experiences. By incorporating culturally responsive practices, educators can ensure that the curriculum fosters a sense of belonging and respect for diversity through critical consciousness. Integrating art in classrooms provides student creativity and nurtures critical thinking skills essential for navigating an interconnected, globalized world. Through visual arts, students can learn empathy, understand how to navigate cultural differences, and develop a better understanding of the world. Incorporating culturally sustaining practices ensures that educational content is relevant and responsive to students' diverse backgrounds and lived experiences.

Key Terms: *critical visual literacy, community, activist art, empathy, culturally sustaining practices*

Inspiring Empathy in Globalized Education: Culturally Responsive Teaching through Activist Art and Young Adult Fiction

The Importance of Critical Global Literacy

Educators across the country are being met with the challenge of bridging the literacy gap. Schools are spending exorbitant amounts of money on scripted curricula and textbooks to address struggling classroom readers. While explicit lesson plans and modules aligned with state standards are fundamentally necessary, there has been a decline in teachers' overall self-efficacy and a growing disconnect from students' needs (Dresser, 2021). How can we ensure that students are engaged in reading, want to read, understand, and can comprehend the text put on their desks? Critical visual literacy is a popular pedagogical method that culturally sustainable educators use to enable students to connect with visual stimuli and foster critical thinking. By integrating critical visual literacy into the curriculum, these educators prepare students to navigate and critically engage with the visual information that permeates their daily lives. Critical visual literacy is a popular pedagogical method that culturally sustainable educators use to enable students to connect with visual stimuli and foster critical thinking. By integrating critical visual literacy into the curriculum, these educators prepare students to navigate and critically engage with the visual information that permeates their daily lives. The pedagogical application of Culturally Sustaining Practices (CSP) empowers students to become more discerning consumers and creators of visual media. This empowerment transitions into the ability for students to interpret, question, and understand the underlying messages in visual content, allowing students to make informed decisions and develop opinions. Additionally, by integrating a critically visual approach into the school's curriculum, educators can guide young students to develop diverse perspectives and cultural representations, preparing them to be more engaged.

This teaching approach must first acknowledge that all texts are constructed, rather than neutral, and that they work to position the reader to accept a particular view of the world (Brown and Savić, 2023); critical visual literacy practices embedded in CSP guide students to gain the understanding and capacity, regardless of ethnicity and culture, to connect to background knowledge and build deeper meaning. Globalization literacy allows the required knowledge, skills, and attitudes that schools must encourage in students in a way so that the world around them is digestible and accessible, and they can successfully live, work, and act as educated, empathetic citizens in a world that is universally connected (Zhao, 2010). As a former middle school reading teacher, I argue that students need to be exposed to various topics that have meaning and connection to their lives. When we present a globalized, multicultural-focused curriculum, we allow students the space to view the outside world through windows, mirrors, and sliding glass doors, a metaphor first created by Sims Bishop (1990). The metaphor of "mirrors, windows, and sliding glass doors" describes how literature can serve different functions for readers. I argue that this can be seen through art as well, as the "mirrors" allow readers to see themselves and their own experiences reflected in the stories and visual media, "windows" provide views into the lives and experiences of others, and "sliding glass doors" invite the viewer to step into these different "worlds," fostering empathy and understanding. This metaphor underscores the importance of diverse discussions and promoting cultural awareness and connection.

When we ask what the purpose of school is, ultimately, we are asking what students should learn, who decides this, and how we as educators facilitate these discussions that give students the autonomy to "step into" these different worlds and provide views into the lives of others. Students should be presented with topics that ignite feelings while also being given the chance to question, deconstruct, and analyze symbolism and significance through their lens of understanding. By creating opportunities for students to learn and engage with the world around them, this practice of instilling global knowledge and awareness allows students to think intentionally about intersectionality, a concept drawn from Crenshaw (2005). By exposing students to rich, symbolic, visual media, they can more effectively connect to global conversations, understand diversity, and appreciate the world and the many ways we are all connected (Bender-Slack, 2002). Developing students to think globally is even more relevant now, with the world's events at the forefront of social media. Students with a developed global interconnectedness can see ethical and social problems and develop critical opinions (Crafter and Maunder, 2012). Students can explore various aspects of identity, gaining insight into their and others' identities. This pedagogical practice nurtures cultural competence beyond mere tolerance, fostering empathy and understanding (Ladson-Billings, 1995). Using Ladson-Billings's framework of Culturally Relevant Pedagogy (CRP), culturally sustaining educators can design lessons that promote academic success, develop students' cultural competence, and support their critical consciousness by tapping into their "funds of knowledge," a term first coined by Moll and Gonzalez (1994). The term "culturally sustaining" requires pedagogies to be responsive or relevant to young people's cultural experiences and practices and support them in maintaining their communities' cultural and linguistic competence while providing access to dominant cultural competence. The explicit goal of culturally sustaining pedagogy is to promote multiculturalism in practice and perspective for both students and teachers, aiming to perpetuate and foster linguistic, literate, and cultural pluralism as part of the democratic project of schooling (Paris, 2012).

I argue that education's overall goal is for students to understand the interconnected nature of the world better, recognizing that events in one part of the globe have global implications (Ladson-Billings, 1995). Teachers in all classrooms can incorporate diverse authors and cultural perspectives to better understand these connections between student perceptions of culture and culture themselves. Utilizing the Sims Bishop (1990) model of mirrors, windows, and sliding glass doors, teachers can encourage students to reflect on their own biases, understand differences, and develop empathy, cultivating a sense of global citizenship and responsibility. Including time in classrooms to have students analyze power dynamics, debate, and relate what they are reading, either fiction or nonfiction, to the world around them adds to the fostering of comprehensive and inclusive learning environments and globalized thinking.

Moreover, critical global literacy equips students with the skills to navigate diverse cultural, linguistic, and social contexts, fostering cultural competence and empathy. It empowers students to address pressing global challenges, such as climate change and poverty, by analyzing complex issues and contributing to sustainable solutions on a global scale. Critical global literacy also promotes social justice, encouraging students to recognize and challenge inequalities locally and globally (Huard, 2024). Thinking of international projects using technology, book clubs, and community partnerships also allows students to think and rethink their own perceptions and deviate from their own center of "normalcy." Including activist art as a pedagogical practice allows students to focus on the interpretations of global issues, the understanding of power, access, equity, and overall empathy for others. This pedagogical approach aligns closely with Ladson-Billings's framework of Culturally Relevant Pedagogy, which fosters student empathy by making learning relevant to their lives.

This chapter strongly suggests that art, critical consciousness, and intentional teaching practices should be at the forefront of education, providing a rationale for developing teacher efficacy in the area of critical visual literacy through the utilization of OPTIC, a reading strategy designed to help students connect to background knowledge and develop empathy. The OPTIC Strategy, a mnemonic device representing overview, parts, title and text, relationships, and conclusion, is not only a tool for analyzing visual texts but also a culturally sustaining practice. By systematically guiding students through a critical examination of visual media, OPTIC encourages them to delve into the texts' cultural contexts and underlying messages. This process helps students appreciate and value diverse perspectives and cultural narratives, fostering an inclusive learning environment where all cultural identities are acknowledged and respected. Through the interrelationship component, students explore how different text parts interact and reflect broader societal issues, promoting a deeper understanding of cultural interconnections and global implications. Ultimately, OPTIC empowers students to draw informed conclusions that resonate with their own cultural experiences, enhancing their ability to empathize with others and appreciate differences that make all of us human.

Prongs of Culturally Responsive Pedagogy: Student Achievement, Cultural Competence, and Critical Consciousness

CRP consists of three key prongs that globalized educators can utilize to ensure that the curriculum and pedagogies emphasize the importance of student understanding. The components of CRP are academic success, cultural competence, and critical consciousness. The first prong of CRP is academic success, which focuses on promoting high academic achievement for all students. The second prong of CRP is cultural competence. Educators who utilize CRP in their classrooms ensure a foundation focusing on the importance of students understanding and valuing their cultures while learning about others. The final prong of CRP is critical consciousness. This final component encourages students to question and challenge social injustices, fostering a deeper awareness of societal issues.

When educators apply these prongs of CRP, it empowers students to take ownership of their learning. This approach enhances students' motivation and engagement by helping them find relevance and meaning in their studies. A sense of ownership over their learning is cultivated by giving students the space to take an active role in decision-making and goal-setting and reflecting on their progress. These practices enhance intrinsic motivation and develop critical thinking skills as students make informed choices and solve problems independently. Beyond the academic setting, student agencies prepare individuals for real-world decision-making, fostering autonomy and a sense of responsibility. Educators do this intentionally. Our classrooms customize learning experiences based on our students' strengths and preferences. These experiences further contribute to developing lifelong learning skills (Rahimi & Oh, 2024) and allow students to become empowered with their knowledge. Additionally, by empowering students with agency, educators promote a positive self-image and build confidence to overcome challenges (Campana, 2011).

Connecting history, relationships, place, and the experiences of those at the forefront of the curriculum is part of a critical area that needs growth in schools and institutions. How do educators and educational preparatory programs (EPPs) assist in connecting the intersectional facets of identity and community? While the answer may be found in multiple curriculum and pedagogical textbooks, this chapter highlights the fundamental and absolute necessity of connecting learners to the material as a foundation of their knowledge and comprehensive understanding of self-agency. Hill Pedagogies, first developed by Dr. Gholdy Muhammad, exemplify how institutions can strive to utilize appropriate culturally and historically responsive education. The four components of HILL Pedagogies, history, identity, literacy, and liberation, aim to cultivate students' understanding of their own identities, promote critical literacy skills, and empower them with a sense of liberation and social justice. By integrating these elements, HILL Pedagogies strive to create a more equitable and inclusive educational experience for all students. At the heart of this work is intertwining educational agency with community engagement and comprehension, enabling educators to craft lessons that express truth, justice, and advocacy through visual literacy.

In this educational capacity, teachers catalyze critical thinking and empowerment. Intertwining educational agency through community engagement and comprehension is the heart of this work, as well as how educators craft lessons that express *truth, justice, and advocacy* in their classrooms through visual literacy. In the educational capacity, teachers represent the means for critical change agents because their curriculum, pedagogy, and philosophy have the most significant impact on dismantling inequity and incorporating student voices and experiences in their classrooms (Ainscow, 2020; Min et al., 2021; van Vijfeijken et al., 2024).

Our goal as educators is to facilitate knowledge through lived experiences and the asset-based nature of community development, where the focus is on the global pedagogy that is culturally and community-focused and sustaining. Integrating community models with classroom discourse and dialogue makes it clear how schools and pedagogy can and should incorporate social relationships, networks, and collaborative inquiry through student ownership and engagement (Cunningham, 2002). Following the critical pedagogy of Johnson (1993), we can examine the purpose of embedding activist art and critical literacy into our practices by committing to critical, self-conscious, and aware teaching that philosophically forces educators to reread, reframe, and reinvent their lessons.

Culturally Sustaining Reading Strategies to Foster Student Learning

This chapter's purpose is to provide education on why CRP and CSP are integral to student success and to provide one activity that can support teachers who want to engage in critical conversation in their classrooms—using the OPTIC framework as a best practice to connect to student background knowledge and build familiarity. OPTIC is an inclusive, culturally sustaining visual analysis tool focused on how students connect and understand images paired with texts or on their own. It guides students to seek deeper meaning through visual literacy. Just like written texts, visual texts are intentional (they chose to draw, photograph, or create that image), meant for certain audiences (those images are for certain specific groups or people to see), and purposeful (meant to do something to invoke an emotion, make people think, show a specific event or situation) (k20 Center, 2017). The lesson included in this chapter was used in a 6th grade reading classroom to help my students, predominantly English Language Learners and first-generation students, connect to the novel we were reading. The goal was to do the OPTIC reading strategy to build background knowledge and increase student interest and understanding. For this curriculum unit, I utilized the young adult novel *Other Words for Home* (Warga, 2021), which won the Newbery Honor Award and was a *New York Times* bestseller. The story follows Jude, a Syrian girl sent to America to live with her family. Jude's father and brother stay in Syria while a war occurs. The novel is from Jude's perspective and includes her journey through American schools as a 7th grader. We see America through the eyes of a young girl learning English, as well as the culture and lifestyle in America. We are also privy to her understanding of belonging. As she experiences more of America, we learn that she is grappling with her own identity and the stereotypes that are placed on immigrant children. The students chose this novel due to its themes and personal relevance to their own lives.

As a globalized educator, I wanted to ensure the connections between this novel and student lives were central so students could reflect and critique the presented events. Engaging topics such as immigration, racism, and loss were foundational to the novel. To connect with the community, I incorporated youth activist murals that depict the common themes of immigration, loss, identity, anti-racism, and the meaning of family, which are also present in the book. The murals are also intentional in that they are all painted by immigrant youth who are actively looking for ways their American dream can come to life as they seek refuge in the United States—engaging with CSP practices provided space for students to connect to the experience of reading and the visual usage of the activist murals connected firmly to the lives of the students in my classroom. Using OPTIC to build those connections and thoughts was integral. Ladson-Billings said it best: When teachers envision "the next Nobel laureate, the next neurosurgeon, or the pioneer of social justice, the perspective shifts from a position of sympathy to one of informed empathy" (p. 35). Applying CRP in my classroom, I envisioned a dynamic, *fun* learning environment where students would take their newfound knowledge and discussions back to their communities, engaging in meaningful conversations with their families. This approach requires teachers to reflect deeply on their teaching practices and continuously question the rationale behind the curriculum set by the state, district, and their own choices. By doing so, educators can ensure that their lessons are not only informative but also relevant and impactful. By fostering this critical inquiry, I aimed to cultivate a classroom environment where education is seen as a personal and communal enrichment tool, ultimately empowering students to become thoughtful, informed, and active members of their communities.

Integrating Culturally Sustaining Practices through Student Learning

Culturally sustaining practices are a pedagogical approach that educators can use when focusing on the students in their classroom (Camangian, 2013). Teachers who model this behavior will spend time cultivating relationships and engaging with families to learn more about students' lives. In contrast, educators who do not practice (CSP) will not make the time to allow students to express feelings, emotions, or experiences. Teachers acknowledge student experiences and are committed to respecting the lives and cultures of their students. Gay (2013) argues that teachers should encourage students to think about their communities: "The education of racially, ethnically, and culturally diverse students should connect in-school learning to out-of-school living; promote educational equity and excellence; create community among individuals from different cultural, social, and ethnic backgrounds; and develop students' agency, efficacy, and empowerment" (p. 49). At its core, CSPs amplify students' voices by creating learning opportunities that allow students to express their thoughts and feelings. Teachers play a crucial role in literacy development, necessitating effectiveness in their instructional approaches. Effective teachers create engaging, inclusive learning environments that foster a love for reading and writing.

Additionally, they continuously assess and respond to student progress, providing targeted support and feedback. Newcomer (2018) provides evidence of the benefit of a caring relationship, specifically between students of color and teachers, stating that creating a classroom community that is responsible for each other and supportive of each other, much like a family, can make a positive difference in a student's life. In addition, culturally responsive teaching relies on caring, mainly when "teachers view dialog and attention as integral parts of the teaching and learning process" (Shevalier and McKenzie, 2012: 1095). Culturally responsive and sustaining practices elevate student voices, opinions, and critiques in a way that provides mutual respect for ideas and understandings. Borrowing from Hammond and Jackson (2015), the term "warm demander" creates an environment where students feel challenged and cared for, balancing firmness with empathy. This allows for both student autonomy in individual thought and the structure that students need to do that comprehensive work. Warm demanders communicate clear expectations and provide consistent support, fostering a classroom atmosphere where students are motivated to meet high standards because they believe in their own potential and feel valued. This allows students to reflect and think and promotes a sense of belonging and respect, essential for creating an equitable and effective learning environment. Thus, it empowers students to participate actively in their educational process.

Teacher Pedagogy Utilizing Activist Art for Critical Thought

My classroom experiences as a 6th-grade reading and writing teacher in an urban state capital have deeply influenced my approach as a professor of teacher education. The lessons in humanistic teaching I learned in those early years remain close to my heart. Art, with its ability to provide a visceral and immersive experience, profoundly impacts empathy, bridging linguistic and cultural gaps in ways that traditional methods often through visual, literary, or performance mediums, art allows individuals to step into the emotional landscapes of others, fostering a deep connection with diverse perspectives and experiences. Artistic expressions, whether conveying joy, pain, or resilience, create a shared space where viewers can empathize with the depicted narratives.

Engaging with art prompts students to reflect on their own emotions and, consequently, develop a deeper understanding of the emotions of others. This practice aligns with an ethical basis of teacher citizenship, emphasizing teachers' responsibility to themselves, their students, and other democratic stakeholders. By fostering empathy through artistic engagement, teachers fulfill their role as co-citizens and contribute to shaping students as informed, empathetic citizens in the making (Fraser-Burgess, 2020). This empathetic engagement is particularly potent when art addresses social issues, sparking a heightened awareness of injustice or inequality (Scott Shields and Fendler, 2023). Whether through stirring visual imagery, poignant narratives, or evocative performances, art catalyzes empathy, encouraging individuals to see the world through different lenses and fostering a sense of interconnectedness and understanding (Koo et al., 2024). To foster a desire in students to develop empathy as global citizens, they need opportunities and dialogue to process and think critically about global issues (Andreotti, 2006).

Assessing a student's global competence is critical as it encourages reflection on their own biases, feelings, and understanding of global events, people, and cultures (Klein, 2013). This reflection is essential for fostering deeper connections between students and the material they encounter. Gangi (2008) highlights that while White children often have more opportunities to make text-to-self, text-to-text, and text-to-world connections due to the representation of their experiences in books, children of color may face barriers to such connections. This disparity underscores the need for a pedagogy that goes beyond merely addressing these issues. Berchini (2017) argues that to advance truly, educators must engage in a pedagogy that openly and honestly grapples with paradoxes, double binds, and diverse contexts (p. 473). Integrating these insights, educators can enhance global competence by ensuring that all students see themselves reflected in the texts and discussions, fostering a more inclusive and equitable learning environment that acknowledges and addresses these complex dynamics.

In a study by Titchnor-Wagner et al. (2016), educators were asked to illustrate how global competency was demonstrated in classrooms at the elementary, middle, and high school levels. Findings ranged from educators reading nonfiction passages on global topics to creating music, writing, and other forms of expression. When educators facilitated the learning process in a meaningful and rich way, rather than merely addressing surface-level culture, students were able to develop empathy and gain a deeper understanding. Middle school students in Titchnor-Wagner et al. (2016) could grasp and consider global issues on a large scale; themes such as overpopulation, war, socioeconomic struggles, and the marginalization of women's rights allowed students to develop a more significant understanding of the world around them. In another example, educators discussed their integration of global topics, with one high school teacher using essential questions to guide class discussions broadly. Students were asked, "How are we the same? How are we different? How are we interconnected?" Similarly, art, specifically activist art, fosters a connection to community and global citizenship. The purpose of activist art is to harness the transformative power of creative expression for social and political change.

Beyond aesthetics, activist art serves as a potent vehicle for raising awareness about pressing issues, inspiring action, and amplifying the voices of marginalized communities. By challenging existing power structures, fostering empathy, and catalyzing meaningful conversations, play a crucial role in cultural transformation and care (Noddings, 2012). It serves as a visual language for dissent and resistance, expressing opposition to injustice and contributing to the formulation of more equitable policies. Activist art celebrates diversity, inclusivity, and cultural richness, challenging stereotypes and advocating for a more tolerant society. In essence, the purpose of activist art is to engage viewers emotionally and intellectually, motivating them to question the status quo, participate in social movements, and contribute to pursuing a more just and compassionate world (Beyerbach and Ramalho, 2011). In these ways, educators can engage. We make that intentional time for students to argue, evaluate, and live in discomfort as we bring up *real* issues that our current society is grappling with and mobilize them.

> Our concerns for social justice mobilize us to challenge conditions that menace human survival. Many of us are conscious of injustices and want to do something about them … poverty, hunger and food security, environmental degradation, displacement, landlessness, and precarious working conditions of rural workers; the history of genocide, survival, and self-determination of Native Americans; resistance and organizing in poor urban communities; racism; the invisibility of women's contributions to society, and the troubling of gender and sexual orientation. All of the issues are local but interconnected globally; their relationships simply cannot be disentangled (Beyerbach and Ramalho, 2011: 202).

Understanding that our students come from different backgrounds, have been exposed to different experiences, and have the capability and desire to dialogue about these critical factors, we as educators need to become the facilitator of discussion, not the director, enforcer, indoctrinator, of the critical literacy process and give students the space to sit with these critical issues (Burn and Menter, 2021). Noddings (2012) argues that an essential task for teachers is to "connect the moral worlds of school and public life" (p. 779). As educators and education trainers, we have the perfect opportunity to show the power of care and demonstrate how we can expose students to global concepts, foster critical thinking, and do all through a framework of culturally sustaining practices.

Understanding the OPTIC Visual Literacy Strategy as Practiced Pedagogy

The OPTIC reading strategy, an acronym for Overview, Parts, Title, Interrelationships, and Conclusion, is a visual analysis tool employed in academic settings to enhance comprehension and critical thinking skills when engaging with visual texts. Developed as a pedagogical approach to deconstructing and interpreting visual information, OPTIC provides a systematic framework for analyzing images, charts, graphs, photographs, and other visual elements commonly found in academic texts. At its heart, OPTIC is designed to occur before any reading occurs. OPTIC's purpose is to serve as a lesson's introduction and to allow students time to process and consider the themes present in the novel before reading. This strategy is a creative way to use reflection and dialogue to help process visual cues and assist with the connection to language.

Recommendations for this strategy suggest using art connected to a larger theme, unit, or novel. Once students are exposed, they can use this strategy to analyze symbolism, break apart themes, reflect on the conversation, and tell a story through a narrative or conclusion paragraph.

Using the OPTIC Reading Strategy for Comprehension

The first component of the OPTIC strategy, "Overview," encourages readers to initially glance at the visual text to gain a broad understanding of its content and purpose. This step involves identifying key elements, such as the main subject, overall composition, and any apparent patterns or themes. By obtaining a general sense of the visual text, readers establish a foundation for more in-depth analysis. Pedagogically, I would show an image and let students look intently for 15–20 seconds before asking them to write a complete sentence about the image. This stage is supposed to be surface-level understanding and literal.

Following the overview, the "Parts" stage involves a detailed examination of the individual components within the visual text. The visual is brought back for students to examine. At this stage, I encourage students to identify specific elements, such as shapes, colors, symbols, and text, and understand how they contribute to the overall meaning. I encourage students to look closely at the background and foreground and list all the visual aspects of the art presented. Analyzing the parts allows readers to delve into the specific nuances of the visual representation and identify essential elements that may have particular significance or convey specific messages that align with the themes this unit covers. Students are then given time to expand their own list of "parts" as they work with shoulder partners and group mates. After 2–3 minutes, I typically ask students to "yell" out the things they have discussed, and I write them on a whiteboard. Students are encouraged to add any words that they did not initially have.

The third part of OPTIC focuses on the words in the image or the title and caption. The "Text" component emphasizes the importance of the title or caption associated with the visual text. Students are asked to consider how the title informs their understanding and comprehension of the visual content. Questions like, "How does this title change the meaning?" are often asked as they provide another level of understanding. Titles often provide context, framing the viewer's perspective and influencing the initial interpretation of the visual text. This step encourages a thoughtful consideration of the relationship between linguistic and critical visual elements.

The fourth step in OPTIC is the "Interrelationships" stage, which encourages students to explore the connections and interactions among different elements within the visual text. I typically ask students to focus on the characters in the art, their physicality, and their body language. By this point in the activity, students clearly understand what is occurring or can make a generalization of what is happening in the art. Educators can push this further by asking students to analyze the interrelationships and uncover subtleties and complexities in the visual representation, fostering a deeper understanding of its significance.

The final stage of the OPTIC strategy, "Conclusion," prompts readers to incorporate their observations and insights into a comprehensive interpretation of the art. We ask students to draw conclusions that are justified by the visual art. We ask students to find the intended message or purpose of the visual text and push them to consider how the various "parts" and "interrelationships" work together to convey meaning and their own interpretation. By arriving at a thoughtful conclusion, readers engage in a critical interpretation that goes beyond surface-level observations.

To begin using OPTIC, the teacher will show an image. We will use Reyna Garcia's Voices of Hope/Voces de Esperanza (Figure 5.1) for this example: Part 1. The intention is to guide students to understand the layered meanings and symbolism behind art. This piece resonates with the similar themes of family, loss, and immigration and can establish a deeper meaning behind the very people who leave their home country and strive to survive in America; this is a hook meant to connect this visual piece with the text that we will utilize for our curriculum unit.

Figure 5.1 Voices of Hope/Voces de Esperanza: Part 1. Artist Reyna Garcia (Garcia, 2024)

Example of OPTIC Visual Literacy Activity Template

Using this image allowed students to think as they connected meaning to the visual. The image above elicited melancholy responses from the students, who felt a profound sense of the man's sadness. The somber tones and the man's lack of expression conveyed a deep emotional weight that resonated with the students participating. This connection was reinforced by the stark, muted background, which amplified the sense of isolation and despair. Consequently, students reported feeling as though they could empathize with the man's sorrow, finding the visual cues in the image to be powerful indicators of his emotional state. Phrases like, "the yellow background should feel warm, like love, but instead feels burning, like missing his family is burning him alive," students also suggested, "he doesn't have a face, maybe he doesn't because he is wearing a mask to pretend he is happy," and "he looks like he is stepping into another life and world. He really is leaving his family behind." These written and verbal comments came from eleven-year-olds who also disclosed their unhappiness at leaving their *home*. While they were young, the desire to go back was a common theme among my students. By including student voices, perspectives, and experiences, educators can acknowledge the uniqueness of each student in their classroom (Gay and Kirkland, 2003). This philosophical practice validates and empowers students to engage more and can inspire the motivation to connect deeply to the rich discussion presented in classrooms (Gere et al., 2009). Teachers might view the inclusion of student voices and perspectives as crucial for validating and engaging students, leading to deeper participation and motivation. Students appreciate how these practices foster a sense of equity and inclusivity, making every student feel respected and valued. However, some might also face practical challenges, such as finding time and resources to implement these practices while maintaining a cohesive curriculum effectively; thus, using reading strategies that allow conversation, reflection, and peer connection is a vital resource to empower student thoughts.

Overall, teachers likely see the benefits of this approach but may seek additional support to navigate the complexities involved. Democratic educational practices promote equity and inclusivity (Morrison, 2008). Students, regardless of background or identity, deserve opportunities to express themselves, share their insights, and contribute to shaping the educational environment. As educators make space for student voice, they enrich the learning experience and cultivate a sense of community and collaboration within the classroom, ultimately preparing students to be active and informed participants in a diverse, interconnected, and globalized world. The OPTIC reading strategy enhances visual literacy by guiding students through a structured analysis of visual images, which is crucial for understanding activist art. Students can critically engage with activist art's complex messages and social commentary by breaking down an image into its Overview, Parts, Title and text, Interrelationships, and Conclusion (Table 5.1). This method enables students to connect deeply with the visual elements and emotional undertones, fostering a greater appreciation for the artwork's impact on social issues.

Table 5.1 OPTIC Reading Strategy

Component	Description
O–Overview	Write a brief **overview** of the image: in one complete sentence, what is this image about?
P–Parts	Identify and examine individual elements within the visual, such as people, objects, and any other significant details.
T–Text	Use the **title** to clarify the subject of the image. Consider both literal and metaphoric meanings. What does the title suggest? Is there any **text** in the image—a caption, or words in the image itself?
I–Interrelationships	Analyze how the parts of the visual are related to each other. Look at how the elements interact, connect, and contribute to the overall meaning or narrative of the visual.
C–Conclusion	Summarize the analysis by drawing a conclusion about the overall meaning, message, or impact of the visual based on the observations made during the previous steps. Consider how the parts come together to create a mood or convey an idea or argument.

Note: This table outlines the critical components of the OPTIC reading strategy, which is designed to enhance students' critical visual literacy by providing a structured approach to analyzing and interpreting visual media.

The OPTIC reading strategy enhances students' critical visual literacy by providing a structured framework for analyzing images and visual media. This method encourages students to systematically break down and examine visual elements, promoting a deeper understanding of how images convey meaning and influence viewers. Students learn to grasp the general context and setting by starting with an Overview. Analyzing the Parts helps them focus on specific details and components, fostering attention to detail and considering the Title, which aids in understanding the creator's intent and the visual's thematic focus. Exploring Interrelationships between elements allows students to see how different parts interact and contribute to the overall message. Finally, drawing a Conclusion helps students synthesize their observations and form a cohesive interpretation. The OPTIC strategy aims to equip students with the skills necessary to critically engage with visual information, enhancing their ability to interpret and evaluate images they encounter in daily life.

Discussion

Incorporating activist immigrant art into educational settings held significant power and potential for enriching students' learning experiences on multiple levels. As an educator, I watched my students connect closely to relevant books and topics. There was a concerted effort to connect our curriculum units to students' desires. As a democratic educator, I tried to value student interests, which led me to use activist art to engage students in the world around them. Activist art, rooted in diverse cultural backgrounds, not only offers a visual representation of immigrant communities' unique narratives, traditions, and perspectives but also catalyzes fostering cultural awareness, empathy, and critical thinking among students. Activist art also nurtured critical thinking skills by asking students to analyze, interpret, and evaluate visual messages. Implementing strategies like the OPTIC reading strategy enables students to approach activist art systematically, examining the visual representation's overview, parts, title, interrelationships, and conclusion. This analytical process enhances visual literacy and cultivates a deeper understanding of the nuanced narratives embedded in activist artworks.

In the OPTIC template above, students could see how the artist Reyna Garcia told a story of heartache, loss, and hope. Students then wrote their conclusion paragraphs, discussing their experiences with heartache, loss, and hope. They wanted to look at more of her art, which we did, and they wanted to learn more about how to paint stories and tell their own story. Their joy, love, and engagement were gifts because my students wanted to read *Other Words for Home; they* did not mind writing. The integration of activist art within the framework of culturally sustaining practices, coupled with the systematic application of the OPTIC reading strategy, represents a powerful approach to fostering critical engagement and cultural inclusivity in educational settings. Activist art catalyzes dialogue, challenging dominant narratives and prompting discussions that amplify marginalized voices. By embracing culturally sustaining practices, educators acknowledge the importance of diverse cultural perspectives, actively incorporating them into the learning environment. As a visual analysis tool, the OPTIC reading strategy complements this approach by providing a systematic and structured method for students to deconstruct and interpret visual texts. Activist art encompasses art created to promote social change and raise awareness about social justice issues. It is a dynamic tool for encouraging students to explore and express their perspectives on global and local issues. By incorporating this form of art into the curriculum, culturally sustaining educators can create a culturally relevant learning experience that resonates with students' lived experiences and cultural backgrounds, allowing students the space to connect and comprehend what they are engaging in within the curriculum.

The OPTIC reading strategy further enhances this approach by providing a structured method for students to analyze visual and textual information critically. This strategy encourages students to take an active role in their learning by closely examining the elements of a text or artwork, understanding the relationships between its parts, and drawing informed conclusions. By systematically applying OPTIC, students develop critical thinking skills and become more adept at interpreting complex information. Through the combination of activist art and the OPTIC reading strategy, students gain proficiency in visual literacy and develop a deeper understanding of the societal issues embedded within artistic expressions. This dual approach encourages students to explore interrelationships within visual texts, discerning nuanced meanings and contributing to a more comprehensive understanding of the cultural context.

Moreover, emphasizing student voice within this framework ensures that learners actively participate in critically examining activist art, contributing their perspectives to the broader discourse. The power of connection between activist art, culturally sustaining practices, and the OPTIC reading strategy aligns with the broader goals of education—promoting critical thinking, cultural competency, and social awareness. By fostering a learning environment that values diversity, empowers student voices, and embraces critical visual analysis, educators pave the way for a more inclusive and socially conscious generation capable of navigating the complexities of our globalized world. This pedagogical approach equips students with the skills and awareness to navigate and contribute positively to an increasingly diverse and interconnected world.

Questions to Consider

1 How does integrating critical literacy and activist art within pedagogical practices influence students' educational experience and development?
2 How do culturally responsive and sustainable practices impact a student's engagement with global issues through critical literacy and activist art?

References

Ainscow, M. (2020). Promoting inclusion and equity in education: Lessons from international experiences. *Nordic Journal of Studies in Educational Policy, 6*, 7–16. https://doi.org/10.1080/200 20317.2020.1729587.

Andreotti, V. (2006). Soft versus critical global citizenship education. *Policy and Practice: A Developmental Education Review, 3*, 40–51.

Bender-Slack, D. (2002). Using literature to teach global education: A humanist approach. *English Journal, 91*(5), 70–5.

Berchini, C. N. (2017). Critiquing un/critical pedagogies to move toward a pedagogy of responsibility in teacher education. *Journal of Teacher Education, 68*(5), 463–75.

Beyerbach, B., and Ramalho, T. (2011). Chapter fifteen: Activist art in social justice pedagogy. *Counterpoints, 403*, 202–17.

Bishop, R. S. (Summer 1990). Mirrors, windows, and sliding glass doors. *Perspectives: Choosing and Using Books for the Classroom, 6*(3).

Brown, C. W., and Savić, M. (2023). Practising critical visual literacy through redesign in ELT classrooms. *ELT Journal, 77*(2), 186–96. https://doi.org/10.1093/elt/ccac049.

Burn, K., and Menter, I. (2021). Making sense of teacher education in a globalizing world: The distinctive contribution of a sociocultural approach. *Comparative Education Review, 65*(4), 770–89. https://doi.org/10.1086/716228.

Camangian, P. R. (2013). Teach like lives depend on it. *Urban Education, 50*(4), 424–53. https://doi.org/10.1177/0042085913514591.

Campana, A. (2011). Agents of possibility: Examining the intersections of art, education, and activism in communities. *Studies in Art Education, 52*(4), 278–91. https://doi.org/10.1080/0039 3541.2011.11518841.

Crafter, S., and Maunder, R. (2012). Understanding transitions using a sociocultural framework. *Educational and Child Psychology, 29*(1), 10–18. https://doi.org/10.53841/bpsecp.2012.29.1.10.

Crenshaw, K. (2005). Mapping the margins: Intersectionality, identity politics, and violence against women of color (1994). In R. K. Bergen, J. L. Edleson, and C. M. Renzetti (Eds.), *Violence Against Women: Classic Papers*, pp. 282–313. Pearson Education New Zealand.

Cunningham, F. (2002). *Theories of Democracy A Critical Introduction*. Routledge.

Dresser, R. (2021). The impact of scripted literacy instruction on teachers and students. *Issues in Teacher Education, 21*(1), 71–87.

Fraser-Burgess, S. (2020). Accountability and troubling the caring ideal in the classroom: A call to teacher citizenry. *Educational Studies, 56*(5), 456–81. https://doi.org/10.1080/00131946.2020.17 99216.

Gangi, J. M. (2008). The unbearable whiteness of literacy instruction: Realizing the implications of the proficient reader research. *Multicultural Review, 17*(1), 30–5.

Garcia, R. (2024). Voices of Hope 1 [Acrylics on Canvas 44x60]. Reynas Gallery, Michigan.

Gay, G. (2013). Teaching to and through cultural diversity. *Curriculum Inquiry, 43*(1), 48–70. https://doi.org/10.1111/curi.12002.

Gay, G., and Kirkland, K. N. (2003). Developing cultural critical consciousness and self-reflection in preservice teacher education. *Theory into Practice, 42*(3), 181–7. https://doi.org/10.1353/tip.2003.0029.

Gere, A. R., Buehler, J., Dallavis, C., and Haviland, V. S. (2009). A visibility project: Learning to see how preservice teachers take up culturally responsive pedagogy. *American Educational Research Journal, 46*(3), 816–52. https://doi.org/10.3102/0002831209333182.

Hammond, Z., and Jackson, Y. (2015). *Culturally Responsive Teaching and the Brain: Promoting Authentic Engagement and Rigor Among Culturally and Linguistically Diverse Students*. Corwin.

Huard, M. (2024). Review of teaching and assessing social justice art education: Power, politics, and possibilities. *Studies in Art Education, 65*(1), 109–14. https://doi.org/10.1080/00393541.2023.2285212.

Johnson, M. (1993). *Education on the Wild Side: Learning for the Twenty-First Century*. University of Oklahoma

k20 Center. (2017). *K20 Learn | optic: A Reading Strategy Recipe*. OPTIC: A Reading Strategy Recipe. https://learn.k20center.ou.edu/lesson/240 (accessed October 26, 2025).

Kibbey, J. S. (2011). Chapter four: Media literacy and social justice in a visual world. *Counterpoints, 403*, 50–61.

Klein, J. D. (2013). Making meaning in a standards-based world: Negotiating tensions in global education. *The Educational Forum, 77*(4), 481–90.

Koo, A., Lim, K., and Song, B. (2024). Belonging pedagogy: Revisiting identity, culture, and difference. *Studies in Art Education, 65*(1), 63–80. https://doi.org/10.1080/00393541.2023.2285206.

Ladson-Billings, G. (1995). Toward a theory of culturally relevant pedagogy. *American Educational Research Journal, 32*(3), 465. https://doi.org/10.2307/1163320.

Ladson-Billings, G. (2011). "Yes but How do We Do It?" Practicing culturally relevant pedagogy. In *White Teachers/Diverse Classrooms: Creating Inclusive Schools, Building on Students' Diversity, and Providing True Educational Equity*. essay, Taylor & Francis.

Min, M., Lee, H., Hodge, C., and Croxton, N. (2021). What empowers teachers to become social justice-oriented change agents? Influential factors on teacher agency toward culturally responsive teaching. *Education and Urban Society, 54*, 560–84. https://doi.org/10.1177/00131245211027511.

Moll, L., and Gonzalez, N. (1994). Lessons from research with language minority children. *Journal of Reading Behavior, 26*(4), 23–41.

Morrison, K. A. (2008). Democratic classrooms: Promises and challenges of student voice and choice, part one. *Educational Horizons, 87*(1), 50–60.

Newcomer, S. (2018). Investigating the power of authentically caring student-teacher relationships for Latinx students. *Journal of Latinos and Education, 17*(2), 179–93.

Noddings, N. (2002). *Educating Moral People: A Caring Alternative to Character Education*. Teachers College Press

Noddings, N. (2012, December). The caring relation in teaching. *Oxford Review of Education, 38*(6), 771–81.

Paris, D. (2012). Culturally sustaining pedagogy: A needed change in stance, terminology, and practice. *Educational Researcher, 41*(3), 93–7. https://doi.org/10.3102/0013189x12441244.

Rahimi, R. A., and Oh, G. S. (2024). Rethinking the role of educators in the 21st Century: Navigating globalization, technology, and pandemics. *Journal of Marketing Analytics, 12*, 182–97. https://doi.org/10.1057/s41270-024-00303-4.

Scott Shields, S., and Fendler, R. (2023). Developing civically engaged art education. In K. N. Denzin and D. M. Michael (Eds.), *Global Shifts in Qualitative Inquiry: New Directions New Challenges*, pp. 55–72 (1st edn.). Routledge.

Shevalier, R., and McKenzie, B. A. (2012). Culturally responsive teaching as an ethics-and care-based approach to urban education. *Urban Education, 47*(6), 1086–105.

Sorensen, T. B., and Dumay, X. (2021). The teaching professions and globalization: A scoping review of the Anglophone research literature. *Comparative Education Review, 65*(4), 725–49. https://doi.org/10.1086/716418.

Tichnor-Wagner, A., Parkhouse, H., Glazier, J., and Cain, J. M. (2016). Expanding approaches to teaching for diversity and social justice in K-12 education: Fostering global citizenship across the content areas. *Education Policy Analysis Archives*, *24*(59). http://dx.doi.org/10.14507/epaa.24.2138T.

van Vijfeijken, M., van Schilt-mol, T., van den Bergh, L., Scholte, R. H., and Denessen, E. (2024). An evaluation of a professional development program aimed at empowering teachers' agency for social justice. *Frontiers in Education*, *9*, 1–14. https://doi.org/10.3389/feduc.2024.1244113.

Warga, J. (2021). *Other Words for Home*. Seedlings Braille Books for Children.

Zhao, Y. (2010). Preparing globally competent teachers: A new imperative for teacher education. *Journal of Teacher Education*, *61*(5), 422–31. http://dx.doi.org/10.1177/0022487110375802.

6

Religious Diversity and Culturally Responsive-Sustaining Learning and Teaching in a Global Context

Yooyeun Hwang

Abstract

A group of US college students in a teacher-education program served for six weeks as conversation partners for college students in Turkey through a weekly online video communication program. The American participants were first-year students in a teacher-education diversity course at a Christian college in the Midwest. The Turkish students, with various years in college and studying to be English teachers, were from a relatively conservative Islamic region of Kurdish-Turkey. Throughout the three years of implementation, this program demonstrated that digital technology can allow us to expand the zone of encountering diversity. The program exhibited at least four benefits for these American pre-service teachers. First, it provided the participants with a global cultural learning experience. Second, the encounter with Kurdish-Turkish students helped the American students improve their religious literacy and reduce their prejudice against and ignorance about Islam. Third, through the experience, the American students constructed an authentic understanding of what culturally responsive and sustaining teaching is. Last, they had an opportunity to infer how a harsh environment could affect the psychosocial development of oppressed groups in a society. The ultimate goal was to increase the future teachers' self-efficacy in teaching diverse pupils and to convince them that culturally responsive-sustaining teaching is an effective pedagogy.

Key Terms: *Religious diversity, Culturally responsive-sustaining teaching, Global learning*

Introduction

America is racially and ethnically diverse and becoming even more so, with PK-12 classrooms increasingly multicultural (National Center for Education Statistics, 2024). As a teacher-educator, I see the necessity of preparing future teachers for this ever-increasing diversity. At the same time, with fast-developing technology, it has become easier to expose ourselves to the world, look at the cultures and affairs of people in distant places, and observe the dynamic changes in the twenty-first century. Wars are raging in several corners of the world, and nations are supporting, trading with, negotiating with, competing with, and destroying each other. Do these global cultures and events affect our classrooms? What can we learn by talking to people on the other side of the earth? What might be the benefit of having the courage to talk to strangers who speak different languages, practice different religions, and have different values and traditions? Will such an experience help our future teachers prepare for their classrooms' domestic diversity in a globalized world? This chapter is about a program that began to answer such questions by connecting American and Kurdish-Turkish future teachers.

It would be ideal if all pre-service teachers had direct cross-cultural experiences in training to become culturally responsive-sustaining teachers. However, many teacher-education programs have limited capacities to provide genuine multicultural experiences (Leckie and Buser, 2020; Merlin-Knoblich and Dameron, 2021; Pewewardy, 2005; Williams and Glass, 2019). It is even more challenging to encourage direct global experiences because of geographical, social, political, and financial reasons. To overcome such limitations, some universities have utilized technology to create alternative methods for providing intercultural experiences for pre-service teachers. For example, several researchers investigated the effect of online programs on fostering foreign-language learning and cultural sensitivities in classroom diversity (e.g., Cherrez and Gleason, 2022; Park, Ryu, and McChesney, 2019; Sardegna and Dugartsyrenova, 2021).

In this chapter, I explore the impact of intercultural experiences when two groups of teacher candidates from different ethnicities, languages, and religious traditions meet through online technology.

According to Pew Research (2022), from the 1990s to 2022, the share of US adults who identified as Christian has fallen from 90 percent to 63 percent, the percentage of adults who say they are religiously unaffiliated has grown from 5 percent to 29 percent, and the percentage of adults who practiced other religions was about 7 percent in 2022. These numbers show that Christians are still the majority in the US, but religious diversity is growing. The religious diversity in public schools (i.e., students, teachers, and administrators) may reflect a similar ratio and is becoming more diverse. However, no one will deny that Christianity is the mainstream culture in North America. Ferber (2012) defines it as Christo-normativity. It is the domination of Christian ideology in a society's day-to-day customs, rules, and activities, such as the BC/AD dating system and the Christmas holiday.

The current K-12 students were born in the twenty-first century, and some people may say that religion is not a daily concern for people of the contemporary world. However, while there are few studies on religious diversity in the multicultural education literature or in culturally responsive-sustaining teaching research (Aronson, Amatullah, and Laughter, 2016; McCorkle and Rodriguez, 2021; Sloane and Petra, 2021), religion and religious diversity are still relevant internationally and domestically in our lives and classrooms. Religious differences still cause conflict and domestic violence in many corners of the world. The conflict between pro-UK Protestants and pro-secession Catholics in Northern Ireland, the violence between Hindus and Muslims in India and Pakistan, the Communist Chinese government's repression of Muslims in Xinjiang, and sectarian disputes among various Islamic sects comprise just some of the evidence (Maoz and Henderson, 2020).

Within the US, many experience violence based on their religious affiliation. For example, after 9/11, Muslim communities and individuals suffered much blatant, overt discrimination and microaggression (Jamal and Naber, 2022). The FBI's 2022 Hate Crimes Statistics show that 17.55 percent of hate crimes are in fact motivated by religion, mainly anti-Jewish, anti-Muslim, and anti-Sikh sentiments (US Department of Justice, 2023). In addition, White-evangelical and Black-church Christians participate frequently in antagonistic political rhetoric and events, and these groups seem to have significant voting powers (Banks, White, McKenzie, 2019; Martin, 2023).

Most North American perspectives of non-Christian religions are influenced by media such as news, TV shows, and movies, which are often inaccurate or superficial. For example, although most Americans don't know much about Islam, they often hear the names of organizations such as the Taliban, ISIS, Hamas, and Hezbollah in the media through the most negative of images. And it is so easy for them to misperceive Islam altogether and construct a stereotypical representation. Panjwani (2017) argues that people in many parts of the world recognize Muslims as a monolithic group. In reality, just like Christians, Muslims comprise a spectrum of people from secular, cultural, or progressive to conservative and religious. Toles-Patkin (2021), in her study on media portraits of Jewish people, argued that the images of other religious and social groups are exaggerated and simplified and that the resulting stereotypes marginalize less powerful groups and establish a boundary between *us* and *them*. The surface message of these shows and movies may inspire "inclusion and tolerance, but the latent message underscores exclusion and difference" (p. 937).

This chapter describes an approach that creates a space for Christian and Muslim pre-service teachers to encounter and learn from each other through video communication programs. The goal is to provide these college students with authentic experiences to more deeply know the other group and prepare them for teaching in and contributing to religiously diverse classrooms and global society.

Literature Review

Cross-cultural Experience via Online Technology

During the last two decades, many studies utilized online programs to provide pre-service teachers cross-cultural experiences while engaging in other academic tasks.

Although foreign-language learning programs were most frequent, some studies employed telecollaboration within other subject areas (O'Dowd, 2016; Sardegna and Dugartsyrenova, 2021). For example, Park, Ryu, and McChesney (2019) enabled Korean and American pre-service teachers to collaborate on virtual-classroom simulation design through an online studio. Other research studies provided opportunities for pre-service teachers from different countries to encounter and engage in virtual intercultural exchanges (Cherrez and Gleason, 2022; Journell and Dressman, 2011). In another study, Leh, Grau, and Guiseppe, J. A. (2015) utilized online intercultural exchange to mediate a cross-cultural project between pre-service teachers from an American and a German university. The participants created a multicultural project to address the importance of diversity in education. Kopish and Marques (2020) also used online technology and intercultural dialogue to foster global citizenship and global competence in future teachers in America and Brazil.

These studies concluded that online communication programs are functional tools for providing an intercultural environment while achieving other academic goals. Specifically, the participants who were pre-service teachers benefited from the experiences, and these online programs positively contributed to their cross-cultural understanding and competencies in global citizenship. Cultural appreciation and responsiveness include various aspects of culture, including religious diversity. Researchers investigated P-12 teachers' attitudes and practices toward Christianity and other faith communities.

Religious Diversity in the Classroom

The United States Constitution mandates the separation of church and state in public education (Heinrich, 2015). Despite this mandate, US culture has primarily originated from Christianity, and its ideology dominates American society, including public schools. This phenomenon is known as Christo-normativity (Ferber, 2012). Puchner and Markowitz (2020) argue that the consequence of Christo-normativity is Christian privilege. However, many teachers do not recognize the invisible Christian privileges present in North American schools. Blumenfeld and associates (Blumenfeld, 2006; Blumenfeld and Jaekel, 2012) demonstrated how pre-service and in-service teachers are oblivious to Christian privilege. Blumenfeld (2006) explained, "Christian privilege as constituting a seemingly invisible, unearned, and largely unacknowledged array of benefits accorded to Christians, with which they often unconsciously walk through life as if effortlessly carrying a knapsack tossed over their shoulders" (p. 195). Christian privilege promotes secular and not-so-secular Christian hegemony in public schooling and the larger society (Blumenfeld and Jaekel, 2012). One of the Christian privileges in schools is that the school calendar and activities revolve around Christian holidays such as Easter, Halloween, Thanksgiving, and Christmas. Puchner and Markowitz (2020) interviewed K-12 school teachers and administrators to investigate their awareness of Christo-normativity and its Christian-privilege consequences. Specifically, the authors discussed with the participants the celebration of Christmas in classrooms. The researchers found that some teachers and administrators were aware of Christo-normativity. They were sensitive to religious diversity in their classrooms, so they either did not celebrate Christmas in class at all or were apologetic about the related activities. However, more than half of the participants were less aware, non-apologetic, or promoted the celebration regardless of religious diversity in the classrooms.

Other research studies demonstrated that K-12 schools and higher education institutions in the US and Canada are not meaningfully accommodating religious diversity in classrooms. For example, Cobb (2012) documented the process of a failed attempt to provide a Ramadan music accommodation for his Muslim students at a school in Canada. Through his struggle with colleagues and administration, Cobb recognized that "Some of the challenges I encountered were logistical in nature while others, such as the opposition voiced by some of my colleagues, were more attitudinal" (p. 14). The teachers were culturally unresponsive. Pouraskari, Dika, and Frankovich (2023) found that hijabi Muslim students' level of adherence to the Islamic dress code was associated with lower perceived support from peers and faculty, and these students experienced more microaggressions in colleges and universities. Amjad (2018) investigated elementary school students' experiences in Canada, and she found that "some Muslim students perceive most of their teachers not only as inefficient in combating racism, discrimination, and Islamophobia but also as promoting injustice through their teaching methods and curriculum" (p. 327).

The above studies demonstrate that educators should do a better job of addressing the existing inequity in religious diversity in our educational institutions. In this chapter, I present an approach that employs technological tools to create a zone for pre-service teachers from different faith traditions in which to encounter each other. Through the experience, they discover each other and construct what culturally responsive and sustaining teaching means.

Methods

A university professor in Turkey and his American friend created the Turkish Students Conversation Partners (TSCP) program during COVID-19. They sought to overcome the pandemic's limitations so that his students could practice English speaking and listening skills. They decided to use an online program through which Turkish and American college students met and talked in English. Through that, Turkish students could practice their English oral language skills while American students practiced ELL tutoring skills. Thus, they initiated a new program involving pre-service teachers from both countries, and in this chapter, I discuss the program, its results, and its educational implications.

Participants

The Americans were first-year students at a Christian liberal arts college and were taking their diversity class in the teacher-education program. Even though the student body of this college is not made up entirely of devout Christians—it includes atheists to extremely conservative Christians—most come from at least nominally Christian families. Over the years, I learned they have minimal experience interacting with people of different faith communities. According to the college admission, about 83 percent of the student body of this college are European-American descendants. However, over 90 percent of the participants in the present study were European Americans. This college is in the Midwest, where the population is predominantly conservative Christians.

The Turkish students, with various years in college, were studying at a large Turkish university to become English teachers. The university is in a relatively conservative Islamic region in eastern Kurdish-Turkey. Kurds are an ethnic minority group in Turkey that has a distinct culture, including language, food, and other traditions. According to Baysu, Coşkan, and Duman, Y. (2018), there are approximately 20–25 million Kurds across the Middle East, and Kurds make up around 18 percent of Turkey's population. In addition, historically, the Kurdish people's resistance and their desire to create an independent state have been dishonored politically and forcefully by the Turkish government. Therefore, Kurds are often targets of prejudice and discrimination in Turkey (Protner, 2018; Religion and Public Life, 2023). I refer to this group as Turkish students except when I explain their unique experience, in which case I use the full description, Kurdish-Turkish students.

These two groups of college students interacted through online programs (e.g., Zoom, WhatsApp, and other programs). Specifically, American college students served as English conversation partners for Turkish college students weekly for six weeks. In many ways, these two groups of students were from different worlds, including their religions (Christians vs. Muslims), language (English vs. Turkish/Kurdish), and ethnicity (American vs. Turkish). However, they shared common characteristics, such as being college students, preparing to be teachers, and being brave enough to choose to talk to strangers through an online program. For the American students, participating in this project was an option for their course's cultural-experiences requirement, six hours of outside events to encourage future teachers to immerse themselves outside their comfort zones and experience new cultural environments. For the Turkish students, participation offered an opportunity to improve their English speaking and listening skills in education classes. In both settings, participation in the program was a voluntary way to complete class requirements. However, since the American students were from a small liberal arts college and the Turkish students were from a large university, the number of students participating reflected that. Specifically, 20 to 25 American students and about 70 to 80 Turkish students were involved each semester.

Procedure

To begin, a coordinator conducted an orientation/training meeting on Zoom for American students only. First, the coordinator provided brief information on the geographical, historical, and political background of the Kurdish population in Turkey. He then prepared the American students to be effective conversation partners by offering tips for initiating and carrying on conversations and supplying some icebreakers (i.e., questions/prompts). At the second meeting, all participants met on Zoom first, and the coordinator announced the base groups, which included three to four Turkish students and one American student. They then had private small-group time to talk for an hour. After this initial meeting, each group met once (or twice if some groups preferred) a week by themselves for four weeks for about an hour or so. During these four weeks, faculty members did not interfere with any meetings except by asking how it was going in casual conversations. Although the first meeting was through Zoom, the individual groups set up their meetings using whatever online program they preferred. In the sixth week, all participants met together on Zoom first before they had small-group talk sessions for about fifty minutes. All students returned to the big group at the end to share feedback on the experiences and bid farewell.

We have completed the third year of administering the program, and the results have been steadily positive. The program has demonstrated that digital technology can allow us to expand the zone of encountering diversity on a global scale, and it can happen using a relatively convenient method in one's own space. Second, students' feedback has revealed that they enjoyed their experiences and benefited from them. The participating students completed brief journal (or log) entries for each session. The American students also submitted their reflections and reviews   of the overall experiences upon program completion. The current chapter draws data from three sources: students' journals/logs and reflective reviews, and my accumulated observations and informal conversations with those students over the past six semesters.

My Turkish counterparts, a colleague, and I also conducted an empirical study to assess the program's effect by administering a survey before and after the experience, and we presented the results in an academic journal (Hwang, Wolthuis, Kasap, and Peterson, 2024). However, I have not included the results of that study in this chapter. The Turkish students, of course, also learned about Americans and American culture. Their feedback after the program was positive, according to their professor. Not every Turkish student presented their reflections/reviews in English, so incorporating their data would have involved the process of complicated translation. In addition, their professor investigated a separate topic, anxiety in foreign-language learning. We are in the process of designing a study to look at both groups with the same focus.

I read American students' logs and reviews at the end of each semester and compiled their responses and comments to categorize recurring themes. Upon analyzing the three data sources (i.e., students' journals/logs, reflective reviews, and my observations and informal conversations with those students), I have concluded that the American students benefited from participating in the program in at least four ways. First, it was a global learning opportunity for these future teachers. They talked about their American culture while also hearing about the Kurdish-Turkish culture. Second, both groups of students, Muslim and Christian, had opportunities to confront and demystify their religious prejudices and stereotypes. Third, while serving as conversation partners and English tutors for second-language speakers, the American students constructed a personal meaning of culturally responsive-sustaining teaching. Last, the American students heard the authentic voices of people who are oppressed for their ethnicity. In the following, I discuss these four benefits, especially from the American students' perspectives.

Researcher Positionality. I have been teaching diversity courses for twenty-eight years, and I consider myself socially conscious and sensitive to the issues related to diversity in classrooms. My knowledge of educational psychology and experiences in teaching diversity classes equipped me to analyze the students' written responses and verbal feedback. However, I am a Roman Catholic who teaches at an ecumenical Christian Liberal Arts college, and I was not familiar with Islamic culture in any sense at the beginning of the program. The last three years have been a learning journey for me, also. I visited the university in Turkey and became friends with the professor who created the program and his family. I fell in love with the landscape of the Kurdish-Turkish region, its people, and the culture, including its great food. I also visited several mosques in Istanbul and admired the tranquility and beauty of these spiritual places. All this has led me to develop more empathy toward the situation of the Kurdish people and their culture, including religion. It has added to my ability to take perspectives from both sides and analyze the data more sensibly. Thus, I have genuinely encouraged my students to participate in this program, and I have sincerely appreciated the program's positive impact on my students.

Results

Global Learning

The program provided a global learning opportunity for college students who want to be teachers. Specifically, the American students learned about many aspects of Kurdish-Turkish culture, encompassing geographical, political, and historical conditions, the religion of Islam, food, cultural traditions, socialization, and daily life. Before participating in this TSCP program, most of the American students said that they did not know anything about Turkey, not to mention the ethnic Kurdish minority who live there. They had probably heard the name, but many students did not even know in which part of the world Turkey is located. For many students, it was an exciting opportunity to learn about something new, while, for some, it was sailing in an uncharted sea, and they were hesitant. Each semester, only a little more than half of the class participated in the program, even though it was enthusiastically encouraged. Perhaps those hesitant students would benefit more from a program like this than the excited ones. However, participation has always been optional and voluntary.

Although the first meeting was awkward for both countries' students, they soon warmed up to each other. They became comfortable talking about various topics and issues, such as college-age females and males, classes, future careers, dating, marriage, music, movies, food, family, traditions, etc. In the beginning, they asked questions to get to know each other. Gradually, they became friends, and the conversations were more personal and in-depth. Some even talked about sensitive issues such as religion. A student shared the following experience:

I loved talking about a variety of topics. We were able to talk about food, TV shows, culture, gender roles, household roles, wedding and funeral traditions, Christianity, Islam, the US, Turkey, travel destinations, our families, our futures, and more! I loved hearing their perspectives and comparing what was similar and different regarding all of our topics. (Spring 2024 participant)

Many American students were surprised to find out how many commonalities they shared. For example, many Turkish students listen to the same Western pop music, watch the same movies, and use the same social media programs. These Turkish students knew about famous American pop-culture artists, such as singers, actors, and actresses. The American students learned that Turkish students also have anxiety about their future careers and wishes for dating and marriage, common concerns for people of that age, regardless of their geographic location and culture. However, it would be an exaggeration to say that all discussions were informative or meaningful. According to some reports, occasionally, discussions were not smooth or were relatively superficial. One student wrote in his report that in every session, he and his Turkish students talked about different types of exercise (e.g., workouts and weight-lifting) they had done that day.

The students also learned about differences. For example, the American students' new friends introduced different kinds of music popular in Turkey. Also, they talked about some Turkish or Kurdish foods and showed pictures of them. The American students also learned about different qualities of family relationships and expectations, including traditional Turkish wedding ceremonies. Several American students were surprised that a typical Turkish wedding ceremony can last a few days, unlike American weddings that take place all in one day. One student said that she was wearing a T-shirt, an ordinary style for American college students, but noticed the Turkish students in her small group wore shirts that did not show much flesh except their faces. She then became self-conscious about her shirt and felt a little uncomfortable. Through learning these kinds of differences, they recognized aspects of their own culture more clearly.

Unexpectedly, American students discovered their ethnocentrism and that they take things for granted. Some students said that they were embarrassed because the Turkish students knew so much about America and American culture while they knew nothing about Turkish culture. Throughout the program, students reported that they did learn about Turkish culture, helping them gain some insights into the influence of culture and reflect on themselves and their cultural identity. Several students were surprised to discover that Thanksgiving is celebrated only in America. A student confessed that she thought American cities were the most developed. She had visited Chicago recently and showed her Turkish partners a picture of such a metropolitan city. She was expecting the Turkish students to be impressed, but their responses were lukewarm. They said Chicago looked like Istanbul, a historical place with beautiful architectural treasures. American students did not question some Turkish students' belief that America seemed an ideal place to live. One student was surprised when a Turkish student mentioned hearing that some Americans have a lot of debt and do not live in pleasant places. A student reflected on the experience:

I learned that Turkey is currently suffering from very high rates of inflation. To me this seems like Turkey must be at a financial disadvantage, but I also learned, when talking about American economics, that the Turkish students believe Americans to have very high amounts of debt. It was hard to explain this knowing that I myself am accumulating debt right now due to the high cost of secondary education. Therefore, financial disadvantage might not be as cut and dry as I thought. Perhaps it depends on culture and perspective. I was biased in assuming that people from other countries think America is better. So many stories about people coming to "the land of freedom" have bolstered my pride in my country, but perhaps made me blind to the pride that others have in their own countries. It was surprising to hear my students discuss some of the problems about America like debt or hear that they would greatly prefer to live in Turkey. I learned that Turkey is a very beautiful country, more than I had expected actually. I was biased in perceiving the Middle East as arid and dry, but it actually is vibrant and full of life depending on the places you visit. I also learned that the hijab is very beautiful as well, I love seeing my student [Student A] shine with confidence when she wears it. (Fall 2023 participant)

The American students also realized economic and environmental privileges. While almost all of them have laptop computers and have easy internet access anywhere on the college campus and in their homes, not every Turkish student can afford a laptop computer, which means many have to use smartphones to connect and carry on their conversations. Complicating the problems, the internet service in particular areas in Turkey is less reliable. Many Turkish students have to go to other places for a better connection, which also causes other issues.

These meetings also revealed the convenience of technology in their encounter with cultures. Beyond their face-to-face conversations, they could have a virtual dorm tour using a computer or smartphone, compare living spaces, and quickly upload pictures of objects and places they talked about. Many American students mentioned who wore a hijab and who did not, which was not a significant aspect of their interaction at all. (I discuss religious issues later in the chapter.) They could also read moods on the faces of their new friends. These live interactions offered what books or video clips could not.

As the sessions went on and they became more comfortable, the American students were able to talk with their partners about the more sensitive issues of prejudice and discrimination against Kurdish people. They learned about different political systems and the power to control people. Not all the Turkish students would talk about this in depth. However, for some American students, it was their first time learning about the historical, political, and geographical environment of the Kurdish people in Turkey. They felt empathetic about where their new friends came from.

Will such knowledge about Kurdish-Turkish culture help American students in any way besides the intellectual benefits? What will this newly acquired global knowledge and these new experiences do for their classroom teaching in the future? The implementation of this knowledge is uncertain. However, I can imagine that they may no longer react based on their ignorance toward the people from the Middle East. Moreover, they may transfer their experiences and become more confident when interacting with new immigrants or diverse students in their future classrooms. The following reflection of a participant is encouraging:

I may have a bias in the sense that my worldview simply isn't big enough yet. There is so much to learn about cultures across the globe! [Student B] helped me look up a local Turkish restaurant I could visit so that I could understand the foods that she was trying to tell me about. Without her influence, I would have never been interested in going there. I've noticed that there are many restaurants and stores in my community that I've been ignoring because they are part of a culture that is out of my comfort zone. [Student B] and [Student C], my two students who came consistently, took a big leap in order to learn about American culture, speaking the English language and trying it out in conversation with an American student. Perhaps I would benefit from taking bigger leaps of my own, not only in continuing to learn about Turkey but also in learning about all of the cultures my peers and future students will associate with. Getting out of my comfort zone will allow me to have more growth and experiences to make my worldview broader. (Fall 2023 participant)

Religious Diversity

Another significant impact was on participants' religious literacy. American students who grew up in a predominantly Christian culture became friends with people from an Islamic culture and had an opportunity to confront their prejudices against Muslims through friendship. Kurdish-Turkish students who grew up Muslim in conservative Islamic regions also had a chance to meet Christians who were probably inconsistent with the images portrayed in their media.

Americans are very diverse, and their diversity includes religion. As such, classrooms combine students from various faith communities and traditions. However, statistics show that around 80 percent of K-12 teachers are middle-class European Americans (National Center for Education Statistics, 2023), and while not all are Christians, most grew up in a mainly Christian culture. Many teachers are unaware that the American school system is also rooted in this Christian culture. The school calendar itself is set up around Christian holidays. These holidays are considered natural parts of life in America, while the holidays of other faith communities, such as Ramadan, Hanukkah, Full Moon's Day, and Kwanzaa, are considered exotic or unusual. A participant of TSCP expressed the following reflection:

I never really thought about other holidays outside of Christianity and Judaism, so learning about one of the Muslim holidays was very interesting to me. At first, I found it a little crazy that they got a lot of days off for the end of Ramadan, but then I thought about all the days we get off for our holidays, especially Christmas. It makes me wonder how many Muslim students have to sacrifice their school time for holidays, which is something you should never have to choose between. When I am teaching, I will do my best to bring awareness to other cultures in order to take steps towards them getting the days off that they deserve. (Spring 2024 participant)

In addition, Americans, including college students, tend to perceive people, even other Americans, who practice other religions as foreigners (Hwang, Wolthuis, Kasp, and Peterson, 2024). This structure creates a cultural/religious hegemony for people from other than Christian cultures (Aronson, Amatullah and Laughter, 2016). Moreover, American schools offer European-American students limited opportunities to acquire basic religious literacy and develop social skills to be comfortable with people from different faith traditions. This can even be the case at the college level, especially at a Christian college.

This lack of religious literacy, combined with minimal exposure to racial and ethnic diversity, also affects college students by creating fear of the unknown (Alderman and Moore, 2021). In their TSCP program review, several American students confessed that they worried their Muslim-student conversation partners would not like them at the beginning of the program. Often, their experiences with non-Christians and racially diverse people come from their Christian summer and spring-break mission trips to places stricken with poverty. Although these are in many respects awakening experiences for some students, such short trips can also foster an unconscious or inflated sense of superiority or even a false burden of responsibility that diverse people require their help. Therefore, it can be highly inaccurate for them to imagine what interactions with Turkish students might be like.

According to Allport's intergroup interaction theory, people benefit most from intergroup interaction when it has four specific conditions for optimal (or appropriate) contact: equal group status, common goals, intergroup cooperation, and authority support (Allport, 1954; Pettigrew, 1998). First, participants in a beneficial group interaction have similar or balanced social status. Sports teams, clubs (e.g., robotics, chess, debate, choir, band, etc.), or the army would be typical examples. Second, the group members have a common goal. For example, a group wants to win a game, a competition, or a war, or they want to acquire common learning skills. Third, the members of the group need to work together and support each other to achieve their goal. And fourth, the group needs the support of authorities, such as coaches of sports teams, advisers of clubs, or the hierarchy within the army.

I believe the TSCP program has met these four conditions of Allport's intergroup interaction, and their discussions have facilitated the process of reducing prejudices and ignorance against particular religions (i.e., Christianity and Islam), languages (English vs. Turkish), and ethnicities (American and Kurdish-Turkish). The two groups of college students have had a similar status in their society: educated people who are part of a higher-education system. Second, their majors have been in the same discipline (i.e., education), and all have been pursuing becoming teachers. In other words, they have had similar career goals and aspirations. Third, their meetings as conversation partners have fostered the Turkish students' English listening and speaking skills while enhancing the American students' scaffolding skills in teaching English-language learners. Therefore, they have worked together to achieve their goals while enjoying their time together. Finally, professors from both countries have created the environment and strongly supported the interactions. These students have enjoyed the experiences, and some have continued to meet even after the program ended.

The American students learned about Islam and Muslims, and the Turkish students learned about Christianity and Christians. The students talked about their religion and asked about the others' religion without meaning to proselytize (or evangelize) their new friends. A student shared the following experience:

We finally got to the point in our friendship where we felt comfortable sharing about our religions and how we practice them. The two young ladies who I talked to today are both Muslim, while I am Catholic, so our worship looks very different even when our prayers are to the same God. I was biased in my expectation for how our discussion about religion would go. In the US, it can be rather taboo to share your faith and people easily start arguments with each other. Considering some of the tension in the Middle East, I assumed this discussion could go the same way. Instead, I found more acceptance talking about Christ with Muslims than I do talking about Christ with other Christians. (Fall 2023 participant)

Religion may have been a salient factor in the beginning of the program. However, their religious differences did not interfere with their forming friendships. Many students reported that they talked about their religions, Christianity and Islam, and some American students even became knowledgeable about Islam and certain practices, such as various holidays, the pillars of Islam, etc. I also noticed the American participants were respectful of the religion of Islam during class discussions. For example, one student explained that wearing a hijab was a personal choice made by women to feel closer to God, and several students explained to their classmates that fasting during Ramadan is a spiritual experience rather than a painful experience of being hungry all day.

More importantly, they realized that not every Muslim is like the stereotypical images in the media. There is a wide variety, just like among Christians. Some Muslims are conservative, some are liberal and progressive, and some are in the middle. And just like students at this primarily Christian college are not all practicing Christians, not every Turkish student is a practicing Muslim, and religion is not necessarily a significant part of their identity. American students also learned that Turkey is much more secular than other Islamic countries and with more religious diversity. In any case, religion was not their prime interest in their conversations. It faded into the background and did not interfere in beginning their friendships. They talked more about typical college-student topics and were able to transcend their religious differences.

Will they transfer this knowledge and these experiences to their understanding of other religions (e.g., Buddhism, Hinduism, Judaism)? There is no way to be sure. However, they may at least have recognized that they are religiously illiterate and that they cannot judge other people's faith based on ignorance. They also realized that they can be friends with others regardless of their religion. Again, it is not clear whether they will apply this understanding to future teaching in a religiously diverse classroom. But the experience may have prepared them to be humble and less uncomfortable around their future students and parents from different faith traditions.

Culturally Responsive-Sustaining Learning and Teaching

The third benefit of the TSCP program for future teachers was that through the experience, students had chances to construct authentic knowledge about culturally responsive and sustaining learning and teaching (Alim and Paris, 2017; Ladson-Billings, 2021; Gay, 2018).

According to Gay, the basic definition of culturally responsive teaching is that "instructions are grounded in positive beliefs about the cultural heritage and academic potential of diverse students" (Gay, 2018: 29). This implies that teachers' understanding and valuing of who their students are in terms of their language, culture, and life experiences, and utilizing them in their teaching, will facilitate students' academic-skills and healthy psychosocial development.

Many American students who participated in the program wrote in their reflections that they worried that the Turkish students may not speak English well. These future teachers were uncomfortable talking to someone whose English was not fluent. However, most likely, they will have students who are English-language learners in their classrooms in the future. Moreover, many Americans tend to believe that the level of fluency in speaking English is an indication of intelligence (Dabach, 2014; Garcia, Sulik, and Obradovic, 2019; Sanatullova-Allison and Robinson-Young, 2016). They often think people who communicate in broken or inarticulate English are less intelligent than native or eloquent speakers. A study in England showed that second-language speakers (or English-language learners) pick up on that belief, which in turn affects their behaviors and relationships. Specifically, the study demonstrated that "experiencing language-based stigma can (1) incite a stereotype threat response from nonnative speakers, and (2) damage their relationship with native speakers on an interpersonal and intergroup level" (Birney, Rabinovich, Morton, Heath, and Ashcroft, 2019). A teacher who believes students are not intelligent because of their status as English-language learners will probably have low expectations for them. This may then negatively affect the students' learning and achievement because of the Pygmalion effect (Howard, Tang, and Austin, 2015; Szumski and Karwowski, 2019). In addition, it can also have harmful effects on the students' relationships with their teacher and peers.

Some students mentioned they were surprised when Turkish students spoke fluent English. However, not all the Turkish students spoke English well and struggled to convey their thoughts, but several American students said they enjoyed talking with students who were not fluent in English. Some even said they liked to hear the Turkish language when the Turkish students talked among themselves to find the right English words in the middle of a conversation. A student shared the following reflection:

> Before having these conversations, I didn't really have any sense of where Turkey was or anything about the country. I had a bias that the United States' education system was working well, and I didn't fully realize how lenient we are and the differences that other countries have. For example, all of the girls shared that they knew multiple languages and were surprised when I shared that I had only been taking French for 4 years. (Fall 2023 participant)

Another student wrote the following in her review:

> Before this experience I knew nothing about Turkey or its culture. This helped me to better understand their country through the eyes of someone my age rather than what a textbook or media could provide. It also allowed me to be more comfortable around those who aren't fluent in English. It amazed me (and was honestly a little embarrassing) how much they knew about America and how little I knew about their country. I feel that as a teacher I will need to expand my knowledge on other countries to better support my students. (Fall 2023 participant)

They seemed to appreciate these Turkish students' efforts to learn a new language. And some students even said that the experience inspired them to learn a new language. The American students witnessed that learning another language is complicated and challenging and that those who could learn and speak two languages were in fact intelligent. Some of the Turkish students could even speak more than two languages. Research actually confirms that knowing more than one language facilitates brain development and that bilingual and multilingual brains allow one to be a more effective learner (Gullifer, Pivneva, Whitford, Sheikh, and Titone, 2023; Singh, Fu, Tay, and Golinkoff, 2018). Therefore, some American students developed a newfound respect for second-language speakers.

While conversing with the Turkish students, American students recognized that communication involves more than just language skills. It also involves cultural knowledge from both sides. To communicate effectively, the American students had to reflect on their own culture to explain themselves to Turkish students and learn about Turkish culture. This was the same for the Turkish students. It also involved some linguistic conventions and other cultural practices in communication. As Gay argues, "teaching is most effective when ecological factors, such as prior experiences, community settings, cultural backgrounds, and ethnic identities of teachers and students, are included in its implementation" (Gay, 2018). The American students experienced what involving ecological factors means in real-life circumstances. They learned that to be an effective conversation partner, they need to know who their Turkish students are as individuals, their life circumstances, and where they are from, including Kurdish-Turkish cultures.

Recognizing the importance of culture in learning language and communication, appreciating the culture itself, and respecting people's ability to learn another language are critical aspects of culturally responsive-sustaining teaching. The TSCP program has been an opportunity for American students to implement what they have learned in theory to teach English-language learners. Through the experience, they gained insight into what this truly means and why it is a necessary practice. They had a meaningful opportunity to construct the value of culturally responsive-sustaining learning and teaching through their interactions with Turkish students and tutor them to improve their English-speaking skills.

Will these teacher candidates generalize and apply this newly constructed understanding to their teaching practices in the future? Chances are they will have ELL students in their classrooms, since the ELL population in K-12 schools is increasing (National Center for Education Statistics, 2023). This experience may help them develop higher self-efficacy in teaching second-language speakers and become advocates of culturally responsive-sustaining teaching.

Racism and Classism in Psychosocial Development

The fourth benefit of the TSCP program was that the American students heard additional narratives that helped them recognize the role of environment in psychosocial development (Brummelman, Thomaes, Orobio de Castro, Overbeek, and Bushman, 2014; Erikson, 1972; Pajares, 2010). Our development is a product of the interaction between hereditary and environmental factors (Bindman, Pomeranz, and Roisman, 2015; Chen, Chung, and

Hsiao, 2009; Rothbart, 2011; Strelau, 2008). The students had learned this psychological theory in classes and heard about it through media and other public discourse. However, by interacting with people from a starkly different culture, they could infer that our characteristics, sense of self, and quality of human relationships are the result of layers of environmental influences.

Diversity courses typically emphasize or argue that critical environmental factors such as racism and classism negatively affect the development of ethnically and racially diverse children and children from low socioeconomic demographics (Dishion and Tipsord, 2011; Kiang, Witkow, Champagne, 2013; Yip, 2014). However, middle-class European-American college students do not always readily make the connection between developmental-psychology theories and the realities of racism and classism. The students who participated in the TSCP program, an option for diversity class assignments, encountered a live example of the theory. One goal of the diversity class was to foster an understanding of the relationship between a harsh environment and human development.

For the past three years, each semester, approximately half of my diversity course has actively participated in the TSCP program, engaging in meaningful discussions on prejudice and discrimination with their new Kurdish-Turkish friends. In other words, they listened to first-hand experiences of unjust treatment and powerless situations. It is not clear how much the Kurdish-Turkish students shared their experiences. However, based on their reviews, the American students did learn about the situation of Kurdish people in Turkey as well as their strong ethnic identity. A student shared her reflection:

> Going into this experience, I was honestly so scared I would come off as a snobbish American, so I tried everything in my power to not. I dreaded the experience because I did not know how hard or how easy it would be. I guess my bias would have been that these students were just like me with similar experiences. It was made clear that while there are some common human experiences that we all do and do not enjoy, there are some pretty vast distances between experiences. Again, I still reflect on just how privileged I am, and for certain this experience deeply humbled me. (Spring 2024 participant)

Do the American students make the connection between domestic cases of racism and classism and their Kurdish friends' experiences? Do these mostly middle- and upper-middle-class American students see the dynamics of majority and minority and more and less powerful groups within a country? Having been placed in an optimal environment for intergroup interaction (Allport 1954; Pettigrew, 1998), the concept of prejudice and discrimination may become more concrete for these college students to grasp. They have heard domestic and international stories now, which may broaden and deepen their understanding of the complex meaning of diversity. Since the environment is a powerful element that affects human development, the hope is that the TSCP experience will help the American students respond to their future diverse students more sensitively and equitably. In other words, this knowledge and understanding is meant to equip them to encounter their future students with empathy and sustain an excellent learning environment and pedagogy.

Limitation

I was very fortunate to have the international connection to be involved in the program, and I am grateful that my students and the Turkish students had meaningful and practical experiences. However, by no means was the program perfect. We had so many students participate each semester that we did not have enough resources to provide scaffolding to make each meeting more conducive. We also had to rely on students being responsible for communicating and setting up weekly meetings. Most groups managed the task well, but some had challenges with the time difference between the US and Turkey and attendance. We keep talking among ourselves to improve the logistics for higher-quality experiences for future semesters.

This program is not a controlled empirical study to prove a research hypothesis. So, while I am excited to disseminate the findings to other educators and researchers, I would not claim any generalizability of the results.

Conclusion

I began this chapter with the idea of exploring the answers to these questions. Do global cultures and events affect our classrooms? What do we learn by interacting with people from a different part of the world? What might be the benefit of having the courage to encounter cultures with unfamiliar languages, religions, values, and traditions? Will such an experience help our future teachers prepare for their classrooms' domestic diversity in a globalized world?

After three years of facilitating this cultural exchange through the TSCP, we have achieved consistent success each semester. Most students who participated in the program appreciated the opportunity and became enthusiastic supporters. Their reviews reflected this positive experience. Many formed friendships with the Kurdish-Turkish students from the other side of the world, despite growing up in substantially different cultures.

What benefits did these students garner from participating in the TSCP program? In this chapter, I have analyzed them mainly from the American student side. The TSCP experience has provided them with four key benefits. It was a global learning opportunity to learn about Kurdish-Turkish people and culture while students learned about Islam and grew to respect it as it truly is. They constructed a personal meaning of culturally responsive-sustaining teaching through interaction with English-language learners. They also had a real-life immersion experience in which they heard the narratives of victims of prejudice and discrimination. What might be the implications of these four benefits? The goal is that the TSCP experience will increase the self-efficacy and competency of future teachers teaching in diverse classrooms. It will be even more fulfilling, and it is my sincere wish, if this is a small step toward understanding and peace among religious groups.

The program's success has also demonstrated that digital technology (i.e., video communication programs) can be a practical and affordable tool to create global learning opportunities for any group of students. In our case, it has offered meaningful interactive experiences for groups of pre-service teachers to reduce their ignorance and prejudices and prepare them to teach in ever-increasingly diverse American classrooms and ever-shrinking global relationships and communication.

Questions to Consider

1 What specific "cultural zones" do you currently lack access to, and how could digital tools help you create an authentic encounter with those communities?
2 How does learning about a student's specific sociopolitical or "harsh" environment shift your role from a standard instructor to a culturally responsive advocate?

References

Alderman, I., and Holt Moore, K. (2021). Terror management and religious literacy in the classroom. *Electronic Journal for Research in Science and Mathematics Education, 25*(3), 68–76.

Alim, H. S., and Paris, D. (2017). What is culturally sustaining pedagogy and why does it matter? In D. Paris and H. S. Alim (Eds.), *Culturally Sustaining Pedagogies: Teaching and Learning for Justice in a Changing World*, pp. 1–21. Teachers College Press.

Allport, G. W. (1954). *The Nature of Prejudice*. Addison-Wesley.

Amjad, A. (2018). Muslim students' experiences and perspectives on current teaching practices in Canadian schools. *Power and Education, 10*(3), 315–32. https://doi.org/kvzz.

Aronson, B., Amatullah, T., and Laughter, J. (2016). Culturally relevant education: Extending the conversation to religious diversity. *Multicultural Perspectives, 18*(3), 140–9.

Banks, A. J., White, I. K., and McKenzie, B. D. (2019). Black politics: How anger influences the political actions Blacks pursue to reduce racial inequality. *Political Behavior, 41*(4), 917–43. https://doi.org/10.1007/s11109-018-9477-1.

Baysu, G., Coşkan, C., and Duman, Y. (2018). Can identification as Muslim increase support for reconciliation? The case of the Kurdish conflict in Turkey. *International Journal of Intercultural Relations, 64*, 43–53. https://doi.org/10.1016/j.ijintrel.2018.02.002.

Bindman, S. W., Pomerantz, E. M., and Roisman, G. I. (2015). Do children's executive functions account for associations between early autonomy-supportive parenting and achievement through high school? *Journal of Educational Psychology, 107*(3), 756–70. https://doi.org/10.1037/edu0000017.

Birney, M. E., Rabinovich, A., Morton, T. A., Heath, H., and Ashcroft, S. (2019). When speaking English is not enough: The consequences of language-based stigma for nonnative speakers. *Journal of Language and Social Psychology, 39*(1), 67–86. https://doi.org/10.1177/0261927X19883906.

Blumenfeld, W. J. (2006). Christian privilege and the promotion of "secular" and not-so "secular" mainline Christianity in public schooling and in the larger society. *Equity and Excellence in Education, 39*(3), 195–210.

Blumenfeld, W. J., and Jaekel, K. (2012). Exploring levels of Christian privilege awareness among preservice teachers. *Journal of Social Issues*, 68(1), 128–44.

Brummelman, E., Thomaes, S., de Castro, B. O., Overbeek, G., and Bushman, B. J. (2014). "That's Not Just Beautiful—That's Incredibly Beautiful!": The adverse impact of inflated praise on children with low self-esteem. *Psychological Science*, 25(3), 728–35. https://doi. org/10.1177/0956797613514251.

Chen, X., Chung, J., and Hsiao, C (2009). Peer interactions and relationships from a cross-cultural perspective. In K. H. Rubin, W. M. Burkowski, and B. Laursen (Eds.), *Handbook of Peer Interactions, Relationships, and Groups*, pp. 432–51. Guilford.

Cherrez, J. N., and Gleason, B. (2022). A virtual exchange experience: Preparing pre-service teachers for cultural diversity. *Journal of Digital Learning in Teacher Education*, 38(3), 126–38. https://doi-org.ezproxy.hope.edu/10.1080/21532974.2022.2083732.

Cobb, C. (2012). Throwing out the culturally unresponsive cookie cutter: Collaborations, concessions, and curricula in a Ramadan music accommodation. *Canadian Journal of Action Research*, 13(3), 3–18. https://journals.nipissingu.ca/index.php/cjar/article/view/58/39 (accessed October 28, 2025).

Dabach, D. B. (2014). "I Am Not a Shelter!": Stigma and social boundaries in teachers' accounts of students' experience in separate "sheltered" English learner classrooms. *Journal of Education for Students Placed at Risk*, 19(2), 98–124. https://doi-org.ezproxy.hope.edu/10.1080/10824669.201 4.954044.

Dishion, T. J., and Tipsord, J. M. (2011). Peer contagion in child and adolescent social and emotional development. *Annual Review of Psychology*, 62, 189–214. https://doi.org/10.1146/ annurev.psych.093008.100412.

Erikson, E. H. (1972). Eight ages of man. In C. S. Lavatelli and F. Stendler (Eds.), *Reading in Child Behavior and Child Development*, pp. 19–30. Harcourt Brace Jovanovich.

Ferber, A. L. (2012). Color-blindness, post-feminism, and Christonormativity. *Journal of Social Issues*, 68(1), 63–77, https://doi.org/10.1111/j.1540-4560.2011.01736.x.

Garcia, E. B., Sulik, M. J., and Obradovic, J. (2019). Teachers' perceptions of students' executive functions: Disparities by gender, ethnicity, and ELL status. *Journal of Educational Psychology*, 111(5), 918–31. https://doi-org.ezproxy.hope.edu/10.1037/edu0000308.

Gay. (2018). *Culturally Responsive Teaching: Theory, Research, and Practice* (3rd edn.) Teachers College Press.

Gullifer, J. W., Pivneva, I., Whitford, V., Sheikh, N. A., and Titone, D. (2023). Bilingual language experience and its effect on conflict adaptation in reactive inhibitory control tasks. *Psychological Science*, 34(2), 238–51. https://doi-org.ezproxy.hope.edu/10.1177/09567976221113764.

Heinrich, J. (2015). The Devil is in the details: In America, can you really say "God" in school? *Educational Review*, 67(1), 64–78. https://doiorg.ezproxy.hope.edu/10.1080/00131911.2013.826 179.

Howard, L. W., Tang, T. L.-P., and Austin, M. J. (2015). Teaching critical thinking skills: Ability, motivation, intervention, and the Pygmalion effect. *Journal of Business Ethics*, 128(1), 133–47. https://doi.org/10.1007/s10551-014-2084-0.

Hwang, Y., Wolthuis, R., Kasap, S. & Peterson, R. (2026). Religious diversity and culturally responsive learning and teaching for teacher candidates. *Multicultural Learning and Teaching*, 21(1), 83–108. https://doi.org/10.1515/mlt-2023-0040.

Jamal, A. A., and Naber, N. C. (Eds.). (2022). *Race and Arab Americans Before and After 9/11: From Invisible Citizens to Visible Subjects*. Syracuse University Press.

Journell, W., and Dressman, M. (2011). Using videoconferences to diversify classrooms electronically. *The Clearing House*, 84(3), 109–13. https://doi.org/10.1080/00098655.2010.538757.

Kiang, L., Witkow, M. R., and Champagne, M. C. (2013). Normative changes in ethnic and American identities and links with adjustment among Asian American adolescents. *Developmental Psychology*, *49*(9), 1713–22. https://doi.org/10.1037/a0030840.

Kopish, M., and Marques, W. (2020). Leveraging technology to promote global citizenship in teacher education in the United States and Brazil. *Research in Social Sciences and Technology*, *5*(1), 45–69.

Ladson-Billings, G. (2021). Culturally relevant pedagogy: Asking a different question. Culturally Sustaining Pedagogies Series. In *Teachers College Press*. Teachers College Press.

Leckie, A., and Buser De, M. (2020). The power of an intersectionality framework in teacher education. *Journal for Multicultural Education*, *14*(1), 117–27. https://doi-org.ezproxy.hope.edu/10.1108/JME-07-2019-0059.

Leh, J. M., Grau, M., and Guiseppe, J. A. (2015). Navigating the development of pre-service teachers' intercultural competence and understanding of diversity: The benefits of facilitating online intercultural exchange. *Journal for Multicultural Education*, *9*(2), 98–110. https://doi-org.ezproxy.hope.edu/10.1108/JME-12-2014-0042.

Maoz, Z., and Henderson, E. A. (2020). *Scriptures, Shrines, Scapegoats, and World Politics: Religious Sources of Conflict and Cooperation in the Modern Era* (1st edn.). University of Michigan Press. https://doi.org/10.3998/mpub.11353856.

Martin, L. A. (2023). *The Gospel of J. Edgar Hoover: How the FBI Aided and Abetted the Rise of White Christian Nationalism*. Princeton University Press.

McCorkle, W., and Rodriguez, S. (2021). When nationalism supersedes belief in religious freedom: An analysis of teachers' beliefs. *Educational Studies*, *57*(2), 182–201.

Merlin-Knoblich, C., and Dameron, M. L. (2021). An examination of educator multicultural attitudes before and after a diversity dinner dialogue. *Journal for Multicultural Education*, *15*(1), 85–96. https://doi-org.ezproxy.hope.edu/10.1108/JME-05-2020-0042.

National Center for Education Statistics. (2023). *Characteristics of Public School Teachers*. https://nces.ed.gov/programs/coe/indicator/clr/public-school-teachers (accessed October 26, 2025).

National Center for Education Statistics. (2024). *Racial/Ethnic Enrollment in Public Schools*. https://nces.ed.gov/programs/coe/indicator/cge/racial-ethnic-enrollment (accessed October 26, 2025).

O'Dowd, R. (2016). Learning from the past and looking to the future of online intercultural exchange. In R. O'Dowd and T. Lewis (Eds.), *Online Intercultural Exchange: Policy, Pedagogy*, pp. 273–93. Taylor & Francis.

Pajares, F. (2010). Toward a positive psychology of academic motivation. *The Journal of Educational Research (Washington, DC)*, *95*(1), 27–35. https://doi.org/10.1080/00220670109598780.

Panjwani, F. (2017). No Muslim is just a Muslim: Implications for education. *Oxford Review of Education*, *43*(5), 596–611. https://doi.org/10.1080/03054985.2017.1352354.

Park, S., Ryu, J., and McChesney, K. (2019). Collaborative studio experiences between South Korean and American pre-service teachers: A case study of designing culturally-responsive virtual classroom simulation. *TechTrends: Linking Research and Practice to Improve Learning*, *63*(3), 271–83. https://doi-org.ezproxy.hope.edu/10.1007/s11528-019-00392-4.

Pettigrew, T. F. (1998). Intergroup Contact Theory. *Annual Review of Psychology*, *49*, 65–85.

Pew Research Center. (2022, September 13). *How U.S. Religious Composition Has Changed in Recent Decades*. https://www.pewresearch.org/religion/2022/09/13/how-u-s-religious-composition-has-changed-in-recent-decades (accessed October 26, 2025).

Pewewardy, C. (2005). Shared journaling: A methodology for engaging white preservice students into multicultural education discourse. *Teacher Education Quarterly*, *32*(1), 41–60. https://doi.org.ezproxy.hope.edu/https://www.teqjournal.org/backvols/2005/32_1/volume_32_number_1.htm.

Pouraskari, N., Dika, S., and Frankovich, J. (2023). Experiences of belonging and Islamophobia among hijabi Muslim college students in the United States. *College Student Affairs Journal*, *41*(2), 1–15. https://doi.org/10.1353/csj.2023.a916688.

Protner, B. (2018). The limits of an "open mind": State violence, Turkification, and complicity in the Turkish-Kurdish conflict. *Turkish Studies*, *19*(5), 671–96. https://doi.org/10.1080/14683849. 2018.1514494.

Puchner, L., and Markowitz, L. (2020). Christmas in U.S. K-12 schools: Categorizing and explaining teacher awareness of Christo-normativity. *Discourse: Studies in the Cultural Politics of Education*, *41*(4), 545–58. https://doi.org/10.1080/01596306.2018.1512074.

Rothbart, M. K. (2011). *Becoming Who We Are: Temperament and Personality in Development*. Guilford.

Sanatullova-Allison, E., and Robison-Young, V. A. (2016). Overrepresentation: An overview of the issues surrounding the identification of English language learners with learning disabilities. *International Journal of Special Education*, *31*(2).

Sardegna, V., and Dugartsyrenova, V. (2021) Facilitating preservice language teachers' intercultural learning via voice-based telecollaboration: The role of discussion questions. *Computer Assisted Language Learning*, *34*(3), 379–407. http://doi.org/10.1080/09588221.2020.1871028.

Singh, L., Fu, C. S. L., Tay, Z. W., and Golinkoff, R. M. (2018). Novel word learning in bilingual and monolingual infants: Evidence for a bilingual advantage. *Child Development*, *89*(3), e183–e198. https://doi-org.ezproxy.hope.edu/10.1111/cdev.12747.

Sloane, H., and Petra, M. (2021). Modeling cultural humility: Listening to students' stories of religious identity. *Journal of Social Work Education*, *57*(1), 28–39.

Strelau, J. (2008). *Temperament as a Regulator of Behavior: After Fifty Years of Research*. Eliot Werner Publications.

Szumski, G., and Karwowski, M. (2019). Exploring the Pygmalion effect: The role of teacher expectations, academic self-concept, and class context in students' math achievement. *Contemporary Educational Psychology*, *59*, 101787. https://doi.org/10.1016/j. cedpsych.2019.101787.

Toles-Patkin, T. (2021). Hallmarking Hanukkah: flawed attempts at diversity in cable television Christmas movies. *The Journal of Popular Culture*, *54*(5), 914–40. https://doi.org/10.1111/ jpcu.13062.

United States Department of Justice. (2023). Hate crimes: Facts and statistics. https://www.justice. gov/hatecrimes (accessed October 26, 2025).

Williams, J. A., III, and Glass, T. S. (2019). Teacher education and multicultural courses in North Carolina. *Journal for Multicultural Education*, *13*(2), 155–68. https://doi-org.ezproxy.hope. edu/10.1108/JME-05-2018-0028.

Yip, T. (2014). Ethnic identity in everyday life: The influence of identity development status. *Child Development*, *85*(1), 205–219. https://doi.org/10.1111/cdev.12107.

7

Critical Global Citizenship Education by South Korean Civic Organizations: Implication for Multiculturalism in South Korea

Seeun Jeon

Abstract

The chapter examines how civil society organizations (CSOs) in South Korea are practicing global citizenship education (GCED) in K-12 schools. Through interviews with people involved in CSO's GCED, the author addresses how GCED has been contextualized into South Korea and how they work with schools. First, the chapter briefly shares trends and critical approaches to GCED. Then it points out South Korea's strong national identity as a racially and ethnically homogeneous country and how that should be a key factor to situate diversity and GCED there. Introducing two GCED programs targeting K-12 learners, (1) Deep-Rooted World Heritage from Seoul Youth Center for Cultural Exchanges (MIZY) and (2) Ubuntu GCED from Africa Insight—the author will elaborate unique features of those programs to fill in the gaps from traditional GCED, as well as how schools take part in it. Through stories of GCED CSOs and analysis, the author manifests how GCED practice can look different in South Korea and why it is important. Ultimately, it suggests Korean GCED's future direction, strengthening connections between school and CSO to collaboratively discuss and embed GCED in class more consistently. The chapter hopes that GCED becomes a platform for critical self-reflection that helps take a step toward a meaningful multicultural society, pondering what diversity in South Korea would look like and building their identity as a global citizen.

Key Terms: *Critical Global Citizenship Education, South Korea, Multiculturalism, Civil Society Organization*

Trend of GCED

The United Nations Educational, Scientific, and Cultural Organization (UNESCO) defines global citizenship as "the idea that we are connected not just with one country but with a broader global community. (…) A global citizen understands how the world works, values differences in people, and works with others to find solutions to challenges too big for any one nation" (UNESCO, n.d.). It is also indicated in Sustainable Development Goal (SDG) 4.7, which indicates global citizenship, and appreciation of cultural diversity and of culture's contribution to sustainable development (United Nations, n.d.). Both mean acknowledging diversity on a global scale as well as national level internally.

With these different aspects of global citizenship, GCED is aiming for a more critical and contextualized viewpoint nowadays. Essentially, GCED is a way to comprehend the relationship between local and global surroundings by incorporating global perspectives into the curriculum. Yet, its origin and development and existing narratives are Europe and North America centered; therefore, there are suggestions for GCED to be more inclusive with more diverse environments and values (Hatley, 2019; Vries, 2020). There has been growing attention to intersectionality as well, such as the way Goren and Yemini (2017) analyze the lack of GCED education access and learner demographics on socioeconomic status. Opportunities for exposure to or for access to global perspectives and experience can be hard to get, and without enough resources and prior knowledge, it is not possible for people to comprehend one's own background and cultural settings.

GCED has been also critically assessed at the theoretical level. With the vague concept of what citizenship is, who gains the citizenship within which boundary of nationality, and how GCED is mostly organized and implemented by government with top-down approach, some studies indicate GCED often becomes a tool to fulfill national interest to raise socioeconomically competent labor forces in the capitalistic and elitist global environment (Hou, 2020; Goren and Yemini, 2017; Schippling, 2020). Dreamson (2018) asserts the need to tackle the binary of cosmopolitan and particularity of culture, stating to go beyond "dualistic understanding of global citizenship by undermining its exclusiveness and othering and facilitating intercultural interaction" (p. 77). Most importantly, there is a concern around GCED being another tool for neo-colonization, dividing Global North and Global South, further standardizing what it means to be a developed country (de Vries, 2020; Goren and Yemini, 2017). With this awareness, there are several efforts to make GCED more critical and inclusive. De Andreotti (2014) contrasts soft and critical GCED to discuss "historical/cultural production of knowledge and power in order to empower learners to make better informed choices—but the choices of action and meaning" (p. 30). Vries's (2020) intersectional method embraces divergent identities that affect GCED, and the distancing strategy suggested by Swanson and Gamal (2021) is a big step to recognize the hegemonic power of the English language, and ethnic based thinking that has been affecting education and GCED paradigm.

Another issue to focus on is around teacher education for GCED. According to UNESCO (n.d.), while teachers are aware of the importance of GCED, only one in five teachers have the resources and confidence to lead GCED for their students, and the lack of relevant resources has been one of the biggest barriers to facilitating GCED. Kim (2019) points out South Korean teachers' perception of GCED, mentioning that it wouldn't suit the current South Korean education system that centers around standardized tests and successful college admission, as well as lack of teaching resources and training for teachers around GCED. Therefore, this chapter addresses not only how GCED has been adopted in South Korea, but also how civic groups took a critical approach to organize it and how they can collaborate with schoolteachers for more consistent and sustainable GCED.

GCED in Korean Society

It is crucial to assess Korean society to understand how GCED has been working. As a racially/ethnically homogenous country, the concept of "*Hanminjok* [한민족]," which means "Korean," is still entrenched. Often it becomes a barrier for immigrants (Chung and Lim, 2016; Denney and Green, 2021). According to Kim (2020), "in order to be considered Korean, one must be of Korean lineage, speak and utilize the Korean language, and look Korean. Koreans have long believed themselves to be a *danil-minjok* ('single-race people/ nation'), sharing a common bloodline" (p. 84). The concept of social cohesion—especially around sufferings from the Japanese colonization era, Korean War, and modern economic development—through shared history is at the core to form national identity and tradition in South Korea (Kim, 2017: 14). This has been evident in several history, social studies, and ethics textbooks in South Korea, highlighting nationalism and solidarity (Moon and Koo, 2011) and foreigners' sameness—both physical and social—as prerequisite of inclusion to Korean society (Olneck, 2011).

This emphasis has been gradually diluted since the 2000s with the influx of more foreigners and global interaction with other countries. According to the Ministry of Justice in South Korea (2023), there are 2,507,584 foreigners residing in South Korea, which consists of 4.89 percent of the whole population in the nation. Different types of foreigners living in Korea such as marriage immigrants, foreigners married to Korean nationals, workers, or students studying abroad are constantly increasing over the years. With more interaction with other countries and involvement in global society such as Official Development Assistance (ODA) or joining international organizations, GCED can focus on multiculturalism and cultural diversity. However, literature identifies that people's confidence in communicating with foreigners or representing Korea in a global setting remains low (Lee and Misco, 2014; Roh, 2014). Tension exists between the realization of multiculturalism on a national level and its practical application into daily life (Watson, 2012), since much multicultural and diversity education is geared toward a broad global scale that deals with the binary of developed and developing countries and immigrants and their children and contains a message of assimilation into Korean society. Most importantly, GCED in Korea, which is government centered, is Eurocentric and follows international guidelines rather than gazing inward toward characteristics of South Korean society and adjusting properly (Kim, 2019).

Despite efforts of different levels and sectors to promote diversity and welcome foreigners—such as implementation of centers and educational programs for settlement, more participation and advocacy for foreign workers' rights, and establishment of a Master Plan for Immigration Policy—there is a long way to go because the meaning of multiculturalism is not thoroughly explored and there are not enough sources for South Koreans to get to know foreigners' background and cultures. This justifies the author's effort to investigate civic engagement and how those groups are working with schools to conduct GCED that overcomes the limitations of the traditional GCED in South Korea.

Positionality

I was born and raised in South Korea and have been studying abroad in the US since college. Recollecting K-12 school experience in South Korea, I have never been in a school with a friend who is an immigrant themselves or has a foreigner parent. Even without affluence, I was very fortunate to have a variety of experiences to encounter different cultures from a young age. In middle school, I was selected for a UNESCO cultural heritage policy research trip to the Czech Republic and represented Korean teenagers in a global forum in Israel. I also went to a Global High School, which has English and social studies intensive curricula providing trips to other countries and cultural awareness and exchange programs.

However, mirroring the critiques to South Korean GCED, I realize the hidden curriculum that centers around and solidifies Korean identity. Every week in elementary school, I had to say out loud a pledge to the flag that promises to be loyal to the country and Korean people. My high school motto is "Heart in Korea, Eyes to the World," thus while learning global surroundings, there were extensive programs and narratives to learn about Korean heritage and be proud of it as well. My first encounter with GCED was in middle school, learning about Millennium Development Goals (MDGs), which are now called Sustainable Development Goals (SDGs). Based on Korea's experience of rapid economical development and democratization, MDGs education was focused on how Korea should help developing countries more. Essentially, it carried a lesson that Koreans should be proud of the history of overcoming colonization and war, thus developing countries can learn from it.

I have rarely questioned those messages centering around Koreans—ethnically, historically, and linguistically homogeneous Korean (Kim, 2020)—until I encountered MIZY's Deep-Rooted World Heritage (DRWH) program and Africa Insight in high school senior year. Despite lots of opportunities to interact with foreigners and their culture, I have never imagined what it is like living in Korea as a foreigner, since foreigners were not present where I was brought up. Yet being an instructor for DRWH and working with Nigerian and Tanzanian partners and other foreign instructors, I heard numerous first-hand anecdotes from them about how they came to Korea and what they have gone through coming into a new space. Through Africa Insight's African Region Professional Development program, I reflected on how much media and limited knowledge shaped my unconscious prejudice and limited view on African countries. It revealed to me the need to develop a more critical lens and engage in more opportunities to get to know different cultures. Living as an international student for seven years in the US, I am constantly learning that what I am seeing about other countries and people from my own pool of news and resources is never enough, and how much I want to expand this and spread the value of a global perspective from real experience. As such, I always do my best to be cognizant and represent South Korea, volunteering for local global citizenship programs, visiting elementary schools, and introducing Korean culture, just like DRWH. Gaining a deeper understanding about GCED and how I could apply that into my precious past experience with MIZY and Africa Insight would be meaningful.

Interviewees and Organizations

I conducted one-to-one virtual interviews with five people who are involved in the GCED program from civic organizations, targeting K-12 students in South Korea; three instructors and a director of the DRWH program from Seoul Youth Center for Cultural Exchange (MIZY) and the founder of NGO Africa Insight. I myself have participated in the DRWH program at MIZY as an instructor in 2017, thus I have connected with the director to find a few instructors who were interested in doing an interview. As the instructor group is made up of Koreans and foreign nationals, I made sure to have at least one foreign instructor to get their perspective as well. I have also been involved in Africa Insight since 2016 with its lecture series and journalist program. Since Jae-seong, the founder, is the one who has been leading the GCED program and is the only one familiar with the program among current staff, I conducted an interview with him. Qualitative interviewing has been selected to have interviewees expand interactive inquiry involving both researcher and participants (Agee, 2009: 432).

MIZY is a youth community center—established in 2000 by the Seoul metropolitan government but now managed by Daesan foundation—that targets youth international cultural exchange. DRWH is one of their signature programs that has been in place for more than ten years. Through DRWH, foreigners living in Korea and Korean instructors are paired up and visit 4th to 6th grade classrooms in Seoul for two-hour sessions. Su-ji has served as the director of DRWH since 2021, and oversees the program, coordinating with schools and selecting and training instructors each semester. Among three DRWH instructor interviewees, two of them are Koreans: Ji-hee has participated in DRWH twice, teaching with Chinese and Ugandan instructors, and Hye-jin, who led a class with Turkmenistan partners. They were drawn to the DRWH program around their majors—Chinese literature and culture and anthropology. Another is Kriti who is an Indian instructor for DRWH. Kriti has been living in Korea for twelve years so she is familiar with Korean society and how to narrate her culture in Korean context.

Je-seong, from the non-governmental organization Africa Insight, joined for the interview. Since 2013, Africa Insight has been working on relieving prejudice toward Africa and promoting its diverse culture, as well as advocating for African people living in South Korea. They organize annual festivals in Seoul to promote African culture in a more engaging way, post different materials around the problematic depiction of African people and culture in Korean media, or work with governments to advise partnering with African countries. As one of the founding members of the organization, Je-seong has been organizing and leading Ubuntu Africa GCED for diverse learners since 2014, from elementary school to professional developments for teachers and corporate workers, mainly in metropolitan areas. Recognized with a strong and unique curriculum to raise cultural awareness and discuss global issues around the African area for different types of learners, Ubuntu Africa GCED earned UNESCO certification of Education for Sustainable Development (ESD) in 2022.

Findings

Characteristic of Programs

Both DRWH and Ubuntu Africa GCED programs are very meaningful as they involve different parties and narratives. For DRWH, Kriti (personal communication, January 21, 2024) says the program is unique in that it invites foreigners into the program and gives agency to design a class to share about their culture, and to get to know about the country and form a positive first impression with actual interaction rather than simple internet browsing. Hye-jin (personal communication, January 23, 2024) also says DRWH is a special GCED led by youth. And all the interviewees from MIZY expressed that it was a meaningful experience to form a community of instructors of different identities and learn from each other. Considering the close relationship between cultural sensitivity with hands-on experience and how traditional GCED lacks giving confidence to actually communicate and respect other cultures (Roh, 2014; Lee and Misco, 2014), DRWH has been a great platform that is guided by youth and for youth themselves.

A critical approach is adopted in Ubuntu GCED in Africa Insight. Jae-seong (personal communication, January 21, 2024) states that their GCED is about the connection between the African area and other current global issues, ultimately shedding light on underrepresented narratives of Africa and how that happened, tying into the Korean context. This relates to several publications that assert inclusion of non-Western areas and their framework of GCED (Dreamson, 2018; Drerup, 2020). Ubuntu GCED's pedagogy takes an inquiry-based pedagogy, which is the core part for practicing intersectional GCED to raise critical awareness and counter-narratives (Swanson and Gamal, 2021). The class starts with a question "What comes to mind when you think about Africa?" Asking further about how they came up with a response to the question, students question themselves where those ideas and images come from and how those stereotypes are created. Ultimately, it touches on the critical insight about who gets to have power to control what to say about Africa and why often they are being misrepresented. At the end of the class, students go back to the response to the initial question, and leave with the lesson that Africa is not about a single image and story but divergent cultures and people. Likewise, DRWH and Ubuntu GCED set great examples of having people learn from the process of designing class, consider different audiences of the program, as well as tune into marginalized voices. Meanwhile, among characteristics of DRWH, language use of the classroom shows a connection to Olneck (2011)'s dilemma of difference. Ji-hee says

> Since a few years ago, DRWH has been selecting foreign instructors who can communicate in Korean language as well. (…) I think it worked out much better than I expected, because when foreigners speak in English and Korean instructors translate, students acknowledge them as an outsider and not easily get close to them. When my Ugandan partner spoke in Korean, kids approached first and asked questions and stuff. (personal communication, January 18, 2024)

How Civic Organization GCED Program Works with Schools

Getting to know how MIZY and Africa Insight are communicating with schools and operating programs gives an idea of the importance of calling for GCED and opens up discussion about who should be in charge of GCED. Despite positive feedback and follow ups from participants after classes, both MIZY and Africa Insight are not doing thorough meetings with teachers or school personnel prior to visits to onboard them with what their program is about, other than sharing brief written documents of lesson plans. That is evidenced by the DRWH instructor's anecdote from the class. Ji-hee shares that

> "My Chinese partner instructor and I were setting up the 6th grade class with Chinese flags. And one of the students loudly said, 'I hate China!' and some other peers said 'It's rude saying that in front of teachers,' but the homeroom teacher reacted 'Why is that a problem, a person has a right to say their opinion …' (Meanwhile) when my Ugandan partner instructor introduced that they can speak different tribal languages, a student said 'I dare you to speak all of them' in an offensive tone. And thankfully the homeroom teacher responded 'What if we try asking it in a more polite way?' and things turned out well." (personal communication, January 18, 2024)

Likewise, as teachers' sensitivity to GCED mattered in the classroom experience, instructors sometimes struggled to respond to situations that are offensive to foreigners and their culture without prior knowledge about the classroom and students. Interviewees also mention that teachers' familiarity with foreign instructors and culture vary between school districts. According to Seoul Open Data (Seoul Metropolitan Government, 2024), the population of foreigners residing in Seoul is concentrated in a few districts. This means teachers in those districts would have more experience communicating with immigrant students or second-generation immigrants in Korea, while others would not get enough chances to meet foreign students and feel the need of GCED. This further explains the disparity between school classrooms and GCED mentioned by Kim (2019), as teachers might not have concrete strategies and resources to bring GCED.

Fortunately, many teachers and administrators have expressed interest in GCED and look for more GCED opportunities after the visit, seeing how much students enjoy engaging activities and learning new things. Jae-seong (personal communication, January 21, 2024) states that the hardest step is before the visit, having people to realize the need for GCED and learning about Africa which is far away and seems too different from Korean culture. Su-ji also puts a lot of effort emphasizing the importance of the DRWH visit to school administrators, as it might be the one and only chance to talk to a person from another country and get to know their culture, which could change their worldview.

Meanwhile, when asked how teachers in the school can seamlessly integrate GCED into the existing curriculum and consistently practice it, a majority of the interviewees said that it should not be a task for teachers to do. With the centralized national curriculum to follow, and many other clerical tasks and mandatory training—schoolteachers in South Korea are counted as government officials—on top of caring and teaching students different subjects, interviewees think carving out time to do GCED class and preparing would be too much work. Therefore, rather than having teachers to design and get trained to do their own GCED, supporting more civic organizations to develop unique GCED and visit schools for a long period is preferred. Although there are practical issues to be figured out such as complex processes to gain access to schools, more longitudinal relationships between schools and civic organizations, even including student families who are immigrants themselves, would be a good way to strengthen school–local community bonds and broaden the contents and sustainability of GCED.

With the question about the importance of GCED, significant features of South Korean society and young students were addressed from responses. At a broad level, Korea has been geographically and ethnically isolated, thus interviewees are feeling the lack of opportunities for awareness of other cultures with hands-on experience, as well as confidence to approach and communicate fluently with foreigners. Having been living in Korea for a long time, Kriti mentions "I feel like they (Koreans) don't know how to treat them (foreigners), so they're kind of afraid to, you know, go up and talk to them or learn more about it" (personal communication, January 21, 2024). Providing a platform for people to be exposed to divergent cultures and interact with others from different backgrounds, GCED is a way for South Korea to keep the pace for rapid globalization, especially with increasing population of foreigners and participation in the global arena. Korea has a great potential to contribute to the GCED field with its unique history. Je-seong states that Korea has gone through very compressed development in a few decades, being the only case that has become a developed country from the developing country. And that can be a key for South Korea to understand and connect both Global North and Global South, pondering what global citizenship mindset that Koreans can have.

Responses also center around what GCED means for young elementary school students. All the interviewees expressed that young people have a relatively flexible and open mind with less bias, thus it is easy to adapt to a new environment and learn new things from foreigners through GCED. Interesting enough, even though the younger generation is in constant contact with social media platforms, it does not necessarily lead to their development of critical lenses to assess and accept foreigners. This is because it is a challenge to mitigate bias online via catered algorithms and with strong-stimuli shorter media forms—YouTube shorts, TikTok, etc.—it is hard to assess reliability of authors and contents (Steinfield and Lev-on, 2024). Therefore, interacting with foreigners and learning their culture and stories from them is crucial and it will enrich their knowledge encounter different cultures in appropriate ways. Most importantly, GCED can tackle current issues around the Korean education system. Su-ji (personal communication, January 17, 2024) shares that as Korean education has been focusing too much on standardized tests, its holistic aspect to cover humanism is being neglected. With that, GCED highlighting morality and respect for each other to collectively address global issues can achieve socioemotional learning and communication skills. Hye-jin adds that GCED education like DRWH can be beneficial for students from a low socioeconomic background, providing chances to experience the other culture without traveling or going to private institutions (personal communication, January 23, 2024). Likewise, it is apparent that GCED is essential and will have a positive impact on the South Korean educational system and society. Targeting younger students can be viewed as the audience with the most potential to influence their flexible developmental stages with respect to having the ability to achieve equity of education.

Discussion—Future of GCED in South Korea

One of the last questions asked was to have interviewees envision their own ideal GCED in the future. The first overarching theme is improving the quantity and quality of GCED. In terms of quantity, there is a desire to have more GCED programs like DRWH where students can closely meet and gain first-hand experience from foreigners, as well as make classroom visits longer and more regular. In addition, since programs interviewed for this project are based on Seoul metropolitan area, interviewees were curious about what other regions' GCED look like with expanded GCED opportunities nationally, considering the inconsistent proportion of the foreigner population. Unequal financial resources and access to quality GCED and connection by regions and school districts was brought up, too. Hye-jin shares

> I felt that even within Seoul there is a big wealth gap between districts. Some schools have very distinct educational resources, facilities, numbers of students and their attitudes towards treating foreigners. So I wondered after this GCED, how this would impact their future perceptions and careers, or how this current state might be related to parents' socio-cultural assets. With that, I believe GCED should be equally provided for all the students" (personal communication, January 23, 2024).

In fact, students, teachers, and schools in Seoul are gathered in a few districts, which also have the highest household incomes (Seoul Metropolitan Office of Education, 2023; Korea

Statistics Information Service, 2024). Su-ji says "regardless of the wealth of the area, GCED should be a precious learning moment that any students can enjoy rightfully, not just with one time visit but on a long-term and national wide level" (personal communication, January 17, 2024). Likewise, there should be more discussion about how GCED can be expanded.

Quality wise, interviewees asked for more seamless GCED and GCED with divergent goals. Instead of carving out time specifically for GCED, Jae-seong argues that it should be incorporated into other existing curriculum to keep the interest consistent (personal communication, January 21, 2024). As a person who gets lots of news about different policies around schools and teenagers, Su-ji noticed that there is more focus on the technology STEM field while there is lack of positioning teenagers in the globalized world and socioemotional learning and character building from education that can facilitate communication with others from different identities (personal communication, January 17, 2024). This reiterates the importance of different entities around education—students, teachers, families—to be on the same page about the needs of GCED. A holistic approach to GCED and its goals, and incorporating them into different aspects of curriculum, would not only help South Korean GCED be more enriching but also help tackle the gaps in the existing system.

Limitation

There is room for improvement and calls for further research around GCED and the South Korean context. First is about the interview group size. Five people, especially the majority of them from the same program and organization, might not be sufficient to represent general GCED state and experience. Geographical elements should be more considered. Interviewees and the organization are based in Seoul, capital city of Korea, yet certain areas are conglomerated with specific groups of immigrants—for instance, many marriage immigrant women from Southeast Asian countries live in rural areas. Therefore, future projects could investigate GCED programs in other areas and how their backgrounds affect people's perception of GCED.

Another issue is about the different subfields of GCED. With the goal to nurture global citizenship, there are numerous ways to narrate it, including global partnership through SDGs, and cultural diversity is only one part of it. Therefore, it would be worth looking at as to whether any other organizations are doing GCED with a different focus and how they narrate global citizenship, as well as how those are adapted to South Korea.

Conclusion

The chapter looked at how the South Korean context—specifically strong social cohesion around shared history and culture—and GCED are affecting each other, through the interviews with GCED civic organization personnel who visit schools. This shows while GCED has a common goal for global understanding and respect, it is essential to have diverse pedagogies that are considerate to each situation and what kind of things are grounded to plant the seed of global citizenship.

I asked interviewees to describe GCED in one word. Su-ji (personal communication, January 17, 2024) says it is "etiquette," which refers to a social commitment to live with others in harmony, based on mutual respect. Jae-seong used the word "Ubuntu," which means "I am because you are" in Swahili. Likewise, GCED program organizers share the importance of GCED in terms of highlighting relationality with others and learning from each other. Yet Ji-hee thinks that GCED is "swan," reflecting all the hard and intricate work behind it in order to achieve an ideal global society (personal communication, January 18, 2024). These reflect not only the passion of civil society to incorporate diversity into Korean society but also recognize that these efforts require much planning and effort to implement.

In fact, Korea has been part of globalization for many years. Queen Heo, married to King Suro, the founder of the Gaya Kingdom, is considered the first international marriage recorded in Korean history. Dutch man Yeon Park is the first person to be officially naturalized to Korea in the seventeenth century. Acknowledging this history and expansion of venues and modalities of connecting with others, GCED can facilitate going beyond space and give time to reflect to recognize one's own unconscious bias and rethink what diversity means.

Questions to Consider

1 In what ways can Global Citizenship Education (GCED) serve as a platform for critical self-reflection, helping individuals envision and embrace a meaningful multicultural society? How can this education shape their understanding of diversity and influence their development as global citizens, particularly with the evolving demographic landscape?

2 In countries with strong social cohesion rooted in shared history and culture, how does the integration of GCED impact both educational practices and the formation of global citizenship? What are the challenges and opportunities that arise when fostering a sense of global responsibility in societies that prioritize a unified national identity, and how can education systems balance these dynamics effectively?

References

Agee, J. (2009). Developing qualitative research questions: A reflective process. *International Journal of Qualitative Studies in Education, 22*(4), 431–47.

Chung, G. H., and Lim, J. Y. (2016). Marriage immigrant mothers' experience of perceived discrimination, maternal depression, parenting behaviors, and adolescent psychological adjustment among multicultural families in South Korea. *Journal of Child and Family Studies*, *25*, 2894–903.

de Vries, M. (2020). Enacting critical citizenship: An intersectional approach to global citizenship education. *Societies*, *10*(4), 91.

Denney, S., and Green, C. (2021). Who should be admitted? Conjoint analysis of South Korean attitudes toward immigrants. *Ethnicities*, *21*(1), 120–45.

Dreamson, N. (2018). Culturally inclusive global citizenship education: Metaphysical and non-western approaches. *Multicultural Education Review*, *10*(2), 75–93.

Drerup, J. (2020). Global citizenship education, global educational injustice and the postcolonial critique. *Global Justice: Theory Practice Rhetoric*, *12*(1), 27–54.

Goren, H., and Yemini, M. (2017). Global citizenship education redefined—A systematic review of empirical studies on global citizenship education. *International Journal of Educational Research*, *82*, 170–83.

Hatley, J. (2019). Universal values as a barrier to the effectiveness of global citizenship education: A multimodal critical discourse analysis. *International Journal of Development Education and Global Learning*, *11*(1), 87–102.

Hou, Y. (2020). Comparative global citizenship education: A critical literature analysis. *Beijing International Review of Education*, *2*(4), 537–52.

Kim, H. A. (2020). Understanding "Koreanness": Racial stratification and colorism in Korea and implications for Korean multicultural education. *International Journal of Multicultural Education*, *22*(1), 76–97.

Kim, H., Oh, H. G., and Lee, S. J. (2017). Determining the quality of life of marriage migrant women in Korea. *Journal of Policy Studies*, *32*(3), 83–104.

Kim, K. L. (2017). Korea and the gender construction of female marriage immigrants. *Pastoral Psychology*, *66*, 13–25.

Kim, Y. (2019). Global citizenship education in South Korea: Ideologies, inequalities, and teacher voices. *Globalisation, Societies and Education*, *17*(2), 177–93.

Korea Statistics Information Service. (2024). Yearly Earned Income by City and District. https://kosis.kr/statHtml/statHtml.do?orgId=133&tblId=DT_133001N_4215&conn_path=I2 (accessed October 26, 2025).

Lee, L., and Misco, T. (2014). All for one or one for all: An analysis of the concepts of patriotism and others in multicultural Korea through elementary moral education textbooks. *The Asia-Pacific Education Researcher*, *23*, 727–34.

Ministry of Justice. (2024). *Statistics on Foreigners Residing in South Korea*. Ministry of Justice. https://www.moj.go.kr/moj/2412/subview.do (accessed October 26, 2025).

Moon, R. J., and Koo, J. W. (2011). Global citizenship and human rights: A longitudinal analysis of social studies and ethics textbooks in the Republic of Korea. *Comparative Education Review*, *55*(4), 574–99.

Olneck, M. R. (2011). Facing multiculturalism's challenges in Korean education and society. *Asia Pacific Education Review*, *12*, 675–90.

Roh, S. Z. (2014). A study on the factors affecting the intercultural sensitivity of middle and high school students in Korea. *Advanced Science and Technology Letters*, *47*, 266–9.

Schippling, A. (2020). Researching global citizenship education: Towards a critical approach. *Journal of Social Science Education*, *19*(4), 98–113.

Seoul Metropolitan Government. (2024). Population of foreigners residing in Seoul. Seoul Open Dat. http://115.84.165.40/dataList/10745/S/2/datasetView.do (accessed November 12, 2025).

Seoul Metropolitan Office of Education. (2023). 2023 Seoul Educational Statistics.

Steinfeld, N., and Lev-on, A. (2024). Exposure to diverse political views in contemporary media environments. *Frontiers in Communication*, 9, 1384706.

Swanson, D. M., and Gamal, M. (2021). Global Citizenship Education/Learning for Sustainability: Tensions, "flaws," and contradictions as critical moments of possibility and radical hope in educating for alternative futures. *Globalisation, Societies and Education*, 19(4), 456–69.

United Nations. (n.d.). 17 Goals. *United Nations*. https://sdgs.un.org/goals (accessed October 26, 2025).

United Nations Educational, Scientific, and Cultural Organization. (n.d.). What you need to know about global citizenship education. *United Nations Educational, Scientific, and Cultural Organization*. https://www.unesco.org/en/global-citizenship-peace-education/need-know (accessed October 26, 2025).

Watson, I. (2012). Paradoxical multiculturalism in South Korea. *Asian Politics & Policy*, 4(2), 233–58.

8

The Impact of School Organizational Structure: A Case Study of Administration of Special Education to Young Children of Immigrants

Cady Landa

Abstract

All students should have access to a global curriculum, an affirming and integrated school community, differentiated instruction, and opportunities for development. Some recent studies show that immigrants' children are not benefiting from entitlements that provide students with disabilities access to school curricula in inclusive settings. This chapter reports on a case study of a public elementary school that examined how school organizational structures contribute to this outcome. The study finds that school structures that do not provide enough support for within-staff and staff–parent coordination on behalf of individual students contribute, in the case of immigrants' children, to significantly delayed identification of disabilities, overly restrictive segregated placement, and denial of appropriate language services. The chapter provides recommendations for the design of organizational structures in elementary schools that can support school staff in effectively including all students in school-based learning. The study finds that to equitably serve immigrants' children, staff–parent coordination structures must include timely availability of language interpretation and translation and provision of systems knowledge that empowers parents to fully participate in their child's education and obtain from the school or broader community the services their child may need for optimal health and development.

Key Terms: *immigrants' children, special education entitlements, elementary school, organizational structure, case study*

In the US, the number and proportion of children with at least one foreign-born parent have grown rapidly, from 8.2 million (13 percent of the child population) in 1990 to 18.0 million (26 percent of the child population) in 2021 (MPI, 2023). During this period, immigrants increasingly dispersed to areas that are not traditional gateways for newcomers. As a result, more jurisdictions have acquired expanded or new responsibilities for educating immigrants' children. This has created both challenges and prospects for PK-12 public schools. The increasing diversity of children and their families within schools provides rich and important opportunities for children and the school community to learn about other cultures and experiences, hear a wider variety of perspectives, and become comfortable with difference. Districts are challenged, however, to adapt long-standing practice to changing student populations.

One of the prominent challenges schools face is the increased language diversity of students and students' parents. While 14 percent of immigrants' children have limited English proficiency (The Urban Institute, 2024), a larger proportion live in homes in which a non-English language is spoken. In 2016, 55 percent of immigrants' children lived in a home with parents who had difficulty speaking English (The Annie E. Casey Foundation, 2024). Immigrant families speak many different non-English languages at home. While 62 percent of the people who speak a non-English language at home speak Spanish, immigrant families in the US speak a total of at least 350 other languages (C. Suarez-Orozco et al., 2015).

Another significant challenge for PK-12 schools, not as readily apparent, is the failure of US immigration policy and US state and local governments to provide infrastructure to fully incorporate all immigrants living in the US (Bloemraad and de Graauw, 2012; Fix, 2007; Jones-Correa and de Graauw, 2013). This aspect of our public policies toward immigrants may mean that immigrant parents struggle more than US-born parents to meet their children's service needs in a timely manner. Services that identify and address disabilities for children in the US are particularly complex to access—difficult for even US-born parents to navigate (Resch et al., 2010). Immigrant parents are learning the systems of a new country, often have a non-English first language, and often face numerous other barriers associated with their migration and status that are likely to obstruct access to these services.

A handful of empirical analyses have examined immigrants' children's access to the Individuals with Disabilities Education Act (IDEA) special education program, which provides entitlements to a free and appropriate education (FAPE) in least restrictive settings to eligible children with disabilities. These analyses suggest that immigrants' children are less likely to receive special education than children of US-born parents, particularly in the early elementary school years (Child Trends, 2015, 2018; Conger and Griogorenko, 2010; Hibel and Jasper, 2012; Landa, 2023). Landa (2023) also finds that when immigrants' children do receive special education in Massachusetts elementary schools, they are less likely than children of US-born parents to be placed in integrated settings and are more likely to be placed in substantially separate settings. Landa (2023) demonstrates that having an immigrant parent significantly affects young children's access to special education and inclusive settings, even after accounting for factors such as students' race, English language proficiency, family low income, grade level, and gender. These findings are concerning because they indicate that newcomers' children who have disabilities are vulnerable to not receiving the services and resources they need to access curricula in integrated settings. This may lead to marginalization and repeated experiences of failure detrimental to development and academic trajectories. Researchers note that xenophobia and negative racial/ethnic/ religious stereotypes often challenge immigrants' children's self-esteem and sense of belonging (Coll and Marks, 2009; Suarez-Orozco and Suarez-Orozco, 2001). It is imperative that those who need services and accommodations to progress in school receive inclusive, affirming, non-stigmatizing support that facilitates growth, self-worth, and belonging.

This chapter reports on a case study that examines how school organizational structures impact the capacity of school staff to administer special education entitlements to immigrants' children. As such, it has implications for understanding how organizational structure contributes to the capacity of school staff to equitably meet needs of culturally and linguistically diverse students. The study explores three IDEA entitlements: Child Find, Least Restrictive Environment (LRE), and access to English language (EL) services. The Child Find provision requires schools to identify and evaluate, subject to parental consent, all eligible students. The LRE provision requires that students are educated in the least restrictive settings best for them, and that they are not separated from students without disabilities unless learning in regular classes cannot be achieved with supplementary aids and services (IDEA, 2004). Federal laws require that schools "must provide EL students with disabilities with both the language assistance and disability-related services to which they are entitled" (US DOE and DOJ, 2015: 24).

How School Organizational Structures Matter

The predominantly bureaucratic structures of today's PK-12 schools are a product of late nineteenth/early-twentieth-century ideas of scientific management and the social efficiency movement that became popular in the developing field of education administration in the context of urbanization and industrialization. At that time, education administrators adopted scientific management to introduce efficiencies in coping with increasing numbers of students stemming from large-scale immigration, the movement of people from rural areas to cities, the need for higher levels of literacy and numeracy, and the spread of compulsory school attendance (Graham, 2005; Skrtic, 1991). Common bureaucratic features of today's schools continue to include hierarchical relationships; exclusion of teachers from policy development; highly structured teaching scripts; departments with specialized functions and structures supporting vertical, as opposed to horizontal, cross-departmental, coordination; hierarchical relationships between school staff and parents; sorting and tracking of students for delivery of standardized programs; teachers working in relative isolation; and compliance paperwork (Darling-Hammond, 1997; Kalyanpur et al., 2000).

Skrtic (1991) and Darling-Hammond (1997) expressed concern that these bureaucratic structures do not allow educators to provide "individually appropriate teaching" (Darling-Hammond, 1997: 38) or to respond to needs of diverse learners, or to "prevent students from falling 'through the cracks'" (Darling-Hammond, 1997: 65). Darling-Hammond attributed successful student outcomes to relational organizational structures that enable teachers to work collaboratively in teams focused on small groups of shared students; to work collaboratively on other teams focused on curriculum; to participate in school governance; and to regularly share rich information with parents.

Recent research compares the impacts of bureaucratic vs. relational organizational structures in schools. August and Hakuta (1998) noted that schools that were most effective with students not proficient in academic English facilitate collaboration between language and mainstream classroom teachers and allow these teachers to customize their educational strategies to the needs of individual students. Serpa (2011) noted problematic implications for students when departmental silos do not support collaboration between EL and special education staff on behalf of dual language learners with disabilities. Hehir and Katzman (2013) found schoolwide structures supporting teachers' collaboration in innovative problem-solving around individual students' needs to be the distinguishing characteristic of schools with superior student outcomes and inclusive practices for students with disabilities. A cross-national study of schools with large numbers of immigrant students found promise in relational attributes including teacher teams responsible for small groups of shared students engaged in collaborative curriculum planning and efforts to understand and meet the needs of individual students (Suarez-Orozco et al., 2013).

Theoretical Frameworks

Building on this literature, the study described in this chapter uses relational coordination (RC) and relational bureaucracy (RB) theories to examine the impact of school organizational structure on a school's administration of the special education program to immigrants' young children. RC theory holds that effective coordination of work is carried out through relationships of shared goals, shared knowledge, and mutual respect reinforced by communication that is frequent, timely, accurate, and problem-solving (Gittell, 2006).

RB theory extends RC theory to propose that organizational structures can be designed to scale, replicate, and sustain reciprocity among work roles based on shared goals, shared knowledge, and mutual respect among staff (relational coordination), between staff and leaders (relational leadership), and between staff and their clients (relational coproduction). RB theory hypothesizes that these three kinds of reciprocal interactions allow for an integration of perspectives that can produce caring, timely, and knowledgeable responses to individuals served (Gittell and Douglass, 2012).

There are several advantages to using these theoretical frameworks to shape data collection and analysis in the case study. RB theory focuses on attributes that are consistent with the educational needs of students with disabilities: the degree to which there are timely, well-informed, and individualized responses to individuals, and the degree to which there is coordination among staff from different departments or having different specializations within school districts. Moreover, RB theory models the relationship between staff and clients (parents) as a coproduction process in which parents are members of the team serving the child. Unlike the traditional bureaucratic paradigm in which the parent is in a subordinate position to professional staff, RB proposes coproduction as a process through which staff and parents work together. In the case of children experiencing difficulty in school, the parent is likely to be the most passionate and caring advocate for the child, while staff will be pulled by the interests of others in the context of limited resources. Additionally, parents have key information about the child's history and out-of-school context and may be able to access critical resources outside of the school.

The coproduction construct of RB theory is particularly relevant to educational equity for immigrants' children. In their theory of "distributional effects of coproduction," Jakobsen and Andersen (2013) note that in contexts in which coproduction helps determine the quality of services, there is danger that unequal resources for participation among coproducers will, if not remedied, have the effect of widening disparities among those served. Failure to provide resources immigrant parents need to equitably participate on behalf of their children, such as language access and systems knowledge, can lead to poorer services and thus, poorer outcomes for immigrants' children.

Finally, RB theory is relevant to organizations that must cope with environmental change. RB substitutes for the top-down management structure of traditional bureaucracy, a more horizontal structure that facilitates constant collaborative problem-solving to address the needs of individuals served by the organization. This horizontal, constant collaborative problem-solving approach to the needs of individuals is hypothesized to support a bottom-up process of organizational learning and innovation (Godwyn and Gittell, 2012) that can enable schools to adapt to changes in the population they serve.

Methods

A case study provides an opportunity for in-depth how and why understanding of phenomena in the contexts in which they occur (Yin, 2009). The unit of analysis in this study is a public elementary school in Massachusetts. The study explores explanatory mechanisms shaping the school's response to newcomers' children through in-depth examination of the approach of staff to eleven children of immigrants who were, from their parents' perspectives, experiencing difficulty in school. The study was designed to generalize to theory in ways relevant to policy and practice.

The full case study sought to understand (1) the results of studies showing inequitable administration of special education to immigrants' children, (2) the impact of school organizational structures and public policies on school capacity to respond in appropriate and timely ways to newcomers' children struggling in school, and (3) the experiences of immigrant parents navigating the school system on behalf of their children. This chapter focuses on the impact of school organizational structure on the administration of special education to immigrants' children.

Selection of Study School

Selection of the school was purposeful (Maxwell, 2013) to maximize the likelihood of recruiting a sufficient number of participants meeting study criteria. Recruitment focused on superintendents in Massachusetts cities with the highest numbers of foreign-born, unnaturalized residents with incomes below 200 percent of the federal poverty level (FPL). The superintendent who volunteered to participate selected the study school in consultation with principals.

The school selected had grades pre-K through 5. In 2016–2017, when the study was implemented, it had approximately 450 students with a 10:1 student-to-teacher ratio. It was a Title I school that housed a district-wide program for students with autism. All the school's teachers were licensed and considered to be highly qualified in their area of teaching. Per pupil expenditure for the school's district was approximately $20,600.

Almost half the school's students were Hispanic and just over a third were White. Approximately half had a first language other than English—mostly Spanish plus twenty additional languages. Just over a quarter were categorized as English learners (ELs). The parents of 37 percent of the students requested school communications in Spanish. An additional thirteen parents requested communications in nine other non-English languages. Approximately a third of students were categorized as economically disadvantaged. Almost a quarter of the school's students received special education—higher than the district's 18 percent because of the school's autism program through which the district sought to place all elementary students with autism regardless of home address.

Overall, the school had a traditional structure. The autism program had one separate classroom, with a special education teacher and several paraprofessionals, at each grade level, for students diagnosed with autism. During the study year, the third-grade class in the autism program temporarily included students without disabilities and was staffed by a general education teacher, a special education teacher, and paraprofessionals. At the time of study implementation, Massachusetts law required that all public PK-12 students be taught in English in English-language classrooms.

Selection of Study Students, Parents, and School Staff

Criteria for selecting study students and parents included that parents had immigrated to the US after age sixteen and had concerns about their child's performance at the study school. Additionally, their child had to be eligible for free- or reduced-price lunch (FRPL). Students were eligible for FRPL, regardless of family immigration status, if family income was within 185 percent of the FPL.

The study school and a district parent literacy program distributed fliers about the study to parents in English, Spanish, Haitian Creole, and Portuguese, and the study was presented to parents at a Special Education Parent Advisory Council meeting facilitated by a parent bilingual in Spanish and English. Thirteen parents requested informational meetings, which were assisted by trained bilingual interpreters and written information in parent languages. Parents were told they would not be asked about their legal status and were offered language interpretation and $20 gift cards from a local supermarket for each hour of interview. The parents of eleven children consented to participate in the study.

The eleven students who became the focus of the study, five girls and six boys, were all born in the US and spanned grades pre-K through five. Five were receiving special education—four through the school's autism program. Ten spoke Spanish as a first language. One student was reported by the district to speak English as a first language, but his parent spoke a low-incidence language[1] and struggled greatly with English. Six were categorized as EL students, and the parents and school staff expressed concerns about the English language skills of three additional students not categorized as EL. All students were covered by the Medicaid program. Eight had been in pre-K programs, and four had received Early Intervention services.

The fourteen parents participating in the study came from six countries. None spoke English as a first language. For all but one parent, Spanish was the first language; the other parent spoke the very low-incidence language and struggled with English. All except one of the parents whose first language was Spanish had requested school communications in Spanish. The parent speaking the very low-incidence language had not requested school communications in her language. Parents' formal educational experience varied widely, from no school through holding a college degree. Four were single mothers. They had lived in the US for seven to twenty years. The twelve educators who participated in the study, all with the parents' consent, were identified by the parents or other staff as working with study students.

Data Collection

Data consisted of federal, state, and district documents and semi-structured in-depth interviews with the school principal, parents, and school staff serving each of the study students. Trained bilingual interpreters were used for interviews with the parents of nine students.

Data Analysis

Transcriptions of audio-recorded English words of the interviewer, interpreters, parents, and school staff were coded and grouped by student in Atlas.ti, version 8. Transcripts were coded deductively with constructs from RC and RB theories. Pattern matching (Yin, 2009) was used to compare the theories with empirical data.

Results

The findings describe how organizational structures affecting intra-staff and staff–parent coordination shaped three areas of the school's administration of special education to immigrants' children: Child Find, LRE, and access to appropriate EL services. They show that insufficient structures for within-staff and staff–parent coordination played a role in delaying special education evaluations of immigrants' children for one and a half to three years, placing those receiving special education in overly restrictive settings, and not providing them with appropriate language services.

Coordination among Staff on Behalf of Students

Organizational structures affecting staff were more bureaucratic than reciprocal. The formal structures that regularly brought staff together tended to focus on the delivery of curriculum to groups rather than on individual students. In addition, structural features discouraged or only tenuously supported the integration of general education, EL, and special education staff on behalf of students requiring services from all three.

Child Find

Only one formal structure regularly supported the coordination of staff on behalf of individual students not receiving special education. This was the child study team that was responsible for deciding whether students would be referred by staff to be evaluated for possible disability. As constituted, this team was unable to function in a timely way. It contributed to delays of one and a half to three years in providing special education evaluations to four study students who were later found to have disabilities once they were evaluated. The team met weekly for ninety minutes to discuss students brought to the team by teachers concerned about their progress. To bring a student to the team for discussion, teachers had to submit the required paperwork on the student to the team. The team, consisting of the referring teacher, the reading specialist, an EL teacher, a general education teacher, the principal/assistant principal, a special education teacher, the coordinator for special education evaluation, speech and occupational therapists, and the adjustment counselor, would discuss the student and recommend an intervention. The teacher would implement the intervention and return to the group in six to eight weeks to report on the student's progress. It was school policy that the team would not request a special education evaluation for a student until it had met three times on the student, and the student had failed to progress with prescribed interventions.

Teachers expressed concern about the timeliness of this structure and described a front-end process that added to the length of the process. They said the extensive paperwork required to bring a student to the team resulted in delays and described long student queues resulting in a three- to four-month wait between submission of the paperwork and initial discussion of the student. This meant the full team process required for referral to an evaluation for disability was likely to require eight months following a teacher's submission of paperwork—which might extend the study team process into a second school year.

Teachers explained that a policy of waiting years for students to acquire more English before evaluating them for disability had further added to these delays in the case of evaluating study students. However, delaying special education evaluations to await further English development is specifically barred by the US Department of Education (DOE) and Justice (DOJ) (US DOE and DOJ, 2015).

Appropriate Language Services

Interviews indicated that organizational structures siloing special education and EL programs and staff had the effect of depriving three study students in the autism program of language services they needed. The first and home language of each of these students was not English. Special educators working in the autism program reported that EL teachers were not permitted to work with students in the autism program. Teachers expressed concern about this policy. One stated, "I have suggested that some of my students would benefit from EL services, but have been told that because they receive support through the [autism] program, additional services would not be provided."

Coordination between Staff and Parents

Data revealed that structures shaping staff–parent relationships were primarily bureaucratic, placing parents in a subordinate role regarding the education of their child, as opposed to the partnership proposed by RB theory. Inadequate supports for staff–parent communication and tremendous gaps in staff and parents' knowledge of students' performance and contexts at school and of school operations contributed to delays in evaluating students, overly restrictive placement, and lack of student access to appropriate language services.

Child Find

There were years-long delays in evaluating four study students not receiving special education whose teachers thought they might have a disability. These delays resulted from structures failing to provide parents with sufficient knowledge of their child's performance at school, of the special education program, or of the right of parents to request a special education evaluation of their child.

Interviews with these children's parents and staff revealed that parents had not been aware of the depth of concern that staff had about their child's performance at school or that their teachers had long thought their child might have a disability. School structures for staff–parent communication and knowledge-sharing regarding student progress at school included a Parent Information Center (PIC), parent–teacher conferences, and report cards. The PIC provided district-wide language translation and interpretation services to support staff–parent communication. When registering their children for school at the

PIC, parents could indicate whether they would need to have written communications from school translated into a non-English language. Staff could contact the PIC via the internet to request language interpreters or translation for their communication with parents. General education teachers were required to be available for one parent–teacher conference per student per year and were given three early release days for this purpose. Report cards were issued three times a year, but they had a college reading level per the SMOG readability index and assumed knowledge of the concept of educational standards. Students were graded as "not yet progressing toward," "progressing toward," "meeting," or "exceeding" "the standard."

Interviews revealed that the PIC was inconsistent in providing the interpretation and translation that staff and parents needed to communicate. Although interpreters frequently attended the one annual parent–teacher conference, interviews revealed this was not always the case. Staff interviews revealed that PIC operations reduced the frequency, timeliness, and accuracy of their communication with parents. Teachers said being unable to communicate with parents in English meant they could not use email or phone to communicate with them. They said it could take two weeks to obtain an interpreter through the PIC. Two of the study parents had requested and needed, but did not receive, Spanish translation of report cards.

Also a barrier to timely special education evaluation of the children was the fact that the child study team did not tell the parents or include them when their child had been brought to the team with their teacher suspecting the child might have a disability. When their child's disability evaluation was being delayed to await further development of English, parents were not informed.

The four parents whose children's evaluations were long-delayed did not know of the special education program, what it is, or that they could themselves request an evaluation for their child at any time. The district's elementary school handbook, which was printed in English and the district's two most commonly spoken non-English languages, had a section on the special education program. However, it had a twelfth-grade to graduate school reading level per the SMOG readability index, and it did not state that parents could request an evaluation.

The parents of two students expressed great distress when they learned during interviews for this study about the special education program and that they could have requested and obtained an evaluation of their child for a disability at any time. At the end of her son's kindergarten year, one of these parents received a request from the teacher to consider retaining him for a second year. She had not known, during the school year, that he was experiencing such difficulty and struggled to understand and discuss with the teacher whether retention would be the best option. She said the teacher did not tell her about special education or the option to have her son evaluated. She explained that had she known, she would have asked to have him evaluated to understand whether promotion to the first grade with supports would have been better for him than a second unsupported year in kindergarten. "If they had told me, I would have said yes, to evaluate him." She was particularly distressed because she was then asked by the subsequent teacher, at the end of her son's second year of kindergarten, during which he again did very poorly, to have him evaluated. She had seen her son experience pain during his second year of kindergarten because he was ridiculed by other students for repeating. "My son … would tell me how the kids who were in the first grade … would make him feel bad."

After three years of seeing her daughter struggle with school, the other mother wept when she learned that she could have requested a special education evaluation for her daughter at any time. "I didn't know that parents could ask for an evaluation." The father said, "The child missed out on a lot of help they need." The mother added, "And that's something very hurtful … I wish we could have helped her be in a better position, a better place." These parents had volunteered to participate in the study because their daughter, then in the fifth grade, had developed debilitating anxiety about school. Interviews with school staff revealed that this student, recently found to be eligible for special education, had been brought to the school's child study team over each of the previous three years with concern that she might have a disability, but this and decisions not to evaluate had never been shared with the parents.

Least Restrictive Environment

Interviews revealed that study students receiving special education were not in least restrictive placements in part because none of their parents had knowledge of the LRE entitlement, did not know where their children were placed and what the options were, and were unaware of their right to participate in Individual Education Program (IEP) development, including decisions about their child's placement. The special education section of the elementary school handbook contained a statement that the district "seeks" to provide the most appropriate programs in the least restrictive settings, but the reading level of the handbook was quite high, the handbook did not state that LRE is an entitlement, and it was not translated into eighteen lower-incidence languages spoken by parents.

Three parents of students receiving special education did not know where their child was or was proposed to be located during the school day or with whom. For the parent of one child, this lack of knowledge was the result of poor spoken communication during a meeting that she did not know was a special education eligibility/IEP meeting and the inaccessibility of the IEP which no one had helped her understand. When she saw nine professionals at the table, "I was so nervous … I was there by myself with so many people. I turned to the interpreter and said, 'I don't think this is a meeting where I should be by myself.'" She said the interpreter did not translate her words to the school staff attending the meeting and instead advised her to let the meeting proceed. The parent reported feeling overwhelmed. She left the meeting without understanding that she had been told her daughter had a learning disability and had been found eligible for special education, that there was a proposed IEP, or what the proposed IEP contained in terms of goals, services, accommodations, or placement.

A second parent also described not knowing what was being proposed for her son at her first special education eligibility/IEP meeting.

Everyone was talking to me at the same time. The teachers were talking to me, and then the other ones were talking to me while the interpreter was talking to me. It was a lot of information at once … It was too fast. … I would begin answering one, and [the interpreter] would be moving towards … the fourth question … I was so overwhelmed. They told me in one hit, he's going to need help, he has a problem … I left that meeting on the verge of tears … To hear that your child needs help is devastating … I was crying. They told me my son has issues … and at the end, I really don't even know what the issue is … I was very confused.

Parents reported that IEPs, even when translated, were difficult to understand due to their technical language, abbreviations, and acronyms. Some evaluations and IEPs were not translated before the IEP meetings, and some important words were incorrectly translated.

The third parent who did not understand her son's placement spoke the very low-incidence language, had never asked the PIC to translate documents for her, and had not been provided with language interpreters to assist her communication with her son's teachers. Her son's special education teacher said, "Parent involvement has been … difficult … because the language barrier is challenging. Our communication between home and school is limited because of that." Her son, who was in the autism program and in the temporary integrated class during his third-grade year, was to be transferred to a separate autism classroom for the fourth grade, although his teachers expressed that this was contra-indicated for him. His parent did not know that he was to be transferred from an integrated to a separate setting or that his teachers believed this was not in his interest.

With the exception of one parent who had received support from an external advocate, the study parents of children receiving special education were unaware of their right to participate in decision-making about their child's IEP. They did not understand the role they could play in shaping an IEP, did not know they were entitled to receive all evaluation reports and proposed IEPs in their language within a prescribed timeframe, or that they could accept, reject, or partially reject an IEP. They did not understand the significance of their signature on the IEP form or their procedural rights. Spanish-speaking parents had received from the school a copy of the state's procedural safeguards notice in Spanish that explained parents due process rights in IEP development. However, the technical, legalistic nature of the language, dense format, and high reading level (15th grade on the SMOG readability index) made it difficult for parents to access, and staff had not tried to explain its contents to parents.

Appropriate Language Services

Insufficient school structures for communicating and sharing knowledge with parents in the study also affected the school's implementation of EL policy to study students. In the 2016–2017 school year, Massachusetts law required school districts to inform parents, in a language the parents could understand, of their right to apply for a waiver from sheltered English immersion. Although the district elementary school handbook contained this information, with an instruction to contact the district's EL office for information on waivers, none of the parents interviewed for the study knew of this opportunity. The section of the handbook that contained information on the waiver had a graduate school reading level on the SMOG readability index. It was not translated into eighteen lower-incidence languages spoken by the school's parents. None of the parents in the study who expressed concerns about their child's English proficiency knew how language was addressed with their child at school. Parents of children in the autism program were not aware that their children were treated as ineligible for EL services provided to other students in the school.

Discussion

The findings from this case indicate that school organizational structures affected coordination among staff and between staff and parents in ways that delayed and obstructed evaluation of eligibility for special education, least restrictive placement, and delivery of appropriate language services to students in this study. These barriers to educational entitlements reduced students' access to curriculum and an included social experience.

The weekly ninety-minute child study team meeting was the only organizational structure in the school outside of the special education program that brought staff together to discuss individual students who were having difficulty in school. Because the queues of students submitted for team discussion were very long, the team was unable to recommend disability evaluations in a timely way. Teachers explained that a special education evaluation could not occur for any student until approximately seven to eight school months after the teacher submitted the required paperwork on the student, which teachers described as extensive and difficult to complete in a timely way given their other responsibilities. This timeline was routinely extended for students with a first language other than English to wait for their further development of English language.

Organizational structures shaping coordination between staff and parents also contributed to delayed or reduced special education participation of study students because the structures were not allowing parents to fully understand how their child was performing in school or to learn about the special education program or how to access it. Teachers and parents had very little opportunity to meet and timely, accurate language interpretation and translation were often not provided when needed. Report cards were not always translated for parents requesting this, and the phrases on report cards describing student performance relied on knowledge of systems and insider language unfamiliar to study parents.

Parents did not know there was a child study team, and there was no procedure to inform parents when it met to determine whether their child, suspected of having a disability, was to be evaluated or not and when that evaluation would occur. When decisions were made to delay disability evaluation to await further development of the child's English, parents were not informed.

The elementary school handbook did contain information on special education, but the handbook was not available in all parent languages, was written at a high reading level, and did not state that parents could initiate an eligibility evaluation for their child. Study parents were not aware of any other school or district procedure to inform them of the special education program and how it could be accessed for their child.

School organizational structures for coordination between staff and parents did not support least restrictive environments for students participating in the special education program. None of the study parents were aware of their child's right to a least restrictive placement, and many of the parents were unaware of their child's context at school—when they were with other children considered not to have disabilities and when they were not. The lack of effective language interpretation and translation to facilitate communication at IEP meetings and the inaccessibility of completed IEPs contributed to this lack of knowledge. Study parents were unaware of their right to play a significant role in developing their child's IEP, including the location of their child when accommodations and services are provided, and they were unaware that they could reject or partially reject a proposed IEP. They were unaware of their due process rights. These rights were spelled out in the highly inaccessible state procedural safeguards notice that the school distributed to parents without explanation.

Departmental silos that prevented coordination among general, special education, and EL educators and weak structuring of communication between staff and parents resulted in students not receiving language services they needed and to which they were legally entitled. EL educators could not provide services to students in the autism program, parents were not aware of how school staff approached language with their child, and parents were unaware of their entitlement to request waivers from sheltered English immersion.

In addition to showing the impact of organizational structure on the administration of special education to immigrants' children, the study revealed that the school's failure to adhere to public policy mandates in its work with immigrants' children and their parents was also a contributing cause of substantial delays in evaluating students' eligibility for special education, failure to provide appropriate language services, and overly restrictive placement of study students receiving special education. Failure to adhere to federal policy in administering special education to immigrants' children emerged in several consequential ways: delaying special education evaluation to wait for further English development of students whose first language was not English; not providing language services to students because they were participating in the autism program; inconsistent provision of language interpretation and translation to parents with limited English; and not providing informed parent participation in special education eligibility determination, service planning, and due process protection of students.

The IDEA requires timely non-discriminatory special education evaluations that consider English and other language proficiency in selecting the assessments and evaluation methods that will yield the most accurate results for each child. It requires school districts to provide students receiving special education with language services to which they are entitled under federal law. In addition, current federal policy requires public schools to provide information to parents with limited English in their native language. This policy, required for all students, is also included in the IDEA for students receiving or being evaluated for eligibility for special education. Special education policy requires informed parent participation and consent in special education eligibility processes, service planning, and protecting children's due process rights. The examples, found in this study, of a school's failure to adhere to these policy mandates with respect to immigrants' children, suggest that in addition to the structural initiatives recommended below, equitable administration of special education to immigrants' children may also require federal and state monitoring and efforts to ensure that schools and districts have the capacity to implement these mandates on behalf of these students.

Recommendations for the Organizational Structure of Elementary Schools

This study's findings suggest that RB structures that regularly support coordination among staff and between staff and parents on behalf of individual students may, while potentially benefiting all students, if supplemented by structures that provide language access and systems knowledge to immigrant parents, improve schools' capacity to identify disabilities experienced by immigrants' children and support the delivery of FAPE to them in least restrictive settings with appropriate approaches to language. The findings provide evidence of the Jakobsen and Andersen (2013) theory regarding the distributional effects of coproduction; failure to ensure that immigrant parents have resources to effectively participate contributed to their children not receiving educational services to which they were entitled. Equity for immigrants' children requires schools to provide the language access and systems knowledge needed by immigrant parents to partner with school staff to include their children and promote their fullest development.

To build the capacity to universally meet the educational needs of each young learner in a school population, elementary schools can work to implement the organizational features detailed below.

1 Develop staffing and scheduling that enable educators to collaborate with one another and parents to differentiate for individual students in integrated settings. This should enable the integration of general education, EL, and special education staff as needed.
2 Implement structures for staff and parents to share information on student progress and context frequently and with timeliness.
3 Provide language translation and interpretation to support timely and accurate communication between school staff and parents with limited English. These services should be provided by trained and qualified personnel in all languages, including all low-incidence languages, spoken by parents with limited English.
4 Ensure that school districts have the capacity to provide culturally and linguistically competent special education evaluation to all students in the district who require it.
5 Ensure that processes for determining whether students require special education evaluation are timely and do not await students' development of English language skills.

6 Provide to all parents, including immigrant parents, complete and accessible information on the school system, education entitlements, and school and community services for children and families. This information should empower parents to access school and community services to meet their children's needs.

Through attentive collaborative work focused on individual students, school staff will learn about the changing populations they serve. Through exercising relational leadership of the school community, administrators can facilitate inclusive processes in which this knowledge is used in ongoing adaptation of schoolwide practice to the students served.

Questions to Consider

1 Why do immigrants' children have inequitable access to entitlements provided by the Individuals with Disabilities Education Act?
2 How can school organizational structure be designed to increase the capacity of school staff to meet the needs of each student and prevent inequitable administration of educational services to immigrants' children?
3 How can schools and community organizations improve their outreach and support strategies to ensure that immigrant parents, particularly those who are English learners, fully understand and access available educational and social services for their children? What role can culturally responsive practices and multilingual resources play in bridging gaps and enhancing overall engagement and support?
4 What factors contribute to the inequitable access that immigrants' children may experience to entitlements provided by the Individuals with Disabilities Education Act, and how can these barriers be addressed to ensure fair access for all students?

Note

1 A low-incidence language is spoken by a relatively small number of people within a community. People speaking low-incidence languages often face insufficient resources due to their small number.

References

The Annie E. Casey Foundation. (2024). *KIDS COUNT Data Center*. https://datacenter.aecf.org (accessed October 28, 2025).

August, D., and Hakuta, K. (Eds.). (1998). *Educating Language Minority Children*. National Academy Press.

Bloemraad, I., and de Graauw, E. (2012). Immigrant integration and policy in the United States. In J. Biles and J. Frideres (Eds.), *Intercultural Perspectives*, pp. 205–33. McGill-Queen's University Press.

Child Trends. (2015). *Individualized Education Plans*. http://www.childtrends.org/databank/indicators-by-topic-area/education (accessed August 1, 2019).

Child Trends. (2018). *Immigrant Children*. https://www.childtrends.org/indicators/immigrant-children (accessed August 1, 2019).

Coll, C. G., and Marks, A. K. (2009). *Immigrant Stories*. Oxford University Press.

Conger, D., and Grigorenko, E. L. (2010). Special educational needs of children in immigrant families. In E. Grigorenko and R. Takanishi (Eds.), *Immigration, Diversity, and Education*, pp. 170–87. Routledge.

Darling-Hammond, L. (1997). *The Right to Learn*. Jossey-Bass.

Fix, M. (Ed.). (2007). *Securing the Future*. MPI.

Gittell, J. H. (2006). Relational coordination: Coordinating work through relationships of shared goals, shared knowledge and mutual respect. In O. Kyriakidou and M. Ozbilgin (Eds.), *Relational Perspectives in Organizational Studies*, pp. 74–94. Edward Elgar Publishers.

Gittell, J. H., and Douglass, A. (2012). Relational bureaucracy. *Academy of Management Review*, *37*(4), 709–33. https://doi.org/10.5465/amr.2010.0438.

Godwyn, M., and Gittell, J. H. (Eds.). (2012). *Sociology of Organizations*. Pine Forge Press.

Graham, P. A. (2005). *Schooling America*. Oxford University Press.

Hehir, T., and Katzman, L. (2013). *Effective Inclusive School*. John Wiley & Sons.

Hibel, J., and Jasper, A. D. (2012). Delayed special education placement for learning disabilities among children of immigrants. *Social Forces*, *91*(2), 503–29. https://doi.org/10.1093/sf/sox092.

Individuals with Disabilities Education Act, 20 U.S.C. §§ 1412(a)(3) & (5). (2004).

Jakobsen, M., and Andersen, S. C. (2013). Coproduction and equity in public service delivery. *Public Administration Review*, *73*(5), 704–13. https://doi.org/10.1111/puar.12094.

Jones-Correa, M., and de Graauw, E. (2013). The illegality trap. *Daedalus*, *142*(3), 185–96.

Kalyanpur, M., Harry, B., and Skrtic, T. (2000). Equity and advocacy expectations of culturally diverse families' participation in special education. *International Journal of Disability, Development and Education*, *47*, 119–36. https://doi.org/10.1080/713671106.

Landa, C. (2023). Differential access of young children of immigrants to special education in Massachusetts. *Developmental Disabilities Network Journal*, *3*(1), 120–44. https://doi.org/10.59620/2694-1104.1066.

Maxwell, J. A. (2013). *Qualitative Research Design* (3rd edn., vol. *41*). Sage Publications.

Migration Policy Institute. (2023). *Frequently Requested Statistics on Immigrants and Immigration in the United States*. https://www.migrationpolicy.org/article/frequently-requested-statistics-immigrants-and-immigration-united-states#children-immigrants (accessed October 28, 2025).

Resch, J. A., Mireles, G., Benz, M. R., Grenwelge, C., Peterson, R., and Zhang, D. (2010). Giving parents a voice: A qualitative study of the challenges experienced by parents of children with disabilities. *Rehabilitation Psychology*, *55*(2), 139–50. https://doi.org/10.1037/a0019473.

Serpa, M. d. L. B. (2011). *An Imperative for Change*. University of Massachusetts Boston. https://scholarworks.umb.edu/gaston_pubs/152 (accessed November 12, 2025).

Skrtic, T. M. (1991). The special education paradox. *Harvard Educational Review*, *61*(2), 148–206. https://doi.org/10.17763/haer.61.2.0q702751580h0617.

Suarez-Orozco, C., Abo-Zena, M. M., and Marks, A. K. (Eds.), (2015). *Transitions: The Development of Children of Immigrants*. NYU Press.

Suarez-Orozco, C., Martin, M., Alexander, M., Dance, L. J., and Lunneblad, J. (2013). Promising practices. In R. Alba and J. Holdaway (Eds.), *The Children of Immigrants at School*, pp. 204–52 NYU Press.

Suarez-Orozco, C., and Suarez-Orozco, M. (2001). *Children of Immigration*. Harvard University Press.

The Urban Institute. (2024). *Data from the Integrated Public Use Microdata Series Datasets Drawn from the 2005–2023 American Community Survey.*

US Departments of Education & Justice. (2015). *Dear Colleague Letter: English Learner Students and Limited English Proficient Parents.* http://www2.ed.gov/about/offices/list/ocr/letters/ colleague-el-201501.pdf (accessed October 28, 2025).

Yin, R. K. (2009). *Case Study Research* (4th edn., vol. 5). Sage Publications.

9

Exploring Experiential Learning: A Duoethnographic Study on US Pre-service Teachers in Costa Rica

Ekaterina Koubek and Olman Vargas Rojas

Abstract

This duoethnographic study (Norris, 2008) examines the collaborative journey of a US teacher educator and a Costa Rican bilingual school principal, focusing on the experiential learning of US pre-service teachers during two summer study abroad programs in Costa Rica. Using continuous data generation and analysis, we served as both participants and research sites, drawing on our own experiences to enhance our understanding of the research focus. Through reflective dialogue, we explored the transformative encounters, challenges, and cultural adjustments faced by pre-service teachers as they taught academic content and English in a bilingual school setting. Our findings reveal the profound impact of cross-cultural interactions on both the pre-service teachers and the host communities. We highlight the crucial role of intercultural exchange in developing future educators' intercultural competence (Beutel and Tangen, 2018), cultural humility (Lund and Lee, 2015), and culturally responsive teaching practices (Gay, 2018; Villegas and Lucas, 2007). The study concludes by discussing the implications of our findings for educational practice and raising future research questions.

Key Terms: *duoethnography, experiential learning, pre-service teachers, study abroad, reflective dialogue*

Introduction

As educators, we aimed to explore our connections to and beliefs about study abroad programs for pre-service teachers (PSTs). Our shared professional and personal international experiences fueled our curiosity, as we sought to unravel the complexities of study abroad programming and broader global engagement. We employed duoethnography, "a collaborative research methodology in which two or more researchers juxtapose their life histories to provide multiple understandings" (Norris and Sawyer, 2012: p. 9). Farquhar and Fitzpatrick (2016) further elaborate: "Participants collaborate in a method of inquiry, sharing and exploring differences and understandings about themselves in relation to a particular topic of concern" (p. 240). We embarked on our study with an expectation of holding each other accountable and remaining critical when examining our experiences with the study abroad programs that took place in Costa Rica during the summers of 2022 and 2023.

Despite our international experiences, we welcomed this research study as an opportunity to reflect on our approaches to global education for PSTs and to highlight areas for centering local community voices in pedagogy and program management. Given the increasing number of US students studying in Latin America (Institute of International Education, 2024), we were reminded that study abroad programs should not replicate colonial patterns that are rooted in the historical legacy of US–Latin American relationships (Pirbhai Illich and Martin, 2019; Sharpe, 2015). As Sharpe (2015) stated, "Post-colonial scholarship draws attention to the ways that education abroad operates in ways that maintain oppressive power relations between host and visitor," situating the host "as the needy other" (p. 228). We aimed to challenge the hegemony of Eurocentric education and to consider the sociopolitical, cultural, and historical context in which education takes place.

Without critical reflection, study abroad programs may inadvertently reinforce inequities and the unequal distribution of power, particularly when involving US students and higher education institutions. Bucar (2023) argues, "Although the rhetoric of international education centers civic engagement and cross-cultural respect, the ways programs are presented to American students reinforce their sense of entitlement, consumerism, and individualism" (para. 9), which poses an obstacle to learning. These programs may also reinforce simplistic notions about knowledge and knowing by neglecting whose voices are being heard and valued.

Sharpe (2015) states that postcolonial scholarship has critiqued how study abroad promotional materials portray the host culture as ethnically different from the students' culture. Likewise, students are interested in participating due to their desire to make a difference, which indicates that the host's culture needs help or fixing. Zemach-Bersin (2007) posits that study abroad programs are imperialistic as an endeavor, as the "missionaries, colonizers, anthropologists, and humanitarian aid workers who have served as 'goodwill ambassadors'" (p. 24). Therefore, in marketing and course design, educators must go beyond a rhetoric of authentic firsthand experiences and require students to engage in "the hard work of experiential learning," focusing on reflecting on preexisting notions and beliefs. Without this, students may believe that "they are entitled to master and domesticate 'the other'" by solely traveling to an international location (Bucar, 2023, para. 11).

Consequently, as educators, we partnered to hold each other accountable in our reflection on PSTs' experiential learning in a bilingual school in Costa Rica. One researcher, being a native of Costa Rica, ensured our reflections were grounded and free from cultural appropriation. Despite our diverse backgrounds and years of experience organizing study abroad programs discussed below, we were united in our desire to challenge the hegemony of Eurocentric education and to work together to decolonize our study abroad programs.

Our International Experiences as Context

Given our extensive backgrounds in study abroad programming and our experiences as international students, we believed these experiences could enable us to critically reflect on the experiential learning outcomes of US PSTs in Costa Rica. As Cushner (2007) states, "Research continues to point to the critical role that firsthand, person-to-person immersion experiences play in helping people become more effective in their intercultural understanding" (p. 35). Experiential learning connects an experience with cognition and is essential to learning about culture. Therefore, we aimed to explore the US PSTs' experiential learning outcomes through reflection on our experiences.

One of the authors, Ekaterina, is a White, cisgender, female teacher educator at an R2 university in the mid-Atlantic region of the United States. She has organized and led twelve study abroad programs, with the last two being part of this research. Originally from the Soviet Union, Ekaterina grew up in both her home country and Czechoslovakia (now the Czech Republic) due to her father's employment. At nineteen, she stayed in the Czech Republic to continue her college studies while her family returned to their home country. Ekaterina graduated with bachelor's and master's degrees in Czech and English linguistics from Charles University in Prague. She then worked as a teacher of English as a Foreign Language in a Czech public school. After three years, she immigrated to the United States when she got married. A year later, she began a doctoral program in Nebraska, studying second language acquisition and foreign language education, and earned her doctoral degree in 2002.

In 2004, Ekaterina was hired as an assistant professor of Teaching English to Speakers of Other Languages (TESOL) at a small liberal arts university in the Midwest. Her responsibilities included designing and teaching both undergraduate and graduate TESOL programs, mentoring and advising students, and serving on both university and professional organization committees. Her interest in studying abroad led her to organize six study abroad programs to Central and South America, as well as Europe. In 2014, Ekaterina joined a mid-sized university, recently reclassified as an R2, in the mid-Atlantic region where she continued similar responsibilities and led six more study abroad programs to Europe and Central America. The final two programs, which included PSTs from her TESOL minor program, took place in Costa Rica during the summers of 2022 and 2023.

Olman is a cisgender male educator and a Costa Rican native. He studied psychology at the University of Costa Rica and completed postgraduate studies in England in 1988–1989, specializing in youth guidance. Olman obtained a master's degree in educational leadership from Framingham State University in Massachusetts, USA, where he studied for a year and a half. Additionally, he received certification as an administrator from the International Baccalaureate Organization, allowing him to serve as a director of international schools. Olman has been an educator since 1991 and has held the position of director of international bilingual schools and colleges in San José, Costa Rica, since 2005. Currently, he serves as the director of a private bilingual school in Costa Rica, where he teaches psychology and philosophy, provides educational consultations, and oversees instructional personnel.

As a school counselor and college adviser, he has been actively involved in various international programs with colleges and universities from the US, Canada, and Europe. His training as an international adviser was obtained from the College Board Organization, with support from different institutions such as Georgetown University, University of Miami, Savannah College of Art and Design, Harvard College, and all Costa Rican universities. Since 1995, he has facilitated the experience of bringing US college students to Costa Rica, contributing significantly to his career as an international educator. Furthermore, Olman's role as the founder and general administrator of the International Center of Torchbearers in Costa Rica from 1991 to 1998 exposed him to a rich multicultural environment. The center specialized in teaching Spanish to English-speaking students, further enhancing his cross-cultural expertise.

Despite having over fifty-five combined years of experience working as educators, we continue to seek out professional development on global teacher preparation, interrogate our teaching practices to promote educational justice for all, and raise awareness of social and racial justice issues among students and colleagues. Our goal is to disrupt normative narratives in teacher education and promote a more inclusive and equitable approach. Therefore, we decided to embark on this study to interrogate our beliefs and experiences related to US PSTs' experiential learning in Costa Rica.

Study Context

The Beginning

The groundwork for our first study abroad program began in 2018 when an alumna from our TESOL minor program, who was the Head of the English Department at a bilingual school in Costa Rica, reached out to Ekaterina with an opportunity to collaborate between our teacher education program and her school. In 2019, as part of the preparation, Ekaterina traveled to Costa Rica to spend a week at the school, experiencing its context, meeting local teachers and students, and gathering information for her PSTs. Her son, then a fourth-grade student from a bilingual school in the US, accompanied her to gain firsthand experience as a student there. When reflecting on his daily encounters with his peers and teachers, he conveyed enthusiasm about the school culture by repeatedly mentioning "how nice the kids are here" and "how much everyone cares about each other." Her son's experience as a bilingual student there coupled with Ekaterina's reflections on classroom observations, interactions with local students, teachers, and administrators, and excursions to natural reserves solidified her desire to establish her new study abroad program there. Gillespie et al. (2020) emphasized that faculty leading study abroad programs found a renewed interest in their work, reported being more multidisciplinary, and deeply reflected on their identity; thus, these programs allow faculty to develop new pedagogical and administrative skills.

Additionally, this trip reconfirmed Ekaterina's commitment to supporting her PSTs in becoming global citizens. The school and its local community were deemed to be situated in the best location to experience intercultural learning and to present PSTs with challenges to test their beliefs and perspectives. Whatley et al.'s study (2021) revealed characteristics associated positively with global perspectives, such as studying with faculty, reflection, internships, and in-country travel. All these features were part of the proposed study abroad program in Costa Rica. As the program was ready to launch in 2020, the global pandemic erupted, resulting in the cancellation of all programs for two consecutive years.

Overview of Two Cohorts of Pre-service Teachers

Despite the initial setback, the program became a reality in the summer of 2022. Eight PSTs embarked on a month-long journey to Costa Rica, spending three weeks supporting bilingual students' English language and content development in the school and one week exploring the country's biodiversity. The first cohort was a diverse group of females, ages eighteen to twenty-one, including three bilingual Latinas fluent in Spanish and English, a student of Asian descent, a student of Native American descent, and others who identified as White. All were TESOL minor students and chose this program to fulfill four credits of this minor.

The program continued in the summer of 2023 with a second cohort of eight students, ages eighteen to twenty-two. This group primarily consisted of White and monolingual females, with one male participant, reflecting the typical student population of Ekaterina's university. All except the male student were part of the TESOL minor program; he subsequently declared the minor after completing our study abroad program. All students except him had taken a prerequisite course, Second Language Acquisition, with Ekaterina as their instructor a semester or two prior to their study abroad.

In both iterations of the program, students signed up for a three credit-hour TESOL methods course and a one credit-hour practicum. Ekaterina taught this course daily for three weeks in Costa Rica, with a special emphasis on bilingual education during the second iteration. She also supervised her PSTs in their practicum, allowing them to apply newly acquired knowledge and skills to support bilingual students at the school.

The School Description

This bilingual private school is situated in a rural area of the northern part of Costa Rica. It consists of 260 children of both national and international descent and employs twenty-eight instructors and staff members. The school spans all levels, including preschool, elementary, middle, and high school programs. The preschool program is designed for three- and four-year-old children and runs from 7 a.m. to noon each day. Other programs start at the same time and end at 2:20 p.m. The school has three one-story buildings for preschool and elementary children, while the middle and high school programs are situated in a two-story building on the same premises. The school is protected with a monitored gate and a fence.

A cafeteria, an administrative building, two playgrounds, and a soccer field are part of the school. The open-air cafeteria, located between the two elementary school buildings, features a covered area. Children can choose to buy breakfast, lunch, and snacks there or bring their own meals. From an early age, they are taught to take care of their surroundings by washing their dishes by hand and cleaning up after themselves. One playground, located behind the cafeteria, is available for elementary children during recess. The other playground is attached to the preschool building. The administrative building, which faces the school entrance, houses the offices of the principal, assistant principal, school owner, as well as a registration desk and the teacher's lounge. The soccer field, situated between the preschool and elementary buildings, serves as a space for physical education (PE) classes and recess activities. It is also used after school for dance, soccer, and other clubs.

The curriculum is divided into courses taught primarily either in English or Spanish. Elementary students receive math instruction in both languages to ensure they are prepared for standardized assessments in Spanish at the end of the year. Students are required to purchase textbooks, school uniforms, and PE clothes. On Fridays, they can wear other clothes for a small fee, which the school uses for fundraising. As this is a private school, students also pay tuition for their education. Upon arriving at school, students are greeted by name and wished a good day by school personnel. During pickup, their names are called to ensure a safe and orderly departure.

Pre-departure Preparation

Research has suggested that a pre-departure orientation is a necessary component for each study abroad program's success (Medora and Roy, 2017; Woods et al., 2017). Goldoni (2015) recommended pre-departure orientation preparatory activities that explore students' own identity, by stating: "Students' integration and engagement in the host community becomes truly successful when learners understand their individual and collective identity, and how it interacts with people from other cultures and societies" (p. 4).

Therefore, preparation for each program began three months in advance with weekly meetings to discuss cultural norms, expectations, travel arrangements, and other relevant topics. The assistant principal of the school, who is a university alumna and the former Head of the English Department at that school, played a crucial role in the program's success. She coordinated host families, planned cultural excursions through her Costa Rican spouse's travel agency, arranged practicum placements with local teachers at her school, and managed in-country transportation. Before each trip, she introduced PSTs to their host families and familiarized them with the school culture. She also joined our weekly meetings via Zoom to explain cultural norms and share her experiences as an English-speaking native working and living in Costa Rica. She contributed to the successful execution of this program by highlighting cultural similarities and differences between the US and Costa Rica, encouraging PSTs to step out of their comfort zone to learn about a local community and school culture, and providing logistical information needed for each iteration of the program's delivery.

At that time, student pairs were assigned to host families and connected with their hosts via WhatsApp, through which they were able to share about their backgrounds and learn about each family's composition and occupations. Doing this contributed to building a sense of community prior to departure. Additionally, students were briefed on the expectations for the study abroad courses and the program overall, including required assignments, readings, and reflections.

Both researchers emphasized the crucial role of pre-departure preparation. They welcomed the assistance of the assistant principal, who had lived in both the US and Costa Rica, to share cultural and school norms with PSTs. Reflecting on the steps to successful study abroad programs, Olman stated:

> La estrategia principal que se debe de utilizar para evitar inconvenientes en este tipo de cursos de estudio en el extranjero en relación a la comunidad en la que se desarrolla, es mantener una planificación muy detallada y ofrecer una eficaz orientación a los estudiantes con varios meses de anticipación. [To circumvent potential issues in such study abroad courses, especially in relation to the host community, it is crucial to adhere to meticulous planning and provide students with comprehensive guidance several months ahead of time].

Furthermore, upon arrival, Olman provided an in-depth orientation on the school's short- and long-term goals and policies. He highlighted the rich diversity of both local students and teachers, emphasizing the mutual learning as a cornerstone of cross-cultural exploration.

Methods

From the moment each cohort landed in Costa Rica, we initiated a reflective process on our PSTs' experiential learning. Sharing the same household throughout the program, we engaged in extensive daily dialogues on PSTs' learning experiences. Initially, these reflections were casual and verbal. However, as time passed, we recognized the need for a more structured approach, which led us to adopt individual and collaborative journaling. This duoethnographic dialogue journaling, along with our PSTs' reflective narratives, became our primary data source. By focusing on ourselves as study participants rather than the local population, we disrupted traditional research norms. This decision compelled us to maintain a critical lens when recounting and recording our experiences, exposing our vulnerabilities in the process (Norris, 2008). We drew on constant comparative analysis to find meaning in our narrative data. Our analyses were co-constructed, incorporating data from our conversations, email exchanges, journaling, and introspection since returning to our respective employments.

Findings

Perspectives on Benefits of Study Abroad Programs

When reflecting on the role and benefits of study abroad programs for PSTs and community members, Ekaterina shared her insights: "I feel study abroad programs could potentially disrupt some of the PSTs' preconceived notions about their role as educators and the role of their students." She added, "Through mentorship and critical reflection, PSTs might challenge conventional practices that position English as the dominant language. They might also question monoglossic practices, where each language is taught in isolation."

Ekaterina held the conviction that their study abroad program could also be beneficial for local teachers and students. Having taken courses in contemporary pedagogy as part of their teacher preparation program, PSTs could share their newly acquired knowledge and skills with local teachers. Additionally, local students could benefit from the presence of PSTs as teaching assistants, enhancing their English language proficiency and content comprehension.

Olman echoed some of Ekaterina's sentiments while also offering a broader perspective on the mutual advantages for all participants. He shared his reflections on the benefits of having PSTs in the school:

- Crear una atmósfera internacional en las familias anfitrionas [Create an international atmosphere in the host families].
- Permitir a los maestros locales actualizarse con los estudiantes de la universidad visitante [Allow teachers to update their practices with the students from the visiting university].
- Crear ambiente colaborativo entre estudiantes y maestros [Create collaborative environment between students and teachers].
- Los estudiantes tienen la oportunidad de compartir la experiencia del aprendizaje con otra maestra (o) nativo [Students have the opportunity to share their experiences with another native teacher].
- Establecer programa de desarrollo profesional (capacitaciones) para los maestros (o) locales. [Establish a professional development program (training) for teachers].
- Los estudiantes visitantes pueden de primera mano experimentar el proceso de enseñanza-aprendizaje en un país de habla hispana y lo que culturalmente eso significa. [Visiting students can experience firsthand the teaching-learning process in a Spanish-speaking country and what it means culturally].
- Los estudiantes universitarios podrán aplicar parte de sus conocimientos en un ambiente completamente bilingüe [University students will be able to apply some of their knowledge in a complete bilingual environment].

Overall, Olman's insights highlighted mutual benefits that hosting PSTs could bring to host families, local teachers, local students, and PSTs alike, enriching the educational experience for all involved and fostering a culture of collaboration, cultural exchange, and professional growth. Hauerwas and Creamer (2018) also discovered that their study abroad program in Italy provided benefits for reciprocal capacity building. However, they asserted that the impact of such partnerships on host communities needs further research.

Perspectives on Schooling and Educational Systems

Centering our reflections on PSTs, we devoted substantial time to exploring their cultural adaptation and experiential learning. We both observed that each cohort consisted of PSTs who were eager to embrace the cultural norms of the bilingual school, including its everyday operations, teachers' instructional methods, classroom management, and parental engagement. However, some PSTs chose to view the school through the US-centric norms, thereby challenging the local personnel's approaches to schooling.

In her role as program director and faculty, Ekaterina found herself confronted with some negative remarks from her PSTs in the first cohort. Comments such as "if this had happened in the US, parents would've sued the school" and "teachers don't really know how to manage kids here" prompted a necessary group discussion with Olman, the school principal. Despite Olman's explanations about the school's policies and cultural norms, many PSTs continued to perceive the system as "wrong" and "inadequate," overlooking the rich experience and expertise of the host country's educators. Notably, one Latina PST held the most negative views about the school, views that remained unchanged despite numerous dialogues. On the other hand, some PSTs countered their peers, reminding them that "it's not our place since we're guests here" and "we don't know how the system works in order to judge it."

Olman also noticed a similar disposition among some PSTs toward the education system in his country. He remarked, "Los estudiantes universitarios podrían asumir una actitud prepotente creyendo que 'saben mucho' y que la educación que ellos han recibido en USA es superior a la de las y los maestros costarricenses, lo cual es una falacia" [University students might adopt an arrogant attitude, assuming that "they know a lot" and that the education they received in the USA surpasses that of Costa Rican teachers, which is a fallacy]. He further elaborated on his point, noting:

> Uno de los principales desafíos que puedan encontrar los estudiantes universitarios al llegar a nuestro país es definitivamente el 'choque cultural' y además hay que destacar que nuestra institución se encuentra en una zona rural del país la cual no representa en su totalidad la vida y las costumbres del costarricense. Además, se deben de enfrentar que hay un mundo afuera del territorio de USA y que la educación que se ofrece en nuestro país es de un alto nivel, aquí debemos de destacar que Costa Rica desde el año 1948 eliminó el ejército y el presupuesto que se pueda utilizar en lo militar se emplea para la educación. [One of the main challenges that university students may encounter when arriving in our country is definitely the 'cultural shock.' It is important to note that our institution, situated in a rural area of the country, does not fully encapsulate the life and customs of Costa Ricans. Moreover, these students must confront the reality that there is a world beyond the USA, and the education offered in our country is of a high caliber. An important point to highlight is that since

1948, when Costa Rica dismantled its military, it has reallocated its corresponding budget to education].

Moreover, some PSTs struggled to connect to foreign or Costa Rican English teachers.

Their reluctance to voice their difficulties in hearing or understanding these teachers often led to missed learning opportunities. While some were more forgiving toward newer foreign teachers, they believed these teachers should have demonstrated better control over their students and teaching practices. This perception seemed to be influenced by the PSTs' comparison of these teachers with their experiences in the US educational system and their preconceived ideas about non-native English teachers. For example, when a new international English teacher joined the school, most of the PSTs in the second cohort perceived her as less proficient in both language and teaching skills. This judgment persisted even with Costa Rican English teachers who often held higher qualifications than some of their US counterparts.

Cohort Dynamics and Community Integration

Perceptions on schooling in Costa Rica varied among the PSTs across the two cohorts, as did their attitudes toward the host community. The first cohort, which included three bilingual Latina students, embraced the opportunity to explore the community independently, often inviting their peers to join them. Some host families, proficient in English, chose to converse in Spanish with these PSTs, fostering closer bonds. This cohort engaged deeply with their host families, joining in their children's athletic and extracurricular activities, and accompanying them on shopping trips and meals out. Our interactions with school personnel and host families revealed that the community members formed deeper relationships with the first cohort, which they attributed to the PSTs' outgoing personalities and eagerness to learn from and with the community. Furthermore, their proficiency in Spanish and familiarity with local cultural norms facilitated stronger connections with community members.

In contrast, the second cohort, who were all monolingual, had a harder time connecting with community members. They were more reserved and less willing to explore the community on their own. They preferred to stay home to catch up on their sleep, homework, or conversations with family and friends back home. This decision prevented them from learning about the community outside of school and being fully integrated into host families' activities. In our interactions with host families about the second cohort, we discovered a shared sentiment: "They are different. They don't seem as eager to get to know us or spend time with us, unlike the previous students." Some families attributed this to the students' limited knowledge and/or lack of effort to learn Spanish and engage in cultural events. Despite these challenges, these PSTs were able to form some connections with community members through their host families and school personnel. However, these connections were not as strong as those formed by the first cohort.

We firmly believed that both parties reaped mutual benefits from their interactions. The PSTs' engagement with host families' children outside of school fostered a language-rich environment, bolstering their English proficiency. Conversely, the children imparted some Spanish to the PSTs and offered a glimpse into their schooling experiences and community life. Olman highlighted these reciprocal advantages by noting:

> Crean un vínculo con las familias anfitrionas y se da una relación de familia costarricense (tica) con el estudiante en todo el sentido de la palabra, donde el modo de vivir de la familia anfitriona debe de prevalecer con él o la estudiante y viceversa. La apertura hacia la asimilación cultural debe de ser un ejercicio en ambas direcciones. Las familias se ven influenciadas en la mejoría de la comunicación bilingüe y en la comprensión de la vida de una persona extranjera. [A bond is forged with the host families, establishing a genuine Costa Rican (Tico) family relationship with the student. The lifestyle of the host family takes precedence, influencing the student and vice versa. Openness toward cultural assimilation must be a two-way journey. This interaction enhances bilingual communication within the families and depends on their understanding of a foreign individual's life].

While the second cohort of PSTs may have had a less noticeable impact on the community outside of school, their influences on students at the school was profound and enduring. Our dialogues with both PSTs and local students revealed a deepening connection, fueled by genuine interest and curiosity about each other, emerging from their interactions. Olman, reflecting on the PSTs' influence on his students, noted: "El estudiante se ve permeado por la interacción bilingüe al 100%" [The student is immersed in 100% bilingual interaction]. He further expounded: "Es una influencia positiva ya que permite que la comunidad estudiantil y docente puedan abrirse a una experiencia transcultural sin tener que incurrir en gastos financieros para nuestros docentes" [It is a positive influence as it enables the student and teaching community to embrace a transcultural experience without incurring financial costs for our teachers].

Fostering Culturally Responsive Teaching

This experiential learning shaped PSTs' views on pedagogical processes in a bilingual educational setting, cultivating their emerging understandings of culturally responsive teaching (Gay, 2018; Villegas and Lucas, 2007). As Gay (2018) posits, this pedagogical approach includes "using the cultural knowledge, prior experiences, frames of reference, and performance styles of ethnically diverse students to make learning encounters more relevant to and effective for them" (p. 36). Immersed in this study abroad experience, the PSTs prioritized harnessing student strengths, interests, and background knowledge, thereby placing students at the heart of their instruction. They also wrestled with the concept of translanguaging and its potential impact on students' bilingual development.

Tasked with studying and discussing culturally responsive pedagogy in their methods course, the second cohort of PSTs seemed to wholeheartedly adopt its principles in their thought processes and practice. As articulated by this PST, "One of our responsibilities as teachers is to overcome the bias and stigma that has prevailed throughout time and help ELL [English language learner] students in particular realize their talent and abilities through encouraging translanguaging." Ekaterina's classroom observations revealed that, despite not knowing Spanish themselves, the second cohort of PSTs frequently encouraged their students to share their emerging understandings in Spanish with their classmates. The PSTs often attempted to use Spanish words or phrases to provide comprehensible input for their learners, thereby validating their linguistic abilities and affirming their identities.

Based on Ekaterina's observations of PSTs in various classrooms, she noted their commitment to fostering strong, positive relationships with all students. They achieved this by learning about each student's background, interests, hobbies, and experiences, which in turn enhanced their learning experiences. The PSTs discovered that these relationships were foundational for students' success, as noted by one of them: "Teachers and students had a bond of respect at [this school], which directly contributed to the classroom environment. Teachers looked at students holistically not just at their grades and test scores." The PSTs shared several strategies for building relationships, such as: "Learning about culture, home life, favorite movies and even topics as small as one's favorite color helps to build connections and ultimately build relationships as well with the students."

Unsurprisingly, the most profound influence on the PSTs' understanding of teaching and learning came from the learners at this bilingual school. The PSTs expressed deep appreciation for the experiences provided by both the school and the country. One PST shared, "I really enjoyed getting to know as much as possible about the students and their lives. I took away so much cultural knowledge and teaching knowledge and cannot wait to return hopefully." Another PST reflected on the transformative nature of the experience:

> My experience at the school and Costa Rica was life changing. I was provided with a new perspective to teaching, had firsthand experience teaching a second language to students, and made connections that will last a lifetime. I am so grateful I had the opportunity to work and study in Costa Rica, and I can't wait to come back and see how much the students will continue to grow.

Moreover, this experience served as a transformative catalyst for one of the PSTs from the second cohort, as she shared: "I have walked away with a greater understanding of how to best teach my future ELLs through affirming their language, culture, and identities. I have walked away completely changed." The experience fueled her desire to become a TESOL major student instead, the major she declared during the final day of the program.

Discussion and Implications

Our duoethnographic research highlighted our collaborative experiences, focusing on the experiential learning of US PSTs during two summer study abroad programs in Costa Rica. We observed their commitment to local students from diverse backgrounds. The PSTs expressed a keen interest in learning from them, fostering meaningful relationships, and challenging the monoglossic perspective on bilingualism. By embracing the unique communication styles and engagement methods of the students, PSTs cultivated a deeper sense of cultural humility, a concept expounded upon by Lund and Lee (2015). These scholars argued that "teacher education must move toward an approach that requires a sense of humility in how pre-service teachers bring into check the power imbalances that exist in education, classrooms, and the broader community" (Lund and Lee, 2015: pp. 9–10). When reflecting on their own experiences, some PSTs wrestled with their preconceived notions regarding the language skills of non-native teachers of English, the role of translanguaging, and their view on the educational system of Costa Rica.

Furthermore, PSTs attempted to implement culturally responsive teaching, drawing on the works by Gay (2018) and Villegas and Lucas (2007). Through translanguaging and affirming learners' identities, PSTs capitalized on students' assets and established nurturing relationships. Witnessing their understandings of students' funds of knowledge (González et al., 2005) and their adept leveraging it both within and beyond the classroom was profoundly gratifying for us, as educators. As Moll (2023) eloquently asserted, "The purpose is to facilitate a sense of personal belonging, especially in an academic setting, and a sense of appropriation and control of the practices and outcomes of learning" (p. 35). Our PSTs diligently endeavored to cultivate such an environment within their classrooms.

While PSTs demonstrated increased cultural humility and tried to engage in culturally responsive teaching, their intercultural competence, especially among monolingual PSTs, was still emerging. Beutel and Tangen (2018) underscored the multifaceted nature of intercultural competence, which included "elements such as respect and valuing other cultures, openness and curiosity about others as well as cultural self-awareness and adaptability to adjust to new cultural situations" (p. 169). The extent of PSTs' engagement with the local community varied based on prior intercultural experiences and linguistic abilities. Some were proactive in seeking personal and educational interactions with locals, while others were less involved. Proactive efforts to embrace new cultural norms, actively engage with local communities, and critically evaluate preconceived notions were pivotal in fostering intercultural competence among PSTs.

Furthermore, we believe teacher educators play a crucial role in equipping PSTs with the knowledge and skills necessary to navigate the complexities of global education. Guiding PSTs to critically examine their beliefs and attitudes toward diverse school populations in a host country challenges biases and promotes social and educational justice. Encouraging PSTs to reflect on their privilege and preconceived notions fosters transformative thinking and practices rooted in equity and inclusion. Critical reflection on the teaching-learning process is imperative to ensure equitable and inclusive educational experiences for all students. Without such reflection, study abroad programs risk perpetuating imbalances in resource distribution and power dynamics, especially involving US students and institutions (Bucar, 2023).

Furthermore, US students may bring and impose their cultural norms, values, and practices, sometimes without sufficient respect or understanding of local cultures. We encountered this with some students from our first cohort, who imposed their preconceived ideas about how local educators should manage and instruct students. To address this issue, we facilitated whole-class discussions with the principal and assistant principals throughout our stay, aiming to help our students understand and appreciate the local cultural and school norms.

Finally, US institutions typically control the curriculum, research agendas, and methodologies, which may not align with local priorities or perspectives. This can create a one-sided educational experience that prioritizes Western knowledge and frameworks. Simultaneously, the immersion in a different cultural and linguistic environment can prompt a reevaluation of sociocultural identities, values, and learning objectives (Goldoni, 2017). To mitigate these risks, it is essential to design study abroad programs that are equitable, respectful of local cultures, and sustainable. This involves engaging local communities in the planning process, ensuring mutual benefit, and promoting a more balanced exchange of knowledge and resources.

Teacher educators must model and facilitate critical reflection in a supportive environment to nurture the reflexivity of future educators. This will allow PSTs to openly share their evolving beliefs and attitudes. Furthermore, it is crucial for teacher educators to understand how PSTs perceive sociocultural factors and their impact on a child's holistic development. Guiding PSTs to recognize the influence of their beliefs and actions on a child, and how this influence positively or negatively affects the child's performance, is key to nurturing them into reflective educators (Koubek and Wasta, 2023).

We advocate for a thorough analysis of initial pre-departure procedures to support the transformation of PSTs and to minimize potential cross-cultural misunderstandings. One of Olman's suggestions emphasized the importance of fostering PST-teacher relationships:

> Si existiese algún rol que pueda desarrollarse para apoyar a los estudiantes que aplican al curso de estudio en el extranjero, creo que podría ser el de nombrarle con anticipación al maestro con quién van a trabajar en nuestro país, de esa forma crearán un vínculo previamente a su llegada al país., eso también servirá como parte de la orientación que deben de tener. [If there is a role that could be developed to support students applying for the study abroad course, it could be to introduce them in advance to the teacher they will be working with in our country. This would allow them to establish a connection before their arrival, servicing as a crucial part of their orientation].

Despite Ekaterina's emphasis on pre-departure training on cultural norms for the second cohort, aimed at mitigating negative perceptions of the school's operation, there is a need to strengthen this training to better equip PSTs' understanding of their role in the host country.

As we reflect on future study abroad programs, several questions emerge: Beyond critical reflections under faculty mentorship, what other instructional strategies could effectively foster changes in PSTs' beliefs and attitudes toward a host country's educational system and culture? Apart from the pre-departure items already utilized in our study, what additional topics should be addressed to better prepare PSTs for their experiential learning? How can we ensure the implementation of culturally responsive teaching practices in PSTs' future classrooms?

Questions to Consider

1 How can authentic cross-cultural interaction take place in spaces where there is resistance from candidates? How can teacher educators help candidates identify "blindspots" related to cultural humility that would assist in diminishing the hesitance to engage with others?

2 What type of preparation and planning would you consider before planning an intensive cultural immersion program in another country? What would be your most valuable asset? What would be your biggest challenge?

References

Beutel, D., and Tangen, D. (2018). The impact of intercultural experiences on preservice teachers' preparedness to engage with diverse learners. *Australian Journal of Teacher Education*, *43*(3), 168–79.

Buzcar, L. (2023, May 19). *Avoiding Curricular Pitfalls of Study Abroad*. Inside Higher Ed. https://www.insidehighered.com/opinion/views/2023/05/19/avoiding-curricular-pitfalls-study-abroad (accessed October 28, 2025).

Cushner, K. (2007). The role of experience in the making of internationally-minded teachers. *Teacher Education Quarterly*, *34*(1), 27–39.

Farquhar, S., and Fitzpatrick, E. (2016). Unearthing truths in duoethnographic method. *Qualitative Research Journal*, *16*(3), 238–50.

Gay, G. (2018). *Culturally Responsive Teaching: Theory, Research, and Practice*. Teachers College Press.

Gillespie, J., Gross, D., and Jasinski, L. (2020). *Faculty as Global Learners: Off-campus Study at Liberal Arts Colleges*. Lever Press. https://doi.org/10.3998/mpub.11923682.

Goldoni, F. (2015). Preparing students for studying abroad. *Journal of the Scholarship of Teaching and Learning*, *15*(4), 1–20.

Goldoni, F. (2017). Race, ethnicity, class and identity: Implications for study abroad. *Journal of Language, Identity & Education*, *16*(5), 328–41. https://doi.org/10.1080/15348458.2017.1350922.

González, N., Moll, L. C., and Amanti, C. (2005) *Funds of Knowledge: Theorizing Practices in Households, Communities, and Classrooms*. Lawrence Erlbaum Associates.

Hauerwas, L. B., and Creamer, M. (2018). Engaging with host schools to establish the reciprocity of an international teacher education partnership. *Journal of Higher Education Outreach and Engagement*, *22*(2), 157–87.

Institute of International Education. (2024). *U.S. Study Abroad: Latin America & Caribbean*. OpenDoors. https://opendoorsdata.org/data/us-study-abroad/all-destinations (accessed October 28, 2025).

Koubek, E., and Wasta, S. (2023). Preservice teachers' experiences on becoming culturally responsive educators: An action research case study. *The Journal on Efficiency and Responsibility in Education and Science (ERIES Journal)*, *16*(1), 12–25. http://dx.doi.org/10.7160/eriesj.2023.160102.

Lund, D. E., and Lee, L. (2015). Fostering cultural humility among preservice teachers: Connecting with children and youth of immigrant families through service-learning. *Canadian Journal of Education/Revue Canadienne de L'éducation*, *38*(2), 1–30.

Medora, N., and Roy, R. N. (2017). Recruiting, organizing, planning, and conducting a 3-week, short-term study abroad program for undergraduate students: Guidelines and suggestions for first-time faculty leaders. *International Journal of Humanities and Social Science Research*, 3, 1–11. https://doi.org/10.6000/23711655.2017.03.01.

Moll, L. C. (2023). Funds of knowledge in practice in international contexts. In M. Esteban-Guitart (Ed.), *Funds of Knowledge and Identity Pedagogies for Social Justice*, pp. 4–37. Routledge.

Norris J. (2008). Duoethnography. In L. M. Given (Ed.), *The SAGE Encyclopedia of Qualitative Research Methods*, pp. 233–6. SAGE.

Norris J., and Sawyer R. (2012). Toward a dialogic method. In J. Norris, R. Sawyer, and D. Lund (Eds.), *Duoethnography: Dialogic Methods for Social, Health, and Educational Research*, pp. 9–40. Left Coast Press.

Pirbhai Illich, F., and Martin, F. (2019). Decolonizing teacher education in immersion contexts: Working with space, place, and boundaries. In D. Martin, and E. Smolcic (Eds.), *Redefining Teaching Competence Through Immersive Programs: Practices for Culturally Sustaining Classrooms*, pp. 65–93. Palgrave Macmillan.

Sharpe, E. (2015). Colonialist tendencies in education abroad. *International Journal of Teaching and Learning in Higher Education*, 27(2), 227–34.

Villegas, A. M., and Lucas, T. (2007). The culturally responsive teacher. *Educational Leadership*, 64(6), 28–33.

Whatley, M., Landon, A. C., Tarrant, M. A., and Rubin, D. (2021). Program design and the development of students' global perspectives in faculty-led short-term study abroad. *Journal of Studies in International Education*, 25(3), 301–18.

Woods, A. L, Sipple, S. M., Otten, M. R. M., and Roos, M. E. (2017). Navigating uncharted waters: Study abroad pre-departure activities and the 2-year-college student. *Community College Journal of Research and Practice*, 41(12), 867–80. https://doi.org/10.1080/10668926.2016.1242439.

Zemach-Bersin, T. (2007). Global citizenship and study abroad: It's all about U.S. critical literacy: *Theories and Practices*, 1(2), 16–28.

Part III

Conclusion, Recommendations, and Resources

10

Invitation to the Process: Applying an Integrative Global-CRSP Framework

Rochonda Nenonene, Novea McIntosh, and Christina Wright Fields

In the end, it's the "So what? Now what?" questions that Ladson-Billings urges educators to consider as we navigate our work in education. These questions push us beyond surface-level discussions to consider the deeper implications and actionable steps our insights demand. Action not words. It's not enough to simply identify issues or analyze disparities; the true test lies in translating understanding into concrete action. We echo Ladson-Billings' call for action of moving from awareness to advocacy, recognizing that words are only as powerful as the steps they inspire. Thus, as educators, we are called to continuously ask ourselves: "What is my responsibility to myself, my students, my community, and the world at large?" "What will I do to challenge inequities and create meaningful change within my own spheres of influence?"

Consider our framework as your starting point for action as you seek to develop a critical and reflexive lens. The five fundamental practices from our globalized integrative framework should inform praxis, shifting one's pedagogical orientation to be inclusive of both global and domestic diversity. An orientation that expands conceptions of knowledge, challenges normative policies and practices, while advocating for equitable student outcomes. Let this framework inspire you to reimagine, create, and sustain a truly globally and linguistically diverse learning environment that nurtures and supports all students.

The framework offers a five-step process for examination and utilization of practices that become a catalyst for powerful learning, liberation, and transformation (see Figure 10.1). The entry point for the process is understanding. Do we as educators have an unbiased awareness and comprehension of the histories, cultures, narratives, lived experiences, and other contextual factors that impact students and communities? This knowledge of local and global contexts leads to the second step, examine. Through critical interrogation and analysis of borderless environments, consider what power dynamics and hegemonic practices create, perpetuate, and sustain disproportionality in educational systems? Commit is the third step. How does one activate a new frame of reference and dismantle

Box 10.1 Integrative Global-CRSP Framework

1. Understand the multifaceted dynamics of cross-cultural interactions grounded in responsive and sustaining equitable educational practices.

   a. Create environments that nurture criticality, encouraging individuals to explore diverse perspectives to cultivate mutual understanding, and promote personal and collective growth.
   b. Engage in critical, reciprocal, and mutually beneficial partnerships that promote purposeful, sustainable, and productive lives for all to thrive through education.

2. Examine local, global, and intercultural issues while developing socio political consciousness for understanding and critique of educational systems and policies.

   a. Analyze how integrative global education can be applied both within and beyond traditional classroom spaces to cultivate sociopolitical consciousness.
   b. Recognize the complexity of bridging the local, national, and global education landscape to foster sociopolitical consciousness.
   c. Support identity development and self-awareness to foster intercultural competence across differences.

3. Commit to an inclusive pedagogical framework that values social perspective taking, cultural appreciation, and decolonizing education.

   a. Engage in practices to actively dismantle institutional policies that have marginalized underrepresented groups.
   b. Reimagine a curriculum that fosters critical thinking, reflection, and action, while embracing multiple intellectual traditions and ways of knowing; and acknowledges the cultural wealth of both students and teachers.
   c. Utilize approaches such as Universal Design for Learning to develop, restructure and reimagine curriculum, scaffold content, and identify key conceptual benchmarks, fostering a more nuanced understanding of intersectionalities in educational settings.

4. Harnesses the power of collectivism through which community cultural assets foster belonging, well-being, and cohesion.

   a. Decenter dominant culture, to establish a new inclusive and globally centered frame of reference.
   b. Provide space for community engagement and agency to promote transformative learning and action in educational spaces.
   c. Empower students, as cultural translators and bridge-builders, to facilitate understanding and connection between diverse cultures.

5. Design academic outcomes that directly correlate to the implementation of relevant cultural and global instructional and assessment practices.

    a. Center student academic success and well-being as the primary focus of education facilitated through the use of a variety of relevant, culturally rich materials, modalities, activities, and experiences.

    b. Reconceptualize assessment practices to draw on the globally diverse assets students bring to the classroom to promote academic achievement.

Five Practices for Developing Global-CRSP

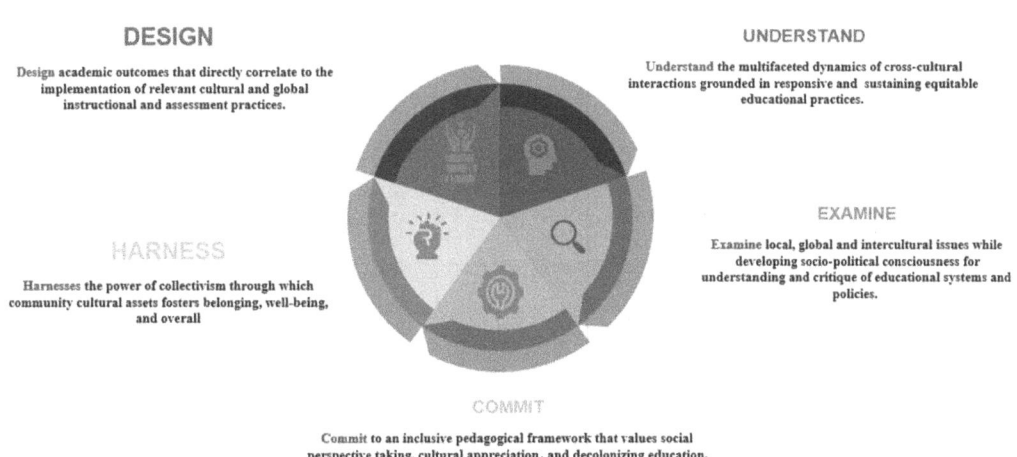

DESIGN
Design academic outcomes that directly correlate to the implementation of relevant cultural and global instructional and assessment practices.

UNDERSTAND
Understand the multifaceted dynamics of cross-cultural interactions grounded in responsive and sustaining equitable educational practices.

HARNESS
Harnesses the power of collectivism through which community cultural assets fosters belonging, well-being, and overall

EXAMINE
Examine local, global and intercultural issues while developing socio-political consciousness for understanding and critique of educational systems and policies.

COMMIT
Commit to an inclusive pedagogical framework that values social perspective taking, cultural appreciation, and decolonizing education.

Figure 10.1 Five Practices for Developing Integrative Global CRSP. *Created by the authors.*

colonized ways of educating? Step four is harness. Garnering the strength of collectivism, how do we mobilize to maximize the assets of the community to uplift, empower, and embrace the beauty of multiplicities of cultures? Finally, design. What are the essential elements of curriculum, instruction, and assessment that lead to emancipatory praxis while liberating students, espousing joy, and elevating achievement?

Operationalizing the Framework

The chapters in this text have offered a means of understanding how to incorporate an Integrative Global-CRSP framework in PK-12 settings, educator preparation programs, and partnerships with community partners. Table 10.1 has been designed as a reference to help the reader identify optimal ways in which the framework has and can be utilized. A check mark indicates the usage of the practice in a significant way that furthers the embedding of

Integrative Global-CRSP framework. The absence of a check mark indicates the practice may not be fully integrated or was not the focus or intention of the program detailed in the chapter. Our hope is that you view these chapters as exemplars to support your own work in embedded practices, as well as utilize them as case studies for candidates to consider in terms of curriculum development, student engagement, teacher advocacy, and transformative learning.

If you are reading this book, you understand the urgency of this work. The ability to understand others, transcend boundaries, and recognize the interconnectedness of our pluralistic society is needed now more than ever. We invite you to consider and contribute

Table 10.1 Integrating a Global-CRSP Framework in PK-12 Education and Community Partnerships

Chapter	Understand	Examine	Commit	Harness	Design
Storytelling for an Anti-Conquest Curriculum: Nurturing Epistemological Diversity in the Global Education Ecology	✓		✓	✓	✓
Borderless Curriculum: Shaping Instruction through Re-imagined Pedagogies and Practices for a Global Community	✓	✓			✓
Collaborative Mathematical Endeavors as Pillars of Global Education	✓		✓	✓	✓
Developing Empathy through Activist Art, Young Adult Texts with Culturally Sustaining Practices	✓		✓	✓	✓
Conflict and Peacebuilding in Northern Ireland and the United States: A Comparative Educational Study	✓	✓			
Developing Empathy through Activist Art, Young Adult Texts with Culturally Sustaining Practices	✓		✓	✓	✓
Religious Diversity and Culturally Responsive-Sustaining Learning and Teaching in a Global Context	✓	✓			
Critical Global Citizenship Education by South Korean Civic Organizations: Implication for Multiculturalism in South Korea	✓	✓		✓	
The Impact of School Organizational Structure: A Case Study of Administration of Special Education to Young Children of Immigrants	✓	✓			
Exploring Experiential Learning: A Duoethnographic Study on US Pre-service Teachers in Costa Rica	✓	✓		✓	

*A checkmark *indicates the presence of a practice (espoused, reflected, and/or illustrated)*

to the evolution of culturally relevant teaching and culturally sustaining pedagogy, by explicitly including the global understanding, narrative, and perspective. You can make a measurable difference in your local community using global considerations. Educator preparation must shift to recognize the relevance and importance of preparing candidates to have a global frame of reference. These competencies include (1) examining local, global, and intercultural issues, (2) understanding and appreciating the perspectives and worldviews of others, (3) taking action for collective well-being and sustainable development, and (4) engaging in open, appropriate, and effective interactions across cultures (OECD/Asia Society, 2018). Including such competencies becomes a new standard for transformative and culturally responsive teacher preparation.

Invitation to Unlock the Borderless Possibilities

This book builds on bell hooks' outsider inside framework. Readers will grapple with the notions of emic (*insiderness*) and etic (*outsiderness*), while negotiating how domestic diversity and global diversity can coexist simultaneously. People are looking outside and not within, when there is a diverse population within our classrooms in the United States and whose cultures are not represented, acknowledged, or valued in their respective educational spaces. Now is the time for educator preparation programs to not only reframe but also restructure current practices by centering global competencies within the core of diversity, equity, inclusion, and belonging. The authors are insiders because we are researchers in the academy, but conversely, we are also outsiders because of how we often hold marginalized identities within the hegemonic practices in education. We are in the system, but not of the system, trying to work to dismantle the system through a dualistic global and domestic diversity integrative approach. Lastly, this book encourages diverse counter storytelling from scholars, activists, students, and practitioners to not only name, but give voice to their lived experiences, in hopes of providing alternative ways of bringing the global within the canon.

What conditions are necessary to be able to fully accept our invitation to develop a knowledge base and skill set that embraces and actively engages in an Integrative Global-CRSP framework? Consider utilizing our Integrative Global-CRSP Framework Audit to assess an organization or individual's culturally sustaining global education acumen. Are you engaged in work to promote and sustain global inclusive practices? Recognizing that teaching is multifaceted and requires the possession and demonstration of complex and complementary skills and actions. We start with the primary supposition that educators must fundamentally believe that all students have value, can learn, and deserve the highest quality of education that we can provide. Furthermore, consider utilizing this book's unit lesson plan to develop dynamic and interculturally rich engaging lessons that are achieved within the context of a welcoming, inclusive, and supportive environment.

Along with our vision that educators must operate from a set of foundational beliefs, we also maintain that there are specific conditions that must be present to fully apply our framework with fidelity. The conditions we recommend are critical to building capacity, optimizing the use of our framework, and creating inclusive learning environments. We are purposeful with the use of the word optimize. When you enhance something, it becomes fully functional and operates at its highest potential, enabling educators, students, and classrooms to operate at peak performance. This is what is needed in schools today. Optimization will lead to strong educational outcomes and provide the momentum needed to close achievement gaps and reduce disparities. It is upon this foundation that we overlay our Integrative Global-CRSP framework, illuminating the four conditions for optimizing that we recommend are not panaceas. But, they are non-negotiables (see Box 10.2).

Box 10.2 Recommended Conditions for Optimizing the Integrative Global-CRSP Framework

Condition One: Knowledge

- Employ a global mindset with local sensitivity, foster one's ability to think and respond globally to issues to promote student learning.
- Commit to becoming a life-long learner and seeker of knowledge.
- Possess the ability to think in new ways including questioning, inquiry probe, and exploration.

Condition Two: Dispositions

- Be open to continuous learning and adaptation, due to the ever-evolving nature of global challenges impacting educators, students, and communities.
- Engage in a community-centric approach because the global-CRSP curriculum is not just developed for students, but also with students actively involved in its creation.

Condition Three: Skills

- Demonstrate awareness, sensitivity, and respect for diverse populations, cultures, and environments.
- Be sensitive and knowledgeable about demographics and social factors within the community and understand the cultural context.
- Demonstrate a belief that all children can learn at high levels, regardless of race, gender, ethnicity, socioeconomic status, special learning needs, or national origin.
- Demonstrate an appreciation for the artistic, social, and intellectual contributions of various cultural groups.

Condition Four: Reflection

- Engage in continuous self-examination of one's own teaching and learning as a reflective, practical, and realistic practitioner.
- Accept constructive criticism and have a willingness to learn.
- Teach from an evolving personal understanding of self-philosophy and practice.

11

Committing to the Integrative Global CRSP Practices through Unit Plan Development

Novea McIntosh, Christina Wright Fields,

and Rochonda Nenonene

Implementing the Integrative Global CRSP framework will require educators to restructure and reimagine the curriculum to meet the needs of their diverse student populations represented in their classrooms. In this section, we present a unit planning template designed under the Integrative Global CRSP framework, as well as a sample unit as an exemplar demonstrating its usage.

The unit plan outlined below is based on the five practices for developing the Integrative Global CRSP framework (see Figure 11.1), encapsulating the practices, core elements, and

Five Practices for Developing Global CRSP

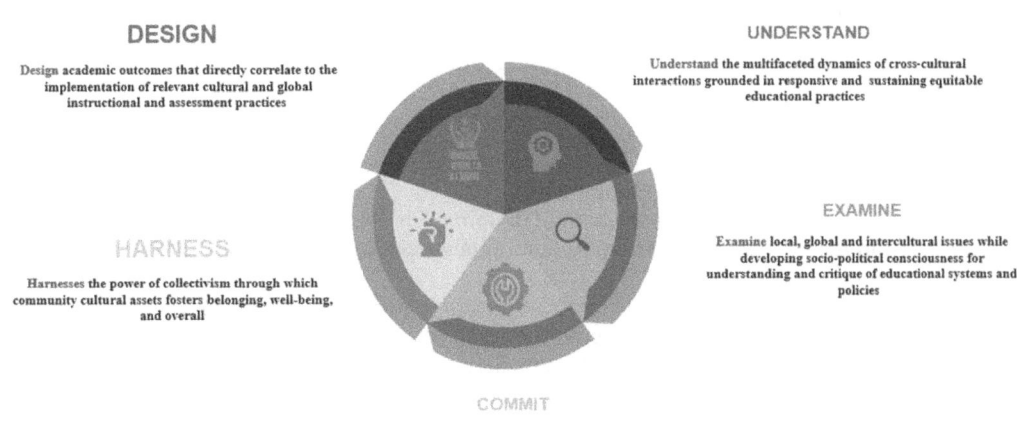

DESIGN
Design academic outcomes that directly correlate to the implementation of relevant cultural and global instructional and assessment practices

UNDERSTAND
Understand the multifaceted dynamics of cross-cultural interactions grounded in responsive and sustaining equitable educational practices

EXAMINE
Examine local, global and intercultural issues while developing socio-political consciousness for understanding and critique of educational systems and policies

HARNESS
Harnesses the power of collectivism through which community cultural assets fosters belonging, well-being, and overall

COMMIT
Commit to an inclusive pedagogical framework that values social perspective taking, cultural appreciation, and decolonizing education

Figure 11.1 Five Practices for Developing Integrative Global CRSP. *Created by the authors.*

teacher moves that support meaningful integrative global CRSP learning. First, we offer practices as a means to transform beliefs into actions, recognizing that teachers' actions in their classrooms are driven by their core beliefs and values about education. Critical to the process of teachers embracing and creating classrooms grounded in integrative global CRSP practices is the development of a mindset of the teacher. Utilizing the five practices helps facilitate the integration of cultural and global considerations into the context of professional learning and growth. Core elements provide for the thoughtful and consistent application of Integrative global CRSP tenets throughout the planning process. When used in tandem, the core elements enable the inclusion and expression of culture in the classroom. Whereas teacher moves are intentional actions, strategies, and decisions to facilitate and engage students effectively and purposefully. As with all good lesson planning, the alignment with relevant state or national standards is essential to ensure instruction is purposeful and standards-based. Thus, not only meeting the academic benchmarks but also respecting and incorporating diverse cultural backgrounds and funds of knowledge leads to making learning relevant and engaging for all students. Lessons created utilizing this template should employ scaffolding, guided practice, hands-on learning activities, and reflections to promote, foster, and sustain student cultural identities and social-emotional well-being in educational spaces. The lesson plan encourages the use of varied assessments which highlight different modalities, expressions, and ways of knowing. Lastly, the teacher reflection at the end encourages educators to reflect on the unit's effectiveness as a means to improve the conception, design, and execution of the lesson. Reflection with the intention that lessons remain student-centered, equity-focused, and aimed toward continuous improvement and adaptation.

By employing the unit plan, it can serve as a comprehensive guide for educators to strategically integrate these practices into their classrooms, fostering a learning environment that is interculturally engaged but also academically rigorous, maximizing students' funds of knowledge in a collectivist classroom community. The unit plan structure (see Table 11.1) is designed to reflect a thoughtful balance between re-envisioning, redesigning, and liberating traditional, rigid, and conventional education boundaries, thus setting a precedent for a borderless curriculum.

Table 11.1 Integrative Global CRSP Framework Unit Plan Template *Adapted from the Community-Engaged Anti-Racist Education Project Rutgers University-New Brunswick*

Unit Title:
Unit Summary:
Integrative Global CRSP Framework Practices **Practice 1 (P1): Understand the multifaceted dynamics of cross-cultural interactions grounded in responsive and sustaining equitable educational practices.** 1. Create environments that nurture criticality, encouraging individuals to explore diverse perspectives to cultivate mutual understanding and promote personal and collective growth. 2. Engage in critical, reciprocal, and mutually beneficial partnerships that promote purposeful, sustainable, and productive lives for all to thrive through education. *Teacher Moves: Problem-based learning, Leveraging cultural assets, Differentiation, Accommodations, and Modifications*

Unit Title:
Unit Summary:

Practice 2 (P2): Examine local, global, and intercultural issues while developing sociopolitical consciousness for understanding and critique of educational systems and policies.

1. Analyze how integrative global education can be applied both within and beyond traditional classroom spaces to cultivate sociopolitical consciousness.
2. Recognize the complexity of bridging the local, national, and global education landscape to foster sociopolitical consciousness.
3. Support identity development and self-awareness to foster intercultural competence across differences.

Teacher Moves: Develop Critical Intercultural Literacies (CIL): Reflection, Prior knowledge activation, Self-assessment tools (Pre/Post, Journaling)

Practice 3 (P3): Commit to an inclusive pedagogical framework that values social perspective taking, cultural appreciation, and decolonizing education.

1. Engage in practices to actively dismantle institutional policies that have marginalized underrepresented groups.
2. Reimagine a curriculum that fosters critical thinking, reflection, and action, while embracing multiple intellectual traditions and ways of knowing; and acknowledge the cultural wealth of both students and teachers.
3. Utilize approaches such as Universal Design for Learning (UDL) to develop, restructure and reimagine curriculum, scaffold content, and identify key conceptual benchmarks, fostering a more nuanced understanding of intersectionalities in educational settings.

Teacher Moves: Diversify materials and resources (texts, audio, videos, multimedia), Content grounding and Curriculum audit.

Practice 4 (P4): Harness the power of collectivism through which community cultural assets foster belonging, well-being, and overall.

1. Decenter dominant culture, to establish a new inclusive and globally centered frame of reference.
2. Provide space for community engagement and agency to promote transformative learning and action in educational spaces.
3. Empower students, as cultural translators and bridge-builders, to facilitate understanding and connection between diverse cultures.

Teacher Moves: Collaborative strategies (Small groups, Think-pair-share, Group projects, translanguaging & story circles) and Socio-Emotional Learning (SEL) practices in the classroom

Unit Title:
Unit Summary:
Practice 5 (P5): Design academic outcomes are directly correlated to the implementation of relevant cultural and global instructional and assessment practices. 1. Center student academic success and well-being as the primary focus of education facilitated through the use of a variety of relevant, culturally rich materials, modalities, activities, and experiences. 2. Reconceptualize assessment practices to draw on the globally diverse assets students bring to the classroom to promote academic achievement. *Teacher Moves: Establish language and content objectives, Assessment literacies, Utilizing diverse assessments, Performance-based assessment, Group projects, Outdoor learning, Cultural mapping, Community engagement*
Core Elements (Should be present in every unit, but may not be applicable to every lesson): Core elements ensure the recognition and affirmation of students' cultures, identities, and assets. • **Centering Intercultural Experiences in Standards and Objectives**—deconstruct and infuse curricular standards to include identities of students, diverse intellectual traditions, and ways of knowing. Planning to include place-based learning, community-engaged opportunities, field trips, cultural immersions, and student and community historiographies. • **Cultural Joy**—Students will celebrate and appreciate each other's cultural backgrounds, identities, and experiences in educational settings. They can engage in story circles to foster a sense of belonging and pride in their heritage. • **Varied Forms of Expression**—Students express themselves through writing and drawing, in addition to recording videos. They create posters and books, and collaboratively compose a letter to the principal as part of an advocacy project. • **Varied Media and Texts/Multilingual Resources**—Students engage with texts (including student-created materials), music, and videos in multiple languages and with a diverse representation of characters. Bilingual picture dictionaries will be provided. • **Varied Assessments**—Students engage in diverse student-centered assessment events drawing on their cultural funds of knowledge. They demonstrate mastery through authentic assessments, projects, presentations, debates, visual and artistic representations, storytelling, music, scientific experiments, etc.
Grade Level(s):
Subject(s):
Suggested Length (Days/Estimated Time for Lesson):
Alignment to Standards:
Content Objectives: Students will be able to do the following:
Enduring Understandings: Describe the takeaways for students. How might students apply this content to real-world applications? **Essential Question(s):**

Unit Title:				

Unit Summary:

Assessment:
Pre-assessment includes:
Formative assessment includes:
Summative assessment includes:

Vocabulary: What are the key components for language learning? What are the relevant terms?

Unit Vocabulary (itemized):

Practice Identification: Select which practice(s) will be utilized in each lesson.

	P1 - Understand	**P2** - Examine	**P3** - Commit	**P4** - Harness	**P5** - Design
Lesson 1					
Lesson 2					
Lesson 3					
Lesson 4					
Lesson 5					

Lessons Overview
Lesson 1: Title
Description
Methods/Instructional Strategies

Lesson 2: Title
Description
Methods/Instructional Strategies

Lesson 3: Title
Description
Methods/Instructional Strategies

Lesson 4: Title
Description
Methods/Instructional Strategies

Lesson 5: Title
Description
Methods/Instructional Strategies

Unit Core Instructional Resources and Materials
(Indicate which you may employ based on appropriateness, access, and availability)
Texts:
Videos:
Locations:
Artifacts:
Local expert/Community Partner:
Additional Materials:

Unit Title:
Unit Summary:
Differentiated Instruction: How will you differentiate instruction to meet the needs of diverse learners (i.e. multilingual, immigrants, refugees, culturally linguistically diverse, special education, and/or gifted students)?
Extensions or Follow-Up Activities: Engagement opportunities in class or for students to engage independently to enhance/enrich their learning.

Reflection (for teacher use): After completing the unit, reflect on the following:
 	
1. **Teaching Strategies:** After delivering the lesson, reflect on how the integrative global CRSP practice was addressed.
 	
    a. How well did the students engage with the practice(s) that was utilized?
    b. Were students able to connect the lesson to their own cultural backgrounds? What insights were shared?
 	
2. **Adapting the Lesson:**
Consider ways to adapt the lesson for diverse learners or different grade levels.
 	
    a. How could you make the lesson more accessible for students with limited reading skills?
    b. What additional scaffolding might be needed for students?
 	
3. **Feedback and Improvement:**
Based on your experience, think about any adjustments you would make in future lessons to further support students' engagement and understanding of integrative global-CRSP topics.
 	
    a. Did you allow students an opportunity to reflect and provide feedback on their learning?

12

Designing a Unit Plan Utilizing the Integrative Global CRSP Framework

Christina Wright Fields, Rochonda Nenonene, Novea McIntosh, and Jennifer Wu-Pope

Global CRSP educators are everywhere. In postsecondary education, K-12 education, government, administration, and non-profit organizations. Global CRSP education is not just an academic concept—it's embedded in the cultural tapestry of our world. It lives in the stories we tell, the traditions we honor, and the ways we connect every day. This knowledge shapes who we are and how we interact with one another.

Sometimes, the universe allows global CRSP educators to not only meet to share their work but to collaborate and engage in intentional opportunities that transcend boundaries—geographical, cultural, developmental, and even disciplinary. This approach dismantles silos and ensures that learning and teaching is enriched by the lived realities and cultural wealth of all involved. Within this context, I, Christina, believe it is important to personally share another moment of happenstance where I believe there was an alignment between our work and what a K-12 educator of color, Jennifer was teaching in the field. I met Jennifer through a qualitative research project focused on bringing teachers and other educators of Color from throughout the United States to share about their experiences in P-12 schools. The section below provides Jennifer's story of how she designs with an integrative global CRSP mindset that honors cultural traditions and makes the learning relevant and meaningful for both herself and her students.

Integrative Global CRSP Unit Plan in Action

Jennifer–Several years ago, I took a course. on intercultural communication and education and the professor shared a poignant anecdote with the class. He had attended a Finnish conference where East Asian participants were the guests of honor. For refreshments, the conference organizers decided that the guests, being from East Asia, would prefer to drink tea and thus organized the refreshments in such a way that the East Asian participants had access to tea and the Finnish participants had access to coffee. To the disappointment of the East Asian participants, they had been looking forward to drinking coffee in Finland.

In many ways, both implicit and explicit, a world language class can deepen students' intercultural communication skills or it can serve to promote superficial stereotypes about cultures and peoples. In this unit on food and dining (see Table 12.1), I wanted to go beyond the tropes of Chinese cuisine and Chinese festivals and allow students to grapple with the presence of identity and values that exist within these topics. By the end of the unit, students will not only develop their language skills, but they will also be familiar with how the cultural practices reflect various values, such as humility and respect, and reflect the influence of historical periods, such as the periods of colonization and international trade. Finally, they will link these understandings with a reflection about their own cultural identity and food practices.

Table 12.1 Integrative Global CRSP Framework Unit Plan Template, 去餐厅吃饭 (Eating at a restaurant)

Unit Title: 去餐厅吃饭 **(Eating at a restaurant)**
Unit Summary: In this 8th-grade Mandarin Chinese unit, students will learn how to communicate in a restaurant or dining setting and interact in culturally relevant ways. Students had previously learned to name various ingredients and foods, as well as express likes and dislikes. They had also completed a prior unit on Chinese festivals. In this unit, they will add to their knowledge of food vocabulary and develop skills, such as reading menus, ordering food, and providing opinions about food. They will also reflect and share about their own understandings of what defines cuisines and think deeply about connections between food and special occasions. This unit is designed for the novice proficiency level in Mandarin Chinese (see ACTFL world language performance descriptors).
Integrative Global CRSP Framework Practices **Practice 1 (P1): Understand the multifaceted dynamics of cross-cultural interactions grounded in responsive and sustaining equitable educational practices.** 1. Create environments that nurture criticality, encouraging individuals to explore diverse perspectives to cultivate mutual understanding and promote personal and collective growth. 2. Engage in critical, reciprocal, and mutually beneficial partnerships that promote purposeful, sustainable, and productive lives for all to thrive through education. *Teacher Moves: Problem-based learning, Leveraging cultural assets, Differentiation, Accommodations, and Modifications* **Practice 2 (P2): Examine local, global, and intercultural issues while developing sociopolitical consciousness for understanding and critique of educational systems and policies.** 1. Analyze how integrative global education can be applied both within and beyond traditional classroom spaces to cultivate sociopolitical consciousness.

Unit Title: 去餐厅吃饭 (Eating at a restaurant)

Recognize the complexity of bridging the local, national, and global education landscape to foster sociopolitical consciousness.

2. Support identity development and self-awareness to foster intercultural competence across differences.

Teacher Moves: Develop Critical Intercultural Literacies (CIL): Reflection, Prior knowledge activation and, Self-assessment tools (Pre/Post, Journaling)

Practice 3 (P3): Commit to an inclusive pedagogical framework that values social perspective taking, cultural appreciation and decolonizing education.

1. Engage in practices to actively dismantle institutional policies that have marginalized underrepresented groups.
2. Reimagine a curriculum that fosters critical thinking, reflection, and action, while embracing multiple intellectual traditions and ways of knowing; and acknowledges the cultural wealth of both students and teachers.
3. Utilize approaches such as Universal Design for Learning (UDL) to develop, restructure and reimagine curriculum, scaffold content, and identify key conceptual benchmarks, fostering a more nuanced understanding of intersectionalities in educational settings.

Teacher Moves: Diversify materials and resources (texts, audio, videos, multimedia), Content grounding, and Curriculum audit.

Practice 4 (P4): Harness the power of collectivism through which community cultural assets foster belonging, well-being, and overall.

1. Decenter dominant culture, to establish a new inclusive and globally centered frame of reference.
2. Provide space for community engagement and agency to promote transformative learning and action in educational spaces.
3. Empower students, as cultural translators and bridge-builders, to facilitate understanding and connection between diverse cultures.

Teacher Moves: Collaborative strategies (Small groups, Think-pair-share, Group projects, translanguaging & story circles), and Socio-Emotional Learning (SEL) practices in the classroom

Practice 5 (P5): Design academic outcomes are directly correlated to the implementation of relevant cultural and global instructional and assessment practices.

1. Center student academic success and well-being as the primary focus of education facilitated through the use of a variety of relevant, culturally rich materials, modalities, activities, and experiences.
2. Reconceptualize assessment practices to draw on the globally diverse assets students bring to the classroom to promote academic achievement.

Teacher Moves: Establish language and content objectives, Assessment literacies, Utilizing diverse assessments, Performance-based Assessment, Group projects, Outdoor learning, Cultural mapping, and Community engagement

Unit Title: 去餐厅吃饭 **(Eating at a restaurant)**

Core Elements (Should be present in every unit but may not be applicable to every lesson):
Core elements ensure the recognition and affirmation of students' cultures, identities, and assets.

- **Centering Intercultural Experiences in Standards and Objectives**—deconstruct and infuse curricular standards to include identities of students, diverse intellectual traditions, and ways of knowing. Planning to include place-based learning, community-engaged opportunities, field trips, cultural immersions, and student and community historiographies.
- **Cultural Joy**—Students will celebrate and appreciate each other's cultural backgrounds, identities, and experiences in educational settings. They can engage in story circles to foster a sense of belonging and pride in their heritage.
- **Varied Forms of Expression**—Students express themselves through writing and drawing, in addition to recording videos. They create posters and books, and collaboratively compose a letter to the principal as part of an advocacy project.
- **Varied Media and Texts/Multilingual Resources**—Students engage with texts (including student-created materials), music, and videos in multiple languages and with a diverse representation of characters. Bilingual picture dictionaries will be provided.
- **Varied Assessments**—Students engage in diverse student-centered assessment events drawing on their cultural funds of knowledge. They demonstrate mastery through authentic assessments, projects, presentations, debates, visual and artistic representations, storytelling, music, scientific experiments, etc.

Grade Level(s): 8th grade

Subject(s): Mandarin Chinese

Suggested Length (Days/Estimated Time for Lesson):
4 weeks

Alignment to Standards:
New York State Learning Standards for World Languages (Modern Languages)
https://www.nysed.gov/sites/default/files/programs/world-languages/nys-learning-standards-for-world-languages-2021.pdf

Content Objectives
Students will be able to do the following:

- identify main ingredients on menus (NYS Standard 1—students will be able to interpret what they see on a menu).
- reflect on the multifaceted nature of Chinese cuisine (NYS Standard 4—students will identify the communities and dishes connected to this cuisine).
- name some popular dishes in Chinese cuisine (NYS Standards 1 and 2—students will identify these dishes on a menu and be able to order it in a restaurant setting).
- demonstrate Chinese dining etiquette (NYS Standard 4—students will participate in role play to demonstrate Chinese dining etiquette and identify the values behind various behaviors).
- describe what they and their families like to eat (NYS Standards 2 and 3—students will communicate their food preferences).
- provide opinions about food (NYS Standards 2 and 3—students will communicate their opinions).
- describe foods that they eat for special celebrations or holidays and compare their personal traditions with Chinese festival traditions (NYS Standards 3 and 5—students will present about foods they eat and compare with food traditions during Chinese festivals).

Unit Title: 去餐厅吃饭 (Eating at a restaurant)

Enduring Understandings:

– Students will understand how Chinese dining etiquette reflects values such as humility and respect. With this understanding, they can participate in Chinese dining situations in culturally relevant ways.
– Students will understand the complexity in defining Chinese cuisine and the multicultural and multiethnic identities that are involved. Thus, students can develop a deeper appreciation and curiosity for Chinese cuisine.

Essential Question(s)

– In a Chinese cultural context, how does one communicate and interact in culturally authentic ways in a restaurant or dining situation?
– What defines a cuisine of a given culture? Who decides on that definition?
– What representation do specific foods have during special celebrations?
– How might Chinese food and dining etiquette compare and contrast with that of your home culture(s)? What are the shared values in these cultures?

Assessment:
Pre-assessment includes:
In-class activities that identify foods and sharing about food experiences with families.

Formative assessment includes:
In-class activities and homework assignments that use various modes of communication—reading, writing, speaking, and listening. In-class activities include:

– Dining at a restaurant role play
– Reading a menu
– Asking questions and ordering food

Summative assessment includes:
1 Project: Students will create a food scrapbook where they share three dishes that are important to them and that they eat for special occasions. Using Mandarin Chinese, they will introduce these dishes and describe the traditions and values associated with the special occasions. They will also compare one of their traditions with a Chinese festival tradition.
1 Test
1 Quiz

Vocabulary: What are the key components for language learning? What are the relevant terms?
Unit Vocabulary
Unit Vocabulary 1
Unit Vocabulary 2

Practice Identification: Select which practice(s) will be utilized in each lesson.

	P1 - Understand	**P2** - Examine	**P3** - Commit	**P4** - Harness	**P5** - Design
Week 1			✓		✓
Week 2		✓			✓
Week 3	✓	✓		✓	✓
Week 4	✓			✓	✓

Unit Title: 去餐厅吃饭 (Eating at a restaurant)

Lessons Overview

Week 1: What do you want to order at the restaurant?
Description
This week, students will expand their food vocabulary in ways that will help them identify dishes
   on a restaurant menu. They will read different menus and practice ordering food and drink from
   the menus.
Methods/Instructional Strategies
Prior knowledge activation, self-assessment of prior knowledge, focus on literacy strategies.

Week 2: How do you order at the restaurant?
Description
They will learn about dining etiquette in a Chinese dining setting and participate in restaurant role
   play situations.
Methods/Instructional Strategies
Role play

Week 3: Why is it called "Chinese" cuisine?
Description
Students will learn about ingredients and dishes that are typically perceived to belong to Chinese
   cuisine. Although many dishes are subsumed under the general label of "Chinese," some of
   these dishes have origins with specific regional or ethnic groups. In China alone, there are fifty-
   five officially recognized ethnic groups in addition to the largest ethnic group, the Han Chinese.
   Students will begin to reflect about the connections between food, values, and identity.
Methods/Instructional Strategies
Journal writing, group sharing

Week 4: How does what we eat reflect our values and identities?
Description
Students will have more opportunities to reflect about the expression of cultural identity in
   cuisine. They will compare and contrast Chinese festival foods with their own food cultures.
Methods/Instructional Strategies
Scrapbook project

Unit Core Instructional Resources and Materials
(Indicate which you may employ based on appropriateness, access, and availability).
Texts: Restaurant menus, restaurant dialogues, and short descriptive paragraphs on food
   preferences.
Videos: Videos about cuisine from a variety of perspectives in Chinese-speaking areas.
Locations: School and Flushing, Queens.
Artifacts: Dining utensils.
Local expert/Community Partner: CUNY Queens College is organizing the Spring Gala and is
   offering specific showtimes for school groups.
Additional Materials:

Unit Title: 去餐厅吃饭 (Eating at a restaurant)

Differentiated Instruction: How will you differentiate instruction to meet the needs of diverse learners (i.e. multilingual, immigrants, refugees, culturally linguistically diverse, special education, and gifted students)?

Through formative assessment, I will be able to assess the needs of individual learners (e.g., heritage learners, learners without Chinese family background, individual learner differences). Using that information, I will be able to provide individualized feedback and design activities that will address specific learner needs (e.g., improvement in writing the characters, strengthening vocabulary knowledge, establishing clarity in pronunciation, etc.).

Extensions or Follow-Up Activities: Engagement opportunities in class or for students to engage independently to enhance/enrich their learning

Field trip to a Spring Festival Gala in Flushing, Queens, and lunch at a Chinese restaurant. The Spring Festival is also known as Chinese New Year, and it is the most important celebration in Han Chinese culture. It is celebrated with various festivities for a period of two weeks and is a time for families to gather together.

Reflection (for teacher use): After completing the unit, reflect on the following:

1. **Teaching Strategies:** After delivering the lesson, reflect on how the integrative global-CSRP principle was addressed.

   a. How well did the students engage with the practice(s) that was utilized?

   Since activation of prior knowledge, self-assessment, and use of literacy strategies are common practices for my students, they were familiar with the activities. With regards to role play, they were highly motivated since they were able to use props for a dining situation, including chopsticks. This particular class had positive social dynamics since all of them were friends, and this allowed group sharing and reflection activities to progress smoothly.

   b. Were students able to connect the lesson to their own cultural backgrounds? What insights were shared?

   Students were quite eager to share about their food experiences. It is often a topic of high interest to them, and they enjoyed making connections to their own food cultures.

2. **Adapting the Lesson:**

   Consider ways to adapt the lesson for diverse learners or different grade levels.

   a. How could you make the lesson more accessible for students with limited reading skills?

   Since the Chinese language uses characters, and not an alphabet, it is highly dependent on the imagery of the character. For students with limited reading skills, they need additional time and support in mastering the new characters. This could take the form of deconstructing the character into its component parts and focusing on the meaning component of the character (i.e., the radical). Students could also benefit from literacy support activities, such as sight word exercises that build automaticity and fluency since reading the characters relies upon visual recognition, rather than the sounding out of a word.

   b. What additional scaffolding might be needed for students?

   Identity and values are abstract concepts that middle school students may find challenging to identify, especially when introduced in an academic setting. I recommend providing students with multiple examples of identities and values, and clarifying the difference between an identity and a value.

Unit Title: 去餐厅吃饭 (Eating at a restaurant)

3. **Feedback and Improvement:**

Based on your experience, think about any adjustments you would make in future lessons to further support students' engagement and understanding of integrative global-CRSP topics.

a. Did you allow students an opportunity to reflect and provide feedback on their learning? Depending on students' comfort level with their peers, they may not want to share all of their identities and values with their classmates, and may only keep their reflections general. I recommend that the teacher models an example of themselves sharing about their identity and values, both for students to understand what the task involves and also to see the teacher being authentic with them, as they are expecting the students to be with the teacher. Overall, everyone should have an understanding that they should only share what they are comfortable sharing, and the teacher should ensure that students have the space to feel safe in reflecting about these topics within the class.

13

The Quilted Classroom Poem: Harnessing Poetry to Cultivate Global and Cultural Awareness

Novea McIntosh, Christina Wright Fields, Rochonda Nenonene, and Isabella Lundgren

Poetry is a useful modality for expressing one's identity and perspectives. Using poetry in teacher education to explore global and cultural awareness can be engaging, transformative, and liberating. Poetry has the power to evoke emotions, stimulate critical thinking, develop empathy, and foster deep reflection, all of which are essential in developing cultural sensitivity and global awareness. Poetry and our Integrative Global CRSP framework were utilized with Urban Teacher Academy (UTA) teacher candidates to process and reflect on the works of scholars who focus on the next generation of culturally responsive pedagogy, and make connections between the research and their future work as educators. Students were encouraged to use non-traditional means of sharing their reflections, specifically using mediums of artistic expression to connect theoretical concepts, experiences as they engage with the learning. Ultimately, their reflections were expressed using their cultural asset, what they love to do, what represented them stepping out of the typical assessment box.

The UTA is a program at the University of Dayton created to recruit, train, and support pre-service teachers who have expressed an interest in teaching in diverse urban school settings. UTA is committed to helping candidates develop into teacher activists who promote social justice, advocate for all students, and create inclusive equitable classrooms. The Urban Teacher Academy is designed to deepen understanding of critical issues facing urban educators. Students examine the context of how issues such as poverty, institutional racism, and societal inequities impact students, families, and schools. Additionally, the program helps cultivate and strengthen the candidates understanding of the importance of culturally responsive/sustaining teaching practices to help close what Ladson-Billings calls the "education debt" gap. Self-interrogation regarding the concept of cultural identity in relation to professional practice and classroom management as well as knowledge of community resources are key focus areas in the program. Candidates learn and demonstrate culturally responsive instructional, assessment, and management strategies that encourage the learning and development of efficacy, risk-taking, sociocultural awareness, contextual interpersonal skills and self-understanding through integrated readings, discussions, field experience, and presentations. Inherent in this deepening of understanding is the development of reflective thinking and writing and problem-solving strategies.

This poem is a UTA student's journal response after being exposed to and immersed in theoretical frameworks and content from diverse scholar activists. One of the goals of the course is to develop sociocultural awareness in a pluralistic society. This student used the Integrative Global CRSP framework to elucidate her vision of a future elementary classroom where students are accepted, respected, honored, and seen as a part of the fabric of society. Hence, the quilt, the comfortable, collective classroom where students thrive, find joy, and are embraced.

The Quilted Classroom

Isabella Lundgren
University of Dayton, Urban Teacher Academy Student

In the classroom,
Our threads intertwine, gently woven,
With each hand-sewn stitch,
A clearer image begins to unfold.

As I step back, I see the design—
A tapestry stretched, vast and wide,
Where cultures meet and stories collide.
Threads of lives, vibrant and true,
Each one adding its unique hue,
Patches working together to shape the view.

This quilt tells a story of global embrace,
Honoring each voice, each time, each place.
The knowledge we gather, both near and far,
Guided by love, our steady North Star.

Collectivism sings its resounding call,
A harmony rising to uplift us all.
Together we harness its boundless might,
Sewing our stories well into the night.

Framed by justice, stitched with care,
Empathy binds the edges we share.
Through new lenses, we start to see
The beauty in our shared humanity.

Decolonizing minds, we clear the slate,
Rewriting stories to appreciate.
Cultural appreciation, honest and near,
Brings the world to our students, vivid and clear.

From global challenges to daily strife,
We teach the skills to sustain a life.
Cross-cultural threads begin to show,
How equity's fabric continues to grow.

Understanding sustains the art we make,
A global classroom where all partake.
So let us teach with passion and grace,
Creating a future no walls can erase.

For in the quilted classroom, we see
A masterpiece stitched by you and me—
A world united, in harmony.

Poetry was utilized as a medium for the Integrative Global CRSP framework to illustrate and emphasize that the framework is not rigid; rather, it is flexible and can be adapted to suit a variety of teaching contexts and content areas. We hope that this example serves as a starting point to reimagine and reframe how educators and teacher educators can leverage poetry as a dynamic tool for fostering global and cultural awareness. We challenge educators to not just embrace poetry as an art form, but as a powerful modality for exploring local and global contexts, student identities and experiences, and as a means of cultural appreciation. Although this poem was one outcome of the framework, there are endless possibilities to extend this work. We suggest the below:

Extensions of Using This Poem That Align with the Integrative Global CRSP Framework

1 Students can collaborate on creating a collective poem about global and cultural awareness.
2 Students can create a cultural square that can develop into a classroom cultural community quilt.
3 Students can learn about global literacy traditions by exploring different poetic forms (Haiku–Japanese, Sonnet–Italian or English, Villanelle–French).
4 Students can use poetry to explore global issues such as climate change, human rights, or conflict.

Poetry is incredibly versatile, capable of being utilized in a wide range and contexts. In the classroom, poetry can serve as a gateway to explore personal identity or other diverse perspectives. Its flexibility allows educators to integrate poetry into multiple formats, such as written exercises, group dialogues, performances, or cross-disciplinary projects, all while encouraging reflection and deeper engagement with the material. We provided some strategies below that educators can utilize:

Strategies for Using Poetry and the Integrative Global CRSP Framework

1 Poetry as a tool for reflection—Have students consider their own cultural identities and biases. Have students create mindfulness/restorative justice circles to share how they have experienced and/or witnessed cultural bias in schools or in the community.

2 Poetry for building empathy—Have students read poems that depict experiences of marginalization, displacement, or resilience, such as refugee experiences or the struggles of minoritized groups. Invite community members representing different cultures to share their experiences with students or visit local museums/community organizations and journal about their experiences on the interactions.

3 Poetry as a tool for celebration—Have students share their own cultural, linguistic, expressions and then create a padlet displaying these with others or have a poetry cipher.

4 Poetry as counternarratives—Have students read poems that describe protests or minoritized individuals' history and invite students to write their own and submit to local papers.

There are endless resources both tangible and intangible, that can be used to embody the Integrative Global CRSP framework. We offered an example using poetry, however, we recognize and affirm that resources can be diverse and multifaceted. In most of our communities, there is an abundance of resources, whether as physical artifacts, people, cultural practices, or organizations. These resources, both visible and hidden, provide opportunities to foster intercultural engagement among our students as they learn more about each other beyond the walls of the classroom. By leveraging these resources, educators can expand students' knowledge while fostering curiosity, sparking creativity, and affirming that they belong to the communities in which they reside. Again, we invite you to use the framework we provide as a catalyst for exploration, innovation, and actualization. We hope it inspires educators to experiment with new approaches, to diversify their teaching practice, and to magnify the cultural assets that students bring to the classroom.

14

Examining Organization's Culturally Sustaining Global Education Strategies through an Audit of Integrative Global CRSP Framework

Christina Wright Fields, Rochonda Nenonene,

and Novea McIntosh

A Integrative Global Pedagogical Framework audit is a comprehensive evaluation of an organization's efforts to promote culturally sustaining global education. It is essential to ensure that your organizational practices align with the current globalized educational landscape, diverse classrooms where students identify with multiplicities of cultures and identities. Multiple stakeholders can utilize the audit to identify assets, gaps in your institutional and educational practices and recommend improvements. It is adaptable for K-12 schools, postsecondary institutions, community organizations, NGOs, corporations, and other stakeholders promoting global engagement. The goal is to ensure that the organization is effectively preparing students and stakeholders for a globalized world while fostering a culturally competent and inclusive environment. Ultimately, this audit should evaluate how the organization's culturally sustaining global education strategies and initiatives are structured and executed. Below are key components to consider when conducting a Integrative Global CRSP Framework Audit (see Table 14.1).

After utilizing the audit, organizations could review specific accreditation or program standards to assess how policies and practices measure up. Next, they could explore the organization's mission and vision statement as well as the strategic plan to ensure coherence and direction in optimizing the globalized pedagogical framework. This exploration will identify areas where the organization is exceeding or falling short, which could impact resource allocation, program development/implementation, and policies. Outcomes should reflect opportunities for synergistic or mutualistic collaborations to extend global efforts/outreach, building capacity for transformative, sustainable, and equitable practices to create and cultivate borderless spaces.

Table 14.1 Integrative Global CRSP Framework Audit

Practice 1: Understands the multifaceted dynamics of cross-cultural interactions grounded in responsive and sustaining equitable educational practices			
Criteria/Questions	**No**	**Yes**	**Needs Improvement**
1. Have you created global-centric environments that nurture criticality, encouraging individuals to explore diverse perspectives to cultivate mutual understanding and promote personal and collective growth?			
2. Are you engaging in critical, reciprocal, and mutually beneficial partnerships that promote global awareness that is purposeful, sustainable, and productive for all to thrive through education?			
Suggestions and examples for revisions:			
Action Plan (Responsible stakeholders, proposed timeline, and measurable outcomes)			
Practice 2: Examine local, global, and intercultural issues while developing sociopolitical consciousness for understanding and critique of educational systems and policies			
Criteria/Questions	**No**	**Yes**	**Needs Improvement**
1. Do you integrate global education both within and beyond traditional classroom spaces to cultivate sociopolitical consciousness?			
2. Are critical issues addressed to demystify the local and global dichotomy in the educational landscape, promoting sociopolitical consciousness and transnational understandings?			
3. Are you actively supporting complex, multifaceted identities and self-awareness across different nations to foster intercultural competence and understanding of differences?			
Suggestions and examples for revisions:			
Action Plan (Responsible stakeholders, proposed timeline, and measurable outcomes)			

Practice 3: Commit to an inclusive pedagogical framework that values social perspective taking, cultural appreciation, and decolonizing education			
Criteria/Questions	**No**	**Yes**	**Needs Improvement**
1. Are you engaged in practices to actively dismantle hegemonic systemic practices that have historically and currently marginalized immigrants, first generation, linguistically diverse, and racial minoritized groups?			
2. Have you reimagined the world as a curriculum that fosters critical thinking, reflection, and action, while embracing multiple intellectual traditions and ways of knowing; and acknowledges the cultural wealth of both students and teachers.			
3. Are you utilizing approaches such as Universal Design for Learning to develop, restructure, and reimagine the world as a curriculum centering Sustainable Development Goals while scaffolding content, identifying key conceptual benchmarks, and fostering a more nuanced understanding of intersectionalities in educational settings across the globe?			
Suggestions and examples for revisions:			
Action Plan (Responsible stakeholders, proposed timeline, and measurable outcomes)			
Practice 4: Harnesses the power of collectivism through which community cultural assets foster belonging, well-being, and overall			
Criteria/Questions	**No**	**Yes**	**Needs Improvement**
1. Does the work you do decenter traditional Eurocentric ways of knowing to establish a new inclusive and globally centered frame of reference?			
2. Do you provide space for community engagement and agency to promote transformative globalized learning and action in educational spaces that transcends borders?			
3. Does your work empower students, as cultural translators and bridge-builders, to facilitate understanding and connection between globally diverse cultures?			
Suggestions and examples for revisions:			
Action Plan (Responsible stakeholders, proposed timeline, and measurable outcomes)			

Practice 5: Design academic outcomes are directly correlated to the implementation of relevant cultural and global instructional and assessment practices			
Criteria/Questions	**No**	**Yes**	**Needs Improvement**
1. Do you center student academic success and well-being as the primary focus of education facilitated through the use of global thinking routines that offer a variety of relevant, culturally rich materials, modalities, activities, and experiences?			
2. Do you reconceptualize assessment practices to draw on the globally diverse assets students bring to the classroom to promote academic achievement?			
Suggestions and examples for revisions:			
Action Plan (Responsible stakeholders, proposed timeline, and measurable outcomes)			

Resource Guide: Understanding the Possibilities—Using the Resource Guide for the Integrative Global CRSP Framework

Books

1   Asia Society/OECD. (2018). *Teaching for global competence in a rapidly changing world*. OECD Publishing, Paris/Asia Society. https://doi.org/10.1787/9789264289024-en.

2   Boix Mansilla, V., and Jackson, A. W. (2023). *Educating for global competence: Preparing our students to engage the world*. 2nd edition. ASD.

3   Chrona, J. (2022). *Wayi wah! Indigenous pedagogies: An act for reconciliation and anti-racist education*. Portage & Main Press.

4   Deardoff, D. K., de Wit, J. P., and Adams, T. (2022). *The handbook of international higher education*. Routledge.

5   Gist C., and Bristol T. (2022). *Handbook of research on teachers of color and indigenous teachers*. American Educational Research Association.

6   Howard, T. (2012). Culturally Responsive Pedagogy. *in Encyclopedia of Diversity in Education* (Vol. *1*, pp. 550–2). Sage Publications, Inc.

7   Longview Foundation. (2008). Teacher preparation for the global age: The imperative for change. https://longviewfdn.org/search?q=Teacher%20preparation%20for%20the%20global%20age (accessed October 28, 2025).

8   Love, B. (2019). *We want to do more than survive: Abolitionist teaching and the pursuit of educational freedom*. Beacon Press.

9   MacDonald, V. M. (2004). *Latino education in the United States: A narrated history from 1513–2000*. Palgrave.

10 Maguire, C., and Holt, A. (2022). *Arts and culture in global development practice: Expression, identity and empowerment*. Routledge.

11 McFadden, J., Merry, M. M., and Barron, K. R. (1997). *Guidelines for programs in teacher education*. AACTE.

12 Moraga, C., and Anzaldua, G. E. (Eds.) (1981). *This bridge called my back: Writings by radical women of color*. State University of New York Press.

13 Picower, B. (2021). *Reading, writing and racism: Disrupting whiteness in teacher education and in the classroom*. Beacon Press.

14 Roofe, C. (2022). *The lived curriculum experiences of Jamaican teachers: Currere and decolonising intentions*. Palgrave Macmillan

15 Sinclair S. (2023). *How to say Babylon. A memoir.* Simon & Schuster
16 Smith, L. T. (2021). *Decolonizing methodologies: Research and indigenous peoples.* 3rd edition. Bloomsbury Publishing.
17 Takaki, R. (2008). *A different mirror: A history of multicultural America.* Back Bay Books.
18 Valdés, G. (1996). *Con respeto: Bridging the distances between culturally diverse families and schools.* Teachers College Press.

Articles

1 Boix Mansilla, V. (2016). How to be a global thinker. *Educational Leadership, 74*(4), 10–16.
2 Gutierrez, K. D., and Rogoff, B. (2003). Cultural ways of learning: Individual traits or repertoires of practice. *Educational Researcher, 32*(5), 19–25. doi:10.3102/001318 9X032005019.
3 Hauerwas, L. B., Kerkhoff, S. N., and Sandra B. Schneider, S. B. (2021). Glocality, reflexivity, interculturality, and worldmaking: A framework for critical global teaching. *Journal of Research in Childhood Education, 35*(2), 185–99. http://doi.org/10.1080/02568543.2021.19007 14.
4 Kumashiro, K. K. (2000). Toward a theory of anti-oppressive education. *Review of Educational Research, 70*(1), 25–53.
5 Ladson-Billings, G. (1995). Toward a theory of culturally relevant pedagogy. *American Educational Research Journal, 32*(3), 465–91. https://doi.org/10.2307/1163320.
6 McCarty, T., and Lee, T. (2014). Critical culturally sustaining/revitalizing pedagogy and Indigenous education sovereignty. *Harvard Educational Review, 84*(1), 101–24.
7 Moll, L. C., and Gonzalez, N. (1994). Critical issues: Lessons from research with language-minority children. *Journal of Reading Behavior, 26*(4), 439–56.
8 Paris, D., and Alim, H. S. (2014). What are we seeking to sustain through culturally sustaining pedagogy? A loving critique forward. *Harvard Educational Review, 84*(1), 85–100.
9 Warner, O. (2012). Black in America too: Afro-Caribbean immigrants. *Social and Economic Studies, 61*(4), 69–103.
10 Zarate, A. D., Reese, L., Flores, D., and Villegas, J. (2016). "Making cambios, usando la voz": Addressing ethical dilemmas of education in immigrant contexts. *Issues in Teacher Education, 25*(1), 39–57.

Websites and Online Resources

1 Bigelow, B. (n.d.). Videos with a global conscience. *Rethinking Schools.* https://rethinkingschools.org/books/rethinking-globalization/videos-with-a-global-conscience (accessed October 28, 2025).
2 Edutopia. (2014). Global education: Resource Roundup. https://www.edutopia.org/article/global-education-resources (accessed October 28, 2025).
3 Public Broadcasting Station. (2024). *PBS Learning Media.* https://thinktv.pbslearningmedia.org (accessed October 28, 2025).

4   Smithsonian. (2024). *Smithsonian for educators.* https://www.si.edu/educators (accessed October 28, 2025).

5   United Nations. (2024). *Sustainable development goals.* https://sdgs.un.org/goals (accessed October 28, 2025).

Books for P-12

1   Abdurraqib, H., Choi, F., Khan, P., and Sullivan, D. (Eds.) (2022). *Respect the mic: Celebrating 20 years of poetry from a chicagoland high school.* Penguin Workshop.

2   Alifrenka, C. (2015). *I will always write back: How one letter changed two lives.* Brown & Company.

3   Ansary, C. (2022). *Odyssey of high hopes: A memoir of adversity and triumph.* Lambert Publications.

4   Applegate, K. (2009). *Home of the brave.* Square Fish.

5   Choi, Y. (2003). *Name jar.* Dragonfly Books.

6   Cisneros, S. (1983). *The House on Mango Street.* Random House.

7   Hart, M. (2022). *You are more than magic: The Black and Brown girl's guide to finding your voice.* Dial Books.

8   Hohn, N. (2019). *A likkle miss Lou: How Jamaican poet Louise Bennet Coverly found her voice.* Owlkids Books.

9   Kamkwamba, W. (2010). *The boy who harnessed the wind: Creating currents of electricity and hope.* Harper Perennial.

10   Morris, M. (1982). *Louise Bennett, selected poems.* Sangster

Multimedia Resources

1   Adichie, C. N. (2010). The Danger of a single story. *YouTube.* https://www.youtube.com/watch?v=D9Ihs241zeg (accessed October 28, 2025).

2   Diverse Issues in Higher Education. (2024, September 26). The critical need for global learning initiatives, with Dr. LaNitra M. Berger. #138 [Video]. *YouTube.* https://youtu.be/MRtM40aDSCY?si=iGteocf9PUOEKf_D (accessed October 28, 2025).

3   Bertrand, S., and Procher, K. (Hosts). (2020–present). *Black Gaze* [Audio podcast]. Spotify. https://podcasters.spotify.com/pod/show/black-gaze/support (accessed October 28, 2025).

4   Earp, J. (Host). (2024, July 11). Teaching for creativity across the curriculum (No. 24) [Audio podcast episode]. In *Global Education.* Teacher Magazine. https://soundcloud.com/teacher-acer/teaching-for-creativity-across-the-curriculum?utm_source=clipboard&utm_medium=text&utm_campaign=social_sharing (accessed October 28, 2025).

5   Edwards, C. (Host). (2019). *Introduction to evolving education globally* [Audio podcast]. Spotify. https://podcasters.spotify.com/pod/show/evolveeducation/support (accessed October 28, 2025).

6   Fleischauer, S., and Pinto, L. (Hosts). (2023–present). *Make it mindful: Insights for global education* [Audio podcast]. Spotify. https://open.spotify.com/show/3XMHCQ1IhzWbGUYc9FEIVA (accessed October 28, 2025).

7   Kinch, G. (Host). (2023–present). *The global ed project* [Audio podcast]. Spotify. https://open. spotify.com/show/7qr7mEpBsEUo9RVeS35mpO (accessed October 28, 2025).

8   Levesque, A. (Host). (2024–present). *The global education station presents* [Audio podcast]. Podbean. https://globaledstation.podbean.com (accessed October 28, 2025).

9   UNESCO IESALC. (2022–present). *Perspectivas: Global talks on higher education* [Audio podcast]. Spotify. https://open.spotify.com/show/37q60ycTHfiy9VARdzQ22M (accessed October 28, 2025).

Teaching Tools

1   Blake, M. E., and Cashwell, S. T. (2003). Use of poetry to facilitate communication about diversity: An educational model. *Race, Gender & Class, 10*(2), 96–108.

2   Council on Foreign Relations. (2024). Globalization. *CFR Education Global Matters.* https:// education.cfr.org/teach/globalization-0 (accessed October 28, 2025).

3   Educators' Institute for Human Rights. (n.d.). Where the world's teachers partner to end hate. https://eihr.org (accessed October 28, 2025).

4   Emergence Institute LLC. (2024). Global oneness project. https://www.globalonenessproject. org/about-project (accessed October 28, 2025).

5   Facing History. (2022). 4 Tools for teaching with poetry. https://www.facinghistory.org/ideas-week/4-tools-teaching-poetry (accessed October 28, 2025).

6   Journeys in Film. (2020). Teach with film. https://journeysinfilm.org (accessed October 28, 2025).

7   Marshall, J. (2019). *Integrating the visual arts across the curriculum: An elementary and middle school guide.* Teachers College Press.

8   Woodson, J. (2019). *Brown girl dreaming.* Penguin

Collaborative Online International Learning (COIL) and Virtual Exchange (VE)

1   American Association of Colleges and Universities (AACU). (2024). Virtual Exchange/ Collaborative Online International Learning. https://www.aacu.org/initiatives/virtual-exchange-collaborative-online-international-learning (accessed October 28, 2025).

2   American Higher Education Alliance. (AHEA). (2020). Collaborative Online International Learning. https://www.ahealliance.org/uncategorized/new-outlooks-on-internationalization-at-home-2 (accessed October 28, 2025).

3   Guimarães, F. F., Mendes, A. R. M., Rodrigues, L. M., Paiva, R. S. S., and Finardi, K. R. (2019). Internationalization at home, COIL and intercomprehension: For more inclusive activities in the global south. *Simon Fraser University Educational Review Journal, 2*(3), 89–103. https:// journals.lib.sfu.ca/index.php/sfuer/issue/view/64/41 (accessed October 28, 2025).

Organizations and Networks

1   Asia Society, Global Cities Education Network, https://asiasociety.org/global-cities-education-network (accessed October 28, 2025).
2   Global Community: Uniting for Equity, https://www.gcue.org (accessed October 28, 2025).
3   National Center on Education and the Economy, https://ncee.org (accessed October 28, 2025).
4   Program for International Student Assessment (PISA), National Center for Education Statics, https://nces.ed.gov/surveys/pisa (accessed October 28, 2025).
5   The Tandana Foundation, https://tandanafoundation.org (accessed October 28, 2025).
6   The Varkey Foundation (Global Teacher/Student Prize), https://www.varkeyfoundation.org (accessed October 28, 2025).
7   World Council on Intercultural and Global Competence, https://iccglobal.org (accessed October 28, 2025).

Bibliography

Acevedo, S. M., Aho, M., Çela, E., Chao, J., Garcia-Gonzales, I., Macleod, A., Moutray, C., and Olague, C. (2015). Positionality as knowledge: From pedagogy to praxis. *Integral Review*, *11*(1), 28–46.

Agee, J. (2009). Developing qualitative research questions: A reflective process. *International Journal of Qualitative Studies in Education*, *22*(4), 431–47.

AIEM. (2023). Mathematics Education Forum, *23*(41), Special Issue. https://doi.org/10.35763/ aiem23.

Ainscow, M. (2020). Promoting inclusion and equity in education: Lessons from international experiences. *Nordic Journal of Studies In Educational Policy*, *6*, 7–16. https://doi.org/10.1080/200 20317.2020.1729587.

Al Jazeera. (2020, June 3). India: Unable to access online classes, Dalit girl kills herself. *Al Jazeera*. https://www.aljazeera.com/news/2020/6/3/india-unable-to-access-online-classes-dalit-girl-kills-herself (accessed October 24, 2025).

Alderman, I., and Holt Moore, K. (2021). Terror management and religious literacy in the classroom. *Electronic Journal for Research in Science and Mathematics Education*, *25*(3), 68–76.

Alger, C. F., and Harf, J. E. (1985). *Global Education: Why? for Whom? About What?* Working Paper for the "Guidelines for International Teacher Education" Project of AACTE, pp. 1–30.

Alim, H. S., and Paris, D. (2017). What is culturally sustaining pedagogy and why does it matter? In D. Paris and H. S. Alim (Eds.), *Culturally Sustaining Pedagogies: Teaching and Learning for Justice in a Changing World*, pp. 1–21. Teachers College Press.

Allport, G. W. (1954). *The Nature of Prejudice.* Addison-Wesley.

Amjad, A. (2018). Muslim students' experiences and perspectives on current teaching practices in Canadian schools. *Power and Education*, *10*(3), 315–32. https://doi.org/kvzz.

Andreotti, V. (2006). Soft versus critical global citizenship education. *Policy and Practice: A Developmental Education Review*, *3*, 40–51.

Andreotti, V. (2015). Global citizenship education otherwise: Pedagogical and theoretical insights. In Ali Abdi, Lynette Shultz, and Tashika Pillay (Eds.), *Decolonizing Global Citizenship Education*, pp. 221–30. Sense Publishers.

Andreotti, V. D. O. (2014). Soft versus critical global citizenship education. In S. McCloskey (Ed.), *Development Education in Policy and Practice*, pp. 21–31. Springer.

Andreotti, V. D. O. (2021a). *Hospicing Modernity: Facing Humanity's Wrongs and the Implications for Social Activism.* North Atlantic Books.

Andreotti, V. D. O. (2021b). Depth education and the possibility of GCE otherwise. *Globalisation, Societies and Education*, *19*(4), 496–509. https://doi.org/10.1080/14767724.2021.1904214.

The Annie E. Casey Foundation. (2024). *KIDS COUNT Data Center*. https://datacenter.aecf.org (accessed October 28, 2025).

Aoki, T. T. (2005). Curriculum implementation as instrumental action and as situational praxis. In W. F. Pinar and R. L. Irwin (Eds.), *Curriculum in a New Key: The Collected Works of Ted T. Aoki*, pp. 111–23. Routledge.

Aronson, B., Amatullah, T., and Laughter, J. (2016). Culturally relevant education: Extending the conversation to religious diversity. *Multicultural Perspectives*, *18*(3), 140–9.

Asia Society, Center for Global Education. (2021). *Five Reasons Why Global Competence Matters*. https://asiasociety.org/education/five-reasons-why-global-competence-matters (accessed October 26, 2025).

Ateh, C., and Ryan, L. (2023). Preparing teacher candidates to be culturally responsive in classroom management. *Social Sciences & Humanities Open*, *7(1)*, 100455. https://doi.org/10.1016/j.ssaho.2023.100455.

August, D., and Hakuta, K. (Eds.). (1998). *Educating Language Minority Children*. National Academy Press.

Bajaj, M., Walsh, D., Bartlett, L., and Martinez, G. (2022). *Humanizing Education for Immigrant and Refugee Youth*. Teachers College Press.

Bakuli, E. (2023, July 7). Detroit's $94 million "right to read" lawsuit settlement is finally coming through for DPSCD. *Chalkbeat*. https://www.chalkbeat.org/detroit/2023/7/7/23787399/detroit-public-schools-right-to-read-settlement-whitmer-emergency-management (accessed October 24, 2025).

Baldwin, J. (1963). *A Talk to Teachers*. ESED 5234 Master List. https://digitalcommons.georgiasouthern.edu/esed5234-master/44.

Banks, A. J., White, I. K., and McKenzie, B. D. (2019). Black politics: How anger influences the political actions Blacks pursue to reduce racial inequality. *Political Behavior*, *41*(4), 917–43. https://doi.org/10.1007/s11109-018-9477-1.

Banks, J. A. (2004). Multicultural education: Historical development, dimensions, and practice. In J. A. Banks and C. A. M. Banks (Eds.), *Handbook of Research on Multicultural Education* (2nd edn.), pp. 3–29. Jossey-Bass.

Banks, J. A. (2015). Multicultural education, school reform, and educational equality. In *Opening the Doors to Opportunity for All: Setting a Research Agenda for the Future*, pp. 54–63. American Institutes for Research.

Barakat, M. (2024, May 10). In reversal, Virginia school board votes to restore Confederate names to 2 schools. *The Hill*. https://thehill.com/homenews/ap/ap-top-headlines/ap-an-education-board-in-virginia-votes-to-restore-confederate-names-to-2-schools (accessed October 26, 2025).

Bardon, J. (2011). *The Plantation of Ulster*. Gill & Macmillan.

Barros, S. R., Hadeer, R., and Gajasinghe, K. (2022). Confabulating research: Performing memory-work as inquiry. *International Review of Qualitative Research*, *15*(1), 21–41.

Bartell, T., Yeh, C., Felton-Koestler, M. D., and Berry, R. Q. I. (2022). *Upper Elementary Mathematics Lessons to Explore, Understand, and Respond to Social Injustice*. Corwin Press.

Barton, K., and McCully, A. (2010). "You can form your own point of view": Internally persuasive discourse in Northern Ireland students' encounters with history. *Teachers College Record*, *112*(1), 142–81.

Barton, K., and McCully, A. (2012). Trying to "see things differently": Northern Ireland students' struggle to understand alternative historical perspectives. *Theory & Research in Social Education*, *40*(4), 371–408. https://doi.org/10.1080/00933104.2012.710928.

Bender-Slack, D. (2002). Using literature to teach global education: A humanist approach. *English Journal*, *91*(5), 70–5.

Benjamin, W. (2019). The Storyteller. In H. Arendt (Ed.) and H. Zohn (Trans.), *Illuminations: Essays and reflections*, pp. 26–55. Mariner Books, Houghton Mifflin Harcourt.

Berchini, C. N. (2017). Critiquing un/critical pedagogies to move toward a pedagogy of responsibility in teacher education. *Journal of Teacher Education*, *68*(5), 463–75.

Berger, J. (2016). *Confabulations*. Penguin Books.

Berger, R. (2015). Now I see it, now I don't: Researcher's position and reflexivity in qualitative research. *Qualitative Research*, *15*(2), 219–34. https://doi.org/10.1177/1468794112468475.

Berry, R. Q. I., Conway, B. M. I., Lawler, B. R., and Staley, J. W. (2020). *High School Mathematics Lessons to Explore, Understand, and Respond to Social Injustice*. Corwin Press.

Bertrand, S., and Porcher, K. (2023). Shifting the gaze to Blackness in ELA: Using the Blackgaze framework in literacy teacher education courses. *Language Arts*, *101*(1), 27–39. https://doi.org/10.58680/la202332598.

Beutel, D., and Tangen, D. (2018). The impact of intercultural experiences on preservice teachers' preparedness to engage with diverse learners. *Australian Journal of Teacher Education*, *43*(3), 168–79.

Beyerbach, B., and Ramalho, T. (2011). Chapter fifteen: Activist art in social justice pedagogy. *Counterpoints*, *403*, 202–17.

Biesta, G. (2013a). Receiving the gift of teaching: From "learning from" to "being taught by." *Studies in Philosophy and Education*, *32*(5), 449–61.

Biesta, G. (2013b). Responsive or responsible? Democratic education for the global networked society. *Policy Futures in Education*, *11*(6), 733–44. https://doi.org/10.2304/pfie.2013.11.6.733.

Bindman, S. W., Pomerantz, E. M., and Roisman, G. I. (2015). Do children's executive functions account for associations between early autonomy-supportive parenting and achievement through high school? *Journal of Educational Psychology*, *107*(3), 756–70. https://doi.org/10.1037/edu0000017.

Birney, M. E., Rabinovich, A., Morton, T. A., Heath, H., and Ashcroft, S. (2019). When speaking English is not enough: The consequences of language-based stigma for nonnative speakers. *Journal of Language and Social Psychology*, *39*(1), 67–86. https://doi.org/10.1177/0261927X19883906.

Bishop, A. (2002). Mathematical acculturation, cultural conflicts, and transition. In G. Abreu, A. Bishop, and N. Presmeg (Eds.), *Transitions Between Contexts of Mathematical Practices*, pp. 193–212. Kluwer.

Bishop, R. S. (1990). Mirrors, windows, and sliding glass doors. *Perspectives: Choosing and Using Books for the Classroom*, 6(3).

Bloemraad, I., and de Graauw, E. (2012). Immigrant integration and policy in the United States. In J. Biles and J. Frideres (Eds.), *Intercultural Perspectives*, pp. 205–33. McGill-Queen's University Press.

Blumenfeld, W. J. (2006). Christian privilege and the promotion of "secular" and not-so "secular" mainline Christianity in public schooling and in the larger society. *Equity and Excellence in Education*, *39*(3), 195–210.

Blumenfeld, W. J., and Jaekel, K. (2012). Exploring levels of Christian privilege awareness among preservice teachers. *Journal of Social Issues*, *68*(1), 128–44.

Borooah, V., and Knox, C. (2015). *The Economics of Schooling in a Divided Society: The Case for Shared Education*. Palgrave Macmillan.

Boutte, G., Kelly-Jackson, C., and Johnson, G. L. (2010). Culturally relevant teaching in science classrooms: Addressing academic achievement, cultural competence, and critical consciousness. *International Journal of Multicultural Education*, *12*(2), 1–20.

Brandt, R. (1994). On education for diversity: A conversation with James A. Banks. *Educational Leadership*, *51*, 28–32.

Brantmeier, E. (2011). Toward mainstreaming critical peace education in U.S. teacher education. In C. S. Malott and B. Porfilio (Eds.), *Critical Pedagogy in the Twenty-First Century: A New Generation of Scholars*, pp. 349–75. Information Age Publishing.

Brown v. *Board of Education of Topeka*, 349 U.S. *301* (1955). https://www.archives.gov/milestone-documents/brown-v-board-of-education (accessed October 24, 2025).

Brown, B. A., Boda, P., Lemmi, C., and Monroe, X. (2019). Moving culturally relevant pedagogy from theory to practice: Exploring teachers' application of culturally relevant education in science and mathematics. *Urban Education*, *54*(6), 775–803.

Brown, C. W., and Savić, M. (2023). Practising critical visual literacy through redesign in ELT classrooms. *ELT Journal*, *77*(2), 186–96. https://doi.org/10.1093/elt/ccac049.

Brummelman, E., Thomaes, S., de Castro, B. O., Overbeek, G., and Bushman, B. J. (2014). "That's Not Just Beautiful—That's Incredibly Beautiful!": The adverse impact of inflated praise on children with low self-esteem. *Psychological Science*, *25*(3), 728–35. https://doi.org/10.1177/0956797613514251.

Burn, K., and Menter, I. (2021). Making sense of teacher education in a globalizing world: The distinctive contribution of a sociocultural approach. *Comparative Education Review*, *65*(4), 770–89. https://doi.org/10.1086/716228.

Buzcar, L. (2023, May 19). *Avoiding Curricular Pitfalls of Study Abroad*. Inside Higher Ed. https://www.insidehighered.com/opinion/views/2023/05/19/avoiding-curricular-pitfalls-study-abroad (accessed October 28, 2025).

Byker, E. J., and Putman, S. M. (2019). Catalyzing cultural and global competencies: Engaging preservice teachers in study abroad to expand the agency of citizenship. *Journal of Studies in International Education*, *23*(1), 84–105. https://doi.org/10.1177/1028315318814559.

Camangian, P. R. (2013). Teach like lives depend on it. *Urban Education*, *50*(4), 424–53. https://doi.org/10.1177/0042085913514591.

Cambridge, J., and Thompson, J. (2004). Internationalism and globalization as contexts for international education. *Compare: A Journal of Comparative and International Education*, *34*(2), 161–75.

Campana, A. (2011). Agents of possibility: Examining the intersections of art, education, and activism in communities. *Studies in Art Education*, *52*(4), 278–91. https://doi.org/10.1080/00393541.2011.11518841.

Center for Reaching and Teaching the Whole Child. (2022). Anchor competencies framework. https://crtwc.org/framework (accessed October 26, 2025).

Cerna L., Mezzanotte C., and Rutigliano A. (2021) Promoting inclusive education for diverse societies: A conceptual framework. *OECD Education Working Papers, No. 260*, OECD Publishing. https://doi.org/10.1787/94ab68c6-en.

Chandir, H., and Blackmore, J. (2024). Situated enactments of global competence in three schools in Victoria. *Journal of Education Policy*, *39*(5), 1–21. https://doi.org/10.1080/02680939.2023.2299471.

Chen, X., Chung, J., and Hsiao, C (2009). Peer interactions and relationships from a cross-cultural perspective. In K. H. Rubin, W. M. Burkowski, and B. Laursen (Eds.), *Handbook of Peer Interactions, Relationships, and Groups*, pp. 432–51. Guilford.

Cherrez, J. N., and Gleason, B. (2022). A virtual exchange experience: Preparing pre-service teachers for cultural diversity. *Journal of Digital Learning in Teacher Education*, *38*(3), 126–38. https://doi-org.ezproxy.hope.edu/10.1080/21532974.2022.2083732.

Child Trends. (2015). *Individualized Education Plans*. http://www.childtrends.org/databank/indicators-by-topic-area/education

Child Trends. (2018). *Immigrant Children*. https://www.childtrends.org/indicators/immigrant-children

Childs, K. J., and Staley J. W. (2025). *Teaching Mathematics for Social Justice: A Guide for Moving from Mindset to Action*. Corwin Press

Chomsky, N. (2020). *Internationalism or extinction* (C. Derber, S. Moodliar, & P. Shannon, Eds.). Routledge, Taylor & Francis.

Chung, G. H., and Lim, J. Y. (2016). Marriage immigrant mothers' experience of perceived discrimination, maternal depression, parenting behaviors, and adolescent psychological adjustment among multicultural families in South Korea. *Journal of Child and Family Studies*, *25*, 2894–903.

Clandinin, D. J., and Connelly, F. M. (2000). *Narrative Inquiry: Experience and Story in Qualitative Research*. Jossey-Bass.

Clarke, A. (2023). Teacher inquiry: By any other name. In R. J. Tierney, F. Rizvi, and K. Ercikan (Eds.), *International Encyclopedia of Education* (4th edn.), pp. 232–42. Elsevier. https://doi.org/10.1016/B978-0-12-818630-5.04026-4.

Cobb, C. (2012). Throwing out the culturally unresponsive cookie cutter: Collaborations, concessions, and curricula in a Ramadan music accommodation. *Canadian Journal of Action Research*, *13*(3), 3–18. https://journals.nipissingu.ca/index.php/cjar/article/view/58/39.

Coll, C. G., and Marks, A. K. (2009). *Immigrant Stories*. Oxford University Press.

Collaborative for Academic, Social, and Emotional Learning. (n.d.). What is the CASEL framework? https://casel.org/fundamentals-of-sel/what-is-the-casel-framework (accessed October 26, 2025).

Collopy, R., Tjaden-Glass, S., and McIntosh, N. (2020). Attending to conditions that facilitate intercultural competence: A reciprocal service-learning approach. *Michigan Journal of Community Service Learning*, *26*(1), 19–38.

Conger, D., and Grigorenko, E. L. (2010). Special educational needs of children in immigrant families. In E. Grigorenko and R. Takanishi (Eds.), *Immigration, Diversity, and Education*, pp. 170–87. Routledge.

Cox, A. M. (2023, October). America the traumatized. *The New Republic*, 15–21. https://newrepublic.com/article/175311/america-polarized-traumatized-trump-violence (accessed October 26, 2025).

Crafter, S., and Maunder, R. (2012). Understanding transitions using a sociocultural framework. *Educational and Child Psychology*, *29*(1), 10–18. https://doi.org/10.53841/bpsecp.2012.29.1.10.

Crenshaw, K. (1989). Demarginalizing the intersection of race and sex: A Black feminist critique of antidiscrimination doctrine. University of Chicago Legal Forum, 139–68.

Crenshaw, K. (2005). Mapping the margins: Intersectionality, identity politics, and violence against women of color (1994). In R. K. Bergen, J. L. Edleson, and C. M. Renzetti (Eds.), *Violence Against Women: Classic Papers*, pp. 282–313. Pearson Education New Zealand.

Cushner, K. (2007). The role of experience in the making of internationally-minded teachers. *Teacher Education Quarterly*, *34*(1), 27–39.

Dabach, D. B. (2014). "I Am Not a Shelter!": Stigma and social boundaries in teachers' accounts of students' experience in separate "sheltered" English learner classrooms. *Journal of Education for Students Placed at Risk*, *19*(2), 98–124. https://doi-org.ezproxy.hope.edu/10.1080/10824669.2014.954044.

Darling-Hammond, L. (1997). *The Right to Learn*. Jossey-Bass.

de Sousa Santos, B. (2015). *Epistemologies of the South: Justice Against Epistemicide*. Routledge.

de Vries, M. (2020). Enacting critical citizenship: An intersectional approach to global citizenship education. *Societies*, *10*(4), 91.

Deardorff, D. K. (2006). Identification and assessment of intercultural competence as a student outcome of internationalization. *Journal of Studies in International Education*, *10*(3), 241–66.

Deardorff, D. K. (2020). *Manual for Developing Intercultural Competencies. Story Circles*. Routledge.

Del Carmen Salazar, M. (2013). A humanizing pedagogy: Reinventing the principles and practice of education as a journey toward liberation. *Review of Research in Education*, *37*(1), 121–48. https://doi.org/10.3102/0091732X12464032.

Delpit L. (2006). *Other People's Children: Cultural Conflict in the Classroom*. New Press.

Denney, S., and Green, C. (2021). Who should be admitted? Conjoint analysis of South Korean attitudes toward immigrants. *Ethnicities*, *21*(1), 120–145.

Dimitrov, N., and Haque, A. (2016). Intercultural teaching competence: A multi-disciplinary model for instructor reflection. *Intercultural Education*, *27*(5), 437–56.

Dishion, T. J., and Tipsord, J. M. (2011). Peer contagion in child and adolescent social and emotional development. *Annual Review of Psychology*, *62*, 189–214. https://doi.org/10.1146/annurev.psych.093008.100412.

Dreamson, N. (2018). Culturally inclusive global citizenship education: Metaphysical and non-western approaches. *Multicultural Education Review*, *10*(2), 75–93.

Durmaz, B., and Miçoogullari, S. (2021). The effect of the integrated mathematics lessons with children's literature on the fifth grade students' place value understanding. *Acta Didactica Napocensia*, *14*(2), 244–56. https://doi.org/10.24193/adn.14.2.18.

Egan, K. (1978). What is curriculum? *Curriculum Inquiry*, *8*(1), 65–72.

Ellis, M. W., and Berry, R. Q., III. (2005). The paradigm shift in mathematics education: Explanations and implications of reforming conceptions of teaching and learning. *The Mathematics Educator*, *15*(1), 7–17.

Erikson, E. H. (1972). Eight ages of man. In C. S. Lavatelli and F. Stendler (Eds.), *Reading in Child Behavior and Child Development*, pp. 19–30. Harcourt Brace Jovanovich.

Estellés, M., and Fischman, G. (2021). Who needs global citizenship education? A review of the literature on teacher education. *Journal of Teacher Education*, *72*(2), 223–36. https://doi.org/10.1177/0022487120920254.

Farquhar, S., and Fitzpatrick, E. (2016). Unearthing truths in duoethnographic method. *Qualitative Research Journal*, *16*(3), 238–50.

Fendler, L. (2006). Others and the problem of community. *Curriculum Inquiry*, *36*(3), 303–26.

Ferber, A. L. (2012). Color-blindness, post-feminism, and Christonormativity. *Journal of Social Issues*, *68*(1), 63–77, https://doi.org/10.1111/j.1540-4560.2011.01736.x.

Fix, M. (Ed.). (2007). *Securing the Future*. MPI.

Flores, B. B., and Smith, H. L. (2009). Teachers' characteristics and attitudinal beliefs about linguistic and cultural diversity. *Bilingual Research Journal*, *31*(1–2), 323–58. https://doi.org/10.1080/15235880802640789.

Foxall, F., Sundin, D., Towell-Barnard, A., Ewens, B., Kemp, V., and Porock, D. (2021). Revealing meaning from story: The application of narrative inquiry to explore the factors that influence decision making in relation to the withdrawal of life-sustaining treatment in the intensive care unit. *International Journal of Qualitative Methods*, *20*, 160940692110283. https://doi.org/10.1177/16094069211028345.

Fraser-Burgess, S. (2020). Accountability and troubling the caring ideal in the classroom: A call to teacher citizenry. *Educational Studies*, *56*(5), 456–81. https://doi.org/10.1080/00131946.2020.1799216.

Freire P. (1970). *Pedagogy of the Oppressed*. Continuum.

Fujikane, H. (2003). Approaches to global education in the United States, United Kingdom and Japan. *International Review of Education*, *49*, 133–52.

FutureEd. (2024). Analysis of legislation restricting the teaching of racism. https://www.quorum.us/spreadsheet/external/KBYQbCxNgAheAgQCtQZC (accessed October 26, 2025).

Gangi, J. M. (2008). The unbearable whiteness of literacy instruction: Realizing the implications of the proficient reader research. *Multicultural Review*, *17*(1), 30–5.

Garcia, E. B., Sulik, M. J., and Obradovic, J. (2019). Teachers' perceptions of students' executive functions: Disparities by gender, ethnicity, and ELL status. *Journal of Educational Psychology*, *111*(5), 918–31. https://doi-org.ezproxy.hope.edu/10.1037/edu0000308.

Garcia, R. (2024). Voices of Hope 1 [Acrylics on Canvas 44x60]. Reynas Gallery, Michigan.

Gay, G. (2002). Preparing for culturally responsive teaching. *Journal of Teacher Education*, *53*(2), 106–16.

Gay, G. (2013). Teaching to and through cultural diversity. *Curriculum Inquiry*, *43*(1), 48–70. https://doi.org/10.1111/curi.12002.

Gay, G. (2018). *Culturally Responsive Teaching: Theory, Research, and Practice* (3rd edn.). Teachers College Press.

Gay, G., and Kirkland, K. N. (2003). Developing cultural critical consciousness and self-reflection in preservice teacher education. *Theory into Practice*, *42*(3), 181–7. https://doi.org/10.1353/tip.2003.0029.

Gere, A. R., Buehler, J., Dallavis, C., and Haviland, V. S. (2009). A visibility project: Learning to see how preservice teachers take up culturally responsive pedagogy. *American Educational Research Journal*, *46*(3), 816–52. https://doi.org/10.3102/0002831209333182.

Gershon, W. S., and Helfenbein, R. J. (2023). Curriculum matters: Educational tools for troubled times. *Journal of Curriculum Studies*, *55*(3), 1–19.

Gillespie, J., Gross, D., and Jasinski, L. (2020). *Faculty as Global Learners: Off-campus Study at Liberal Arts Colleges*. Lever Press. https://doi.org/10.3998/mpub.11923682.

Gittell, J. H. (2006). Relational coordination: Coordinating work through relationships of shared goals, shared knowledge and mutual respect. In O. Kyriakidou and M. Ozbilgin (Eds.), *Relational Perspectives in Organizational Studies*, pp. 74–94. Edward Elgar Publishers.

Gittell, J. H., and Douglass, A. (2012). Relational bureaucracy. *Academy of Management Review*, *37*(4), 709–33. https://doi.org/10.5465/amr.2010.0438.

Global North and Global South. (2024, January 7). In *Wikipedia*. https://en.wikipedia.org/wiki/Global_North_and_Global_South (accessed October 26, 2025).

Godwyn, M., and Gittell, J. H. (Eds.). (2012). *Sociology of Organizations*. Pine Forge Press.

Goldoni, F. (2015). Preparing students for studying abroad. *Journal of the Scholarship of Teaching and Learning*, *15*(4), 1–20.

Goldoni, F. (2017). Race, ethnicity, class and identity: Implications for study abroad. *Journal of Language, Identity & Education*, *16*(5), 328–41. https://doi.org/10.1080/15348458.2017.1350922.

González, N., Moll, L. C., and Amanti, C. (2005) *Funds of Knowledge: Theorizing Practices in Households, Communities, and Classrooms*. Lawrence Erlbaum Associates.

González-Salamanca, J. C., Agudelo, O. L., and Salinas, J. (2020). Key competences, education for sustainable development and strategies for the development of 21st century skills: A systematic literature review. *Sustainability*, *12*(24), 10366. https://doi.org/10.3390/su122410366.

Goral, M., and Gnadinger, C. M. (2006). Using storytelling to teach mathematics concepts. *Australian Primary Mathematics Classroom*, *11*, 4–8.

Goren, H., and Yemini, M. (2017). Global citizenship education redefined—A systematic review of empirical studies on global citizenship education. *International Journal of Educational Research*, *82*, 170–83.

Graham, P. A. (2005). *Schooling America*. Oxford University Press.

Guillén-Yparrea, N., and Ramírez-Montoya, M. S. (2023). Intercultural competencies in higher education: A systematic review from 2016 to 2021. *Cogent Education*, *10*(1), 1–14. https://doi.org/10.1080/2331186X.2023.2167360.

Gullifer, J. W., Pivneva, I., Whitford, V., Sheikh, N. A., and Titone, D. (2023). Bilingual language experience and its effect on conflict adaptation in reactive inhibitory control tasks. *Psychological Science*, 34(2), 238–51. https://doi-org.ezproxy.hope. edu/10.1177/09567976221113764.

Halpern, J. (1993). Empathy using resonance emotions in the service of curiosity. In H. Spiro, M. G. M. Curren, E. Peschel, and St. D. James (Eds.), *Empathy and the Practice of Medicine*, pp. 160–73. Yale University Press.

Halpern, J. (2001). *From Detached Concern to Empathy: Humanizing Medical Practice*. Oxford University Press.

Hammond, Z., and Jackson, Y. (2015). *Culturally Responsive Teaching and the Brain: Promoting Authentic Engagement and Rigor Among Culturally and Linguistically Diverse Students*. Corwin.

Haraway, D. (2016). *Staying with the Trouble: Making Kin in the Chthulucene*. Duke University Press.

Haraway, D. (2018). Making kin in the Chthulunene: Reproducing multispecies justice. In A. E. Clarke and D. J. Haraway (Eds.), *Making Kin Not Population*, pp. 67–100. Prickly Paradigm Press.

Haraway, D. (2019). It matters what stories tell stories; it matters whose stories tell stories. *A/b: Auto/Biography Studies*, *34*(3), 565–75. https://doi.org/10.1080/08989575.2019.1664163.

Hatley, J. (2019). Universal values as a barrier to the effectiveness of global citizenship education: A multimodal critical discourse analysis. *International Journal of Development Education and Global Learning*, *11*(1), 87–102.

Hauerwas, L. B., and Creamer, M. (2018). Engaging with host schools to establish the reciprocity of an international teacher education partnership. *Journal of Higher Education Outreach and Engagement*, *22*(2), 157–87.

Haydar, H. N., Kaya, M., and Weaver, J. C. (2023). Promoting interdisciplinary connections and mathematics collaborations through literacy-centered lesson study. In S. Dotger, G. Matney, K. Chandler-Olcott, J. Heckathorn, and M. Fox (Eds.), *Lesson Study with Mathematics and Science Preservice Teachers Finding the Form*, pp. 170–81. Routledge. https://doi. org/10.4324/9781003326434-20

Hehir, T., and Katzman, L. (2013). *Effective Inclusive School*. John Wiley & Sons.

Heinrich, J. (2015). The Devil is in the details: In America, can you really say "God" in school? *Educational Review*, *67*(1), 64–78. https://doiorg.ezproxy.hope.edu/10.1080/00131911.2013.826179.

Hibel, J., and Jasper, A. D. (2012). Delayed special education placement for learning disabilities among children of immigrants. *Social Forces*, *91*(2), 503–29. https://doi.org/10.1093/sf/sox092.

Hou, Y. (2020). Comparative global citizenship education: A critical literature analysis. *Beijing International Review of Education*, *2*(4), 537–52.

Howard, L. W., Tang, T. L.-P., and Austin, M. J. (2015). Teaching critical thinking skills: Ability, motivation, intervention, and the Pygmalion effect. *Journal of Business Ethics*, *128*(1), 133–47. https://doi.org/10.1007/s10551-014-2084-0.

Howard, T. C. (2021). Culturally responsive pedagogy. In J. A. Banks (Ed.), *Transforming Multicultural Education Policy and Practice: Expanding Educational Opportunity*, pp. 137–63. Teachers College Press.

Hsieh, H.-F., and Shannon, S. F. (2005). Three approaches to qualitative content analysis. *Qualitative Health Research*, *15*(9), 1277–88. https://doi.org/10.1177/1049732305276687.

Huaman, E. S., and Swentzell, P. (2021). Indigenous education and sustainable development: Rethinking environment through Indigenous knowledges and generative environmental pedagogies. *Journal of American Indian Education*, *60*(1–2), 7–28. https://doi.org/10.1353/jaie.2021.a840601.

Huard, M. (2024). Review of teaching and assessing social justice art education: Power, politics, and possibilities. *Studies in Art Education*, *65*(1), 109–114. https://doi.org/10.1080/00393541.2023.2285212.

Hughes, J. (2011). Are separate schools divisive? A case study from Northern Ireland. *British Educational Research Journal*, *37*(5), 829–50.

Hull G. A., and Stornaiuolo A. (2014). Cosmopolitan literacies, social networks, and "proper distance": Striving to understand in a global world. *Curriculum Inquiry*, *44*(1), 15–44.

Hult, F. M. (2013). Covert Bilingualism and symbolic competence: Analytical reflections on negotiating insider/outsider positionality in Swedish speech situations. *Applied Linguistics*, *35*(1), 63–81.

Hwang, Y., Wolthuis, R., Kasap, S. & Peterson, R. (2026). Religious diversity and culturally responsive learning and teaching for teacher candidates. *Multicultural Learning and Teaching*, *21*(1), 83–108. https://doi.org/10.1515/mlt-2023-0040

Individuals with Disabilities Education Act, 20 U.S.C. §§ 1412(a)(3) & (5). (2004).

Institute of International Education. (2024). *U.S. Study Abroad: Latin America & Caribbean*. OpenDoors. https://opendoorsdata.org/data/us-study-abroad/all-destinations (accessed October 28, 2025).

Jakobsen, M., and Andersen, S. C. (2013). Coproduction and equity in public service delivery. *Public Administration Review*, *73*(5), 704–13. https://doi.org/10.1111/puar.12094.

Jamal, A. A., and Naber, N. C. (Eds.). (2022). *Race and Arab Americans Before and After 9/11: From Invisible Citizens to Visible Subjects*. Syracuse University Press.

Jilani, Z., and Smith, J. A. (2019, March 4). What is the true cost of polarization in America? *Greater Good Magazine*. https://greatergood.berkeley.edu/article/item/what_is_the_true_cost_of_polarization_in_america (accessed October 26, 2025).

Johnson, B., and Christensen, L. B. (2017). *Educational Research: Quantitative, Qualitative, and Mixed Approaches* (666th edn.). Sage.

Johnson, B., and Christensen, L. B. (2019). *Educational Research: Quantitative, Qualitative, and Mixed Approaches* (7th edn.). Sage.

Johnson, M. (1993). *Education on the Wild Side: Learning for the Twenty-First Century*. University of Oklahoma

Jones-Correa, M., and de Graauw, E. (2013). The illegality trap. *Daedalus*, *142*(3), 185–96.

Journell, W., and Dressman, M. (2011). Using videoconferences to diversify classrooms electronically. *The Clearing House*, *84*(3), 109–13. https://doi.org/10.1080/00098655.2010.538757.

k20 Center. (2017). *K20 Learn | Optic: A Reading Strategy Recipe*. OPTIC: A Reading Strategy Recipe. https://learn.k20center.ou.edu/lesson/240 (accessed October 26, 2025).

Kalyanpur, M., Harry, B., and Skrtic, T. (2000). Equity and advocacy expectations of culturally diverse families' participation in special education. *International Journal of Disability, Development and Education*, *47*, 119–36. https://doi.org/10.1080/713671106.

Kang, H., and Fay, L. (2023). Teacher responsiveness as a core feature of justice- and equity-centered instruction. *The Science Teacher*, *90*(5), 38–43. https://doi.org/10.1080/19434871.2023.12290282.

Kauper, K., and Jacobs, M. (2019). The case for slow curriculum: Creative subversion and the curriculum mind. In C. A. Mullen (Ed.), *Creativity Under Duress in Education? Resistive Theories, Practices and Actions*, pp. 339–60. Springer. https://doi.org/10.1007/978-3-319-90272-2.

Kazemi, E., and Hubbard, A. (2008). New directions for the design and study of professional development: Attending to the co-evolution of teachers' participation across contexts. *Journal of Teacher Education*, *59*, 428–41.

Kelly, A. V. (2009). *The Curriculum: Theory and Practice*. Sage.

Kelly, M., and Wright Fields, C. (2020). Unlocking the doors: Opening spaces for inclusive pedagogy and practice in teacher education. In C. K. Clausen and S. R. Logan (Eds.), *Integrating Social Justice Education in Teacher Preparation Programs*, pp. 1–28. IGI Global.

Kendi, I. (2019). *How to Be an Anti-racist*. Random House.

Kerkhoff, S. N. (2017). Designing global futures: A mixed methods study to develop and validate the teaching for global readiness scale. *Teaching and Teacher Education, 65*, 91–106.

Kerkhoff, S. N. (2018). Teaching for global readiness: A model for locally situated and globally connected literacy instruction. In E. Ortlieb and E. H. Cheek, Jr (Eds.), *Addressing Diversity in Literacy Instruction*, pp. 193–205. Emerald Publishing.

Kerkhoff, S. N. (2022). A pedagogical framework for critical cosmopolitan literacies. *Changing English, 29*(3), 262–84. https://doi.org/10.1080/1358684X.2022.2042673.

Khalil, G., and Khalil, J. (1926). *Beyond Borders*. Simon & Schuster.

Kiang, L., Witkow, M. R., and Champagne, M. C. (2013). Normative changes in ethnic and American identities and links with adjustment among Asian American adolescents. *Developmental Psychology, 49*(9), 1713–22. https://doi.org/10.1037/a0030840.

Kibbey, J. S. (2011). Chapter four: Media literacy and social justice in a visual world. *Counterpoints, 403*, 50–61.

Kim, H., Oh, H. G., and Lee, S. J. (2017). Determining the quality of life of marriage migrant women in Korea. *Journal of Policy Studies, 32*(3), 83–104.

Kim, H. A. (2020). Understanding "Koreanness": Racial stratification and colorism in Korea and implications for Korean multicultural education. *International Journal of Multicultural Education, 22*(1), 76–97.

Kim, K. L. (2017). Korea and the gender construction of female marriage immigrants. *Pastoral Psychology, 66*, 13–25.

Kim, Y. (2019). Global citizenship education in South Korea: Ideologies, inequalities, and teacher voices. *Globalisation, Societies and Education, 17*(2), 177–93.

Kimmerer, R. W. (2013). *Braiding Sweetgrass: Indigenous Wisdom, Scientific Knowledge and the Teachings of Plants* (First paperback edition). Milkweed Editions.

Klein, J. D. (2013). Making meaning in a standards-based world: Negotiating tensions in global education. *The Educational Forum, 77*(4), 481–90.

Knox, C. (2011, April). Tackling racism in Northern Ireland: The race hate capital of Europe. *Journal of Social Policy, 40*(2), 387–412. https://doi.org/10.1017/S0047279410000620.

Kolovou, M. (2022). Embracing culturally relevant education in mathematics and science: A literature review. *The Urban Review, 55*(1), 133–72. https://doi.org/10.1007/s11256-022-00643-4.

Koo, A., Lim, K., and Song, B. (2024). Belonging pedagogy: Revisiting identity, culture, and difference. *Studies in Art Education, 65*(1), 63–80. https://doi.org/10.1080/00393541.2023.2285206.

Kopish, M., and Marques, W. (2020). Leveraging technology to promote global citizenship in teacher education in the United States and Brazil. *Research in Social Sciences and Technology, 5*(1), 45–69.

Korea Statistics Information Service. (2024). Yearly Earned Income by City and District. https://kosis.kr/statHtml/statHtml.do?orgId=133&tblId=DT_133001N_4215&conn_path=I2 (accessed October 26, 2025).

Koubek, E., and Wasta, S. (2023). Preservice teachers' experiences on becoming culturally responsive educators: An action research case study. *The Journal on Efficiency and Responsibility in Education and Science (ERIES Journal), 16*(1), 12–25. http://dx.doi.org/10.7160/eriesj.2023.160102.

Ladson-Billings, G. (1995). Toward a theory of culturally relevant pedagogy. *American Educational Research Journal, 32*(3), 465–91. https://doi.org/10.3102/00028312032003465.

Ladson-Billings, G. (1998). Just what is critical race theory and what's it doing in a nice field like education? *International Journal of Qualitative Studies in Education, 11*(1), 7–24. https://doi.org/10.1080/095183998236863.

Ladson-Billings G. (2004). Culture versus citizenship: The challenge of racialized citizenship in the United States. In J. A. Banks (Ed.), *Diversity and Citizenship Education: Global Perspectives*, pp. 96–126. Jossey-Bass

Ladson-Billings, G. (2009). *The Dreamkeepers: Successful Teachers of African American Children* (2nd edn.). Jossey-Bass.

Ladson-Billings, G. (2011). "Yes but How do We Do It?" Practicing culturally relevant pedagogy. In *White Teachers/Diverse Classrooms: Creating Inclusive Schools, Building on Students' Diversity, and Providing True Educational Equity*. essay, Taylor & Francis.

Ladson-Billings, G. (2021a). Culturally relevant pedagogy: Asking a different question. Culturally sustaining pedagogies series. In *Teachers College Press*. Teachers College Press.

Ladson-Billings, G. (2021b). Three decades of culturally relevant, responsive, & sustaining pedagogy: What lies ahead? *Educational Forum, 85*(4), 351–4. https://doi.org/10.1080/0013172 5.2021.1957632.

Landa, C. (2023). Differential access of young children of immigrants to special education in Massachusetts. *Developmental Disabilities Network Journal, 3*(1), 120–44. https://doi.org/10.59620/2694-1104.1066.

Le Guin, U. K. (1993). *The Ones Who Walk away from Omelas*. Creative Education.

Leckie, A., and Buser De, M. (2020). The power of an intersectionality framework in teacher education. *Journal for Multicultural Education, 14*(1), 117–27. https://doi-org.ezproxy.hope.edu/10.1108/JME-07-2019-0059.

Lee, Jenny J. (Ed.). (2021). *U.S. Power in International Higher Education*. Rutgers University Press.

Lee, L., and Misco, T. (2014). All for one or one for all: An analysis of the concepts of patriotism and others in multicultural Korea through elementary moral education textbooks. *The Asia-Pacific Education Researcher, 23*, 727–34.

Leh, J. M., Grau, M., and Guiseppe, J. A. (2015). Navigating the development of pre-service teachers' intercultural competence and understanding of diversity: The benefits of facilitating online intercultural exchange. *Journal for Multicultural Education, 9*(2), 98–110. https://doi-org.ezproxy.hope.edu/10.1108/JME-12-2014-0042.

Leonard, J. (2008). *Culturally Specific Pedagogy in the Mathematics Classroom: Strategies for Teachers and Students*. Routledge.

Lerer, L. (2024, January 13). On the ballot in Iowa: Fear. Anxiety. Hopelessness. *New York Times*. https://www.nytimes.com/2024/01/13/us/politics/iowa-caucuses-anxiety-fear.html (accessed October 26, 2025).

Lincoln, A. (n.d.). Gettysburg Address. Library of Congress. https://www.loc.gov/resource/rbpe.24404500/?st=text (accessed October 26, 2025).

Loewen, J. (1995). *Lies My Teacher Told Me*. Touchstone.

Love, B. (2019). *We Want to Do More than Survive: Abolitionist Teaching and the Pursuit of Educational Freedom*. Beacon Press.

Loveless, N. (2019). *How to Make Art at the End of the World: A Manifesto for Research-Creation*. Duke University Press.

Lund, D. E., and Lee, L. (2015). Fostering cultural humility among preservice teachers: Connecting with children and youth of immigrant families through service-learning. *Canadian Journal of Education/Revue Canadienne de L'éducation, 38*(2), 1–30.

Lune, H., and Berg, B. L. (2021). An introduction to content analysis. In *Qualitative Research Methods for the Social Sciences* (9th edn.), pp. 349–85. Pearson.

Lynch, R. (2019). *The Partition of Ireland: 1918–1925*. Cambridge University Press.

Mahalingappa, L., Kayi-Aydar, H., and Polat, N. (2021). Institutional and faculty readiness for teaching linguistically diverse international students in educator preparation programs in U.S. universities. *TESOL Quarterly*, *55*(4), 1247–77. https://doi.org/10.1002/tesq.3083.

Mainali, B. R., and Belbase, S. (2023). Job satisfaction, professional growth, and mathematics teachers' impressions about school environment. *Education Policy Analysis Archives*, *31*(22), 1–24. https://doi.org/10.14507/epaa.31.7424.

Maney, G. (2012). The paradox of reform: The Civil Rights Movement in Northern Ireland. In S. Erickson Nepstad and L. Kurtz (Eds.), *Nonviolent Conflict and Civil Resistance*, pp. 3–26. Emerald Group Publishing.

Mansilla, V. B., and Jackson, A. (2012). *Educating for Global Competence: Preparing our Students to Engage the World*. ACSD.

Mansilla, V. B., and Jackson, A. W. (2011). *Educating for Global Competence: Preparing Our Youth to Engage the World*. Council of Chief State School Officers.

Mansilla, V. B., and Jackson, A. W. (2023). *Educating for Global Competence: Preparing our Students to Engage the World* (2nd edn.). ASCD.

Maoz, Z., and Henderson, E. A. (2020). *Scriptures, Shrines, Scapegoats, and World Politics: Religious Sources of Conflict and Cooperation in the Modern Era* (1st edn.). University of Michigan Press. https://doi.org/10.3998/mpub.11353856.

Martin, D. B. (2009). *Researching Race in Mathematics Education. The Teachers College Record*, *111*(2), 295–338.

Martin, L. A. (2023). *The Gospel of J. Edgar Hoover: How the FBI Aided and Abetted the Rise of White Christian Nationalism*. Princeton University Press.

Matthews, L. E., Jones, S. M., and Parker, Y. A. (2022). *Engaging in Culturally Relevant Math Tasks, 6–12: Fostering Hope in the Middle and High School Classroom*. Corwin Press.

Maxwell, J. A. (2013). *Qualitative Research Design* (3rd edn., vol. *41*). Sage Publications.

McCorkle, W., and Rodriguez, S. (2021). When nationalism supersedes belief in religious freedom: An analysis of teachers' beliefs. *Educational Studies*, *57*(2), 182–201.

McCormack, K., and Gilbert, E. (2022). The geopolitics of militarism and humanitarianism. *Progress in Human Geography*, *46*(1), 179–97. https://doi.org/10.1177/03091325211032267.

McCully, A., and Barton, K. (2019). Schools, students, and community history in Northern Ireland. In A. Clark and C. Peck (Eds.), *Contemplating Historical Consciousness: Notes From the Field*, pp. 19–31. Berghahn Books.

McIntosh, N., and Nenonene, R. (2022). Developing culturally responsive antiracist activists. S. Browne and G. Jean-Marie (Eds.), *Reconceptualizing Social Justice in Teacher Education: Moving to Anti-racist Pedagogy*, pp. 215–230. Palgrave Macmillan.

McKittrick, D., Kelters, S., Feeney, B., Thornton, C., and McVea, D. (1999). *Lost lives: The Stories of Men, Women, and Children Who Died as a Result of the Northern Ireland Troubles*. Random House.

Medora, N., and Roy, R. N. (2017). Recruiting, organizing, planning, and conducting a 3-week, short-term study abroad program for undergraduate students: Guidelines and suggestions for first-time faculty leaders. *International Journal of Humanities and Social Science Research*, *3*, 1–11. https://doi.org/10.6000/23711655.2017.03.01.

Merlin-Knoblich, C., and Dameron, M. L. (2021). An examination of educator multicultural attitudes before and after a diversity dinner dialogue. *Journal for Multicultural Education*, *15*(1), 85–96. https://doi-org.ezproxy.hope.edu/10.1108/JME-05-2020-0042.

Merolla, A. J., Neubauer, A. B., and Otmar, C. D. (2024). Responsiveness, social connection, hope, and life satisfaction in everyday social interaction: An experience sampling study. *Journal of Happiness Studies*, *25*(1–2), 7. https://doi.org/10.1007/s10902-024-00710-5.

Mignolo, W. D. (2011). The global south and world dis/order. *Journal of Anthropological Research*, *67*(2), 165–88. http://www.jstor.org/stable/41303282.

Migration Policy Institute. (2023). *Frequently Requested Statistics on Immigrants and Immigration in the United States.* https://www.migrationpolicy.org/article/frequently-requested-statistics-immigrants-and-immigration-united-states#children-immigrants (accessed October 28, 2025).

Milner, H. R. (2020). Disrupting punitive practices and policies: Rac(e)ing back to teaching, teacher preparation, and Brown. *Educational Researcher, 49*(3), 147–60. http://doi.org/10.3102/0013189X20907396.

Min, M., Lee, H., Hodge, C., and Croxton, N. (2021). What empowers teachers to become social justice-oriented change agents? Influential factors on teacher agency toward culturally responsive teaching. *Education and Urban Society, 54*, 560–84. https://doi.org/10.1177/00131245211027511.

Ministry of Education. (2020). *Mathematics: Teaching and Learning Syllabus Primary.* Curriculum Planning and Development Division.

Ministry of Justice. (2024). *Statistics on Foreigners Residing in South Korea.* Ministry of Justice. https://www.moj.go.kr/moj/2412/subview.do (accessed October 26, 2025).

Moll, L., and Gonzalez, N. (1994). Lessons from research with language minority children. *Journal of Reading Behavior, 26*(4), 23–41.

Moll, L., Amanti, C., Neff, D., and Gonzalez, N. (1992). Funds of knowledge for teaching: Using a qualitative approach to connect homes to classrooms. *Theory into Practice, 31*(2), 132–41.

Moll, L. C. (2023). Funds of knowledge in practice in international contexts. In M. Esteban-Guitart (Ed.), *Funds of Knowledge and Identity Pedagogies for Social Justice*, pp. 4–37. Routledge.

Moon, R. J., and Koo, J. W. (2011). Global citizenship and human rights: A longitudinal analysis of social studies and ethics textbooks in the Republic of Korea. *Comparative Education Review, 55*(4), 574–99.

Morrison, K. A. (2008). Democratic classrooms: Promises and challenges of student voice and choice, part one. *Educational Horizons, 87*(1), 50–60.

Moustakas, C. (1994). *Phenomenological Research Methods.* Sage. https://doi.org/10.4135/9781412995658.

Muhammad, G. (2023). *Unearthing Joy: A Guide to Culturally and Historically Responsive Teaching and Learning.* Scholastic.

Mundy, K., Bickmore, K., Hayhoe, R., Madden, M., and Madjidi, K. (Eds.). (2008). *Comparative and International Education: Issues for Teachers.* Economic Policy Institute and Teachers College.

Mystal, E. (2021, June 3). The miseducation of white children. *The Nation.* https://www.thenation.com/article/society/critical-race-theory-white (accessed October 26, 2025).

Nash, K.(2010). *Contemporary Political Sociology Globalization, Politics, and Power.* Wiley.

National Center for Education Statistics. (2023). *Characteristics of Public School Teachers.* https://nces.ed.gov/programs/coe/indicator/clr/public-school-teachers (accessed October 26, 2025).

National Center for Education Statistics. (2024). Racial/Ethnic Enrollment in Public Schools. https://nces.ed.gov/programs/coe/indicator/cge/racial-ethnic-enrollment (accessed October 26, 2025).

Neri, R. C., Lozano, M., and Gomez, L. M. (2019). (Re)framing resistance to culturally relevant education as a multilevel learning problem. *Review of Research in Education, 43*(1), 197–226. https://doi.org/10.3102/0091732X18821120.

Nespor, J. (1987). The role of beliefs in the practice of teaching. *Journal of Curriculum Studies, 19(4)*, 317–28. https://doi.org/10.1080/0022027870190403.

Newcomer, S. (2018). Investigating the power of authentically caring student-teacher relationships for Latinx students. *Journal of Latinos and Education, 17*(2), 179–93.

Newton, C., and Early, F. (2015). *Doing Good … Says Who? Stories from Volunteers, Nonprofits, Donors, and Those They Want to Help*. Two Harbors Press.

Noddings, N. (2002). *Educating Moral People: A Caring Alternative to Character Education*. Teachers College Press.

Noddings, N. (2012). The caring relation in teaching. *Oxford Review of Education*, *38*(6), 771–81.

Norris J. (2008). Duoethnography. In L. M. Given (Ed.), *The SAGE Encyclopedia of Qualitative Research Methods*, pp. 233–6. SAGE.

Norris J., and Sawyer R. (2012). Toward a dialogic method. In J. Norris, R. Sawyer, and D. Lund (Eds.), *Duoethnography: Dialogic Methods for Social, Health, and Educational Research*, pp. 9–40. Left Coast Press.

Nygren, T. (2016). UNESCO teaches history: Implementing international understanding in Sweden. In P. Duedahl (Ed.), *A History of UNESCO: Global Actions and Impacts*, pp. 201–30. Palgrave Macmillan.

O'Connor, K., and Zeichner, K. (2011). Preparing US teachers for critical global education. In Vanessa De Oliveira Andreotti (Ed.), *The Political Economy of Global Citizenship Education*, pp. 208–23. Routledge.

O'Dowd, R. (2016). Learning from the past and looking to the future of online intercultural exchange. In R. O'Dowd and T. Lewis (Eds.), *Online Intercultural Exchange: Policy, Pedagogy*, pp. 273–93. New York: Taylor & Francis.

OECD. (2018). Preparing our youth for an inclusive and sustainable world. In *The OECD PISA Global Competence Framework*. OECD.

Ohlmeyer, J. (2020, December 29). Ireland has yet to come to terms with its imperial past: Some celebrate and some excoriate connections with the British Empire. *The Irish Times*. https://www.irishtimes.com/opinion/ireland-has-yet-to-come-to-terms-with-its-imperial-past-1.4444146 (accessed October 26, 2025).

Olneck, M. R. (2011). Facing multiculturalism's challenges in Korean education and society. *Asia Pacific Education Review*, *12*, 675–90.

Pajares, F. (2010). Toward a positive psychology of academic motivation. *The Journal of Educational Research (Washington, DC)*, *95*(1), 27–35. https://doi.org/10.1080/00220670109598780.

Panjwani, F. (2017). No Muslim is just a Muslim: Implications for education. *Oxford Review of Education*, *43*(5), 596–611. https://doi.org/10.1080/03054985.2017.1352354.

Paris, D. (2012). Culturally sustaining pedagogy: A needed change in stance, terminology, and practice. *Educational Researcher*, *41*(3), 93–7. https://doi.org/10.3102/0013189X12441244.

Paris, D., and Alim, H. S. (2014). What are we seeking to sustain through culturally sustaining pedagogy? A loving critique forward. *Harvard Educational Review*, *84*(1), 85–100.

Park, S., Ryu, J., and McChesney, K. (2019). Collaborative studio experiences between South Korean and American pre-service teachers: A case study of designing culturally-responsive virtual classroom simulation. *TechTrends: Linking Research and Practice to Improve Learning*, *63*(3), 271–83. https://doi-org.ezproxy.hope.edu/10.1007/s11528-019-00392-4.

Pastori, G., Mangiatordi, A., Ereky-Stevens, K., and Slot, P. L. (2018). ISOTIS virtual learning environment. Development, progress and on-going work in WP3, 4 and 5. ISOTIS.

Patiño-Santos, A., and Poveda, D. (2022). Bilingual education: English and the life projects of youth in contemporary Spain. In E. Codó (Ed.), *Global CLIL*, pp. 149–73. Routledge.

Pettigrew, T. F. (1998). Intergroup contact theory. *Annual Review of Psychology*, *49*, 65–85.

Pew Research Center. (2022, September 13). *How U.S. Religious Composition Has Changed in Recent Decades*. https://www.pewresearch.org/religion/2022/09/13/how-u-s-religious-composition-has-changed-in-recent-decades (accessed October 26, 2025).

Pewewardy, C. (2005). Shared journaling: A methodology for engaging white preservice students into multicultural education discourse. *Teacher Education Quarterly*, *32*(1), 41–60. https://doi.org.ezproxy.hope.edu/https://www.teqjournal.org/backvols/2005/32_1/volume_32_number_1.htm.

Pinar, W. F., and Grumet, M. R. (1976). *Toward a Poor Curriculum* (3rd edn.). Educator's International Press, Inc.

Pirbhai Illich, F., and Martin, F. (2019). Decolonizing teacher education in immersion contexts: Working with space, place, and boundaries. In D. Martin and E. Smolcic (Eds.), *Redefining Teaching Competence Through Immersive Programs: Practices for Culturally Sustaining Classrooms*, pp. 65–93. Palgrave Macmillan.

Popkewitz, T. S. (2014). *The Reason of Schooling: Historicizing Curriculum Studies, Pedagogy, and Teacher Education*. Routledge.

Pouraskari, N., Dika, S., and Frankovich, J. (2023). Experiences of belonging and Islamophobia among hijabi Muslim college students in the United States. *College Student Affairs Journal*, *41*(2), 1–15. https://doi.org/10.1353/csj.2023.a916688.

Powell, A. B., and Frankenstein, M. (Eds.). (1997). *Ethnomathematics: Challenging Eurocentrism in Mathematics Education*. State University of New York Press.

Pratt, M. L. (2008). *Imperial Eyes: Travel Writing and Transculturation*. Routledge.

Protner, B. (2018). The limits of an "open mind": State violence, Turkification, and complicity in the Turkish-Kurdish conflict. *Turkish Studies*, *19*(5), 671–96. https://doi.org/10.1080/14683849.2018.1514494.

Puchner, L., and Markowitz, L. (2020). Christmas in U.S. K-12 schools: Categorizing and explaining teacher awareness of Christo-normativity. *Discourse: Studies in the Cultural Politics of Education*, *41*(4), 545–58. https://doi.org/10.1080/01596306.2018.1512074.

Rahimi, R. A., and Oh, G. S. (2024). Rethinking the role of educators in the 21st Century: Navigating globalization, technology, and pandemics. *Journal of Marketing Analytics*, *12*, 182–97. https://doi.org/10.1057/s41270-024-00303-4.

Ramos, K.,Wolf, E., and Hauber-Özer, M. (2021). Teaching for global competence: A responsibility of teacher educators. *Journal of Research in Childhood Education*, *35*, 1–20. 10.1080/02568543.2021.1880998.

Rana, A. (2022, Fall). Our segregation problem. *Dissent*. https://www.dissentmagazine.org/article/our-segregation-problem (accessed October 26, 2025).

Reid A. D., Hart P. E., and Peters M. A. (2014). *A Companion to Research in Education*. Springer.

Reis, H. T., Clark, M. S., and Holmes, J. G. (2004). Perceived partner responsiveness as an organizing construct in the study of intimacy and closeness. In D. J. Mashek and A. P. Aron (Eds.), *Handbook of Closeness and Intimacy*, pp. 201–25. Erlbaum.

Reis, H. T., Itzchakov, G., Lee, K. Y., and Yan, R. (2022). Sociability matters: Downstream consequences of perceived partner responsiveness in social life. In J. P. Forgas, W. Crano, and K. Fiedler (Eds.), *The Psychology of Sociability: Understanding Human Attachment*, pp. 239–257. Routledge. https://doi.org/10.4324/9781003258582.

Religion and Public Life. (2023). Kurds in Turkey. https://rpl.hds.harvard.edu/faq/kurds-turkey

Resch, J. A., Mireles, G., Benz, M. R., Grenwelge, C., Peterson, R., and Zhang, D. (2010). Giving parents a voice: A qualitative study of the challenges experienced by parents of children with disabilities. *Rehabilitation Psychology*, *55*(2), 139–50. https://doi.org/10.1037/a0019473.

Riessman, C. K. (2008). *Narrative Methods for the Human Sciences*. Sage.

Rios-Aguilar, C., Kiyama, J. M., Gravitt, M., and Moll, L. (2011). Funds of knowledge for the poor and forms of capital for the rich? A capital approach to examining funds of knowledge. *Theory and Research in Education*, *9*, 163–84. https://doi:10.1177/14778785114097761.

Roediger, D. (2007). *The Wages of Whiteness: Race and the Making of the American Working Class.* Verso Books.

Roh, S. Z. (2014). A study on the factors affecting the intercultural sensitivity of middle and high school students in Korea. *Advanced Science and Technology Letters, 47,* 266–9.

Rokeach, M. (1972). *Beliefs, Attitudes and Values: A Theory of Organization and Change.* Jossey-Bass.

Romijn, B., Slot, P., and Leseman, P. (2021). Increasing teachers' intercultural competences in teacher preparation programs and through professional development: A review. *Teaching and Teacher Education, 98,* 103236. http://doi.org/10.1016/j.tate.2020.103236.

Rothbart, M. K. (2011). *Becoming Who We Are: Temperament and Personality in Development.* Guilford.

Sanatullova-Allison, E., and Robison-Young, V. A. (2016). Overrepresentation: An overview of the issues surrounding the identification of English language learners with learning disabilities. *International Journal of Special Education, 31*(2).

Sandell, E. J., and Tupy, S. (2015). Where cultural competency begins: Changes in undergraduate students' intercultural competency. *The International Journal of Teaching and Learning in Higher Education, 27,* 364–81.

Sardegna, V., and Dugartsyrenova, V. (2021). Facilitating preservice language teachers' intercultural learning via voice-based telecollaboration: The role of discussion questions. *Computer Assisted Language Learning, 34*(3), 379–407. http://doi.org/10.1080/09588221.2020.1871028.

Schippling, A. (2020). Researching global citizenship education: Towards a critical approach. *Journal of Social Science Education, 19*(4), 98–113.

Schwarzenthal, M., Schachner, M. K., Juang, L. P., and van de Vijver, F. J. R. (2019). Reaping the benefits of cultural diversity: Classroom cultural diversity climate and students' intercultural competence. *European Journal of Social Psychology, 50*(2), 323–46. https://doi.org/10.1002/ejsp.2617.

Scott Shields, S., and Fendler, R. (2023). Developing civically engaged art education. In K. N. Denzin and D. M. Michael (Eds.), *Global Shifts in Qualitative Inquiry: New Directions New Challenges,* pp. 234–39 (1st edn.). Routledge.

Secules, S., McCall, C., Mejia, J. A., Beebe, C., Masters, A. S., L. Sánchez-Peña, M., and Svyantek, M. (2021). Positionality practices and dimensions of impact on equity research: A collaborative inquiry and call to the community. *Journal of Engineering Education, 110*(1), 19–43. https://doi.org/10.1002/jee.20377.

Seoul Metropolitan Office of Education. (2023). 2023 Seoul Educational Statistics.

Serpa, M. d. L. B. (2011). *An Imperative for Change.* University of Massachusetts Boston. https://scholarworks.umb.edu/gaston_pubs/152

Sharpe, E. (2015). Colonialist tendencies in education abroad. *International Journal of Teaching and Learning in Higher Education, 27*(2), 227–34.

Shevalier, R., and McKenzie, B. A. (2012). Culturally responsive teaching as an ethics-and care-based approach to urban education. *Urban Education, 47*(6), 1086–105.

Sims Bishop, R. (2011). Windows, mirrors, and sliding glass doors. *Perspectives: Choosing and Using Books for the Classroom, 6*(3), ix–xi.

Singh, L., Fu, C. S. L., Tay, Z. W., and Golinkoff, R. M. (2018). Novel word learning in bilingual and monolingual infants: Evidence for a bilingual advantage. *Child Development, 89*(3), e183–e198. https://doi-org.ezproxy.hope.edu/10.1111/cdev.12747.

Singh, P. (2020). Mathematics and social justice: How stories can help us understand our roots and our connections. *Mathematics Teacher: Learning and Teaching PK-12, 113*(1), 16–22.

Skrtic, T. M. (1991). The special education paradox. *Harvard Educational Review*, *61*(2), 148–206. https://doi.org/10.17763/haer.61.2.0q702751580h0617.

Sloane, H., and Petra, M. (2021). Modeling cultural humility: Listening to students' stories of religious identity. *Journal of Social Work Education*, *57*(1), 28–39.

Sorensen, T. B., and Dumay, X. (2021). The teaching professions and globalization: A scoping review of the Anglophone research literature. *Comparative Education Review*, *65*(4), 725–49. https://doi.org/10.1086/716418.

Southern Poverty Law Center. (2017, October). *Teaching the Movement: The State of Civil Rights Education in the United States*. https://www.learningforjustice.org/sites/default/files/2017-10/Teaching-the-Movement-2011-v2-CoverRedesign-Oct2017.pdf (accessed October 26, 2025).

Spangler, V. (2023). On positionalities in research with international students. *Journal of International Students*, *13*(4), 234–39. https://doi.org/10.32674/jis.v14i3.6090.

Stanley, J. (2024, June). Education: The end of civic compassion. *The New Republic*, 18–19. https://newrepublic.com/article/181274/end-civic-compassion (accessed October 26, 2025).

Stein, S., Andreotti, V., Ahenakew, C., Suša, R., Taylor, L., Valley, W., Siwek, D., Cardoso, C., Duque, C., Calhoun, B., Sluys, S., Pigeau, D., and D'Emilia, D. (2024). Education beyond green growth: Regenerative inquiry for intergenerational responsibility. *Nordic Journal of Comparative and International Education (NJCIE)*, *8*(2), 1–25.

Stein, S., Andreotti, V., Ahenakew, C., Suša, R., Valley, W., Huni Kui, N., Tremembé, M., Taylor, L., Siwek, D., Cardoso, C., Duque, C. "Azul," Oliveira Da Silva Huni Kui, S., Calhoun, B., Van Sluys, S., Amsler, S., D'Emilia, D., Pigeau, D., Andreotti, B., Bowness, E., and McIntyre, A. (2023). Beyond colonial futurities in climate education. *Teaching in Higher Education*, *28*(5), 987–1004. https://doi.org/10.1080/13562517.2023.2193667.

Steinfeld, N., and Lev-on, A. (2024). Exposure to diverse political views in contemporary media environments. *Frontiers in Communication*, *9*, 1384706.

Strelau, J. (2008). *Temperament as a Regulator of Behavior: After Fifty Years of Research*. Eliot Werner Publications.

Suarez-Orozco, C., and Suarez-Orozco, M. (2001). *Children of Immigration*. Harvard University Press.

Suarez-Orozco, C., Abo-Zena, M. M., and Marks, A. K. (Eds.). (2015). *Transitions: The Development of Children of Immigrants*. NYU Press.

Suarez-Orozco, C., Martin, M., Alexander, M., Dance, L. J., and Lunneblad, J. (2013). Promising practices. In R. Alba and J. Holdaway (Eds.), *The Children of Immigrants at School*. NYU Press.

Swanson, D. M., and Gamal, M. (2021). Global Citizenship Education/Learning for Sustainability: Tensions, "flaws," and contradictions as critical moments of possibility and radical hope in educating for alternative futures. *Globalisation, Societies and Education*, *19*(4), 456–69.

Szumski, G., and Karwowski, M. (2019). Exploring the Pygmalion effect: The role of teacher expectations, academic self-concept, and class context in students' math achievement. *Contemporary Educational Psychology*, *59*, 101787. https://doi.org/10.1016/j.cedpsych.2019.101787.

Tabulawa, R. (2003). International aid agencies, learner-centred pedagogy and political democratisation: A critique. *Comparative Education*, *39*(1), 7–26. https://doi.org/10.1080/03050060302559.

Taylor, S., and Henry, M. (2000). Globalisation and educational policymaking: A case study. *Educational Theory*, *50*(4), 487–503.

The Urban Institute. (2019). *Data from the Integrated Public Use Microdata Series Datasets Drawn from the American Community Survey*. www.urban.org.

Tichnor-Wagner, A., Parkhouse, H., Glazier, J., and Cain, J. M. (2016). Expanding approaches to teaching for diversity and social justice in K-12 education: Fostering global citizenship across the content areas. *Education Policy Analysis Archives*, *24*(59). http://dx.doi.org/10.14507/epaa.24.2138T.

Tichnor-Wagner, A., Parkhouse, H., Glazier, J., and Cain, J. (2019). *Becoming a Globally Competent Teacher*. ASCD

Toles-Patkin, T. (2021). Hallmarking Hanukkah: Flawed attempts at diversity in cable television Christmas movies. *The Journal of Popular Culture*, *54*(5), 914–40. https://doi.org/10.1111/jpcu.13062.

Torres-Olave, B., & Lee, J. J. (2020). Shifting positionalities across international locations: Embodied knowledge, time-geography, and the polyvalence of privilege. *Higher Education Quarterly*, *74*(2), 136–48. https://doi.org/10.1111/hequ.12216.

Tsing, A. L. (2015). *The Mushroom at the End of the World: On the Possibility of Life in Capitalist Ruins*. Princeton University Press.

Tuck, E. (2009). Suspending damage: A letter to communities. *Harvard Educational Review*, *79*(3), 409–28.

U.S. Department of Education. (2022). *Succeeding Globally Through International Education and Engagement*.

US Departments of Education & Justice. (2015). *Dear Colleague Letter: English Learner Students and Limited English Proficient Parents*. http://www2.ed.gov/about/offices/list/ocr/letters/colleague-el-201501.pdf (accessed October 28, 2025).

UNESCO. (2015). *Global Citizenship Education: Topics and Learning Objectives*. Paris: UNESCO.

United Nations. (n.d.). 17 Goals. *United Nations*. https://sdgs.un.org/goals (accessed October 26, 2025).

United Nations. (n.d.). *Sustainable Development Goals*. https://www.un.org/sustainabledevelopment/sustainable-development-goals (accessed October 26, 2025).

United Nations Department of Economic and Social Affairs. (2024). https://sdgs.un.org/goals (accessed October 24, 2025).

United Nations Educational, Scientific, and Cultural Organization. (n.d.). What you need to know about global citizenship education. *United Nations Educational, Scientific, and Cultural Organization*. https://www.unesco.org/en/global-citizenship-peace-education/need-know (accessed October 26, 2025).

United States Department of Justice. (2023). Hate crimes: Facts and statistics. https://www.justice.gov/hatecrimes (accessed October 26, 2025).

Van M, J., and Ferreira, M. M. (2023). An essay about intercultural sensitivity and competence in higher education. *European Journal of Education and Pedagogy*, *4*(2), 149–55. https://doi.org/10.24018/ejedu.2023.4.2.624.

van Vijfeijken, M., van Schilt-mol, T., van den Bergh, L., Scholte, R. H., and Denessen, E. (2024). An evaluation of a professional development program aimed at empowering teachers' Agency for social justice. *Frontiers in Education*, *9*. https://doi.org/10.3389/feduc.2024.1244113.

Villegas, A. M., and Lucas, T. (2007). The culturally responsive teacher. *Educational Leadership*, *64*(6), 28–33.

Voyles, T. B. (2015). *Wastelanding: Legacies of Uranium Mining in Navajo Country*. University of Minnesota Press.

Warga, J. (2021). *Other Words for Home*. Seedlings Braille Books for Children.

Watson, I. (2012). Paradoxical multiculturalism in South Korea. *Asian Politics & Policy*, *4*(2), 233–58.

Wetts, R., and Willer, R. (2022). Anti-racism and its discontents: The prevalence and political influence of opposition to antiracism among white Americans. *SocArXiv*. https://doi.org/10.31235/osf.io/xvcf2.

Whatley, M., Landon, A. C., Tarrant, M. A., and Rubin, D. (2021). Program design and the development of students' global perspectives in faculty-led short-term study abroad. *Journal of Studies in International Education*, *25*(3), 301–18.

Williams, J. A., III, and Glass, T. S. (2019). Teacher education and multicultural courses in North Carolina. *Journal for Multicultural Education*, *13*(2), 155–68. https://doi-org.ezproxy.hope.edu/10.1108/JME-05-2018-0028.

Woods, A. L, Sipple, S. M., Otten, M. R. M., and Roos, M. E. (2017). Navigating uncharted waters: Study abroad pre-departure activities and the 2-year-college student. *Community College Journal of Research and Practice*, *41*(12), 867–80. https://doi.org/10.1080/10668926.2016.1242439.

Xiaotian, Z., and Mingming, Z. (2023). Information and digital technology-assisted interventions to improve intercultural competence: A meta-analytical review. *Computers & Education*, *194*, C. https://doi.org/10.1016/j.compedu.2022.104697.

Yeh, E., and Wan, G. (2018). Intercultural competence for teachers of young ELLs. In G. Onchwari and J. Keengwe (Eds.), *Handbook of Research on Pedagogies and Cultural Considerations for Young English Language Learners*, pp. 192–216. IGI Global. https://doi.org/10.4018/978-1-5225-3955-1.ch010.

Yin, R. K. (2009). *Case Study Research* (4th edn., vol. 5). Sage Publications.

Yip, T. (2014). Ethnic identity in everyday life: The influence of identity development status. *Child Development*, *85*(1), 205–19. https://doi.org/10.1111/cdev.12107.

Zemach-Bersin, T. (2007). Global citizenship and study abroad: It's all about U.S. critical literacy. *Theories and Practices*, *1*(2), 16–28.

Zembylas, M. (2008). *The Politics of Trauma in Education*. Palgrave Macmillan.

Zhao, Y. (2010). Preparing globally competent teachers: A new imperative for teacher education. *Journal of Teacher Education*, *61*(5), 422–31. http://dx.doi.org/10.1177/0022487110375802.

Zhirkov, K., and Valentino, N. (2022). The origins and consequences of racialized schemas about U.S. parties. *Journal of Race, Ethnicity, and Politics*, *7*(3), 484–504. https://doi.org/10.1017/rep.2022.4.

Index

About the Editors

Christina Wright Fields, PhD, is an Associate Professor of Education at Marist University. Dr. Fields' research focuses on culturally responsive pedagogy, urban education, equitable administrative practices, and global education. Prior to joining Marist University, Dr. Fields oversaw a pre-college global infusion project at Indiana University Bloomington with Dr. Amy Horowitz. Dr. Fields received the 2023 Institute for Teachers of Color Fellowship, and 2022 Longview Foundations Global Teacher Education Fellowship. Currently, she is a Visual Studies in Education (ViSE) Research Fellow at Rutgers University-Newark. Also, she was awarded the 2019 Marist College Strategic Plan Grant–Think Global, Act Local: Developing Social Justice Minded Youth, and 2017 NASPA Program Excellence Award in International, Multicultural, Cultural, LGBTQ, Spirituality, and Disability. Dr. Fields served as 2022–2024 co-chair for American Association of Colleges of Teacher Educators (AACTE) Global Diversity Programmatic Advisory Committee and was a member of AACTE's Global Teacher Education Professional Learning Community. Currently, she serves as a Collaborative Online International Learning (COIL) coordinator at Marist University and the co-chair for the American College Personnel Association (ACPA) Commission for Academic Affairs. Dr. Fields has presented at American Education Research Association (AERA), International Conference on Urban Education (ICUE), International Visual Sociology Association (IVSA), Critical Race Studies in Education Association (CRSEA), and American Association of Colleges of Teacher Educators (AACTE). She has published in *Administration Theory & Praxis, Urban Education and Teaching and Teacher Education, Black Education–A Mixtape Journal, Public Integrity, Journal of African American Women and Girls in Education,* and *Journal of Education Human Resources.*

Novea McIntosh, EdD, is an Associate Professor in the School of Education and Health Sciences at the University of Dayton. Dr. McIntosh coordinates the Adolescent to Young Adult program (Secondary education licensure) and co-directs the Urban Teacher Academy. Dr. McIntosh is an Afro-Caribbean human rights scholar practitioner whose research focuses on culturally responsive pedagogy, intercultural competence, decolonization, and internationalization of education. As a global scholar, she collaborates with the University of Dayton Human Rights Center and NGOs such as Determined to Develop and Dandelion Africa leading international interdisciplinary practicum to the continent in Malawi and Kenya. She has led study abroad in Florence, Italy and recently initiated opportunities in her native Jamaica. Dr. McIntosh received the 2024 Longview Foundation Global Teacher Education Fellowship and 2025 Collaborative Online International Learning (COIL) University of Dayton fellowship. Dr. McIntosh served as 2024–2025 co-chair for American

Association of Colleges of Teacher Educators (AACTE) Global Diversity committee and was a member of AACTE's Global Teacher Education Professional Learning Community. She currently serves as the President for the North American Community: Uniting for Equity (NAC:UE) and secretary for AACTE Internationalization of Teacher Education Topical Action Group (TAG). Dr. McIntosh coaches and provides professional development to in-service and pre-service teachers. She presented at American Association of Colleges of Teacher Educators (AACTE), American Educational Research Association (AERA), and the American Educational Studies Association (AESA). Dr. McIntosh's scholarly work has been published in national and international journals. Recent publications include Teacher Preparation Partnerships to Foster Learning for All Students. *Middle School Journal* 55(1); Disrupting and transgressing the canon: Including BIPOC voices in *BIPOC Alliances: Building Communities and Curricula for the Curriculum & Pedagogy*; and Developing Culturally Responsive Antiracist Activists in *Reconceptualizing Social Justice in Teacher Education: Moving to Anti-racist Pedagogy*. Additionally, she has published in *Michigan Journal of Community Service Learning, Understanding and Dismantling Privilege, Journal of Catholic Education, Journal of Interdisciplinary Education, Multicultural Learning and Teaching,* and *International Journal of Educational Reform*.

Rochonda Nenonene, PhD, is an associate professor of education at the University of Dayton. She serves as the First Year Experience Coordinator and the Founding Co-Program Director of the Urban Teacher Academy. Areas of research interests include urban teacher preparation, culturally responsive/sustaining pedagogy, social-emotional learning, and dispositions of teacher candidates. Dr. Nenonene conducts professional development for school districts on culturally responsive teaching, student engagement, classroom management, social-emotional learning, and issues relevant to equity and social justice. Dr. Nenonene has received several fellowships to support her scholarship; 2025–2026 Longview Foundation Global Teacher Education Fellowship; 2022–2023 Institute for Teachers of Color Fellow (ITOC); and 2019 University of Dayton Global Education Fellow. She currently serves as the President for the Global Community: Uniting for Equity (GCUE) and the immediate past Co-chair of the membership committee for American Association of Colleges of Teacher Educators (AACTE). Dr. Nenonene has presented at American Association of Colleges of Teacher Educators (AACTE), American Educational Research Association (AERA), and the American Educational Studies Association (AESA). Recent publications include Social Emotional Learning (In Reiser, R., Carr-Chellman, A., Dempsey, J. (Eds.). *Trends and Issues in Instructional Design and Technology*, 5th edition); Disrupting and transgressing the canon: Including BIPOC voices in *BIPOC Alliances: Building Communities and Curricula for the Curriculum & Pedagogy*; and Developing Culturally Responsive Antiracist Activists in *Reconceptualizing Social Justice in Teacher Education: Moving to Anti-racist Pedagogy*. Additionally, she has published in *Teacher Education Quarterly, Understanding and Dismantling Privilege, Journal of Catholic Education,* and *Multicultural Learning and Teaching*.

About the Contributors

Yetunde S. Alabede is a doctoral student in the Curriculum, Instruction, and Teacher Education (CITE) program at Michigan State University. Her research interest centers on decolonial approach to curriculum planning and implementation, global language and literacy practices especially among Africans, multilingualism, Less Commonly Taught Languages (LCTLs) pedagogy, and home-school-community educational collaboration to enhance children's development and sense of belonging.

Thomas Falk is an Assistant Professor in the School of Teacher Education at the University of Dayton, where he coordinates the Educational Foundations program and teaches courses in Philosophy and History of Education and Comparative Education Studies. He holds a PhD in Philosophy of Education from Ohio State University. His research interests include political economy, phenomenology, and peace studies. He is the contributing editor of *Philosophical Studies in Education*, volume 55, the journal of the Ohio Valley Philosophy of Education Society.

Kasun Gajasinghe is a doctoral candidate in the Curriculum, Instruction and Teacher Education program at Michigan State University. His scholarly interests are in curriculum theory, global education, language and literacy, alternative imaginaries of education, and humanities-oriented methodologies. His research has been featured in the *Language Learning Journal*, *International Review of Qualitative Research*, and *English Teaching: Practice & Critique*, among others.

Colleen Gallagher is an Associate Professor in Teacher Education at the University of Dayton and coordinates the graduate and TESOL programs. She holds a PhD in applied linguistics from Georgetown University. Her research and teaching focus on supporting emergent multilingual students and their teachers in content-based instructional settings. Dr. Gallagher's projects have focused on teacher cognition in teaching multilingual students, professional development in linguistically responsive instruction, and emergent biliteracy development. She has experience teaching and conducting research in elementary, secondary, and higher education settings.

Lindsay A. Gold, PhD, is an associate professor of STEM Mathematics in the Teacher Education department at the University of Dayton and a T³ National Instructor. She currently teaches the undergraduate mathematics methods courses for licenses PK–5 and is program coordinator for the Technology Enhanced Learning master's degree. Her research interests include pre-service teacher education, teacher education, STEAM, financial literacy, SEL, teaching with technology, and professional development.

Dr. Hanna Haydar is an associate professor of mathematics education and chair of the Department of Childhood, Bilingual and Special Education, and head of the childhood mathematics program at Brooklyn College-CUNY. He was previously the curriculum standards and professional development adviser at RAND Education and the Supreme Education Council in Doha, Qatar. His research interests focus on beginning mathematics teachers, inclusion, lesson study, clinical interview, the use of stories as contexts for mathematizing, and the integration of computational thinking in elementary mathematics. He has international experience in Guatemala, Ecuador, Nepal, Qatar, UAE, Oman, Jordan, Spain, and Turkey.

Yooyeun Hwang is a professor of the Education Department at Hope College in Michigan. She holds a PhD in Educational Psychology from the University of Wisconsin, Madison. The 2024/2025 academic year marks her twenty-ninth year teaching at Hope College. She has taught educational psychology and cognitive psychology courses. She now teaches a diversity class and a senior seminar for teacher education students. Her research interests include memory, learning strategies, and single-case studies. Her current research focus is on religious diversity and culturally responsive-sustaining teaching.

Éder A. Intriago-Palacios is a Teaching Assistant Professor in the Department of Curriculum and Instruction at Kansas State University. Before joining Kansas State University, Alfaro de Manabí, in Ecuador, for ten years. In 2014, he was awarded a scholarship to participate in the Go Teacher master's program at Kansas State University, where he also earned a PhD in Curriculum and Instruction. His research interests revolve around Internationalization of Higher Education, English Medium-instruction, Extensive reading, and English language teachers' professional development.

Seeun (Tina) Jeon is a fourth-year PhD student in the Learning Technologies program, College of Education and Human Development at the University of Minnesota. She also has bachelor's degree in education and anthropology/sociology and graduate certificate on Leadership in Technology Integration. She has worked in K-12 school as an education technology integration fellow, teaching computational thinking and digital/media literacy skills for students. She is passionate about teaching Korean to diverse learners. She is interested in what education means in different contexts and how to support teachers and students from diverse backgrounds for better onboarding for educational technology integration.

Dr. Shabina Kavimandan is an Assistant Professor of Curriculum and Instruction at the College of Education, Kansas State University. Her K-12 teaching experience includes international and national experiences within elementary and secondary school settings. Her current research emphasis includes issues specific to global cultural and linguistic competencies, teacher agency and positionality, and culturally responsive literacy development. Shabina teaches graduate-level courses in culture and language and advises and mentors doctoral candidates in Curriculum and Instruction. She has directed and managed several Title III National Professional Development projects funded by the US Department of Education.

Ekaterina Koubek holds a PhD in Second Language Acquisition/Foreign Language Education from the University of Nebraska-Lincoln and a master's degree in Linguistics from Charles University, Czech Republic. She is a Professor and TESOL Coordinator at James Madison University, Virginia, USA. She teaches both undergraduate and graduate courses in TESOL. Her research interests include teacher identify and agency, the use of action research in teacher education, high-impact practices and student engagement, and culturally responsive and sustaining practices.

Cady Landa has a PhD in Social Policy from Brandeis University's Heller School for Social Policy and Management and a Master's in Public Policy from the Harvard Kennedy School of Government. She taught in public schools for ten years. She learned about issues confronting immigrant parents and their children through teaching immigrants' children, managing non-profit agencies serving immigrant families, and volunteering as a public policy advocate with a youth-led immigrant rights organization in Massachusetts. Her research interests include the impact of public policies and programs on children and families, equitable access to education, and inclusion of immigrants and their children.

Amanda Lickteig holds a PhD in Curriculum and Instruction with an emphasis on multiple literacies. Her career began as a secondary language arts and ESL teacher on a non-DOD army installation where she worked with a high transient population of adolescents from around the world. As a teacher educator, Dr. Lickteig currently works in the Global Education Outreach office within the College of Education at Kansas State University where she teaches graduate coursework, develops and facilitates international professional development, works to establish high-impact study abroad experiences, and conducts research within the fields of teacher preparation and international education.

Isabella Lundgren is an undergraduate student in the Early Childhood Education program at the University of Dayton, where she is pursuing a dual license in General and Special Education. A member of the Urban Teacher Academy, Isabella is deeply committed to serving students from diverse backgrounds and cultivating a love for learning. In addition to her work in education, she expresses herself through poetry, often drawing connections between her artistic endeavors and her experiences in the classroom.

Dr. Chadd McGlone is a distinguished leader in mathematics education, currently serving as a board member of the National Council of Supervisors of Mathematics (NCSM) and co-leading its AI and Mathematics Education Task Force. He is also a member of the US National Commission on Mathematical Instruction and leads a TSG committee for

ICME-15. As co-founder of Mathkind, he has spearheaded transformative initiatives in culturally responsive mathematics education across diverse international contexts. His work, including the innovative Global Math Stories resource, reflects a deep commitment to educational equity and excellence. Dr. McGlone has delivered keynote addresses at major conferences in Guatemala, Ecuador, and Nepal.

Mona Menking is a tri-lingual (native proficiency in English, Spanish, and Farsi), extroverted, dynamic, task-oriented professional with a passion for excellence. Born in Iran, her family fled that country to escape religious persecution when she was four years old. After spending four years in England, at the age of 8, her family relocated to Quito, Ecuador. In Quito she secured a scholarship to attend the elite Academia Cotopaxi International Baccalaureate School through the 11th grade. She finished high school in Santa Fe, New Mexico, USA, graduating in the top 10% of her class. Ms. Menking has a bachelor's degree in business administration from The University of New Mexico in Albuquerque (1995), and a master's degree in education from Universidad San Francisco de Quito (USFQ), Ecuador, graduating with honors and a 4.0 GPA (2007). Mrs. Menking has worked in higher education since 2001, serving the Office of the President at USFQ in various capacities, including Director of Institutional Effectiveness & Accreditation, Director of Alumni Relations and Development, and International Summit Coordinator. At USFQ she gained a deep understanding of the Southern Association of Colleges and Schools accreditation process as USFQ prepared for U.S. accreditation. After working for a brief period in Western Kentucky University's Office of Enrollment Management (2008), she began telecommuting as an International Admissions Counselor for the University of Mississippi, with a special emphasis on Latin America and the Middle East and successfully did this for three and a half years. After serving as the Associate Director for International Initiatives for the Center for Intercultural and Multilingual Advocacy of the College of Education at Kansas State University for 9 years, in June of 2021 she was named the Inaugural Director of the Global Education Outreach Office in the Department of Curriculum and Instruction at the same institution. In March of 2025 Ms. Menking was appointed as the Inaugural Director of International Graduate Recruitment at Baylor University in Waco Texas. She resides in China Spring, Texas, with her husband Dr. Cornell Menking, Director of the Global Gateway Program at Baylor University, and her son CJ and daughter Aryana.

Dr. Alyssa Morley is an Assistant Professor of Global Education at Michigan State University. She coordinates MSU's Global Educators Cohort Program, which prepares future teachers to critically engage global issues. She pursues collaborative research projects exploring issues of gender, teaching, and power dynamics in global education. Dr. Morley holds a PhD in Education Policy from Michigan State University, where she also earned interdisciplinary graduate certificates in International Development and Gender, Justice, and Environmental Change.

Dr. Arthur B. Powell is a professor of mathematics education in the Department of Urban Education, Rutgers University-Newark, where he has taught graduate students qualitative research methods and undergraduate courses on mathematics as well as elementary and secondary mathematics curriculum and teaching methods. Internationally, he has taught mathematics education courses in Brazil, Canada, China, Ecuador, Haiti, and Mozambique, as well as mathematics in South Africa. From 2009 to 2019, he was head of his department and, since 2003, with Carolyn Maher, has been the co-director of the Robert B. Davis Institute for Learning, Graduate School of Education, Rutgers University-New Brunswick.

Olman Vargas Rojas estudia Psicología en la Universidad de Costa Rica y después hace estudios de postgrado en Inglaterra con una especialidad en orientación juvenil. Realiza una maestría en Liderazgo Educativo en Framingham State College de Massachusetts, USA. Obtiene certificación como administrador de la organización de bachillerato internacional lo que le permite ser director de colegios internacionales. A partir del año 2005 es director de escuelas y colegios bilingües internacionales en San José, Costa Rica. Actualmente es el director de Green Forest School en Costa Rica donde ha trabajado como consultor educativo y ha dado seminarios y conferencias en diferentes organizaciones.

Translated into English: MA. Ed. Olman Vargas Rojas studied Psychology at the University of Costa Rica and later pursued postgraduate studies in England with a specialization in youth counseling. He completed a master's degree in Educational Leadership at Framingham State College in Massachusetts, USA. He obtained certification as an administrator of the International Baccalaureate organization, which allowed him to serve as a director of international schools. Since 2005, he has been the director of bilingual international schools and colleges in San José, Costa Rica. He is currently the Head Master of Green Forest School in Costa Rica. He has also worked as an educational consultant and speaker at various congresses and seminars.

Elizabeth Wilkins holds a PhD in Educational Leadership and Policy Studies from the University of Oklahoma. She currently serves as an Assistant Professor in the Teacher Education Department at the University of Southern Indiana and is the current director of doctoral programs in education at her institution. Her scholarly work centers on fostering inclusive environments that promote success for all students, embedding the application of humanistic pedagogies in her higher education courses, both undergraduate and graduate. Her area of research specializes in equity, culturally relevant pedagogy, and instructional literacy practices, with a particular focus on supporting English Language Learners and students with exceptionalities.

Jennifer Wu-Pope is a world language teacher in New York State and has over a decade of experience as a classroom teacher. She is an alumna of the Fulbright Distinguished Awards in Teaching Research Program and conducted her research in Singapore. Her professional interests include global competence and performance-based teaching and assessment.